Gypsies

ARLAND REFERENCE LIBRARY OF THE HUMANITIES
OLUME 2039

GYPSIES
AN INTERDISCIPLINARY READER

EDITED BY
DIANE TONG

GARLAND PUBLISHING, INC.
A MEMBER OF THE TAYLOR & FRANCIS GROUP
NEW YORK AND LONDON
1998

Library of Congress Cataloging-in-Publication Data

Gypsies : an interdisciplinary reader / edited by Diane Tong.
         p.   cm. — (Garland reference library of the humanities ; v. 2039)
    Companion volume to: Gypsies : a multidisciplinary annotated bibliography. 1995.
    Includes bibliographical references.
    ISBN 0-8153-2549-5 (hardcover : alk. paper)
    1. Gypsies—Europe—History.   I. Tong, Diane.   II. Series: Garland
reference library of the humanities ; vol. 2039.
DX145.G94   1998
940'.0491497—dc21   98-5257
                                                        CIP

Cover illustration of Greek Gypsy copyright © Diane Tong.

Printed on acid-free, 250-year-life paper
Manufactured in the United States of America

Contents

Acknowledgments

My warm thanks to the authors represented in this volume for taking the time to answer my questions and also for writing such thoughtful and eloquent afterwords to their essays.

The following friends and colleagues offered their expertise, for which I'm very grateful: Michael Kandel, Judith Kuppersmith, Marianna Lee, Kathy Rutter, and Johanna Tani. Special thanks both to Dana McDaniel and to Robert Roth, who generously put aside their own work to share important political insights with me.

My appreciation to everyone at Garland, especially my editor, Phyllis Korper, for her meticulous work on the manuscript, Laurel Stegina, production editor, Donna Pintek, proofreader, and Andrew Galli, publicist. Also, David Barsamian generously granted permission to quote Noam Chomsky in my introduction.

Finally, I am indebted to Paul Sant Cassia, editor of *Journal of Mediterranean Studies*, for first encouraging me to do this book.

Introduction

Down through the centuries the story of what has been done to the Gypsies, or Roma, is an unremitting series of human-rights violations. The dismantling of the Communist regimes in Eastern Europe has unleashed mob violence against Gypsies under the name of nationalism; there are rapes, lynchings, bombings, and torchings of Gypsy neighborhoods. Romani and non-Romani activists worldwide are fighting for dignity and justice for Roma at a time when Roma seeking asylum in Western Europe are being sent back to their countries of origin to be raped, murdered, or tortured. As Noam Chomsky noted, "There's a lot of talk about German racism, and it's bad enough. For example, kicking out the Gypsies [from Germany] and sending them back to Romania is such a scandal you can't even describe it. The Gypsies were treated just like the Jews in the Holocaust, and nobody's batting an eyelash about that because nobody gives a damn about the Gypsies."[1]

Underlying these historical events are the many ways in which Gypsies are trapped inside the dominant culture of the country they live in. Economic repression and institutional racism fuel and are fueled by anti-Gypsy representations and stereotypes, including romantic clichés. Not surprisingly, some of these stereotypes have been internalized by the Roma. What is important is resistance to the images, stereotypes, and racist biases that negate the Gypsies' humanity and ignore both heterogeneity and complexity in Romani culture. Racism is a disease that affects everyone. As James Baldwin said, "It is a terrible, an inexorable, law, that one cannot deny the humanity of another without diminishing one's own: in the face of one's victim, one sees oneself."[2]

Paradoxically, it is also true that "it is a mark of a racist and class-driven society that those who are in a dominant position can easily remain blind to the experience of others and thereby to the reality of their own domination."[3]

* * *

This book of interdisciplinary readings on Gypsies is a companion volume to *Gypsies: A Multidisciplinary Annotated Bibliography* (Garland, 1995). The selected articles are sensitive to the Romani point of view and avoid the prevalent "unexamined white perspective" critiqued by Adrienne Rich.[4] The authors have synthesized passion and scholarship and avoid the exoticization/patronization of the Gypsies and their culture as well as the false notion of objectivity. As Ken Lee has said, "An appeal to 'objectivity' is not just epistemologically outdated, but is a reinforcement of hegemonies of privilege, power, and control."[5]

There are recurrent themes and echoes in the readings presented: the historical oppression of the Gypsies including today's new waves of xenophobia and violence; the nonstatic, heterogeneous nature of Gypsy cultures; the persistence of racist stereotypes; and Gypsy/non-Gypsy relationships, both personal and institutional. All tell stories of the persistence of the Roma in the face of savage atrocities and appalling living conditions. I hope that readers of this collection find the articles as enlightening and thought-provoking as I do.

The first article, "Researching Finnish Gypsies: Advice from a Gypsy," by Finnish Gypsy activist **Saga Weckman**, is a critical analysis of non-Gypsy research. It should be required reading for any member of a dominant culture working with members of an oppressed minority. Weckman's recommendations reflect the obstacles Gypsies have historically faced to doing their own research, and she makes it crystal clear that Gypsies have their own voices and their own analyses of their culture.

"Ways of Looking at Roma: The Case of Czechoslovakia" by **Will Guy** is an empathetic and detailed history of the Roma as a dominated minority in former Czechoslovakia with an afterword describing the stark situation and changes since the "Velvet Revolution" and the "Velvet Divorce." Guy documents how the Roma have always fit into the political agendas of the dominant group and sadly concludes, "As in so many other aspects of Communist practice it was felt that going through the motions of building socialism according to correct principles was enough to ensure success while consciousness was left unexamined. Beneath the outward conformity the old pernicious attitudes lay undisturbed and unchallenged, waiting to reemerge into the open with the ending of Communist rule. This was the true legacy of the Communist regime and one which its successors seem equally unfit to resolve."

Dan Pavel's article, "Wanderers: Romania's Hidden Victims," succinctly reports on what is happening to the Roma in post-Ceausescu Romania. Following a description of the miners' assault on the Gypsies in Bucharest, he notes, "Equally remarkable was what was seen on Romanian television later in the day. In an act of unprecedented courage, Gypsy leaders denounced the attack. Not even the students had yet protested publicly. At that moment two long-standing myths were dispelled: the idealized historical and literary image of Romanians as a peaceful and hospitable people incapable of racism, anti-Semitism, chauvinism, and nationalism; and the popular view of the Gypsies as a non-people incapable of asserting their rights."

"Police Perception of Gypsies in Finland" by **Martti Grönfors** analyzes the hostile attitudes of the Finnish police toward the Gypsies. Essentially, the police feel the Gypsies need "correction" because they are in opposition to the rest of society. In his afterword, Grönfors notes that changes in the police profile since the original article was written have led to improvements.

Gabrielle Tyrnauer, in "'Mastering the Past': Germans and Gypsies," discusses the Gypsy civil rights movement in Germany that began by protesting the silence surrounding the issue of the Gypsies as forgotten victims of the Holocaust. In her afterword Tyrnauer describes the unleashed hatred of the tragic and frightening "new world order."

In "Duty and Beauty, Possession and Truth: 'Lexical Impoverishment' as Control," Gypsy activist and scholar **Ian Hancock** attacks erroneous but pervasive assumptions and a double standard with respect to Romani, the Gypsies' language. These assumptions, for instance that Romani has "stolen" its non-Indic vocabulary, mirror ubiquitous racist attitudes and stereotypes.

Cathy Kiddle's "Pictures of Ourselves" describes teenage English Gypsy photographers and their photographs. "The girls already figured in their family archives of photographs, but now they were being given the opportunity to take control of the process themselves," deciding how they wanted to present themselves and adding texts as an extension and amplification of the image. In this way, as bell hooks has said, they used the camera as "a political instrument, a way to resist misrepresentation as well as a means by which alternative images could be produced."[6]

Thomas Acton in "Using the Gypsies' Own Language: Two Contrasting Approaches in Hungarian Schools" provides an account of two schools with different strategies for language learning for Gypsy students: a multilingual and multicultural approach compared with a segregated situation. To accompany the article, Nidhi Trehan has supplied a description of the current situation for Roma in Hungarian schools, "Roma in the Hungarian Educational System: Still the Invisible Minority."

"Roma (Gypsies) in the Soviet Union and the Moscow Teatr 'Romen'" by **Alaina Lemon** describes the development of the Russian Gypsy theater. Regarding the issue of authenticity, Lemon asserts that "performing Roma must accept and enact images of 'real Gypsies' as Russians define them in order to subsist." She discusses performances within a socialist framework as well as the performances of Roma for Roma.

Bertha Quintana's "'The Duende Roams Freely This Night': An Analysis of an Interethnic Event in Granada, Spain" is about Gitano (Spanish Gypsy) reactions to a complex interethnic event that followed a "familiar and well-worn path." The article highlights Gypsy points of view as well as the exploitation by tourist agencies who take advantage of racist stereotypes of the Gypsies as "exotics."

"Andalusian, Gypsy, and Class Identity in the Contemporary Flamenco Complex" by **Peter Manuel** describes developments in Gypsy flamenco as well as its extramusical political significance to Gypsies and the non-Gypsy poor, including the increasing politicization of flamenco lyrics in the twentieth century.

Carol Miller discusses ritual and symbolic pollution taboos (*marime*) among the Machvaia of California in "American Roma and the Ideology of Defilement." She describes *marime* as both uncleanness and as social disgrace and speaks of the use of *marime* rules to control sexual behavior; child rearing; ideal vs. real practices; sex role differences and the patriarchy; and the non-Gypsy propensity for defilement from a Romani point of view. In her afterword she talks about developments in this system since her article first appeared.

In "Sex Dichotomy Among the American Kalderaš Gypsies," **Rena Cotten (Gropper)** describes a society set up to exclude women from power, in which women are absent from decision-making bodies, and where there is a rigid division of labor. In her afterword Gropper speaks of changes in social conditions and in the status of women.

Milena Hübschmannová's "Economic Stratification and Interaction: Roma, an Ethnic Jati in East Slovakia" confounds some of the stereotypes of Gypsies by offering details of traditional Gypsy occupations based on interviews (quoted in the original Romani in footnotes). Hübschmannová also discusses the Indian concept of jati as it relates to Romani society.

In "Black•Quadroon•Gypsy: Women in the Art of George Fuller," **Sarah Burns** analyzes Fuller's paintings of women of color, including his depictions of Gypsy women in *The Romany Girl* and *Fedalma*, both of which were influenced by literature. As Burns points out, "From his vision of the black woman as peasant and slave to his solemn evocation of the Gypsy as a tragedy queen, Fuller unfolded a rich spectrum of dark, allegedly exotic womanhood, the stuff of nineteenth-century white romantic dreams, though in real social terms the women were peripheral, alienated, and outcast."

Wims Willems and **Leo Lucassen** discuss the development of historically largely unquestioned stereotypes and their ironies and contradictions in "The Church of Knowledge: Representations of Gypsies in Dutch Encyclopedias and Their Sources (1724–1984)." The article shows how these recurring themes were the inspiration for "scientific" rationalizations and how the stereotypes were exploited by the Nazis.

In **Christine Cartwright**'s frank and egalitarian article "Johnny Faa and Black Jack Davy: Cultural Values and Change in Scots and American Balladry," she discusses the ballad "The Gypsy Laddie" and the narrative tension and associations that underlie its "hold upon the emotions and memory of English-speaking people." She explains how the American versions of this tale of a white woman abducted by Gypsies reflect major changes in cultural function and how the ballad is "about decision making, and the importance of choosing on the basis of inner needs and values, rather than on the basis of material needs."

* * *

Because sexism and racism are related and parallel systems, I have encouraged the authors in this anthology to use nonsexist language. However, the final decision was theirs. Sexist and male-centered language in material quoted from written sources remains as in the original texts.

The word *Gypsy*, a proper noun designating an ethnic group, is often misspelled. Since the Gypsies deserve the dignity of an upper-case G, I have edited the word in quoted material to avoid using [sic]. Variant spellings of Romani words reflect different dialects in diaspora and sometimes different spelling conventions based on time or location.

For further research in Romani studies, I refer readers to the bibliographies of the articles included here, to my book *Gypsies: A Multidisciplinary Annotated Bibliography*, and, of course, to the Internet.

I welcome comments, suggestions, and corrections. My address is 67 Park Avenue, New York, NY 10016, U.S.A.

Diane Tong
March 1998

NOTES

1. Noam Chomsky, *Keeping the Rabble in Line: Interviews with David Barsamian* (Monroe, Maine: Common Courage Press, 1994), p. 58.
2. James Baldwin, quoted in David Leeming, *James Baldwin: A Biography* (New York: Knopf, 1994), p. 168.
3. Jill McLean Taylor, Carol Gilligan, and Amy M. Sullivan, *Between Voice and Silence: Women and Girls, Race and Relationship* (Cambridge: Harvard University Press, 1995), p. 7.
4. Adrienne Rich, *Blood, Bread, and Poetry: Selected Prose 1979–1985* (New York: Norton, 1986), p. 162.
5. Kenneth Lee, letter to the editor of *Nationalities Papers*, 25 August 1992.
6. bell hooks, *Art on My Mind: Visual Politics* (New York: The New Press, 1995), p. 60.

GYPSY STUDIES

Researching Finnish Gypsies: Advice from a Gypsy (1983)

Saga Weckman

Before I go into my actual topic, Gypsy research, I would like to remind you also on this occasion about the origin of the Gypsy culture in India and in India's ancient culture. Although our culture—and at the same time the old and valued Indian culture—is looked down upon in Europe, anyone can read about its achievements in history books. We are proud of our Indian origin and of our culture, and under no circumstances would I want to change it to anything else. Being different from the Western culture, our Eastern culture values such things as correct behavior, respect toward the old and their experience, humanity, security among our own people, sincerity, equality, and unselfishness.

There are 6,000–8,000 Gypsies in Finland. From their original home in India they came here via various routes, mainly from the West, from Sweden. Gypsies form the largest ethnic minority in Finland, apart from the language-minority Swedish Finns. The first evidence of their arrival in Finland is from the 1500s. Until recently, we have lived our lives isolated from the Finnish majority and from other Gypsy groups in Europe. Although our culture closely resembles the Gypsy cultures elsewhere, it is natural that the culture of Finnish Gypsies has also developed independently over the centuries. This applies, for example, to our language, which can no longer be understood by other Gypsy groups.

The fast social changes of the last few decades have influenced the Gypsy economic situation in particular. Earlier, the horse formed the most important basis for Gypsy economic life. Gypsies traveled from place to place with horses, which were exchanged with and sold to the settled Finnish folk. Many customs and norms were attached to horses. The care and use of the horse and also the horse trading were men's work. Women sold handicrafts and told fortunes. The disappearance of the horse from agriculture in the last few decades has meant the disappearance of the most important economic basis for Gypsies.

The traditional education which took place inside the Gypsy society and which trained the young in traditional values and activities guaranteed the possibility for a living and a position independent from the majority. Outside education was found meaningless and educational opportunities were not given to the Gypsies even when they wanted them. The disappearance of the traditional means of livelihood and the lack of Finnish-type education forced the Gypsies who were living through a period of change into an intolerable situation. Their earlier independence changed into a dependency upon the majority, a situation which was earlier considered absolutely unsuitable and even shameful.

Increasingly, Gypsies have to resort to social welfare in order to meet their basic needs. Already in 1969, two-thirds of Finland's Gypsy households received at least part of their income in the form of social welfare benefits.

The attitude of the Finnish majority toward Gypsies has been colored with prejudice, discrimination, and violence throughout our stay in Finland. In the main, the situation is unaltered even today. In 1971, a law prohibiting racial discrimination was enacted in Finland, years after Finland had signed the United Nations general agreement on human rights. This, however, has not changed the general attitudes, and blatant prejudice and discrimination are part of the everyday life of all Finnish Gypsies.

The development of the social welfare system has influenced the Gypsies in many ways. Among other things, Gypsies have become a primarily urban group. An estimated 2,500 Finnish Gypsies have moved to Sweden as part of a wider Finnish migration there and as so-called social refugees. The attitudes toward foreigners in Sweden has been less prejudiced than in Finland. Urbanization has made the practice of the traditional occupations and the observance of the traditional culture more difficult. This naturally affects the Gypsy identity and our general social situation—our way of life. At the same time it has speeded up the process of assimilation. In addition, this assimilation is regrettably often into the lower societal strata.

Gypsy Research in Finland

Generally it can be said that the poor situation of Gypsies is also reflected in the meager amount of research on them. Even researchers have not been interested in us. From the small amount of research that there is on the Finnish Gypsies, I shall pick out a few major trends. In the late 1800s and early 1900s, Arthur Thesleff researched the culture and language of our people, using primarily just one Gypsy informant. The work of Thesleff was important as a descriptive account of Gypsy culture, and his thorough international comparisons show serious scholarship. The weaknesses of his work relate to his analyses, which were erroneous and presented the majority point of view. As a direct result of his research, the first official report on the problems of Gypsies came out in 1900. That report utilized primarily Thesleff's material. Thesleff's role in examining the Gypsy culture was typical of its time: Gypsies formed a problem to the governing majority, they should be assimilated. However, at the same time they were defined as qualitatively inferior to the Finnish majority. On the basis of Thesleff's work, the Gypsies were officially defined as a pariah class of Finland. As late as 1955, another state committee report still contained most of the conclusions and suggestions of the earlier report.

The first academic thesis came in 1961, when Raimo Vehmas, a Finnish sociologist, published his doctoral work on the acculturation of the Gypsies. That work relied on interviews with Gypsies. If that work is compared with Thesleff's work, it can be said that it was even more prejudiced, a true outsider and a representative of the governing majority examining the Gypsies. If Thesleff's work made the Finnish Gypsies into an official pariah group, the work of Vehmas affirmed the general prejudiced and incorrect beliefs about the nature of Gypsy culture in Finland. Vehmas belonged to that group of 1950s Finnish sociologists who unashamedly considered that firsthand experience is not necessary in the research of culture. It was enough to put on paper the researcher's own and other people's prejudices, the comments from the subjects serving only a subservient role. The importance of Vehmas's work can be assessed when we discover how it has been used by the majority. In the 1970s, Finnish policemen shot dead two Gypsies in a scuffle which was caused only by the Gypsies' demand to be allowed to eat in a restaurant. When the constables were prosecuted, they successfully utilized Vehmas's work in trying to show, as he did, that Gypsies are quick-tempered and unpredictable, and shooting them was an action claimed to be taken merely to prevent the Gypsies from shooting the policemen.

Only in the 1970s did Gypsy researchers start making use of the real experts on Gypsy culture, Gypsies themselves, in their research. I have been actively involved in Gypsy politics since the 1960s and in that role I have closely followed the work of Gypsy researchers. However, from experience, I can say that although some of them contacted me and wanted information and advice, the relationship between me and them was unequal. My role was that of a passive informant, and if I dared to give my own interpretations or to criticize researchers' analyses, the researchers pointed out the differences in formal schooling between me and them. According to them, only those who had formal university training were able to make interpretations. When I persisted in criticizing some of their wrong interpretations, the relationship ended. In this way, the researchers created "Gypsy culture" which did not correspond to the reality in which the Finnish Gypsies live.

Only in the mid-1970s did a researcher dare to do Gypsy research among the Gypsies as a participant observer, giving the Gypsy point of view, doing research on their terms. . . . I shall not go into greater detail about his work here. What was important from our point of view, however, was that Gypsies took part in his research from the beginning to the end, from the planning and executing to the analyses.

It can be asked now, why have the Gypsies themselves not researched their own culture? One indication of the general inequality of Finnish society is that the possibilities for research lie only with those who have a certain amount of formal schooling; only their work is appreciated. Because of the general discrimination in Finland, university-trained people seldom rise from among the Gypsies, except those who have been forced to deny their origins. This will be true also in the future, I am sure. It is much easier for the majority to take care of the Gypsy problems through handouts than to create opportunities and settings for improving our societal status. The Gypsy politics of the Finnish society is aimed at making the Gypsies passive.

As we are not given opportunities to do our own research into our own culture, we can influence research by outsiders either by cooperating with them or by denying cooperation to them. Fortunately, nobody can force the Gypsies to be research objects. Cooperation is necessary for the success of outsider research when one is researching such a different culture as the Gypsy culture. As a Gypsy, I would like to finish up with some comments on how an outsider might seek successful cooperation with the Gypsies. I am certain that many of my comments can be extended to apply also to other governed minorities and to research on them.

Basic Conditions of Gypsy Research

Although I am not qualified to say much about actual research methods, I would like to point out that not all methods suit the study of Gypsies. When choosing suitable methods, the special features of Gypsy culture must be taken into account. One of those is that the entry into the Gypsy world for outsiders is probably more difficult than that into many other cultures. One should avoid the uncritical use of written sources. Through critical use of the source material, the transference of others' mistakes and inaccuracies is avoided. The researcher should also be aware of his or her own prejudices and attitudes, so that these neither consciously nor even unconsciously interfere with the research processes and analyses. One absolute condition for the success of Gypsy research is an internalization of the essence of Gypsydom, the culture of Gypsies and their life situation. Cooperation with the Gypsies is absolutely necessary for finding the essence of Gypsydom so that this can be passed on also to non-Gypsies. Therefore:

1.   Make yourself familiar with the essential elements of Gypsy cultures and social organization, no matter what the actual research problem you are interested in.
2.   When researching, be genuinely yourself. Do not try to "become a Gypsy," and do not try to overplease us.
3.   Do not pigeonhole us into the framework of the governing majority and its science. It has been attempted for over four hundred years

already, with little success. In some ways we are like other people, but hasty generalizations are dangerous.

4.   Remember that you are the novice in Gypsy culture, not the expert. That is so, no matter how many degrees you have.

5.   As is, I suppose, the case with any research into a culture, there is a common thread running through Gypsy culture. Without discovering that, any research on Gypsies will fail. Remember that you are dealing with a non-European culture. Do not force us into a European mold. We are an Eastern culture, as we come from India.

6.   Never be satisfied with the first answer you get to your question.

7.   Although we use the Finnish language, our Finnish differs sometimes from that of the majority. That is not because our use of the language is inferior to yours, but it is different, with different meanings attached to the same words. Pay attention to meanings, not to words, to avoid misunderstandings. You can also be made fun of through the use of language.

8.   Do not draw too-hasty conclusions, as they may always be the wrong ones.

9.   Come "down" to "our level" from your pedestal. From a platform you can never reach us.

10.   Try to leave your attitudes and prejudices outside the door. Do not compare us with yourself.

11.   Be a humane human being.

12.   Always utilize our expertise about ourselves, but use it and us correctly.

13.   Gypsies love authenticity in all its forms and in every situation. Be genuine, too, when you are working among us.

14.   Never betray the trust shown to you.

To the few representatives from other minorities here, I would like to make an appeal, that we should work together, to respect one another's cultures as equal. Only by working together can we achieve satisfactory results in our common struggle for our rights.

Afterword 1995:

In general there has been some limited progress in researching the situation of the Finnish Gypsies. In the late 1980s a few government-sponsored papers on Gypsy housing conditions and general welfare were published. In addition, a permanent office for the Secretariat for the Gypsy Commission was established—though headed by a Finn. Although the lack of formal schooling continues to reduce the opportunities for Gypsies either to advance in Finnish society or to have a definitive say in what concerns them at both the municipal and government level, overall there has been a growing level of awareness of and sensitivity to Gypsy matters on the part of Finnish decision-makers since the 1980s. Because the Gypsies themselves are not the real decision-makers but only *consulted* on their affairs, however, it remains difficult to translate this increased sensitivity into action. And despite having achieved a higher level of schooling than was possible in the 1980s, only rarely does a Gypsy complete a university education or even reach the point of being accepted into a university.

The lack of higher education acts to hamper even those research findings that might actually improve the lot of the Gypsies. The main reasons for this are that the subjects themselves lack a basic understanding of the nature of research and that they have learned from experience to expect the worst at the hands of outsiders. Thus researchers outside the Gypsy community can either manipulate their subjects in the first instance or in the second may fail to bring about truly benevolent results. A further consequence of this misunderstanding has been the creation of opposing cliques within Gypsy society itself, a fact sometimes welcome to a Finnish majority eager to deny the resources for either research or programs that might aid its minority population. And finally, the difficulty of conducting Gypsy research often drives good researchers to seek out easier fields. This is largely where the situation stands today: the Gypsies oppose *any* research and the researchers do not dare tackle Gypsy topics.

Even in the matter of improving educational opportunities in order to nurture Gypsy culture there is a problem: education can lead to alienation unless it includes Gypsy culture in the curriculum. Some progress has been made in that there are now Romani-language teachers who can teach the language to Gypsy children. In addition, some municipalities have appointed Gypsy liaison officers to mediate between the Finnish and Gypsy segments of the population. Finally, there is now a university with an informal quota for Gypsy entrants.

In conclusion, there is urgent need for further research on the Gypsies. Because our culture is both disappearing and transforming at a rapid rate, the danger of assimilation is imminent if older traditions are eclipsed—despite the fact that the Finnish majority continues to reject Gypsies in their midst.

POLITICS, SOCIAL CHANGE, AND HISTORY

Ways of Looking at Roma[1]:
The Case of Czechoslovakia (1975)

Will Guy

THE IMPORTANCE OF A HISTORICAL APPROACH

The Relevance of Historical Experience

> Class happens when some men, as a result of common experiences (inherited or shared), feel and articulate the identity of their interests as between themselves, and as against other men whose interests are different from and usually opposed to theirs. . . . Class-consciousness is the way in which these experiences are handled in cultural terms: embodied in traditions, value-systems, ideas, and institutional forms.[2]

What Thompson writes about class is equally relevant to minority communities if the positions of being a minority and also a dominated stratum or class coincide, as they so often do. If anything, historical experience can often play an even more crucial role for such minorities in helping them understand their present situation.

The situation of Roma in what is now Czechoslovakia has long been that of a dominated minority. Being a Rom meant for many centuries seeing the world as hostile; as a place where gaining a livelihood was a precarious business, where you were always liable to be beaten up and driven away, where perhaps you and your family might even be drowned, hanged at the crossroads, or burned alive in your hut. It didn't happen all the time, of course, but it had happened in the not too distant past and might happen again—perhaps quite soon—who could know? Even in "good times," being a Rom meant seeing perhaps half of your children die young, of hunger and disease. To spare a weak child the prolonged agony of an inevitable death, nomadic Roma in Czechoslovakia used to plunge their newborn babies into icy water. If they could survive that, they had a chance on the road.

All this must have given these people a rather special way of looking at the world.

Nomadism and Persecution

When writing about Roma in general, two central problems always arise and are, of course, linked—nomadism and persecution.

Despite presenting a wealth of comparative historical data, Jean-Paul Clébert is still able to write that "the Gypsy is primarily and above all else a nomad. His dispersion throughout the world is due less to historical or political necessities than to his own nature."[3]

Where settling has occurred, it is explained as being due to degeneration.

The sedentary Gypsies are generally "excluded" people, groups or families or couples who have founded a family and who have been banned from the clans or made "marimé," that is, "unclean," because of serious violations of the Tradition.[4]

When you realize that the countries with the largest numbers of Roma are in Eastern Europe and that the majority there are "sedentary" and therefore that Clébert's "groups or families or couples" in fact number hundreds of thousands of people, you begin to feel a little uneasy with this explanation. Was it really like that? Who is excluding who? Perhaps Clébert is more a self-appointed custodian of the "authentic Gypsy culture" as he conceives of it rather than a chronicler of choices actually made by Roma in concrete historical situations?

In his careful assessment of the problems facing Europe's Roma today, Grattan Puxon writes of anti-Romani prejudice as "a Europe-wide phenomenon which permeates all strata of society, regardless of political, ethical or religious systems."[5] As a way of stressing the extent and continuity of anti-Romani hostility this is excellent, but it also carries the suggestion that persecution of Roma is somehow undifferentiated and consequently inexplicable in historical terms. If no matter what the conditions, the situation, it was always there, how can you start trying to understand it? And what would be the point anyway, for perhaps it will always be there?

A more fruitful approach to both these problems would seem to be to probe rather the variety of Romani experience in specific historical situations rather than stressing its universal nature. For example: Under what conditions did Roma settle? In what circumstances were Roma persecuted in certain ways?

General answers are difficult to provide but even particular answers are not easy to give, largely because of the way in which much previous data have been presented. Writers on history almost invariably, and understandably, ignore Roma. Writers on Roma frequently, and unforgivably, ignored history. They wrote myopically about these people almost as if the Roma were the sole arbiters of their fate whereas, as a small and vulnerable minority, it was far more likely that their history would be more a tale of what was done to them than of what they themselves had done. Even the tale of what was done to them must be seen in a broad context, for most authorities had far more pressing problems to deal with than complaints against a few Roma, so when they did act against the Roma perhaps they were playing a deeper game. The possibility is worth bearing in mind.

In an important sense the study of Roma is worthwhile not so much for its own sake but for what it reveals about the nature of the societies in which they lived and still live.

To take just one example, the romantic stereotype of the Gypsy, as an exotic and noble primitive, wandering unconstrained as the mood takes her or him, tells us very little about the ways Roma managed to exist in England during the nineteenth century. Yet it comes as a shock to realize that this stereotype was cherished by members of a class which collectively owed its comfortable existence (including the leisure to fantasize about "Gypsy freedom") to the systematic imposition of long hours of daily, repetitive, soul-destroying factory labor on other human beings. This was not perceived as a contradiction.

Fanon (a Black) commented aptly on a comparable romanticizing of Blacks:

> To us, the man who adores the Negro is as "sick" as the man who abominates him. . . . In the absolute, the black is no more to be loved than the Czech, and truly what is to be done is to set man free.[6]

The Important Case of Czechoslovakia

The territory now known as Czechoslovakia should be significant for those interested in Romani history for at least four main reasons. First, it straddles the frontiers of what might be termed the "Western" and "Eastern" areas of Romani development in Europe.

In the Czech lands of Bohemia and Moravia, the development pattern is similar to those of Germany, France, and England, where Roma were more usually seen as useless pests by the authorities, who ignored them or legislated savagely to expel them and deter new immigration. In these areas the Roma remained largely nomadic.

In Slovakia, however, which until 1918 was part of the Hungarian lands, the pattern resembles those of the Danube lands and the Balkans, where Roma were often seen as useful and from their first appearance were permitted, encouraged, and even forced to settle. They were also taxed by local authorities or the state. It is these countries that have the larger Romani populations.

It is not suggested of course that all Roma or all authorities always conformed to these patterns, but that as a model these rough generalizations prove helpful in understanding the varied trends of Romani history in Europe, including developments in particular countries since the Second World War. For this reason a fairly detailed account is given of Romani history in Czech lands and especially Slovakia, the homeland of virtually all of contemporary Czechoslovakia's adult Roma.

Probably the general differences between "Western" and "Eastern" development are related to more fundamental modes of economic development (capitalist industrialization/feudal ruralism) and related methods of state formation (nation-states/multinational states), but this would need careful demonstration.

Second, on this territory were made probably two of the most widespread and systematic attempts to assimilate Roma—by the Hapsburg monarchs Maria Theresa and Joseph II in the second half of the eighteenth century, and by the government of socialist Czechoslovakia from 1958 onward.

Third, we are fortunate in having fairly full documentation of both these attempts as well as having a number of general studies of Romani history in Czechoslovakia. At present the most outstanding work is Emília Horváthová's excellent and painstaking *Cigáni na Slovensku,*[7] to which the following section is greatly indebted.

Finally, Roma are relatively well integrated into Czechoslovak society, especially in comparison with the capitalist countries of Western Europe. For those interested in speculating on possible future developments of Romani communities, the situation in Czechoslovakia, where the majority of Roma participate in the labor market and where there is a small but growing Romani intelligentsia who still see themselves as Roma, should prove stimulating.

THE HISTORY OF ROMA ON CZECHOSLOVAK TERRITORY UNTIL 1945

Roma in the Czech Lands Before 1918

Shortly after the first undisputed reference to Roma in the Czech lands (1399), a large group arrived from the east in 1417 who were later to arouse the attention of Western Europe partly because of their numbers, novelty, and apparent nobility of their leaders but also since they had been granted impressive letters of safe-conduct. After passing through Bohemia[8] they divided and various subgroups traveled to north Germany, Bavaria, Rome, Paris, and Barcelona. They were magicians, fortune-tellers, horse dealers, and apparently petty thieves—occupations compatible with, or even requiring, nomadism.

Their obvious difference from Roma previously settled in Eastern Europe has usually prompted the explanation that they were simply a different tribe of Roma. Štampach, a noted Czech Gypsiologist, believed that they had not come from the Balkans but directly from Asia Minor with the Turks. However, a straightforward account of their appearance as the unplanned intrusion of a primitive nomadic tribe practicing their traditional occupations is inadequate, as Horváthová has convincingly argued, because the newcomers seem more, rather than less, sophisticated than most Roma in the Balkans at that time.

It almost appears as if they made a careful market survey before their arrival, for they knew Western European languages and soon possessed accurate maps and almanacs indicating fairs[9] and they included craftsmen who could make seals and write official letters. Even more remarkable was their initial success in obtaining powerful letters from such rulers as the Holy Roman Emperor Sigismund[10] and Pope Martin V by means of an explanation of their origin and nomadism which was not only plausible but even meritorious in terms of current European values: they claimed to be religious penitents.

Poissonier[11] even suggested that the apparent great difference in wealth between Romani leaders and followers was not so much a reflection of internal social divisions but a collective tactic to give these groups a better negotiating position. Although highly speculative, this view is partially supported by the fact that in France at least Roma imitated aspects of the beggars' guilds, which were, in turn, a parody of feudal society, having their own courts, kings, social divisions, and systems of justice.

Whatever the origin of these Roma, it is important to recognize that in any case contemporary conditions in Western Europe probably would not have permitted them to follow the pattern of Roma in Eastern Europe. In particular the more developed craft industries were better organized to resist penetration by intruders. Likewise, prospects for settling would have been bleak during a period when hordes of beggars, discharged soldiers, and peddlers often wandered the roads.[12]

Although legislation expelling Roma as alleged Turkish spies had been enacted at the end of the fifteenth century in neighboring German lands, it was not until the mid-sixteenth century that similar measures were taken in the Czech lands, when Roma were accused of aiding the Turks by starting the fires which broke out in Prague in 1541. Official lethargy in implementing such laws is evident from their frequent renewal and despite a not unrealistic fear of hired incendiaries, it is probable that the legislation was intended largely as a sop to public fears, a convenient way of demonstrating that the authorities were taking some positive action against the growing Turkish threat. At times popular feeling must have been extreme, for in 1556 it was necessary to forbid the drowning of Romani women and children, yet during the same period there are records of alms and letters of commendation granted to Roma by town councils. Although some Roma were killed or driven out, others continued to travel the Czech lands supplying their usual services of horse trading, fortune-telling, and the like.

The late seventeenth and early eighteenth century is known as the "Age of Darkness" to the Czechs, for the devastation of the Thirty Years War had left the country depopulated, plague-ridden, starving, and continually troubled by serf uprisings and robber bands recruited from discharged soldiers. Meanwhile the Turks (and French) mounted new and more menacing attacks. It was a terrible period for Roma.

Once more the activities of foreign-paid incendiaries, including Roma, in Prague led to the expulsion of Roma, but this time they were accompanied by mass killings. Whole groups were hanged, shot, or drowned and to discourage further immigration scores of Romani bodies hung from trees along frontier roads. Later, signs were erected depicting gallows and bearing the inscription: "This is the penalty for Gypsies entering Bohemia."[13] Youths and girls under eighteen were mutilated; in Bohemia the right ear was cut off, in Moravia and Silesia, the left.

This period of savage persecution came to an end some time after the accession of Maria Theresa to the Hapsburg throne. Starting in 1761 she and her successor, Joseph II, made a systematic attempt to assimilate all Roma by settling them throughout the Hapsburg lands and making serfs of them by prohibiting them from nomadism, horse dealing, having their own leaders, and even from speaking their own language. Probably the most drastic measure was the forcible removal of children from their parents, fostering them with non-Roma to ensure a Christian upbringing.

Compared with what had gone before, these measures were enlightened, being based on the principle that integration would succeed only by settling, employing, and educating the Roma, or, as they were officially renamed, *Neubauern* (new farmers) or *Ujmagyar* (new Hungarians). In the Czech lands several colonies were founded to provide adequate accommodation, with apparently little enduring effect, although one colony in South Moravia remained until the 1930s. But in any case the total number of Roma involved was relatively small; in Slovakia, however, the situation was quite different.

The nineteenth century, like the fifteenth, is remarkable for its lack of reports of Roma. Attempts to assimilate them lapsed with Joseph II's death in 1790, and they were left to wander around the rapidly industrializing Czech lands, apparently causing little more than occasional local aggravation.

> Gypsies often visited the villages, the men selling chains, axes and gimlets, the women telling the fortunes of senseless women from cards or palms and casting spells.[14]

In 1887, however, a "modern" policy of official registration and harassment was introduced. Similar measures were adopted by other Western European countries (for example, Bavaria and France).

Roma in Slovakia Before 1918

Many early Romani immigrants to the Balkans (for example, Serbia) managed to integrate themselves into the wider society, often forming their own quarters in towns and specializing in a limited number of occupations like other ethnic minorities. The commonest early settlement pattern in fourteenth- and fifteenth-century Slovakia, however, was around feudal castles. There are frequent references to Roma as castle musicians and metalworkers, but an even more common occupation was that of soldier, and Hungarian kings commented favorably on Romani troops in 1476, 1487, 1492, and 1496.

Not all Roma settled, for fifteenth-century sources refer to nomadic bands who lived by fortune-telling, magical healing, and theft. Social differentiation was therefore extreme among Roma from their first appearance in Slovakia, for while some lived the precarious life of robbers in the woods, others sought service and protection with the ruling nobility and were fortunate that conditions permitted their skills to be utilized. However, the isolation of each newly settled group of Roma from the Slovak and Hungarian peasantry made them vulnerable to manipulation by their protectors, a situation which feudal lords were not slow to exploit.

In 1514 a major Hungarian peasant uprising was crushed by the Palatine Ján Zápolský. The peasant leader was gruesomely executed by being seated on a heated iron throne and having a red-hot iron crown placed on his head. These torture implements were forged by a group of Romani smiths.

Zápolský was later (1526) an unsuccessful contender for the throne of Hungary and to revenge himself on the Slovak towns which had supported his opponent, he used Roma to set fire (in 1534) to four important East Slovak towns. Some of the Romani incendiaries were caught and confessed that they had orders to burn a further nine Slovak towns.

Such manipulations of Roma in class struggles must have worsened relations with peasants and burghers, but evidently not to the extent of preventing further settlement during the sixteenth century. Roma were generally granted permission to settle beyond the outskirts of towns and villages, where they often made simple implements for local farmers, weapons for night watchmen, and so forth. Larger-scale and more profitable metalworking was monopolized by non-Romani craftsmen.

As in the Czech lands conditions rapidly deteriorated during the seventeenth and early eighteenth centuries as a consequence of the Thirty Years War. There was an influx of vagrants and nomadic Roma fleeing the savage measures of the Czech lands, which in turn provoked retaliatory legislation in Slovakia. Regional authorities passed numerous measures which although referring formally to all Roma, were usually only enforced against "foreign" nomadic groups. The difference between the Czech lands and Slovakia is well illustrated by the signs erected on the borders depicting the execution of Roma. In the Czech lands this fate awaited any Rom who entered the country, while in Slovakia the threat was to "all nomadic Gypsies who did not settle within three weeks."[15]

This differential treatment of Roma cannot be explained by greater devastation in the Czech lands, for Slovakia too was a battleground in the strange triangular struggle between Turks, Hungarians, and Hapsburgs, further complicated by peasant uprisings. However, an economic explanation is strongly supported by contemporary documents showing the extensive taxation of Roma in the Hungarian lands. The slaughter or expulsion of Roma in Slovakia wold have meant a loss of revenue; this deterrent did not apply in the Czech lands.

The accession of Maria Theresa did not lead to any dramatic change in policy toward Roma in the Hungarian lands but rather to an intensification of efforts to assimilate them by settling and employing them under an altered administrative structure. In 1758 the Imperial Council made local Diets of gentry responsible for Roma in their area, reserving a coordinating function for itself.

In spite of a wealth of statistics, it is difficult to assess the success of the policy for, as J. H. Schwicker demonstrated, Diets deliberately falsified their progress reports in the safe knowledge that the Imperial Council had no way of independently evaluating their work.[16]

In any case they enjoyed considerable autonomy, for "Hungary, even in periods of absolutism, was administered by elected committees [Diets] of the country gentry, and these would never operate measures which ran against their privileges."[17]

There is good reason to suppose that the policy was not entirely welcome to the gentry, for although it might appear advantageous to landowners to gain new labor power and feudal rent, this would only be the case if nomadic Roma could be successfully settled and put to work. The initial prohibitively high costs (new housing and training as well as regular payments to foster parents of young Romani children) were to be met entirely by the landowner, while the first rewards went to the Imperial coffers in the form of tax. In view of these factors it is likely that many gentry made a careful assessment of investment prospects before trying to settle groups of nomadic Roma; those who appeared a bad risk were simply moved on, despite Council instructions to admit them to serfs' villages.

Nor is it likely that many Roma were enthusiastic about the policy, for while it is probable that some nomads would have welcomed the opportunity to settle (as they had previously), the harsh conditions, such as losing their children, would have been quite unacceptable. In fact Schwicker found statistical evidence of movement of Roma from regions where the policy was more vigorously enforced to those which were more lax. As well as the nomads, however, those Roma already settled opposed the policy since they probably saw any increase of their numbers in a particular place as a threat to their precarious social position and also to their livelihood through increased competition. They occasionally petitioned Diets to move bands of nomadic Roma from the district, usually with justifying accusations of theft.

The simplistic assessment that "Maria Theresa had very good feelings [but] . . . a complete lack of understanding in regard to Gypsies and their way of life,"[18] fails to appreciate that many Roma were not at all opposed to settling per se, but, more important, overlooks the practical considerations behind the policy. Allowing Maria Theresa her "good feelings," her efforts must also be seen on a different level, as yet another move in the continuous struggle by the Hapsburgs to extract money from their wayward Hungarian lands. As an important part of their jealously guarded autonomy, the gentry paid no direct imperial taxes, although their serfs and the commoners did. To raise money from these lands, therefore, Maria Theresa was forced to use a variety of indirect means, including the imposition of heavy taxes on imports to Hungary. To maximize these taxes Hungarian home industry was intentionally neglected.[19]

While the gentry were prepared to sacrifice the economic development of their country to maintain their own privileged position, they actively resisted more direct ways of raising imperial revenues, and therefore any failure of the policy toward Roma was probably as much due to administrative sabotage by Diets as to resistance by nomadic Roma.

As in the industrializing Czech lands, the nineteenth century is remarkable for the lack of official attention paid to Roma in Slovakia. The country remained predominantly rural under the control of the gentry, but there was a little industrialization (mainly mining) in the east, although not enough to create much hope of a better life among the Slovak peasantry. "Over half a million Slovaks, nearly one-fourth of the population, emigrated to the United States in the quarter-century preceding the First World War. Others streamed to Canada, South America and Russia."[20]

Meanwhile, the numbers of Roma had greatly increased and an 1893 census revealed 36,000 Roma in Slovakia, of whom 2,000 were seminomadic and only 600 nomadic (less than 2 percent). Even though a certain number of nomads must have escaped the census, it is clear that by this time the vast majority of Roma were already settled.

Roma in Czechoslovakia 1918–1945

Although Roma were recognized as a nationality in 1921, little was done to alleviate their poverty. This is hardly surprising, since Slovakia and Ruthenia (now part of Ukraine), where most of them lived, were left undeveloped and in general "were regarded more or less like colonies"[21] during the First Czechoslovak Republic (1918–1939). In 1924 a Slovak local authority complained: "The penalty of imprisonment has no effect on them, because imprisonment only improves their living conditions. It often happens that a Gypsy without resources commits a crime only to escape the pangs of hunger."[22]

Yet the situation of many peasants was often little better, especially in Slovakia where some were forced to become itinerant peddlers and artisans, often working for food, not cash, and sometimes simply bartering fruit for grain. It was against such itinerants, as well as against nomadic Roma, that the 1927 law controlling nomadism was directed. This was based on the old 1887 regulations and required all officially permitted nomads to be registered and carry a nomad's pass, which could be withdrawn at any time. Apparently 36,696 such passes were issued up to 1940[23] although a 1927 census of Roma in Slovakia had shown 60,315 to be settled and 1,877 nomadic.

Some newspapers justified the law as a new and humane approach, but a more reliable picture of the situation of Roma in these times of general unemployment and hunger is given by other contemporary events such as the 1928 Pobedim pogrom where, in reprisal for pilfering crops from the fields, Slovak villagers wounded eighteen and killed six Roma—including two young children. Commenting on this massacre, the influential daily *Slovák* wrote, "the Pobedim case can be characterized as a citizens' revolt against Gypsy life. In this there are the roots of democracy."[24]

A year later a Romani robber band was accused of murder and cannibalism. The second charge was eventually dropped but not before the press had inflamed public opinion with sensational and inaccurate coverage reminiscent of its role at a 1782 trial where forty Roma were tortured and executed, being accused of identical crimes, before an investigation ordered by Joseph II discovered that all of the supposed victims were still alive.

While there is no evidence to suggest that the hostility against Roma was deliberately fomented by the government, nevertheless there appeared little official resistance to such developments and perhaps even some elements within the government welcomed them to divert some of the acute public bitterness over social and economic conditions. It is important to notice that since 1926 the dominant party in the bourgeois coalition had been the Agrarian Party, which eventually took office in 1932. Since this party represented the interests of predominantly landowners and farmers, it was unlikely to have had much sympathy for Roma.

It is a commonplace to point to the manipulation of minorities as scapegoats in times of severe crisis. As might be expected, therefore, pogroms against Roma were not limited to Czechoslovakia during this period but occurred also in Austria, France, and Germany.[25]

Despite the generally bleak outlook it would be wrong to see the situation as entirely hopeless during this period for remarkable, if isolated, efforts were made to integrate Roma, especially in the field of education. After 1925 special schools for Roma were established in several towns in Ruthenia and East Slovakia, and in 1929 a group of Slovak doctors founded what was later known as the "Society for the Study and Solutions of the Gypsy Problem." As well as concerning itself with health matters, the society organized theatrical and musical performances by Roma in principal regional theaters in Slovakia and inspired the formation of a flourishing Romani football club which toured abroad.

The events of the Second World War are simple to relate, but less easy to forget for the Roma.

Soon after the start of the war, a register of Roma (1940) showed 60,000 in Slovakia, while only 6,500 (about 11 percent) lived in the Czech lands.[26,27] Although some Roma in the Czech lands managed to escape the register, these figures reflect the overwhelming prewar concentration of Roma in Slovakia.

Of those 6,500 "Czech" Roma only a few hundred returned from the Nazi concentration camps to which they were sent,[28] while under the puppet Slovak state Roma had been more fortunate. Some had been sent to labor camps; there had been occasional pogroms, burning Roma alive in their huts and machine-gunning them as they burst out with their clothes aflame; fascist Slovak Hlinka Guards had delighted in beating them up—but there had been no mass extermination. The war had ended too soon for that.

ROMANI EQUALITY—BY ASSIMILATION OR INTEGRATION

The "Gypsy Problem" and the 1958 Assimilation Campaign

Immediately after the war what can only be described as a mass migration began as thousands of Roma, often as families, left their isolated settlements in rural Slovakia for the Czech lands. There they settled mainly in the industrial conurbations of north Moravia and north Bohemia, in the larger towns, and in the border areas from which the former inhabitants, Sudeten Germans, had been expelled in 1946. For the first time Roma were participating in the general labor market on a mass scale, usually as unskilled factory or construction workers.

By 1947 of a total Romani population of 101,190, there were 16,752 in the Czech lands. They comprised over 16 percent, a marked increase over the prewar proportion, although for an obvious reason they were virtually all migrants from Slovakia. It was noted that these new migrants were forming Romani concentrations, or even minor ghettos, in the Czech towns rather than dispersing among non-Roma. Probably this was more the result of Councils' policy in allocating houses than anything else.

Also there was considerable re-migration to home settlements in Slovakia where conditions began to improve dramatically as migrants invested their earnings in new brick-built family houses.

Meanwhile, an estimated 6,000[29] nomadic Olach Roma (who regarded themselves and were regarded by other Roma as ethnically distinct) still traveled the republic with horses, carts, and tents.

The migration was viewed officially with mixed feelings. On the one hand, it was acknowledged that it was partially a positive response to new opportunities "which they made use of . . . by taking regular employment and settling permanently,"[30] but on the other hand there were fears that a concentration of Roma, both in their home settlements and in towns, would "perpetuate the backward Gypsy way of life."

Eventually it was decided in 1958 to mount a massive national campaign to raise the socioeconomic level of the Roma by assimilating them into wider Czechoslovak society. To accelerate this process, a policy aim of maximum dispersal was adopted. However, this could only be achieved by adequate control of migration, and for this reason most major measures thereafter related directly to population movement. The timing of the campaign can be explained partly by the fact that the government was previously preoccupied with more important problems, partly by the fact that in the late 1950s Czechoslovakia was preparing for the transition from a People's Republic to a Socialist Republic (declared in 1960), which entailed, among other things, a cultural revolution. Yet "we would not be able to talk of achieving a cultural revolution . . . , if we left the group of our Gypsy citizens with low cultural and living standards."[31]

To make matters more embarrassing, Roma were becoming increasingly visible largely as a result of migration but also because of their rapid population growth. In 1966 the first really reliable census of Roma showed 221,526 (1.55 percent of the whole population). Another census in the following year showed an annual increase of Third World proportions in the Romani population of between 2.6 and 2.8 percent in contrast to the overall national rate of 0.4 percent, itself one of the lowest rates in the world. Stated another way, in 1967 every eleventh baby born in Czechoslovakia was a Rom.

The campaign started with "Law 74/1958 on the permanent settlement of nomads." Although this appeared nominally to be aimed at the 6,000 nomadic Olach Roma, a register of nomads compiled in 1959 also included those non-Olach Roma judged by local authorities to be "seminomads" as well as a few non-Roma. Paragraph one of the law stated that

> local authorities shall provide comprehensive assistance to persons who lead a nomadic life to enable them to adopt a settled way of life; in particular they are obliged to help such persons in finding suitable employment and accommodation and by educational means to aim at making them orderly working citizens. (Law 74)

This was clearly different from the 1927 laws where the livelihoods of Roma were often removed at a stroke without any alternative being offered.

Registered "nomads," who numbered between 20,000 and 27,000, had their identity cards stamped and were to be refused employment in any place other than where registered, unless by mutual agreement between local authorities. If they moved without permission, therefore, they were subject to up to three years' imprisonment as parasites. The elimination of Olach nomadism appears to have been remarkably effective, although some officials were unprepared for the quick-witted Roma. "What do the comrades from Nitra report?" asked a handbook for local authorities. Nitra reported:

> In solving how to settle nomads, we came up against the question of horses. Horses enabled Gypsies to move easily from place to place. We bought them but soon afterwards . . . [some Gypsies] used this money to acquire new horses from agricultural cooperatives that had a surplus as a result of increased mechanization and were selling them off cheaply. We learned a lesson from this.[32]

In a few years, however, it was obvious that Law 74 was singularly ineffective in controlling the movement of "seminomads." This was because employers needing labor usually turned a blind eye to the regulations but more importantly because nonregistered Roma migrated too. Local authorities were usually unwilling to use their powers to register them, since this involved supervising them and providing them with jobs and accommodation. It was simpler to ignore them.

Postwar Romani Population Movement: Nomadism or Migration?

"The Gypsy is primarily and above all else a nomad," we are told. Clébert's view appears to have been shared by many Czechoslovak administrators, although since the key terms "nomadic" and "wandering" were used without any precise discussion of their meaning,[33] it is difficult to impute any firm theory underlying their use.

The 1958 classification of Roma into "nomadic," "seminomadic," and "sedentary" suggests a historical, evolutionary model—a set of progressive stages through which sections of Romani society passed on their road to "ultimate assimilation." Yet the study of Romani history in Slovakia suggests that many Roma settled as long ago as the fourteenth and fifteenth centuries. In any case, most Roma appear to have been settled by the time of Maria Theresa, and the 1893 census showed less than 2 percent of Slovakia's 36,000 Roma to be in any way nomadic—and this at a time when nearly a quarter of all Slovaks were emigrating to the United States! Given this historical development it is absurd to need to discuss "Romani nomadism" any further, but official and popular beliefs about Roma as incorrigible nomads linger on, despite historical evidence to the contrary. It is true that after 1965 government and ministry documents replaced the term "nomadic" with "migrating," and one major 1965 Government Committee report clearly recognized Romani population movement as rural to urban migration.[34] However, this frank treatment was exceptional and as recently as 1971 a Federal Ministry of Labor report explained Romani population movement by the "historically rooted proneness to nomadism in Gypsies."

Local government documents are often little better, although a firm grasp of local history might have been expected. Some list Romani settlements in Slovakia allegedly founded in the 1930s yet which local informants, both Romani and non-Romani, remember as already long established in the 1890s and which parish records show to be at least one hundred fifty years old. There they are in the records, the same Romani family names as nowadays. As for the Roma themselves—you ask them: "When did you first settle here?" Shrugs and puzzled looks. "I don't know—we've always been here."

When—after how many years of being settled—do you cease to be "sedentary" and just become "normal"? If you are a Rom, the answer seems to be—Never!

A leading sociologist of migration wrote:

A social group at rest, or a social group in motion (e.g., nomads) tends to remain so unless impelled to change; for with any viable pattern of life a value system is developed to support that pattern. To analyse the migration of Gypsies, for example, in terms of push and pull is entirely inadequate—no better, in fact, than to explain modern western migration, as Herbert Spencer did, in terms of "the restlessness inherited from ancestral nomads."[35]

Accepting Petersen's point, if it can be shown that certain Roma have been settled for a long period, the positions are reversed, and it is as

inadequate to explain their subsequent movement as "ancestral nomadism" as it is to explain anyone else's.

In addition to the historical evidence, data from fieldwork strongly
support the idea that postwar Romani population movement in Czechoslovakia is a fairly typical case of rural-to-urban migration rather than
any resurgence of nomadism.

Particularly relevant is the prominent feature of chain migration,
although official documents (and popular opinions) sometimes give the
impression that Romani population movement is an aimless swirling
over the face of Czechoslovakia, where any destination is as good as
any other. This is well illustrated in a joke told about Roma.

Gypsy (buying train tickets)	"Two to Bohemia."
Booking office clerk	"To where?"
Gypsy	"To Bohemia!"
Clerk (now irritated)	"Yes—but to where exact-ly?"
Gypsy (turning resignedly to wife)	"You see how stupid these Slovaks are—they haven't even heard of Bohemia!"

In a recent study of Romani migrants in a Czech city[36] it was
clearly demonstrated that certain areas in East Slovakia were heavily
overrepresented. Similarly, fieldwork in Romani settlements in Slovakia
revealed that for each village there were only two or three main
destination areas and that outmigrants originally migrated with relatives
and later usually to destinations where relatives were already established.

In fact, there is nothing unique about such migrations and to give
one example of this point, much of an account of the migration of
Kentucky mountaineers (in no sense nomads) is equally true of
Czechoslovak Roma. In both cases there was chain migration of
relatives and considerable movement between source and destination
areas.

Many . . . families facilitate and encourage migration and provide
in crises "havens of safety." Furthermore "branch families" in the

new communities provide a socio-psychological "cushion" for the migrant during the transitional phase.[37]

Other comparable factors are that:

(i) The pattern of extended families in the home area is related to the social isolation of these people from wider society.

(ii) Migrants travel direct to industrial centers, avoiding intervening farming areas, and perform unskilled labor.

(iii) Although not a pariah group to the same extent as Roma, Kentucky mountaineers are denigrated as ignorant rural primitives beset with social problems (for example, drunkenness, illiteracy).

(iv) This continued although lessened social isolation in towns has tended to broaden bonds among these migrants, gradually replacing extended family networks by wider regional-based ones.

If this categorization of Romani population movement is correct, the implications are profound, for characteristically the main motive for such migration has been the desire for improved economic and social status. Here emphasis must be placed on the migrants' comprehension of their previous poor conditions, their perception of the possibility of changing them, and their desire to better themselves, all concretely expressed in the fact of migration. Petersen explained the puzzling paradox that in certain periods few migrants to the United States came from those European countries where conditions were objectively the worst by stressing that poor conditions, in themselves, are insufficient to trigger off migration. Also necessary is some improvement in conditions in the source country to awaken hope in the would-be migrant of something better.[38]

As has been indicated, the history of Roma in Slovakia shows them not so much as nomadic tribes fiercely defending their independence and "tradition" as settled immigrants seeking a securer place in wider society. What happened in Czechoslovakia, then, to change the objective conditions and to raise the hopes of Roma?

The simple answer is the postwar dominance of the Communist Party. This is not theoretic speculation, it is what many Roma have said—and it makes good sense. In 1927 the Party had opposed the law on nomads and already recruited Romani members during the First

Republic. Later Roma fought alongside Communist partisans, and the arrival of the Red Army is still remembered with affection—the open friendliness of the soldiers toward them and especially their children. These things are important—the Slovak Hlinka guards had beaten them. A Romani woman expressed it all charmingly: "In the castle nearby lived a miserly lord who treated Roma badly. So God sent the Russian army to punish him and drive him out. I think he lives in Vienna now with his rich relatives."

The 1944 Košice government program proclaimed that there would be no more discrimination and while the Roma still preserved their deep suspicion, they felt it was worth taking a chance. When Gottwald (the first Communist president) took power in 1948, the main Romani settlement studied in Slovakia almost emptied as migrating families set off for the Czech lands and a new life.

The 1965 "Dispersal and Transfer" Scheme and Its Aftermath

In 1965 a new "Dispersal and Transfer" scheme was introduced to speed up the stagnant dispersal of what were termed "undesirable Gypsy concentrations." The aim was to replace the continuing "natural migration" by a system of planned population transfers from Romani settlements in Slovakia to parts of the Czech lands with a low density of Roma, that is, to spread them as thinly as possible throughout the Republic. To coordinate the whole operation and Romani affairs in general, a special government committee was established, although it had no powers to control local authorities, only to report to the government on the basis of information supplied to it by local authorities.

Quotas were agreed upon and transfers began. As a Romani spokesperson later expressed it: "They plan how many there should be in each village: horses, cows, and Gypsies."[39] In practice the plan proved difficult to operate and ground to a virtual standstill by the end of 1968. In 1966 the transfer plan was 85 percent fulfilled, in 1967 51 percent, and in 1968 only 20 percent. In all only 494 Gypsy families were transferred from Slovakia to the Czech lands in the period 1966–1968. Meanwhile, control of natural migration had again proved inadequate, for in the same period, 1,096 unplanned family migrations took place.[40]

There had been an attempt to modify Law 74 to make unplanned migration virtually illegal, but the Parliamentary Committee for Constitutional Law had decided: "the proposed solution of restricting the movement of the Gypsy population in fact limits their freedom of residence and therefore is not in harmony with article 31 of the Constitution."[41]

Despite this hostile ruling, the government committee's 1966 "Principles for Organizing Dispersal and Transfer" instructed local authorities that "every unplanned, unorganized, unconfirmed transfer of a Gypsy person or family should be considered as undesirable migration of Gypsy persons and consequently refused. The person or county who arranged the transfer should be charged the costs of returning the Gypsy person or family to the original place of residence."[42] Or in other words, if you were a Rom and not among those 494 families transferred as part of planned quotas, you could not move at all between the Czech lands and Slovakia—in theory anyway.

Little more than a year later, the same government committee reported critically that "local authorities protect themselves . . . by refusing to register these citizens [that is, Romani migrants] as permanent residents. However, the Home Office directive on Law 54/1959Sb. about population registration specifically states that registration as a permanent resident may not be made dependent on any other conditions, especially accommodation, economic, financial, and so forth."[43] Yet these local authorities were only following government committee instructions in refusing unplanned migrants; the committee seemed unaware that it was its own "Principles for Organizing Dispersal and Transfer" which were in conflict with the Home Office directive.

The collapse of the "Dispersal and Transfer" scheme is difficult to explain—not because of the lack of causes but rather their abundance. However, comparison with the previous Hapsburg assimilation attempt is instructive, for then, as now, the main opposition probably came not from the Roma but from local authorities.

Many Roma were eager to exchange their overcrowded wooden houses in Slovakia for houses and flats in the Czech lands. Although they wanted to move to an industrial center where they had relatives and not to some bureaucratically decided agricultural area where they knew no one, these Romani misgivings were not the determining factor. Crucial to the scheme were the Czech local authorities, for they were to provide accommodation for the incoming Roma. Usually skeptical to begin with and soon further discouraged by the cynical way in which some Slovak local authorities unloaded their most troublesome Roma onto them, these authorities began to refuse transfers, pleading lack of adequate accommodation.

They often had some justification, for the overall transfer plan had been prepared with little regard for the national building program, but in any case the government committee, like its Hapsburg predecessor, did not have the resources to evaluate independently such reports or the power to control the reporting local authorities.

With the ending of transfers in 1968, the government committee was disbanded and the whole policy toward Roma reconsidered. As a result permission was given for Roma to form their own sociocultural associations and organize economic cooperatives. This was a complete reversal of the 1958 position that socioeconomic equality could only be achieved by assimilating Roma and instead "recognised Romani national consciousness as a valid motivation for self-help along the new socialist path."[44] For a time Roma were treated virtually as a national minority, although never formally recognized as such, but the experiment was short-lived, and in April 1973 all Romani mass organizations were dissolved.

Rom Identity and the "Gypsy Way of Life"

From 1958 onward official documents frequently referred to "the Gypsy way of life" as a mixture of undesirable remnants of previous social orders, including such elements as nomadism, tribalism, animism, and blood feuds. The 1959 handbook for local authorities declared: "The heavy heritage of the past still stretches like a black cloud over the majority of our Gypsy citizens," or more prosaically:

> As a result of oppression and persecution by the ruling classes, Gypsies were stamped with characteristic features of a way of life and psychological nature which are nowadays an anachronism and must be removed by a process of socialist education.[45]

The argument was that the "Gypsy way of life" (embodying traditions, value systems, and attitudes) which had been formed, or rather deformed, by bitter historical experience, had been carried over into a period and form of society where it had no relevance. Resistance to change was perpetuated merely by the fact that Roma usually lived with other Roma in "undesirable concentrations." The "Gypsy way of life" was no more than a contagious disease and the remedy was isolation from other sufferers.

Looking at Roma in this way, the authorities naturally saw little point in preserving a separate identity for these people. In any case it was felt to be in their own best interest to assimilate, for:

> experience shows that all forms which revive Gypsy national [sic] consciousness, their own special organization and autonomy, preserve the present isolation and separation of Gypsies from the remainder of the population, prevent the penetration of everything progressive from our environment to the life of Gypsies and help conserve the old primitive Gypsy way of life with all its bad habits.[46]

This was the rationale behind the dispersal policy. Yet a theoretical justification was also necessary, for what sort of group were these people?

How Roma should be characterized is a basic problem that faces all administrators and researchers concerned with them. The former tend to describe them as a social rather than an ethnic group as this gives them a freer hand with policy—they are less likely to be accused of discrimination.[47] In this they are aided by the theoretical confusion of the latter, especially social anthropologists who have pursued an inconclusive search for definitive objective criteria of the ethnic group. Fredrik Barth has recently attacked this whole approach, arguing that the ascriptive aspect is logically prior to any objective characteristics of the ethnic group which, for him, consists in "a membership which identifies itself, and is identified by others, as constituting a category distinguishable from other categories of the same order."[48]

To some extent the drafting of Law 74 on nomadism could be interpreted as such an administrative attempt to define Czechoslovak Roma (or at least those who migrated) as a social group, for great care was taken to specify a way of life and avoid mentioning the word "Gypsy." However, the associated ministry directives on implementing the law were not so oblique and soon a solution was found to the problem of designating Roma without referring to them directly in the general adoption of the formula "citizen of Gypsy origin," which enshrined the contradiction in the official attitude toward them. While Rom or Gypsy was no longer to exist as a valid identity, nevertheless a series of measures were enacted which were directed specifically at Roma.

However, little was at stake in conceding Roma ethnic group status; the real problem was whether they could be seen as a national minority, thus qualifying for guaranteed group rights under Marxist-Leninist theory.

Writing of Roma in 1961, Jaroslav Sus, a Czech theorist, explained that

> the assimilation of ethnic communities is one of the pre-conditions which hasten the elimination of class society. . . . Marxism still recognizes at present the necessary existence of the most developed ethnic units—nations . . . Marxism-Leninism recognizes as correct those actions which consciously accelerate the naturally continuing assimilation process.[49]

Sus claimed that since Roma lacked one or more of Stalin's four defining characteristics of a nation—common language, territory, economic life, and psychological makeup manifested in a common culture—Roma were not a nationality but only an ethnic group and should therefore be assimilated. In any case, he argued, they were assimilating naturally.

Although claiming the full authority of Marxism-Leninism, Sus did not give a single quotation or reference from any of the Marxist-Leninist classics to corroborate his analysis. A more important omission was his failure to point out that Stalin differentiated between nation and national minority, the second being a far more flexible category not requiring all four defining characteristics. Nor did he mention the awkward fact that Roma had long been considered a nationality in the Soviet Union, or consider the arguments of Soviet theorists such as Dzunusov, whose position is close to that of Barth.

Not surprisingly, some Roma in Czechoslovakia remained unconvinced by Sus-type reasoning.

If the Gypsies have not been recognized yet as a nationality, the main cause has been fears of the results of granting various rights to the Gypsies as a nationality. Arguments—like the lack of several characteristics (territory, and so forth)—which were employed according to the precepts valid until now, were only a means to prevent recognition of the Gypsies as a nationality.[50]

Their membership in Romani associations was in itself a refutation of Sus, for these Roma were often officially regarded as "assimilated," the successes of the policy. Yet rather than seek to conceal their origin, they believed that the best way to solve the social problems of Roma was to strengthen the positive aspects of Romani identity by what amounted to a "Black Is Beautiful" campaign, led by their own socialist-inspired organizations.

The need for such a campaign may puzzle some people, for it is commonly believed that Roma are unequivocally proud of their identity. In *Stigma*, Goffman accepts that while it is difficult for minorities to maintain positive self-evaluations in the face of denigratory judgments of them by dominant minorities, the Rom might be "protected by identity beliefs of his own, he feels that he is a full-fledged normal human being and that we are the ones who are not quite human."[51]

Fieldwork among Roma in Czechoslovakia does not confirm this; rather one encounters the same deep ambivalence toward their identity that Fanon chronicled for Blacks and Sartre for Jews. Roma are at the same time proud *and* ashamed of being Roma. Proud of their music and dancing into which they pour their pain and joy; ashamed of their drinking and fighting—other ways of coping with the same feelings and the situations that arouse them.

Righteously angry at the hostile stereotypes others hold of them:

"We're not the only ones who drink! The council chairman used to lie drunk in the street, pissing in his pants."

"They say we're always in prison but we read the papers. We see what terrible crimes other people do. Gypsies don't do anything like that."

Unable to resist this stereotype:

"She's so white and beautiful you'd never think she was a Gypsy."

"We're not going to tell lies like Gypsies, are we?"[52]

"I'm not drunk, you understand—just in a good mood" (said by a Rom after collapsing into a snowdrift on his way home from a wedding).

As Sartre put it:

They have allowed themselves to be poisoned by the stereotype that others have of them, and they live in fear that their acts will correspond to this stereotype. . . . We may say that their conduct is perpetually overdetermined from the inside.[53]

These ambivalent attitudes of pride and self-hatred are the theme of many of their songs.

> You were born, my brothers,
> Of a black mother.
> What are you ashamed of?
> Perhaps that you're not white?

> You play at being *gaje*,
> Your own blood isn't good enough.
> Couldn't pride grow then
> In a Gypsy heart?

> People don't treat people
> Just by what they're called.
> The blood of blacks and whites
> Is red just the same.[54]

Understanding Romani Social Organization

The Romani population in Czechoslovakia is known to differ from non-Roma in many ways. Some of these differences have been studied in detail, but no account has yet been given of Romani social organization and its relation to their historical experience within the territory of Czechoslovakia.

This short section is not an account of Romani social organization but an example of the misunderstanding that can occur if Roma are simply seen as a closed community, whose social isolation has led to the preservation of a static, "traditional" social organization. In fact this is usually how they have been seen and also how I thought of them when starting my fieldwork. The plan was to look first at a Romani community and see how it functioned as a whole, then look at an associated non-Romani community and finally ask: What are the relations between the two? How are they connected?

The first thing to look for was the formal power structure, having read about Romani chiefs (*vajda* in Slovak and *čibalo* in Romanes). Yet things didn't seem to work that way at all and questions to Roma met with puzzled looks. Eventually someone remembered:

> Oh yes, the Slovaks chose a *vajda* during the war. They sat him on a ladder, put a red sash around him, and we had to carry him around the settlement.

Not too promising, but perhaps there would be better luck with tribalism and blood feuds. They were there all right!

The main settlement studied in Slovakia was split into two hostile lineage groups—their houses mostly faced each other across the track which served as a main street and the Roma talked of "our side" and "their side." Why was there this hostility?—"We've always hated each other."

An old Slovak told with relish of an incident soon after the war, when the balance of power was upset by migration. The lineage temporarily in the majority attacked their enemies, breaking someone's arm. Immediately a telegram was sent to the Czech lands and the next day the trans-Republic express disgorged returning relatives of the defeated lineage—enough to fill two "war-taxis." The Slovak villagers knew what was coming but they didn't tell the police—they were looking forward to it. The battle raged all night and the next day ambulances were eventually sent in to pick up the casualties.

So after reading *Tribes Without Rulers*[55] by Middleton and Tait, I wrote the following:

> Preliminary findings indicate that in formal organisation the Roma have something resembling a segmentary political system: that is, "lacking ranked and specialised holders of political authority that relations of local groups to one another are seen as a balance of

power maintained by competition between them."[56] This has important consequences for understanding certain aspects of Romani behaviour, currently defined as social problems. For example, the prevalence of fights among Roma could be seen as an integral feature of social systems where violence is a form of self-help and indeed may be "the recognized means of maintaining law in default of a superior judicial authority."[57] Although fighting is often between individuals, it appears from local accounts that conflicts can often escalate into group warfare, where the original participants can call on kinsmen to support them. Detailed study of such conflicts should provide revealing evidence of Romani social organisation.

All that was needed to complete the picture was a leopard-skin chief.

Yet despite the similarities between Romani social organization and rulerless political systems, the crucial point was that the studies in Africa had been made of "indigenous systems, unaffected by European contact."[58] Roma however have never been known as anything other than a pariah minority, so perhaps this should be the starting point, not something to be considered later. As Mick Lineton put it, writing of Travellers:

"Being a Traveller" does not consist simply in having been brought up and living among Travellers, but also in a relationship to settled people. . . . An approach which began with an ethnography of Travellers as a minority group and then related the internal workings and conceptions of the minority group to the outside world would miss the way in which those very "internal" workings and conceptions and the "outside" were part of a *single* situation, interpenetrating in many ways, as mutual reactions, reflections and relationships. Yet many studies of minority groups do start as if they were dealing with cultural or social entities instead of relationships, and while there may be areas in which the context of the total situation can be ignored or added afterwards . . . the situation of Travellers is [not] one that permits such an approach without loss and distortion. We would therefore shift the focus from the minority as such to the point of articulation between the minority and others.[59]

Looking at things from this vantage point, it is clear that these initial explanations artificially limited the total situation of the Roma as they perceived it. So what about chiefs, tribalism, and feuds, bearing in mind the actual historical experience of Roma in Slovakia as a dominated minority?

Horváthová suggests that while an elected *vajda* was important among nomadic Roma, this institution took a changed form among settled Roma. "The vajda of a Gypsy settlement . . . was above all an assistant to the village authorities in matters of local Gypsies."[60] The non-Roma needed someone through whom to exercise control.

Tribalism must be discussed on two levels. Ethnographically Czechoslovak Roma are usually divided into four groups (*Slovak* [Slovak],[61] Olach [nomadic], Sinti [German], and Hungarian), each having its own dialect of Romanes.[62] While these groups see themselves as distinct, this differentiation seems closely linked to the various non-Romani majority groups among whom they lived. This is true of other countries, for example, Britain.

"Tribal" settlements in Slovakia, where perhaps three hundred Roma share a handful of family names, are far more obviously the direct product of their historical situation rather than an age-old Romani tradition. A 1781 census in the region studied showed only one or two Romani families settled near each Slovak village, the men generally working as smiths, the women and children as servants. As described in the historical section above, both Roma and non-Roma would have usually discouraged any influx of new Romani families, and so numbers grew by natural population alone to present levels. It is ironic that these artificially highly immobile communities should later have been characterized as inherently nomadic.

Even today in Slovakia the situation has similarities to that of Maria Theresa's time. For example, it is extremely difficult for a Rom to move from one settlement to another unless by marriage, and the reasons are more or less the same.

Rural Local Official: "There are lots of empty Gypsy houses here but if we were to start accepting Gypsies that aren't ours, we'd soon be swamped."
A Rom: "We don't want any 'foreign' Gypsies here, it would only make things worse. It's better when there are less of us."

The Slovak villagers don't want too many Roma (a painful fact of which the Roma are well aware), although some are useful for odd jobs—shoveling coal or housecleaning. Patron-client relationships still exist as they did formerly, although progressively weakening as the continuing industrialization of Slovakia makes alternative employment available, especially for Romani women.

Feuds possibly arose from competition between families for the desperately scarce resources doled out by their employers. The "colonial" experience of the Roma in Slovakia, however, suggests that such conflicts should not be interpreted as an institutionalized "means of maintaining law" but as expressions of frustration in an unbearable yet insoluble situation. "In a colonial society all violence is turned inward; the natives kill each other rather than the settlers."[63]

This approach is also relevant to contemporary disputes where previous direct exploitation has been replaced by subtler forms of discrimination, justified by hostile stereotyping. Roma often see this quite clearly. They don't need to read sociology books to understand how stereotyping works; they have more direct ways of learning.

Romani member of rural council: I've been round the village making a register (of cattle, and so forth) and some of those outlying Slovak cabins—you should have smelled them! But the whites keep quiet about their own bad examples—yet if any Gypsy is dirty, they point to him and say to us: "That's what you're like, you Gypsies!"

Understanding doesn't seem to help much, though; not if you can't do anything effective to change things. So what you do is silly things, despairing things—and the whites laugh at you all the more. The same man took part in a Romani petition to demand the removal from the settlement of the three families the Roma were most ashamed of. It was senseless, of course; who else would have them? The outcome was predictable—a fight—two Roma got six months in jail and the families still live in the same settlement. And the stereotype was confirmed once more.

While this approach sees the "Gypsy way of life" as a product of their past experience, it also throws some doubt on the claim that in a socialist society like Czechoslovakia this way of life is nowadays entirely an anachronism.

In 1958 there were predictions of a speedy assimilation of Roma, but when these hopes were disappointed the "Gypsy problem" was reported to need several generations for its solution. The slow rate of progress was attributed simply to a cultural time lag, an undynamic view of how traditions, value systems, and so forth, are transmitted. However, with class consciousness, young people do not automatically adopt patterns simply because they are their parents', but also because they find the patterns of their parents relevant to their own experience, they realize their own situation is comparable to that of their parents.

The possibility must therefore be faced that within the socialist framework, which undoubtedly offers better opportunities for Romani integration than have ever been known, there nevertheless may be features which serve to perpetuate the deep-rooted hostility of Roma toward non-Roma, such as continuing discrimination against Roma.

On a local level Roma sometimes encountered severe difficulties in trying to realize their ambitions to buy flats in town or build new family houses, as Sus frankly admitted.

> Frequently either entire local authorities or their individual members . . . try to prevent Gypsy families from moving into empty flats among non-Gypsies. By means of bureaucratic methods they make it difficult for Gypsies to build a family house outside of the Gypsy settlement . . . and often make it impossible for them to obtain a building plot.[64]

Although many complaints were made of such flagrant violations of the official policy, little was done to punish offenders.

More seriously, despite the good intentions of its formulators, certain aspects of the 1958 policy were unwittingly discriminatory. While Roma welcomed the possibility of better houses, they resented the restrictions on their movements. When a recent national census of the whole population was made, the immediate assumption of the Roma in the settlement studied was that it was another "nomads' register" aimed at controlling them. As the Gypsy-Rom Associations pointed out, decisions were made about Roma but never by them.

Similarly, the outright rejection of Romani identity as completely worthless can have done little to help these people to resolve their identity crisis but served to undermine further their self-respect. The situation in Czechoslovakia today is consequently a paradox. In some important respects the aim of socioeconomic equality has almost been achieved. In 1970 the male employment rate for Roma in the Czech lands equaled the national rate and since, as heavy manual workers in a socialist state their wages are generally above average, a recent study showed them to be one of the wealthier ethnic groups in Czechoslovakia.[65] Yet at the same time their rate of criminal convictions was four times the national average (1967 figures) and their alcoholism was comparable.

Some still sing about their experiences—new songs as well as traditional ones—migrant and prison blues to comfort themselves, not for customers. Perhaps they say more than statistics.

> I don't beg for bread
> Even though I'm hungry.
> Just give the Gypsy
> A little respect.[66]

NOTES

1. "Rom" (plural "Roma") is the name used by these people to refer to themselves. Names like the more familiar "Gypsy" and so on were coined by non-Roma.
2. Thompson 1968:9, 10.
3. Clébert 1967:246.
4. Ibid.
5. Puxon 1973.
6. Fanon 1970:8.
7. Horváthová 1964.
8. Hence the French term "bohémien" for Roma.
9. Clébert 1967:68.

10. At Spiš castle in Slovakia.
11. Poissonier 1855, quoted in Horváthová 1964:48.
12. Clébert 1967:63, 134.
13. Jamnická-Šmerglová 1955:50, 51. Similar treatment was sometimes given to vagrants (Horváthová 1964:57).
14. Drobil, quoted in Horváthová 1964:73.
15. Horváthová 1964:113.
16. Schwicker 1883:69, quoted in Horváthová 1964:100.
17. Taylor 1964:17.
18. Clébert 1967:102.
19. Taylor 1964:19.
20. Straka 1964:77.
21. Nováček 1968:22.
22. Horváthová 1964:155.
23. Jamnická-Šmerglová 1955:65.
24. Nováček 1968:25.
25. Ibid., 87.
26. Jamnická-Šmerglová 1955:80.
27. However, a 1939 police report estimates this figure at 13,000. (Kenrick and Puxon 1972:135.)
28. Ibid.
29. 1958 estimate.
30. *Práce mezi cikánským obyvatelstvem* (Prague: ÚPV, 1959) (hereafter cited as "Handbook").
31. "Handbook," 5.
32. Ibid., 12.
33. Law 74's definition is little help here: "§2. A nomadic life is led by someone who, whether in a group or individually, wanders from place to place and avoids honest work or makes his living in some disreputable way. . . ."
34. "The departure of the Rom population to industrial centers is an objective process."
35. Petersen 1970:52.
36. Davidová 1970a.
37. Brown, Schwarzweller, and Mangalam 1970:116.
38. Petersen 1968:287.
39. Quoted in Hübschmannová 1968.
40. Czech Ministry of Labor and Social Affairs 1969.
41. Quoted in Davidová 1970a:306.
42. Quoted in ibid.:296.
43. Quoted in ibid.:295.
44. Puxon 1973:13.

45. "Handbook," 6.
46. Ibid., 28.
47. For example, in English law Gypsies are defined as a social group, whereas researchers see them as an ethnic group.
48. Barth 1970:11.
49. Sus 1961:98.
50. Svaz Cikánů-Romů 1969.
51. Goffman 1968:17.
52. The colloquial verb "to tell lies" in Slovak is *cigánit* (literally "to Gypsy").
53. Quoted in Fanon 1970:82.
54. Quoted Hübschmannová 1960:65.
55. Middleton and Tait 1958.
56. Ibid., 6.
57. Ibid., 20–21.
58. Ibid., 1.
59. Lineton 1973.
60. Horváthová 1964:239.
61. The vast majority and the subject of this essay.
62. Davidová 1970b.
63. Geismar 1971:191.
64. Sus 1961:111.
65. Machonin et al. 1969:537.
66. Quoted in Hübschmannová 1960 and in a different translation in Kenrick and Puxon 1972:209.

REFERENCES

Barth, Fredrik
   1970   "Introduction," in Fredrik Barth (ed.) *Ethnic Groups and Boundaries: The Social Organisation of Culture Difference*.London: George Allen & Unwin.
Brown, J. S., Schwarzweller, H. K., and Mangalam, J. J.
   1970   "Kentucky Mountain Migration and the Stem-family: An American Variation on a Theme by Le Play." In Clifford J. Jansen, ed., *Readings in the Sociology of Migration*, Oxford: Pergamon, pp. 93–120.
Clébert, Jean-Paul
   1967   *The Gypsies*. Trans. Charles Duff. Harmondsworth: Penguin.

Czech Ministry of Labor and Social Affairs
1969   *Zpráva o současném stavu řešení otázek cikánského obyvatelstva v ČSR* (Report on the Current Situation in Solving Questions of Gypsy Inhabitants in the Czech Socialist Republic), 2 December.
Davidová, Eva
1970a   *Cikánské (Romské) etnikum v Ostravě.* Prague: Výzkumní ústav výstavby a architektury.
1970b   "The Gypsies in Czechoslovakia," trans. Will Guy. *Journal of the Gypsy Lore Society* 49(3–4):84–97.
Fanon, Frantz
1970   *Black Skins, White Masks.* Trans. Charles Lam Markmann. London: Paladin.
Geismar, Peter
1971   *Fanon.* New York: Dial.
Goffman, Erving
1968   *Stigma: Notes on the Management of Spoiled Identity.* Harmondsworth: Penguin.
"Handbook"
1959   *Práce mezi cikánským obyvatelstvem.* Prague: Úřad předsednictva vlády, edice časopisu národní výbory.
Horváthová, Emília
1964   *Cigáni na Slovensku.* Bratislava: Vydavatel'stvo Slovenskej akadémie vied.
Hübschmannová, Milena
1960   *Cikánské písně.* Prague: Mladá fronta.
1968   "cikáni = Cikáni?", in *Reportérova ročenka*, Prague: Reportér.
Jamnická-Šmerglová, Zdeňka
1955   *Dějiny našich cikánů.* Prague: Orbis.
Kenrick, Donald, and Grattan Puxon
1972   *The Destiny of Europe's Gypsies.* London: Heinemann.
Law 74
1958   *Zákon č.74/1958 Sb. o trvalem usídlení kočujících osob* (Law 74/1958 on the permanent settlement of nomadic persons), passed by the National Assembly of the Czechoslovak Republic on 17 October 1958 (in "Handbook" 1959:63).
Lineton, Mick
1973   *Proposal for a Research Study on Travellers in Scotland and Ireland* (unpublished proposal to Social Science research Council). Bristol: Department of Sociology, University of Bristol.
Machonin, Pavel et al.
1969   *Československá společnost.* Bratislava: Epocha.

Middleton, John, and David Tait
    1958   *Tribes Without Rulers: Studies in African Segmentary Systems.*
           London: Routledge and Kegan Paul.
Nováček, Josef
    1968   *Cikáni včera, dnes a zítra.* Prague: Socialistická akademie.
Petersen, W.
    1968   "Migration," in D. L. Sills, ed., *International Encyclopedia of the
           Social Sciences.* New York: Macmillan.
    1970   "A General Typology of Migration," in Clifford J. Jansen, ed.,
           Readings in the Sociology of Migration. Oxford: Pergamon.
Poissonier, Alfred
    1855   *Les esclaves Tsiganes dans les principautés danubiennes.* Paris:
           Ferdinand Sartorius.
Puxon, Grattan
    1973   *Roma: Europe's Gypsies.* London: Minority Rights Group.
Schwicker, J. H.
    1883   *Die Zigeuner in Ungarn und Siebenbürgen.* Vienna: K. Prochaska.
Sus, Jaroslav
    1961   *Cikánská otázka v ČSSR.* Prague: Státní nakladatelství politické
           literatury.
Straka, Václav
    1964   *Czechoslovakia Today.* Prague: Artia.
Svaz Cikánů-Romů
    1969   *Program ústavujícího sjezdu svazu Cikánů-Romů v ČSR* (Program of
           the founding congress of the Gypsy-Rom Association of the Czech
           Socialist Republic). Brno: Svaz Cikánů-Romů v ČSR.
Taylor, A. J. P.
    1964   *The Habsburg Monarchy.* London: Penguin.
Thompson, E. P.
    1968   *The Making of the English Working Class.* Harmondsworth: Penguin.

Afterword 1996:

A Brave New World

It is now over twenty years since I first wrote about the experience of
the Roma in Czechoslovakia. Then I had argued in favor of writing
about Roma in specific historical contexts since "as a small and

vulnerable minority, it was far more likely that their history would be more a tale of what was done to them than of what they themselves had done" (above, page 15). Developments since that time confirm the validity of this approach since this is the only way the changing fortunes of Roma can be fully understood.

At the time of my original article only a limited amount of attention had been paid to Roma by Czechoslovak sociologists and social anthropologists, although some carefully researched historical and ethnographic studies had been published. Meanwhile these people had long been scrutinized by ministry and local authority officials, assiduously compiling statistics about population numbers, housing conditions, level of assimilation and, most important, migratory movements. This almost frenzied activity was driven partly by the fear that one day, in the not too distant future, parts of their beloved country would be overwhelmed by the unruly, dark-skinned Roma, who were seen as a foreign and alien race in spite of the fact that they had been settled on the territory of the Republic for over half a millennium.

Since then the world has changed unimaginably for Czechs and Slovaks with the almost miraculous collapse of Communist rule without bloodshed in what they called the "Velvet Revolution" of 1989. For Roma, too, life changed dramatically after the fall of communism for, as so often in their past, they found themselves the pawns of powerful political processes beyond their control. As the new, fledgling states exposed their cumbersome inherited economic structures to the unsentimental forces of market pressures in pursuit of the holy grail of a "market economy" and eventual incorporation into the European Union, the impact on Roma was immediate.

Like their fellow citizens Roma had welcomed the democratic principles of post-communism, but for them the first tangible experience of this brave new world was not of a sudden expansion of civic liberties but of harsh economic realities as many were flung out of their predominantly manual jobs in the now virtually redundant heavy industries. As part of the same broad process some Romani women were driven to take up prostitution, joining the growing numbers of women offering themselves for sale on city streets or at the roadside of main routes leading to the West—the first visible advertisement to tourists and truck drivers of the new freedoms on offer.

It seems ironic that formerly I saw my writing about Roma as bearing witness to the worthily intentioned yet oppressive Communist policy toward Roma and yet now I find myself looking back to this era with a certain measure of nostalgia. This is in spite of the fact that formerly many of the administrative measures were blatantly discriminatory and demonstrably illegal. At times they breached not just the Czechoslovak constitution but amounted to a denial of basic human rights.

But what would the new freedoms bring? An intelligent and highly articulate Rom in his early thirties felt, in 1991, that he could see the writing on the wall, even though he and his wife still had their jobs. "I am going to vote Communist at the next elections," he declared, "and so are all my family and friends. The Communists are the only people who ever cared about the Roma" (Guy 1991). He had not forgotten what had preceded the often forcible attempts to control Romani migratory movement during the years of communism. While Czechs fondly remember the interwar republic as a period of humane liberalism, for most Roma these had been years of grinding poverty, sharpened by the terror of unpredictable racist beatings which occasionally escalated into pogroms. The eventual culmination had been the holocaust when almost all Roma living in the Czech lands had been annihilated.

The Final Years of Communism

Unlike other reforms during the Prague Spring of 1968, the strengthened position of Slovakia survived the reimposition of strict Party control (or "normalization") after the Soviet-led military invasion in August that year. To some extent it was a matter of divide and rule. In this case the devolution of federal powers actually worked directly against Slovak interests for the likelihood of pursuing any nationwide policy toward Roma almost vanished.

Since 1965 a main policy aim of federal officials dealing with the Romani population had been to lighten Slovakia's load by the planned dispersal of families to the Czech lands. Now the Czech government was able to take advantage of the new arrangements. First it dismantled the existing administrative structure and then canceled the previous policy by revoking, unilaterally, a major federal government directive intended to apply to the whole territory of the Czechoslovak state (Czech Socialist Republic 1969 & 1970). The Slovaks protested impotently as these new arrangements were being drafted, regarding them as legitimation at national level of the earlier, near-illegal resistance by Czech local authorities to the dispersal program and, more ominously, as a statement of intent that the Czechs would refuse in future to take equal responsibility for a problem of whole-state dimensions.

> [These changes] . . . perhaps suit the Czech regions where there are about 40,000 Gypsies. In Slovakia, where today we have 170,000 (of which perhaps 100,000 live in quite inhuman conditions), the latest administrative structure for solving the Gypsy question is utterly unsuitable. (Slovak Socialist Republic 1968)

The administrative division of Slovakia from the Czech lands had the further effects of weakening central control over local authorities and disrupting the systematic collection of nationwide statistics. In spite of these developments, attempts were still made to coordinate policy toward Roma in the now separate parts of the Republic under the leadership, in the Czech lands, of the Federal Ministry of Labor and Social Affairs and, in Slovakia, of a special Government Commission for Questions of Gypsy Inhabitants (Komise vlády SSR pre otázky cigánských obyvatelov). Slovakia, indeed, returned to the administrative system which had overseen federal policy from 1965 to 1968. Consequently the treatment of Roma in the twenty years of normalization up to the end of Communist rule is a partially chronicled story of sporadic and uneven development—often dependent on local initiatives rather than stemming from directives sent from the capital cities of Prague and Bratislava.

On reflection, the actual differences that official policy made to the lives of Roma during the two decades between 1969 and 1989, compared with the decade that preceded them, are less distinct than might be thought. Although there was a concerted campaign to disperse and assimilate Roma in the earlier years, these sweeping nationwide policies had been largely ineffectual in achieving their aims, bringing a mixture of benefits, frustrations, and occasionally worse to the Roma caught up in them. The later, more piecemeal approach, due to more disjointed administrative structures, resulted in a pattern of patchy development that matched the reality of the earlier period.

It can also be argued that throughout the years of Communist rule much of the gradual improvement in the living conditions of Roma was due largely to their own efforts in taking advantage of the opportunities provided by economic expansion. Rather than conforming to the Czech and Slovak stereotype of them as passive recipients of state aid, many Roma used their initiative in moving to places where their labor was needed, putting aside much of their earnings and investing these savings in new family houses or flats. In this endeavor they were often opposed by local authorities and reaped the usual bitter rewards of migrant workers (Guy 1975).

In the late 1970s another organization took a keen interest in the situation of Roma in Czechoslovakia and published a report on their conditions. However, this was no official body but Charter 77, a dissident group established in 1977 to bear witness to violations of human rights safeguarded by the 1975 Helsinki Accords to which Czechoslovakia was a signatory. This major report (Charter 77 1979) took a caustic view of the whole of Communist policy toward Roma as well as listing specific aspects of human rights abuses. It maintained that the denial of national minority status to Roma, which underpinned the policy's rationale, "was dictated by the desire of the ruling powers to reduce the size of the minority problem, and subordinate its handling to the alleged interests of the whole of society" (Charter 77 1979a & b).

Most of the contemporary official measures condemned by the report were not new but rather a perpetuation of long-established practices. The illegitimacy of using the 1958 law on nomadism to control the movement of Roma, "who, while not nomads, are forced to migrate on account of living conditions not of their own making" was branded as "racist repression" (Charter 77 1979a:7). In practice this law had failed to stem the continuing flow of economic migrants, although the consequences of being registered as a "nomad" were certainly unpleasant for the 20,000 or more Roma wrongly identified in this way. The most pressing problem for migrants to the Czech lands remained the frequent and illegal refusal of local authorities to register them as residents, debarring them from eligibility for municipal housing and forcing them either to squat in derelict buildings or crowd in with relatives already established in the town (Guy 1975; Charter 77 1979a:7–8).

In Slovakia the perennial problem was that of the primitive living conditions in the many segregated and isolated settlements. The plan had been to eliminate them all by 1990 but there was no hope of this goal being achieved. In the meantime many Slovak councils continued to refuse permission for Roma either to buy existing Slovak-owned village houses or build their own among the Slovaks (Guy 1975).

One dramatic and innovative housing initiative in the 1970s and 1980s was the "experiment" of moving Roma from their previous concentrations in dilapidated urban ghettos or in overcrowded, unsanitary settlements on the edge of town directly into brand-new housing projects. The motivation behind the initiative was to rid the towns concerned of their aggravating eyesores at a stroke, but there had been little practical planning or consultation before the move. Those relocated had little choice in the matter and were often combined in ways that soon led to friction and disillusionment. Although the new blocks of town flats were often spacious and of high quality, the new developments were intended to maintain the segregation of Roma and consequently remained ghettos.

[M]any of these housing projects, among them Chanov in Most (Northern Bohemia), Lunik 9 in Kosice (Eastern Slovakia), and Duzavska Cesta (also called "Black City") in Rimavska Sobota, were demolished by some inhabitants and have become highly publicized examples used by non-Roma to justify initiatives to prevent Roma from moving into non-Romani neighborhoods. (Tritt 1992:56)

Some of the fiercest condemnation in the report was directed against the growing practice of sterilizing Romani women which it characterized as a "planned administrative policy" (Charter 77 1979b:22). There is considerable evidence that during the 1970s and 1980s Romani women were either offered financial inducements to undergo sterilization, or were pressured into agreeing to this procedure, or were even sterilized without their knowledge or consent after giving birth by cesarean section or when having an abortion. While Romani women with several children were the most frequent victims, this was by no means always the case (Tritt 1992:19–32).

A 1972 Decree on Sterilization, issued by the Ministries of Health of the Czech and Slovak Socialist Republics, was careful not to mention Roma by name, but other evidence makes it clear that this ethnic group was a prime target. A 1977 briefing paper for the Slovakian Government Commission referred to what it called the "high unhealthy" level of the Romani population and urged increased grants for sterilization to counterbalance the income from child benefits, since "even a backward Gypsy woman is able to calculate that, from an economic point of view, it is more advantageous for her to give birth every year" (quoted in Tritt 1992:20). In the East Slovakia Region the proportion of all sterilizations involving Roma rose from 25.8 percent in 1983 to 36.6 percent by 1987, while in the Czech lands 25 percent of all sterilization grants in the late 1980s were made to Roma, even though this group constituted only 2 or 3 percent of the total population. The fullest discussion of this topic is in the 1992 Helsinki Watch Report (Tritt 1992) and in a 1990 report investigating Charter 77 charges for the Lau Mazeril Foundation in Amsterdam (Pellar and Andrs 1990).

As with official attempts to control migration, sterilizations were not a new occurrence—but from the early 1970s they did appear to have become more widespread and readily sanctioned. The same was true of other practices condemned by Charter 77. Romani children continued to be transferred to special schools intended for those with severe learning difficulties, creating for many what amounted to an educational ghetto which complemented the physical segregation of their dwellings. An official report revealed that by 1990/91 of all children at such schools in Czechoslovakia 40.7 percent were Roma, while in Slovakia this proportion was a massive 65.3 percent—two out of three (Institute for Educational Information 1991). In Slovakia, even when Romani children attended ordinary schools, they were often seated separately from Slovaks (Tritt 1992:42–44). Meanwhile, in a process familiar in the West, "black" Roma were more likely than "whites" to be sent to prison for the same offense and their prison sentence was likely to be longer (Charter 77 1979b:22; Tritt 1992:91–93).

In spite of well-documented evidence of discrimination against Roma at every level during the period of normalization, this was flatly denied by *Rudé právo*, the Communist party daily (21 June 1986). I language reminiscent of the strident tones of earlier assimilationism, the newspaper dismissed Roma unwilling to adapt to socialist society as "victims of capitalist ways of thinking and vestiges of the past" (Kalvoda 1992:103). The main purpose of the article, however, was to support the government's rejection of the appeal of the World Romani Congress for Roma to be recognized as a national minority as had happened long before in the Soviet Union and more recently in Yugoslavia (1981). At this time Hungary, too, was taking cautious steps in this direction (Puxon 1987:9–12).

Such intransigence was not to last for within little more than a year there were signs, emanating from the higher political ranks, of a more relaxed approach to "questions of Gypsy inhabitants." As it turned out these encouraging signs were irrelevant. Slight shifts in official policy were soon to be overwhelmed by far more momentous changes, which would transform the political map of Central and Eastern Europe and pose a whole new set of problems for the Roma of Czechoslovakia.

The Early Years of Post-Communism

At first the omens seemed promising for Roma when the demoralized Communist leadership relinquished power without a struggle in the face of determined popular resistance. This time, unlike 1968, the hard-liners knew that no help would come from Moscow to shore up their unloved regime.

Roma played an active part in bringing about the changes by joining the mass demonstrations of the 1989 Revolution and the newly formed Romani Civic Initiative Party (ROI) was a partner in the coalition parties which swept to victory in the first post-Communist elections—Civic Forum (OF) in the Czech lands and Public against Violence (VPN) in Slovakia. In 1990 Romani deputies were elected to Federal, Czech, and Slovak Parliaments—and not only as candidates for ROI but for other parties as well. These parties included the Communist party, and it is worth remembering that there had been Rom deputies during the Communist period.

Matching their new political representation the formal status of Roma was reconsidered, and in April 1991 the Slovak government passed resolution 153 "to acknowledge the Roma to be a nationality in the contemporary terminology and to guarantee their political and legal equality of rights" (Tritt 1992:14–16). The Czech and Federal authorities, while moving some way in the same direction, were more hesitant about making such a forthright declaration. At the same time there was a flowering of Romani culture. Newspapers and magazines in the Romani language soon appeared and throughout the Republic over thirty cultural organizations applied for official registration. A museum of Romani culture was founded in Brno, the capital of Moravia, while in East Slovakia a Romani theater opened its doors in Prešov, and an innovatory department of Romani music was established as part of an existing conservatory in Košice. This new beginning was celebrated in Brno, in July 1990, by staging the first World Romani Festival, attended by President Václav Havel.

The election of Havel to the presidency to wide popular acclaim at the end of 1989 was another hopeful sign that life would be better for Roma after the Revolution. Havel had been the leading figure in the Charter 77 movement and soon reaffirmed his earlier commitment to the plight of Roma by speaking out on TV at this festival. Yet Havel's scrupulous adherence to moral principles, which had made him the conscience of the nation during the last decade of communism, now seemed strangely at odds with the thrusting, devil-take-the-hindmost atmosphere of post-communism where his credo of "living in truth" had little place.

Havel's compassionate attitude to Roma was deeply unpopular since the rapid growth of this minority was perceived as an ever-encroaching threat. In 1991 a comparative international poll found that 91 percent of Czechoslovaks held unfavorable views of Roma, a far higher degree of antipathy toward an ethnic group than was expressed by any other European nation included in the survey (Times Mirror 1991). This widespread dislike found public expression in many ways, even emerging in the unlikely context of a beauty contest. When asked on national TV about her ambitions in life, a contestant for the title of Miss Czech-Slovak 1993 replied simply: "I want to become a public prosecutor so that I can cleanse my town of all its brown-skinned inhabitants." In the storm of publicity which followed, university entrant Magdalena Babička explained that it had all been just an embarrassing misunderstanding (Stewart 1993).

The antagonism was not limited to verbal assaults. The confused conditions of rapid economic flux and an uncertain legal interregnum encouraged the emergence of neo-fascist groups which had more direct ways of expressing their feelings. These ranged from skinhead gangs to a Ku Klux Klan and a "White League" (*Bílá liga*). Racially motivated attacks and even murders of Roma began to increase—with accusations that the police sometimes looked on as disinterested bystanders (Tritt 1992:93–109). One neo-Nazi skinhead, proud owner of a Wehrmacht helmet, boasted of shooting Roma with a rifle from his Prague balcony—for sport (David and Serotek 1991).

> On November 24, 1991, several hundred skinheads marched down Wenceslas Square shouting "Gypsies to the gas chamber!" "Blacks raus!" "Czechs for Czechs!" "Oi, oi, liquidate ROI!" (the Romani Civic Initiative Party), "Sčuka [the chair of ROI] will hang!" Eventually they marched through Žižkov, a neighborhood where many Roma live, shouting "White Žižkov!" As they walked, some non-Romani inhabitants clapped and waved out of their windows. (*Lidové noviny*, 25 November 1991, quoted in Tritt 1992:3)

Apart from the racist attacks the most direct and widespread effect of post-communism for Roma was unemployment. In spite of the relatively low overall unemployment rate in the Czech lands—around 3 percent in 1992—this actually represented a rise of 3 percent from the full-employment economy of communism. This meant real hardship for those who were victims of the shake-out—mainly the old, the young, women, and unskilled workers. Many Romani workers came into these categories and, of all ethnic groups, the Roma undoubtedly suffered worst of all.

The situation was even starker in Slovakia with an unemployment rate up to five times that of the Czech lands (Plichtová 1993:18). Here, too, Roma were often laid off and formed high proportions of the newly unemployed. At the end of 1991 in the large town of Rimavská Sobota (Central Slovakia) where Roma were in the minority, almost two-thirds of the 6,530 persons known to be unemployed were Roma (Tritt 1992:78).

Apart from being among the first to lose their jobs, Roma suffered major difficulties in restarting work. On the whole Roma were unskilled workers with few qualifications and therefore at a disadvantage in seeking any new employment resulting from restructuring. A more important factor was that they now suffered discrimination on an unprecedented scale when applying for advertised vacancies—even for unskilled jobs. In spite of regulations forbidding discriminatory hiring practices, many local employment offices openly displayed job details which included stipulations that applicants should not be Roma. This practice was widespread both in the Czech lands and Slovakia (Tritt 1992:76–90; Guy 1991).

These developments had been predicted with chilling accuracy as long ago as 1979 in the Charter 77 report, which accused the Communist administration of deliberately perpetuating the disadvantaged situation of Roma in order to use them as a flexible and compliant reserve pool of industrial labor.

> In the current economic situation, the powers-that-be need the Romani minority to remain in the position which it is in now: uneducated, without clear prospects, and ready to move from one end of the republic to the other in search of unskilled work without knowing where they are going to live. The existence of unskilled labor is not, however, a normal or inevitable consequence of economic development. . . . The demand for unskilled labor will then fall, threatening the Roma with massive unemployment which will expose this ruthlessly urbanized minority to extreme pressures, and fuse their social ostracism and material oppression with a new ethnic consciousness, all the stronger the more cruelly it is today suppressed. (Charter 77 1979b:7)

Political tensions between the two partners in the Republic had been mounting throughout 1992 and were eventually resolved by still further separation in what was dubbed the "Velvet Divorce." On 1 January 1993 the country was divided and Slovakia became a sovereign state for the first time in its history. All too soon these political changes were to have major implications for the life of Roma. In the early 1970s I wrote that Slovakia was "the homeland of virtually all of contemporary Czechoslovakia's adult Roma" (above, page 16) but by the early 1990s Roma had been established in the Czech lands for well over forty years and, in spite of complex patterns of migration, settlement, and remigration, perhaps as many as two-thirds of those living in the Czech lands had been born there (Gross 1994:vi).

The 1991 Census might have thrown light on this matter as Roma were given the right to identify themselves as such for the first time since the interwar republic. As it turned out, less than a third of the estimated 400,000 Roma in Czechoslovakia took this option (Plichtová 1993:17). This small proportion was explained partly by "a low level of ethnic awareness" (ibid.) but, far more plausibly, by the realistic fear that to label themselves in official records as Roma was to invite further bureaucratic repression in the future. Many Roma simply thought it safer to camouflage themselves as Czechs, Slovaks, or Hungarians.

Roma were right to fear more trouble ahead. But, in the event, the strategy of adopting another nationality proved of little help to those living in the Czech lands when a carefully drafted citizenship law came into force with the creation of the new state. As a bizarre consequence of the previous citizenship rules, anyone under forty whose parents were registered as Slovak, was deemed to be Slovak also. Consequently almost all Roma living in the Czech Republic at the start of 1993 were regarded as Slovak citizens, irrespective of where they were born and even of whether they had ever been to Slovakia in their lives (Gross 1993; Borger 1994:13).

For anyone other than an ethnic Czech it was necessary to make a special application and meet stringent conditions in order to gain Czech citizenship. These requirements included proof of permanent registered residence in the Czech lands for at least two years, no criminal record for the previous five years, no criminal proceedings pending in Slovakia, and no taxes owing in Slovakia. All of these posed considerable problems for Roma. Difficulties in obtaining residence registration had not eased with the ending of communism and many were technically ineligible on this count, even though they had lived in the Czech lands for longer than the required period. Likewise many adult Roma, estimated as up to 50 percent, had convictions—though mostly for minor offenses such as pilfering state property—while the last two criteria involved obtaining the relevant documentation from Bratislava. In some cases personal visits were needed and a wearisome trek from office to office to plead with unhelpful officials. This involved process was complicated immeasurably for the Roma by their lack of technical expertise, financial resources and—in many cases—basic literacy (Gross 1993).

This law did attract a limited level of international protest. The CSCE High Commissioner on National Minorities "strongly urged that such legislation be changed," and U.S. Congress members asked the prime minister to alter what they described as "the most extensive revocation of citizenship since the end of the Second World War." Czech Premier Václav Klaus scornfully dismissed these condemnations as "insignificant," and even Havel, now reelected as Czech President, publicly defended the law (Gross 1994).

Reaction to these new measures was very mixed. In Cheb (West Bohemia), where officials were said to be sympathetic, less than 10 percent of the town's Roma appeared to have applied for Czech citizenship seven months after the changes, while in the nearby large industrial town of Plzeň, this figure was estimated to be between 31 and 62 percent (Gross 1993). More important, though, was the response of Czech officials to the many Roma without Czech citizenship. What would happen to them?

Surprisingly, the consequences of national legislation seemed to depend on local interpretation, which varied widely. Shortly before the division of the state a Czech ethnographer, working for the Federal Presidency at the Department of Human Rights and Humanitarian Issues, clearly identified the problem. It stemmed from devolution following the ending of Communist centralism since now "[t]he Federal Government has no legal form by which it can force local authorities to change their decisions, especially in the Czech Republic. Sovereignty of the local government exists in most fields" (quoted in Tritt 1992:10). In this case the democratic transfer of power to local level had resulted in a situation where the constitutional rights of Romani citizens now depended on the opinions of minor functionaries.

Although no wholesale deportations of Roma back to Slovakia were envisaged, some officials hoped that similar results might be achieved by attrition. Various local authorities throughout the Czech Republic told human rights lawyers that Roma without Czech citizenship "would be treated like foreigners in future and would lose their benefits under the law." These could include unemployment, health, welfare, and insurance benefits as well as the loss of rights to vote, obtain passports, and purchase privatization coupons (Gross 1993). A later report showed that these threats were being put into practice (Gross 1994:vi).

In parallel with the new citizenship law the Prosecutor General submitted a national "migration law" in December 1992 to protect places "endangered by migration." This was justified by unsubstantiated reports that month that 2,000 Roma had migrated from Slovakia to beat the deadline for the breakup of Czechoslovakia. The proposed law required visitors to be approved by local councils, to pay a tariff if they stayed for more the five days, and to be subject to police inspection. Unauthorized visitors were liable to eviction and their hosts to imprisonment or fines of more than £2,000. After an outcry from Czech legal experts and accusations of Stalinism, the law was withdrawn, but local authorities still had recourse to their own migration bylaws to carry out evictions. Meanwhile the Minister of the Interior, former dissident Jan Ruml, speculated about reintroducing the previous regulation from Communist times requiring foreigners, now "including Slovaks," to register with the police if they remained longer than three days in spite of assurances about freedom of movement when the "divorce" was being negotiated (Greenberg 1993a).

I had argued earlier that postwar Romani population movement to the Czech lands was best understood as that of migrant workers flocking to work opportunities (above, pages 28–32). Twenty years later here was the corollary of a developed industrial state which had first encouraged such workers, then had outgrown the need for them, and now was attempting to deny them the right to remain where they had labored, raised families, and, in many cases, had been born. It is sadly appropriate that at a time when the Czech Republic is seeking to emulate and join the European Union, it displays some of the most inhuman yet characteristic features of its leading member states. It is significant that in June 1993, the Council of Europe set no conditions on minority rights for admitting the Czech Republic as a member—but it was otherwise for Slovakia.

In Slovakia the effects of the political division of the country were more muted. But here, although Roma were not faced with immediate withdrawal of state benefits as a consequence of the removal of their citizenship, they remained vulnerable to similar threats to be realized in other ways. In September 1993 the Slovak Premier, Vladimir Meciar, paid a visit to the town of Spišská Nová Ves in East Slovakia, the administrative center of a district with one of the highest proportions of Roma in the whole of Slovakia. There he proposed that family allowances of Roma should be lowered to help cut "extensive reproduction of the socially unadaptable and mentally backward population." In the furor that followed international Romani organizations and the Simon Wiesenthal Center accused Meciar of adopting "the thinking and diction of nazism" and called on the Council of Europe to reconsider the membership of Slovakia, its newest member.

Meanwhile the Slovak journalist Karel Hirman, who had reported the story for the official Czech news agency (ČTK), was condemned by Meciar as a tool of an international plot to bring about the "disintegration" of Slovakia and threatened with a libel action and two years in prison (Greenberg 1993b). Since that time Meciar has been more mindful of his public image in the West. In September 1995, for example, he attended a ceremony in the village of Nálepkovo, East Slovakia, where the foundation stone for a new settlement was being laid. Whether such symbolic gestures signify practical intervention to improve the real prospects for Roma is doubtful, as the news report made clear.

> The settlement of forty-six wooden houses [at Nálepkovo] is intended for Roma, who make up half of the unemployed in that area, where factories that once employed them have been closing down or turning to labor from Ukraine. The ČTK report did not say whether Romani organizations considered the project to be a welcome relief and sign of support from the government, or to be a segregationist solution. (Lemon 1995)

Nálepkovo lies only seven miles from Spišská Nová Ves and the surrounding district provides good examples of the wide range of conditions that still exists following the uneven development of the Communist era. When I had undertaken my original research in this district in the early 1970s, the settlement at Letanovce had been one of the most remote with a complete lack of basic amenities. In March 1991, twenty years later, things had hardly changed. In spite of a visit by Havel the previous year with promises of improvement, living conditions were appalling. A cluster of about forty ramshackle wooden huts stood isolated in a sea of mud. A rough field track linked the settlement to the Slovak village over a mile away. In the other direction lay an attractive area of wooded hills and ravines called, by a strange irony, the "Slovak Paradise" (Slovenský Raj). There was still no electricity or sanitation and—even worse—no safe drinking water. Numbers living in these shantytown conditions had increased in the past year since rising unemployment among Roma in the Czech lands had driven some to remigrate to their original settlements where living was cheaper (Guy 1991).

In contrast two-thirds of the Roma living in the equally dilapidated settlement at nearby Žehra, perched on the steep hillside above the main road, had been resettled in October 1990 into a small estate of attractive low-built blocks of family flats. This development was located on the edge of the Slovak village and even included a cultural center for communal use. The Slovak village officials seemed genuinely pleased with what had been achieved—but pointed out that the estate represented the completion of a phase of an earlier Communist project. Now no new funds were forthcoming to improve the situation of those families left stranded in the original settlement (Guy 1991).

Prospects for the Future

One Saturday in May 1995 in the quiet town of Žd'ár nad Sázavou three youths spent the evening drinking and chatted about trying out a new baseball bat. Soon after they broke into the home of a Romani family and started smashing the furniture. When Tibor Berky, the house owner, tried to intervene they beat him to death in front of his wife and children with repeated blows to the back of the head. In this town, about 70 miles east of Prague, there were only 120 Roma out of a total of 26,000 inhabitants. There was no reason why the victim should have been singled out, other than the fact that he was a Rom and lived nearby. When questioned the attackers told police they supported a right-wing skinhead movement (*Lidové noviny* 1995).

This incident was yet another in the spiraling toll of racially motivated attacks in the Czech Republic, 160 during 1994 alone according to a recent Interior Ministry report. The report stated that "most of the crimes were perpetrated by skinheads or youths affiliated to right-wing movements. Most of the victims were Gypsies" (ibid.). The brutal murder of Tibor Berky was widely reported at home and abroad, prompting Premier Klaus to convene a special meeting of government ministers where he gave vent to his frustration: "The situation is untenable and must not continue. . . . [This is] the straw that broke the camel's back." In response the Justice Minister proposed stiffer penalties—life sentences for racially motivated murders and increased sentences from three to five years for hate attacks (ibid.). Whether such measures make much of an impact remains to be seen but in any case they deal with only the most extreme manifestations of racism. Attacks on Roma by skinheads and others might be dismissed as aberrations of a small and deviant minority were it not for the extent to which virulently racist views are held and expressed at every level of Czech and Slovak society. The Helsinki Watch report is one of many sources to give a selection of these, often returning to the recurrent theme of gas chambers. In this context the Czech citizenship law and Meciar's comments about measures to reduce unhealthy overpopulation should be seen as deliberate attempts by both states, sanctioned by the wishes of the majority of their citizens, to use administrative methods to rid themselves of "their" Roma once they had become a burden. Skinhead attacks and the citizenship law are located on the same continuum, and the distance between them is less than might be assumed.

I well remember a conversation in 1986 with the mother of a Czech friend who sharply condemned racism in the West. Fully agreeing with her criticisms I then mentioned discrimination against Roma in Czechoslovakia. Without hesitating for a moment she carefully explained that this was a different matter altogether since "Gypsies are not really human—you only have to see how they behave." She was no skinhead youth but a well-educated, respectable medical specialist in her fifties and in other respects a likable and intelligent person—yet it was not hard to see where her arguments could lead.

The 1979 Charter 77 report had accused the Communists of deliberately preventing the upward social mobility and integration of Roma in order to keep them as a separate, highly vulnerable pool of unskilled labor. According to this view the Communists could be blamed for the predicament of Roma who had been thrown out of employment in post-Communist conditions. While this was undoubtedly the practical outcome of policies ostensibly aimed at assimilation, it is a partial view of Communist intentions. While the Czechoslovak Communists did have a continuing and expanding need for unskilled labor, they had other means of securing this—by attracting labor from less-developed neighboring Communist states and eventually by importing what amounted to indentured workers from Vietnam and Cuba in exchange for arms deals. These dark-skinned workers, too, were to become the target of racist attacks in the new conditions of post-communism (Tritt 1992:2).

The mistake of the Communists was not that they attempted to draw Roma into the labor market, albeit at the lowest level—indeed tens of thousands of Roma were already choosing this path to a better future. The real failure lay in their complete inability to appreciate the extent to which racism at every level of society, including within the Party, was acting to prevent truly effective help reaching the Roma, which alone would enable them to move out of their social and economic ghetto in significant numbers. Even more seriously, in denying any positive value to Romani identity they validated and strengthened existing denigratory attitudes, inflaming the problem rather than sweeping it out of existence as had been the intention. In this way it can be argued that racism lay at the heart of the Communist policy and undermined its many positive achievements.

As in so many other aspects of Communist practice it was felt that going through the motions of building socialism according to correct principles was enough to ensure success while consciousness was left unexamined. Beneath the outward conformity the old pernicious attitudes lay undisturbed and unchallenged, waiting to reemerge into the open with the ending of Communist rule. This was the true legacy of the Communist regime and one which its successors seem equally unfit to resolve.

Legal frameworks and human rights were as much part of the Communist statute books as they are now, enshrined in the new legislation of the democratic Republics. But, as before, the outward semblance of legality is meaningless without the rigorous and conscientious enforcement of constitutional law, combined with an extensive education program to help many Czechs and Slovaks come to an understanding of the endemic racism of their society. Some progress has been made, as in the cessation of coercive sterilizations, but in many other respects the signs are far from reassuring.

As part of this process some protection must be given to the Roma to shield them from the most savage effects of current changes. The danger, already being realized, is that the tumultuous transition to a market economy will reduce many of the most vulnerable Roma to penury, driving them in ever larger numbers to crime, prostitution, and abject dependency on state benefits. This would only serve to confirm the negative stereotype, setting back the timescale for harmonious coexistence by years. Romani political parties, cultural organizations, and media have a crucial part to play at this decisive moment, but there is a fear that they will continue to be vulnerable to the factionalism that has severely weakened their effect in the past.

Looking to the future the potential outcomes for the Roma are symbolized by two diametrically opposed views—the chilling dismissal of their humanity by the well-educated Prague doctor set against the quiet pride of the unsophisticated Slovak village officials from Žehra, who spoke of how the council had acted to transform immeasurably the conditions of "their" Roma. Perhaps the officials' attitude betrayed traces of patronizing condescension, but, more important, it acknowledged that, in Žehra, Slovaks and Roma were fellow villagers and—more broadly— showed a clear recognition that somehow the fate of their two peoples was bound up together.

In both republics the demographic time bomb ticks on as Roma continue to grow in numbers at a far faster rate than Czechs and Slovaks. The problems this expanding minority poses for the proud possessors of their newly minted nation-states will not go away by themselves and must be solved one way or other. It is the "other" that is terrifying.

REFERENCES

Borger, Julian
    1994   "How Many Forms Must a Czech Gypsy Fill In?" *The Guardian*, 23
           September 1994.
Charter 77
    1979   "Dokument 23 o situace Cikánů v Československu." *Listy* 2, 47,
           Prague: Charter 77, and in English trans. by Mark Jackson in *Labour
           Focus*, 1979 March/April (cited as Charter 1979a) & May/June (cited
           as Charter 1979b).

Czech Socialist Republic
1969 *Zákon č.2/1969 Sb. ČSR o zřízení ministerev a jiných ústředních orgánů* (Law no.2/1969 of the Czech Socialist Republic on establishing ministries and other central bodies), 8 January 1969.
1970 *Usnésení vlády ČSR č.279 ke zprávě o současném stavu řešení otázek cikánského obyvatelstva v ČSR* (Government decree no. 279 of the Czech Socialist Republic in relation to the contemporary state of affairs in solving questions of Gypsy inhabitants in the CSR), 25 November 1970.
David, Tomáš, and Filip Serotek
1991 *Punks in Prague*, documentary from an evening of punk films, London: Channel 4 (date unknown).
Greenberg, Susan
1993a "Victims of the Velvet Divorce." *The Guardian*, 26 January.
1993b "Meciar Turns on the Media." *The Guardian*, 27 September.
Gross, Tom
1993 "The World Overlooks Czech Bigotry." *Prague Post*, 27 October.
1994 "A Blot on the Conscience: Czech Attitudes on Citizenship for Gypsies Come under Fire." *Financial Times*, Supplement on the Czech Republic.
Guy, Will
1975 Historical text (no pagination), in Josef Koudelka, *Gypsies*. New York: Aperture.
1991 Field notes from a research trip to East Slovakia, March 1991.
Institute for Educational Information
1991 *Statistika Školství 1990/91, Československá Republika*. Prague: Ústav pro informace ve vzdělávaní.
Kalvoda, Josef
1992 "The Gypsies of Czechoslovakia," in David Crowe and John Kolsti, eds., *The Gypsies of Eastern Europe*. New York: M. E. Sharpe.
Lemon, Alaina
1995 "Slovak Roma Encounter Mixed Political Messages," message to Romnet mailbase from lemona@omri.cz, 15 September 1995 (based on ČTK press report, 6 September 1995).
Lidové noviny
1991 "Máme holé hlavy." *Lidové noviny* 275, IV, 25 November 1991.
1995 "Czechs Alarmed by Rise in Racially Motivated Murders." *Lidové noviny*, reprinted in *The Guardian*, 31 May 1995.
Pellar, Ruben, and Zbynek Andrs
1990 "Statistical Evaluation of Romani Women in East Slovakia," Appendix in Paul Ofner and Bert de Rooij, *Het Afkopen van*

Vruchtbaarheid: Een Onderzoek naar Sterilisatiepraktijecten ten aanzien van Romavrouwen in Tsejchoslowakije (Report on the Examination in the Problematic of Sexual Sterilisation of Romani Women in Czechoslovakia). Amsterdam: Lau Mazeril Foundation.

Plichtová, Jana
1993   "Czechoslovakia as a multi-cultural state in the context of the region: 1918–92." In Minority Rights Group and Third World: EEC, eds., *Minorities in Central and Eastern Europe*. London: Minority Rights Group.

Puxon, Grattan
1987   *Roma: Europe's Gypsies*, 1992 printing. London: Minority Rights Group.

Slovak Socialist Republic
1968   *Plnení harmonogramu práce . . . za I-III štvrt'rok1968 a návrh plánu na 1969* (Completion of the programme of work . . . 1st to 3rd quarters 1968 and proposed plan for 1969), November 1968.

Stewart, Michael
1993   "What Magdalena Said." *Everyman*, London: BBC 1, 2 January 1993.

Times Mirror
1991   Times Mirror Survey, Washington, D.C.: Times Mirror Center quoted in *The Guardian*, 4 October 1991.

Tritt, Rachel
1992   *Struggling for Ethnic Identity: Czechoslovakia 's Endangered Gypsies*. Helsinki Watch report, New York: Human Rights Watch.

Wanderers: Romania's Hidden Victims (1991)

Dan Pavel

Bucharest

Romania's aborted revolution has garnered its fair share of bitterly disappointed reformers but none, perhaps, so disappointed as the Gypsies. They form Romania's largest and most scorned minority. Like many others, they had expectations for change after the elections last May, not least of which was the hope of finally being treated as full citizens. Instead, they're being persecuted more brazenly and brutally than before.

The miners' savage attack on demonstrating students in Bucharest last June 14 and 15 was well covered in the Western media. . . .But not much was written about the miners' gratuitous assault on the Gypsies. According to a report by the Group for Social Dialogue, Romania's most influential dissident organization, immense trucks and buses overflowing with miners bearing hatchets, chains, steel bars, clubs, and other crude weapons—and accompanied by civilian guides (typically Securitate members)—suddenly appeared at the doorsteps of Gypsy homes. Men who were found inside were subjected to rapid executions; some of them had their heads cut off with a single swipe of the sickle. Women were beaten and raped in front of their horrified children and parents, who were themselves tortured in an attempt to force them to reveal hidden merchandise destined for the black market. Some men and women were tied by the hands and feet and lifted onto trucks that took them to unknown destinations. Many never returned. Of those who did, few had the courage to talk about what happened.

At a press conference after the bloody two days, Prime Minister Petre Roman denounced "the Gypsies, the leaders of prostitutes, and the world of the underground" as having been the "instruments of fascist rebellion, of Legionnaires" during World War II. This was his explanation for calling in the miners—an ironic one, since during Ion Antonescu's fascist dictatorship from 1940 to 1944, an unknown number of Romanian Gypsies died in massacres and tens of thousands were deported. Equally remarkable was what was seen on Romanian television later in the day. In an act of unprecedented courage, Gypsy leaders denounced the attack. Not even the students had yet protested publicly. At that moment two long-standing myths were dispelled: the idealized historical and literary image of Romanians as a peaceful and hospitable people incapable of racism, anti-Semitism, chauvinism, and nationalism; and the popular view of the Gypsies as a non-people incapable of asserting their rights.

It is now assumed that the Gypsies originated in the Indus River and began migrating to Europe in the eleventh or twelfth century. Since at least the fourteenth century the Gypsies in Romania were forced to work as serfs on the lands of Orthodox monasteries, whose religion they adopted. They continued to live in one form of peonage or another until 1856, when they were ostensibly emancipated from serfdom. Their social ostracism, however, only increased. After the Communists took power, there was spectacular growth in the Romanian Gypsy population. But they became so marginalized in all areas of society that the issue of equal rights and opportunities was never raised (this despite the Communist constitution, which forbade discrimination on the basis of ethnic origin, religion, social status, sex, or age). Most never finished school and are illiterate. The tiny portion who became members of the nomenklatura (or, grander still, of the Executive Political Committee of the Communist Party), or who obtained high-level posts in the army, militia, Securitate, or administration, or in the professions, did so by hiding their ethnic identity.

The vast majority of Gypsies live in miserable conditions, suffering from want and even famine. Much has been made in the West of the appalling conditions of the Romanian orphanages and of Ceausescu's harsh anti-abortion law. What is generally left untold is that Gypsies constitute the majority of the children. Gypsies have tended to have larger families than the rest of the population, and because of their poverty, more were given up to the orphanages.

Denied access to legal jobs, most Gypsies were forced into the black market and the Mafia-style underground. They sought protection for their illegal activities in two ways: by bribing corrupt cops and by giving information (about dissident intellectuals and disgruntled workers) to the Securitate. This kind of protection, of course, only increased the contempt of the population.

Most Romanians also believed the Gypsies were receiving favorable treatment from Ceausescu, who periodically freed Gypsy prisoners from jail. The frequent amnesties spurred rumors that Ceausescu was a Gypsy and fooled even the Gypsies themselves, who nicknamed him "our daddy." (In the aftermath of the anti-Ceausescu revolution, as part of a cowardly push to cleanse Romanians of any blame for the sins of communism, some journals published "proofs" of Ceausescu's supposed Gypsy origin. The idea was that the Romanian nation could not have produced such a monster.) But the truth is that Gypsies weren't the only Romanians released—there just happened to be a disproportionate number of criminal prisoners who were Gypsies—and the amnesties were used to camouflage the existence of political prisoners, who were officially unrecognized in Romania. Whenever the regime found it politic to release a few political prisoners after pressure from international human rights organizations, it did so under the cover of a wider release of common criminals.

Far from singling out the Gypsies for good fortune, Ceausescu wanted to conceal their existence, especially their extraordinary demographic growth. In the past fifteen years the Gypsies have equaled and probably overtaken the Hungarians as Romania's largest minority; there are 3 million Gypsies, according to their own spokesmen, out of a total Romanian population of 23 million. Yet they had all but disappeared from the annual statistics. Ceausescu never even mentioned them as an ethnic minority. The implication was that the Gypsies had been fully integrated—a line seemingly accepted by the international human rights community, which never took much interest in their plight.

* * *

The Gypsies believed the National Salvation Front offered them the hope of a better life. Although the NSF made no specific promises to them, during the weeks preceding the first "free elections" in May 1990 the newly formed National Committee of Gypsies announced its unconditional support for NSF presidential candidate Ion Iliescu. The NSF promised a free market, which would both legalize the Gypsies' underground activities and open up new entrepreneurial opportunities for them. These promises proved empty: the economic system has hardly altered in the past year.

More devastating is the NSF's policy toward the Gypsies. As in other Eastern European countries, the political tumult in Romania ignited nationalist sentiments, some of them exceedingly unattractive. The difference in Romania is that the government is leading the crusade, and the most retrograde nationalists are acting on their feelings. The primary target of the campaign is the Gypsy population. As scapegoats they feed the resentments of many working people, including the miners, who are suffering from the economic crisis and believe the Gypsies not only are responsible for everybody else's troubles but are prospering on account of them.

The government justifies its harassment as an attempt to eradicate the black market. But the campaign against the Gypsies, as well as the one against the Hungarians for allegedly wanting to take back part of Transylvania, represents nothing more than a new populist ideology that is meant to galvanize the Romanian people. By denouncing the Gypsies as *popor de culoare* (people of color) and the Gypsies and Hungarians as Asians or non-Europeans, the government is attempting to substitute racial ideology for Marxist class ideology.

This is easily confirmed by leafing through a selection of the ultranationalist publications, chauvinistic as well as anti-Semitic, which enjoy the direct or indirect support of the National Salvation Front. These newspapers and magazines—such as *România Mare* (Great Romania), *Azi* (Today), and *Democratia* (Democracy)—are directed by people who made their reputations by promoting the propaganda of the Party and the "personality cult" of Ceausescu. They are also working hand in hand with the reactivated secret police.

What is happening in Romania is obviously not just a local issue. Central and Western Europe have been invaded by Romanian emigrants, with estimates ranging from 300,000 to 1 million. The intelligentsia are leaving, as are students and highly qualified workers. But the largest percentage of those fleeing are Gypsies. For the first time since the fourteenth century, the Gypsies are again becoming nomads, overwhelming the European governments with their numbers and their needs. In Germany they're living in railroad stations. Austria is sending tens of thousands back to Romania. And Czechoslovakia has begun to ask Romanians who want to immigrate or even visit for visas. The plight of the Romanian Gypsies, ignored by the world for the past century, is now everybody's problem.

Trans. Juliana Geran Pilon

Police Perception of Gypsies in Finland (1981)

Martti Grönfors

This essay is concerned with the *social settings* which affect the ways in which the police as an occupational group view their spheres of activity as well as with the social settings of the subsections of the community with whom the police come into more frequent contact in their work. I shall concentrate mainly on the *shared sentiments* of the police with the similarities in their background, ideology, common experiences at work and outside work. In every society, there are certain groups which, more than other groups, are considered to be problematic from the point of view of the conformist sections of society. These "problem" groups often come into contact with the police more than other groups in society do. I maintain that because of the ideology, background, and role of the police, the police see these kinds of groups mainly as a control problem rather than one requiring social policy solutions.

My comments here are based on an empirical investigation I conducted on the relationship between Finnish Gypsies and the police. Material was gathered in two main ways: for eighteen months I worked among the Finnish Gypsies doing participant observation research. The results of this intensive study are not presented here. My original intention, however, was to attempt something similar with the police, but my application to accompany the police in their work activities was turned down on the basis that the police are already doing such dangerous and difficult work that they cannot afford to devote their time to looking after a researcher on their patrols as well. A request to present a large-scale structured questionnaire to a "representative" sample of police officers was similarly refused. This, I was told, would take too much of the policemen's time to complete. However, permission was granted to interview a smaller number of police officers at the discretion of individual section chiefs.

Although research on the police in Finland is rather limited, my not being allowed to participate in the life and work experiences of the police officers was not such a disadvantage as it would have been in the case of the Gypsies. The police are drawn from the majority Finnish culture, which I also come from and know something about. Also, international research on the police has come to some agreement about the main characteristics of police forces, about the recruitment of individual officers, their training and informal socialization, and about the relationship of police forces to the wider society. Therefore, intimate involvement in their work and lives was not so vitally necessary as it was in the case of the Gypsies. In the police interviews, it was decided to attempt to get "off-the-cuff," spontaneous gut reactions from the policemen as to their views about the Gypsies. The rationale for this was that policing is a human activity, which is governed (apart from various rules and regulations and other "objective" criteria) by subjective feelings and attitudes, and that uniformities in those feelings can be discovered.

The representativeness of one's sample is always problematic. It becomes even more acute in research like mine where it was not possible to take random samples, which would give the data at least an appearance of being valid (and it is often only an appearance of "validity" created by accepted statistical manipulations). The police material was gathered during in-depth interviews with 55 male police officers in Finland's two main cities, Helsinki and Tampere, and most (45) came from Helsinki. All Helsinki interviews were conducted by a female research assistant, a psychologist well versed in interviewing techniques. The principal method of interviewing was a nondirective one, in which the interviewer introduced the topic of Gypsies, after which the officer was left freely to air his views on them. The research assistant was deliberately kept more or less totally ignorant of the culture and nature of Gypsies and their society, so that she would not inadvertently introduce any direction to the opinions of the policemen.

Her role was mainly that of getting the policemen to speak freely and recording what was being said.

The sample of policemen is a small one and limited to two major cities, and therefore it could quite justifiably be criticized as a sample from which generalizations can't be made. However, the opinions that the policemen in the sample expressed about the Gypsies had a remarkable unanimity; these 55 policemen generally agreed on the nature of Gypsy society and culture. The differences in opinion were more of degree than of kind and arose largely in the area of what should be done to "correct" the Gypsy society to make it more acceptable. As it was the sectional heads in most cases who selected the interviewees, it is reasonable to assume that the sample has a disproportionate and unrepresentative number of police officers who are considered by their seniors as "reasonable" (not known to be overtly racist) and "Gypsy experts" (those known to get on well with Gypsies). This bias would make the research material "milder" in attitudes toward Gypsies than would have been the case if the interviewer had been able to make the selection. It is my considered opinion that the material presented here underestimates the negative views of the Finnish police toward Finnish Gypsies. An indication that this indeed could be the case came when efforts were made to correct the obvious bias of the selection process. The interviewer was able to get some informants of her own accord through chance encounters with officers at the police stations. The officers with the most hostile attitudes toward Gypsies were, in fact, introduced this way into the study.

Police Background, Recruitment, and Attitudes

International evidence about the social background of police officers indicates that policemen are recruited from lower socioeconomic groups and quite often from a farming background (McNamara 1967; Bowden 1978:32). Evidence from my research supports those findings.

People with a rural and farming background are described by anthropologists as tending to be territorial, respecting patriarchal authority, relying on secure, low-risk sources of livelihood, admiring hard work for its own sake, people who see commercial and sexual adventures and traveling as indications of instability and unreliability (see, for example, Redfield 1956; Wolf 1966). In my sample, those farmers' sons who themselves could not become farmers saw the policeman's job as an acceptable alternative, an occupation which did not conflict but in many respects coincided with the values of the farming community. The focus which the policemen placed on some specific features of Gypsy society in their stated attitudes was in line with the above, and the police unanimously condemned Gypsies on the grounds of their not settling permanently, not putting into the economy what they were seen to get out of it, being different in their sexual attitudes, not being able to control their emotions, and many similar perceived features. Here are some of the statements made by the police in relation to Gypsies:

It is in their blood, the desire to wander. That pulls them on the road, heredity. They seldom stay indoors. And if heredity has nothing to do with this, then the children learn it from their parents. If the parents are rats, the children rarely become anything different.

I have a good example of their lack of desire to work. One Gypsy man worked in a road gang. His only request was that his workmates would tell him in time if there were other Gypsies coming along the road, so that he would have time to hide before they saw him. It obviously is not good to be caught working. I get the feeling that they actually don't appreciate working, or money obtained through regular work.

When the child allowance finishes, then the disability pension starts rolling in. How do they manage that? In full possession of their physical and mental—well, not always mental—faculties. I have often asked them who would take care of things if everybody in this country was drawing a pension. They can't answer that one!

They don't marry in the way everyone else does. All the children have different fathers, but never white men. Gypsy men see to that.

Incest is common among them. The whole kin lives together and breeds together.

They're very emotional people, very quick-tempered. When they're confronted, they resort to violence. They are sort of children of the moment.

In the case of the older officers especially, the policeman's job may also have seemed an attractive alternative to manual work, which their generally low educational standard might have forced upon them. (The educational level of the constables in my study is presented in Table 1.) The older group (over forty years old) grew up into working life during the hard times following the Second World War. For them, as many put it, joining the police was the best option then available; not something which they would have wanted under ideal circumstances, but a "clean and nice" job and, especially, a secure one. Elsewhere also, this has been observed as one reason for joining the forces (see, for example, Bowden 1978:33; Chappell and Wilson 1969:4).

Table 1. Schooling by Age

	Under 30 years (N)	30 to 39 years (N)	40 years or over (N)
Basic schooling only	13% (3)	27% (4)	71% (12)
Medium schooling	52% (12)	60% (9)	29% (5)
Above average schooling	35% (8)	13% (2)	0% (0)
Total	100% (23)	100% (15)	100% (17)

n = 55

With the younger group of officers (under thirty) there was a markedly larger number of policemen who had above-average education (to matriculation level). Although there was little information about the factors which influenced their choice of occupation, there are at least two feasible possibilities. First, the policeman's job could have been taken up for ideological reasons, where the work is seen in larger societal terms. While for many older constables the policeman's job was only "another job," many younger constables saw their work as being important for upholding the more important values of society, and the job was a carefully chosen career. A similar observation has been made in relation to the police in Japan (Bayley 1976:78). Second, with the general increase in educational opportunities in Finland in the last decade or so, people are forced to take jobs which have previously been considered "below" their educational qualifications. So, just as for the older age group of officers with lower educational achievement, the policeman's job could have been a "step up," for "overeducated" younger constables it could have been a "step down." Joining the force for ideological reasons, or joining because "better" opportunities were not available would both, in my opinion, affect the way in which the policemen view their work and act in their job. It is in light of this that the following tables about the general police attitudes toward Finnish Gypsies could be viewed. The division into "hardliners" and "softliners" has been made rather arbitrarily and crudely by comparing the frequency of negative statements and positive statements by a policeman about the Gypsies. As all the policemen had numerous deeply negative statements and very few positive ones, the division could also have been made differently, for example into "hardliners" and "extreme hardliners," but the purpose of these two tables (Tables 2 and 3) is only to show attitude patterns in terms of age and education.

Table 2. Attitude by Age

	Age in years 20–29 (N)	30–39 (N)	40 yrs. or over
Hardliners	74% (17)	60% (9)	35% (6)
Softliners	26% (6)	40% (6)	65% (11)
Total	100% (23)	100% (15)	100% (17)

n = 55

All the officers basically agreed on the features of Gypsy society, and the differences in attitudes were evidenced only in suggestions as to what should be done about the "Gypsy problem," that is, how to alleviate or eradicate this "problem." "Hardliners" suggested, for example, the following:

> Stop the social welfare. It's gone much too far already. Look at when they're collecting empty bottles over there, outside. That requires iron health, not possible for people who claim to be ill. They should have similar obligations for schooling as the whites do. The school inspectors and teachers are powerless. A much tougher line should be taken. All Gypsies should be sent back to where they came from, all those vagrants who only come here to get better social welfare benefits.

Table 3. Attitude by Schooling

	Low (N)	Schooling Medium (N)	High (N)
Hardliners	42% (8)	69% (18)	70% (7)
Softliners	58% (11)	31% (8)	30% (3)
Total	100% (19)	100% (26)	100% (10)

n = 55

> Some have talked about sending them to an uninhabited island. Racial discrimination is practiced in Finland—against the whites! The Gypsies already have the same rights as the rest. Let's hope that their obligations will also be the same, in regard to having to attend school, do army service, and pay taxes. I think that it's wrong that a Gypsy is able to buy a farm, for instance, with the aid of a special loan.

> . . .it might be worth trying to utilize the sorts of labor camps we had during the war.

During Hitler's time, they knew how to take care of Jews and Gypsies.

A bullet through the head is the only cure. That way at least other people would be protected. Perhaps a kind of camp could be established for Gypsies only. That way at least they wouldn't hurt other people. Not quite into cages, but perhaps their own suburb, so that they are not spread over every bloody place.

The "softliners" made the following kinds of suggestions:

If only they could all be given permanent accommodation but not all in the same area. They should be spread so that they could attend school. Otherwise we can't get anywhere, as they're so mobile. Also, if the accommodation was a bit better, perhaps their illnesses would be reduced too.

Sometimes I've thought that something rather drastic has to be done in their case, such as curbing their freedom of movement. So that they could at least attend school, and learn to look at things with a wider outlook, and could stay on a job. Basically what they need is efficient job training. If they could only be taught to work, they might actually get adjusted to society. It won't ever happen if they can do what they please, and everything comes to them for nothing. Only through work.

I wish that they could be absorbed into the mainstream of society as ordinary citizens, so that they have the same obligations and rights as everyone else. As a tribe, of course, they could remain as their own group. Also they should be thought of by others as brothers and sisters, as everyone else is.

I have often thought about how their situation could be improved. The only thing I can think of is how their education standards could be raised, so that they could live normal lives. They should have similar social standards. The housing problem has now of course been solved. If they're ever going to become fit members of society they must be helped. On the other hand, it's important that they should also do something for it themselves. They shouldn't be left to fend for themselves. If their educational standards could be raised, I'm sure that this would help. Unfortunately this isn't happening. These matters are so complicated. However, it's not only that the Gypsies' own attitudes are at fault. Generally the Gypsies are not thought of as human beings.

Shared Socialization

The organization of formal police training, which often takes place in residential training schools, the rigid authoritarian structure of the force, which does not encourage initiative or free expression, the relatively young age at which the career is taken up, long-service record, and the marginal position of the policeman as a person who has the authorized power to coerce his fellow citizens, all make the common process of socialization important when the policeman's perception is examined. These factors, plus the fact that policemen work irregular hours, mean that much of their free time is also spent with other police officers. The police force organization itself in some countries discourages the free association of policemen with others. For example, in New Zealand they are discouraged from drinking in ordinary pubs and bars; drinking and other recreational facilities are provided for them within the police stations.[1] It has been said that because of all this, policemen are somewhat cut off from the realities of life and are unable to follow the changes that take place in society (Skolnick 1966). Also, it has been observed that in police forces there exists a high degree of solidarity and loyalty, even to the extent that the officers are tolerant of each other's crimes as well (Bowden 1978:30).

Shared socialization, together with shared motivation and common backgrounds, must bring the attitudes of the officers even closer to each other through reinforcement. By the same token, whatever differences they may have had initially have little chance of surviving in the kind of situation the policemen find themselves in at work. In light of this, it may appear somewhat surprising that the best indicators of a "racist" constable are young age and higher-than-average schooling. The differences in opinion were most marked in the views concerning the perceived level of violence in Gypsy society, the younger policemen considering Gypsies violent, while a significant proportion of the older constables did not think them any more violent than other Finns. The tougher attitude of the younger officers could possibly be explained by their inexperience and the desire to appear tough.

Recent Finnish research on the police ways of carrying arms lends support to this, the younger officers more often violating the regulations, carrying their arms exposed in cowboy style (Uusitalo 1980). It may also be explained by their reasons for joining the force, those who joined for ideological reasons wanting to bring deviant groups into line with their convictions. Those who joined because better opportunities were not available might want to take out their occupational disappointment by directing against those whom they consider to be scroungers their felt aggression toward the unjust society that did not provide them with an occupation they wanted. The "softer" attitudes of the older and less educated constables may possibly be explained by their being more careful of what to say to a researcher. It is also possible that since for some of them police work was at least as good an occupation as they could hope for, they do not feel occupationally frustrated and have no desire to act out frustrations. Also, it may be that when it comes to the presumed Gypsy violence, where the opinions of the policemen varied by age most of all, it takes years and years of convincing that the stereotype of the violent Gypsy is not in fact true. However, it is primarily the younger officers who carry out the patrolling duties and thus in practice have a better chance than the older ones of acting upon their conceptions of the Gypsies.

The Nature of Police Forces

Police forces have often been compared to military organizations. Three main kinds of characteristics stand out in this comparison: (1) "men" are subordinated to "officers," (2) a rigid chain of command operates between the various ranks, and (3) there is a marked lack of both formal and informal provision for consultation between various ranks (Bowden 1978:31). This must also affect the ways in which policemen think, look at things, and act.

The Finnish material shows that the police officer's environment puts a high premium on law and order in society, and that his sense of order can be easily upset by a variety of deviations. Society is seen largely in terms of black-and-white "normal" and "abnormal."

"Normality" includes concepts such as an individual's responsibilities to society as a taxpayer, as a non-bludger, who is married and raising a family, and is nonprotesting and compliant. The political opinions of the Finnish policemen tended to express criticism of the felt tendency toward socialism, which was seen as providing for people who did not want to earn their keep:

> The state has created a situation where it's not worth going to work these days. Nobody is so crazy as to take a job if he doesn't have to. The old system was much better. If a person didn't want to work he was put in a work camp. Now they're patted on the head [interview response].

Police View of Social Problems

By "social problems" I mean here "the unwilled, largely indirect, and often unanticipated consequences of institutionalized patterns of social behavior" (Merton and Nisbet 1963:ix). This point of view entails the assumptions that social problems are generated by the same structure and culture which also creates conforming behavior and that social problems represent the social costs of a particular organization of social life. It excludes the possibility of the view that "evil causes evil" and invites us to look at the ways in which social arrangements and values in society produce results which are socially condemned. "Social problems," it appears from research on police attitudes, are not viewed by the police as being embedded in the structure of society and not as by-products of the institutional arrangements. Rather, it appears, they are viewed as being threatening to the very structures of the society that produces them, the antithesis of structure and order. Above all, they are seen as issues of morality, of which the police see themselves as guardians. Social problems are seen in a politico-moral framework.

The structure of society, whatever it may be, tends to be self-perpetuating, and the police represent the practical arm of this conservatism, reflecting it in an exaggerated form. It has been said in relation to the police that "Everywhere, it seems they have a tendency to enforce a puritanical morality, no matter what the existing climate of the times" (Bowden 1978:84). Research conducted on the London Metropolitan Police shows that they endorse a social philosophy which supports the politico-moral stand. Most of them agreed on such views as, for example, that drug addicts and alcoholics are in their situation through their own fault and that immigrants should adopt the British way of life (Belson 1975:42). The organizations which harmed relations between the police and the public, according to the police, were those which dealt with citizens' rights, such as the National Council for Civil Liberties, and the immigrants' associations (Belson 1975:58). Such a view of these organizations by the police is not surprising, as these most often allege police malpractice against particular sections of the community, usually blacks and immigrants (see, for example, Bishton and Homer 1978).

Police behavior in strike situations also clearly shows the political direction of police forces all over the world (see, for example Humphry 1972). The "Protestant ethic" governs the way in which the police view social problems, a way which is a moral calculus of work which views people grappling with social difficulties as "scroungers," "layabouts," or "living off the Welfare" (see, for example, Hall et al. 1978:139ff.). In extremist political situations, such as that in Brazil, the role of the police as the practical arm of the state is stretched to its extreme, where a special police killer squad murders and tortures urban slumdwellers (Jakubs 1977). Some subcultures in their entirety are considered deviant in every respect by the police, as they do not fit the established structure of society. The Finnish Gypsies are a good example of this.

Their attitude is against the society. They've been brought up that way.

It's very expensive for the rest of us to keep up such a culture.

If only they could stop wearing their national costume, and come halfway to meet us that way. They must adjust. These days, as there are so many mixed marriages, they should think of the future generations, and shouldn't try to draw too much attention to themselves. They are a whining small group of people for whom too much has already been done—patted on the head, they've been!

Police and the "Problem Groups"

If the police view "social problems" as being signs of either subversion, irresponsibility, or evil, there are groups who, to a greater or lesser degree, are thought of as possessing those kinds of characteristics as groups. This view, I would claim, is a functional way of looking at the work and role of the police in our society. The police act as a practical and symbolic demonstration of the power of the powerful, and for that demonstration certain groups must be lifted up to the public view as examples of the decay that threatens the order in society. Then action can be directed toward them, "evil" is seen to be dealt with, and confidence in the idea of order is maintained. This kind of selective action shows that those in power are in power because of superior morality or superior ideology, and those not in power are not in power because they deserve not to be. For this demonstration it is functional to attach undesirable labels to certain groups.

There are a few concepts which can be utilized to demonstrate this argument. *Marginality* is a concept which refers to the distance between the ideology and culture of the power-holders and those not in power. Those furthest away from the ideology of the state and of the police, that is the "underdogs," form the most marginal groups in society and have also been observed to have "the highest rates of perceived deviance" (Gove 1975:11). The concept of *"moral indignation"* (Garfinkel 1965), as well as the term *"moral entrepreneur"* (Becker 1963:Chapter 8) are both utilized when activation of attention toward particular classes of people by the police has been analyzed. Police belief in their own superior moral standing is sufficient justification for treating the nonconforming differently from the conforming.

> All societies condemn certain groups to being less than equal and to receiving treatment . . . which indicates that they are not considered to be entitled to the same human rights as the upright, property-owning citizen, who is at one with conventional morality and is deferential to the established authority symbolized by the police (Bowden 1978:84).

The examination of police attitudes and stated activities in the case of Gypsies in Finland seems to make this point explicit. The physical *visibility* of the group, of its members, or of its culture, is important for this demonstration of problem groups among "ordered" society. The people belonging to those visible problem groups have an *ascribed deviant status.*

The opposite view to the above would claim that those kinds of groups, such as the Gypsies, earn their treatment and that the inequality they face in the treatment is deserved because of their deviant behavior. However, the police powers to interfere in the lives of other people are very broadly defined by law, at least in Finland, where any form of interference by the police can be justified by the claim that the people acted in a suspicious manner. The Finnish Police Law states, among many other criteria which create power for the police, that the police can "request the information necessary to establish a person's identity, and if the supplied information is suspected to be false, to detain a person for further verification." Also they can "act when a person creates a danger to general order and safety, and . . . detain a person who is thought, from his threats or actions, to be about to commit a crime . . ." Poliisilaki 1966:§13 and §19).

A graphic illustration of the way in which the legal powers for the Finnish police are defined in relation to Gypsies comes from the early 1970s, when police shot dead two Gypsies in a fight. In the court case that followed, the policemen responsible for the fatal shots were discharged. During the trial a social science thesis on the Gypsies written in the early 1960s was produced as evidence to show that Gypsies are prone to spontaneous behavior and that shooting two of them dead was a matter of the police getting in first before they themselves were shot. In another incident, police let a police dog loose among a group of arrested Gypsies, and the dog managed to bite several of them. According to the subsequent inquiry by the Ombudsman, the situation was fully under control before the incident with the dog. The two constables responsible for the dog and also responsible for physically ill-treating the Gypsies were charged in the lower court for assault and were discharged. In the middle court they were sentenced to short terms of imprisonment and lost their jobs. In the Supreme Court the original judgment was reverted to and the constables were reinstated in their jobs.

In an effort to look at how "deserved" is the police stated view of Gypsies as an inherently deviant and criminal group, I looked at all the indictable offenses for which Gypsies had been charged in 1975, the last complete year preceding the interviews, in the Helsinki police district from which most of the police informants came. On the basis of that, it can be said that in the two main areas of criminality where the Gypsies are thought by the police to engage en masse, that is, dishonesty and violence, the offenses were quite minor ones. In all, 54 persons identified as Gypsies were charged for offenses in that year, and the total number of offenses was 121. A group of 28 individuals was held responsible for more than 80 percent of all offenses. Of that group, 11 had been reared from infancy in Finnish-run institutions for Gypsy children, and these institutionally reared Gypsies were held responsible for more than half of all offenses. In the greater Helsinki area there are an estimated 1,000 to 1,500 Gypsies. The most serious dishonesty offense was a grab-and-run theft from a bank, in which four Gypsies got away with 10,000 Fmks (about $2,500), the rest being considerably less serious. None of the victims of violence required hospitalization; most of these offenses were threats of violence in an effort to extort money from the victim without actual violence, which were usually classed as "robbery." According to the Helsinki police, in the sample year there was a special drive to "clean up" the known Helsinki trouble spots, which were also places frequented by some Gypsies. It seems that there was a small group of delinquent Gypsy youngsters who were responsible for the great majority of Gypsy crime in Helsinki in 1975, and although no comparison with Finnish offenders was attempted, it appears that the nature of Gypsy crime is probably not all that different from non-Gypsy crime, where criminal gangs contribute a disproportionate amount to the recorded criminality. In the researched Gypsy crime in Helsinki, most glaringly missing were older Gypsies (25+) and females. The Helsinki police nevertheless alleged that for Gypsies crime is a way of life:

> Their way is living on earnings from illegal activities. Criminality is part of the Gypsies' way of living.

> Stealing and robbery is their work, as is selling booze, which they do quite openly.

> Pilfering is the women's work.

They are unable to accept working for somebody else, and they must get their income from somewhere. So they steal, mainly shoplifting or robbing.

The police admitted that they do apply different standards of control in the case of Gypsies:

> We treat everybody the same. No difference at all. . . .However, Gypsies do find themselves very often stopped by the police when they drive. . . .

> If there is more than one Gypsy in a group, if they're not actually doing something illegal then at least they're planning to.

> Gypsies are much more visible on the streets than are others. Our attitude to them is one of caution. Underneath we're always wondering what they might be up to.

> If we see a group of Gypsies somewhere, we ask their identity, in case they have outstanding fines and are on the run. Ordinary people are not stopped, except when they look suspicious. . . . The Gypsies don't mind being stopped, because they are never in a hurry.

> One reason why we usually take in the entire group is the fact that they don't have identity papers. Then we can fingerprint them here. They are not let out of the station until we are absolutely sure about their identity. . . . We have the entire Gypsy lot against us.

When the police were asked to provide some examples of their own encounters with Gypsy criminals, personal experience was often lacking, such matters being handled by "another department," or by "somebody else," or they "just heard about it." Also, actual personal encounters were hampered because:

> They are pretty clever in the art of disappearing. If they stick a knife into somebody, they soon leave the scene. Non-Gypsies tend

to linger at the scene of the crime for a while after they have knifed somebody.

The most visible of Gypsy crimes is the illegal sale of liquor. . . . But when we arrive at the points where they carry out their business, the Gypsies are never taken by surprise. Two or three Gypsy cars are on the lookout and obviously our approach is immediately relayed to the sellers and the Gypsies vanish.

In Finland everything connected with the Gypsies is seen as being different from the values which the policeman respects and which he sees himself as protecting: the way the Gypsies look, speak, dress, and behave are all seen as opposing the values that are worthy in Finnish society. As the entire culture and social organization of Gypsies is viewed by the police as deviant there was little inhibition felt by the police about disclosing their feelings toward Gypsies. The Gypsies, being different from the rest, have relinquished their right to impartiality. In Finland, other visible minorities, such as blacks, migrants from the Asian subcontinent, migrant workers, and so forth, are not yet conspicuous. The Gypsies are the main group who are seen as being furthest away from the ideology of Finnish society, and therefore they are the targets of police control more than any other group. That this happens has been amply illustrated by this research; the police actually admitted that they treat Gypsies differently from others. The effect on the police of the differential treatment of Gypsies is a confirmation that they were right in the first place, a case of self-fulfilling prophecy. The level of moral indignation that the police feel toward the Gypsies is kept alive. The Gypsies could hardly be perceived as a group of political activists who might overturn the Finnish government. However, they do form the most distinct ethnic minority in the country, with the most distinct culture. They are at the edge of Finnish society, in the society but not part of it. Because of the visibility of Gypsies, the police indignation can be acted upon. The police might feel just as indignant about, say, Stalinist Marxists, but as these cannot be identified with such ease, turning indignation to action would be more difficult. There is a possibility that the mere fact that the Gypsies are *not* a political group may indeed increase their chances of being identified with deviant values in a country like Finland, where political divisions are anyway well established and political diversity reasonably tolerated.

Police Action

In Scandinavia, at least in Denmark, Sweden, and Norway, the police are attempting to create an image which combines social work with control policies. From my evidence of police work in relation to Gypsies in Finland, I find myself very skeptical about such attempts to shift the police image. It is difficult, in my opinion, to talk about the police-client relationship in the majority of police actions. Such a relationship should be voluntary, and should include the idea of help. The relationship between the police and the community is, in the main, a one-way application of coercion on the part of the police, the idea of which is the submission of the recipient. The background of the police officers, the organization of the forces, the socialization into the role of the policeman as well as the role itself, the authoritarian nature of the force, and the possibility of coercion against the public, speaks very loudly against a shift in emphasis from control policies to the area of social work. This unfeasibility is very clearly demonstrated when the relationship of the police to certain ethnic and national minorities is examined, those minorities being often just the sections of the communities which are badly disadvantaged socially.

Police in London see their task in relation to "problem groups" as one which needs traditional police means of handling, rather than viewing the problems as social ones (Belson 1975:42–43). Similarly, the police in Finland see the Gypsies, as the most marginal and visible "problem group" of Finnish society, as a group that should be forced to "toe the line." When drunkenness was defined as a social problem in Finland in 1969 and was decriminalized, prosecutions for resisting the police shot up dramatically (Uusitalo, unpublished lecture notes). It appears possible that even when the political society redefines something as a social problem, the police independently redefine it in accordance with their conception of morality.

Afterword 1995:

I have participated for many years in educating Finnish police officers about minority issues, including an awareness and understanding of the Gypsy segment of the population, which indicates that the police took my critique somewhat seriously. In fact, the police profile has changed a great deal since the material for the present article was collected. Training has improved considerably, thanks to excellent basic schooling. Since only 2% of all applicants are accepted for training, the successful candidates are the best of the lot. And since the mid-1980s the police have been voted the most trusted institution in the country, a situation almost unique in Western democracy. Thus although there is need for further work in promoting understanding between the police and the Gypsies, there is fertile ground in which to do so.

The urbanization of the Finnish Gypsies continues, by far the greatest number living in the southern cities of Helsinki, Espoo, and Vantaa. But since traditional Gypsy culture and urban life make for a poor mix, both assimilation and marginalization are ever-present threats. Gypsies remain the most disliked group in Finnish society, despite the fact that the number of foreigners has risen geometrically since I first wrote the article. Still, Finnish hostility has not taken the extreme form it has taken in certain other European countries. Unfortunately, however, their very marginalization works against them, since it has led, as with other minorities, to alcoholism, criminality, and illness.

On the positive side, there is growing interest in furthering the study of Gypsy culture and language as well as in improving the interaction between the Gypsies and the Finnish society they inhabit. The Romani language, for example, is taught—by Gypsies—to Romani children as part of "mother tongue" instruction. There is as well a "cultural interpreter" project whereby Gypsy experts are called upon as cultural mediators, a function especially important when simple but profound misunderstanding can have a disproportionately drastic effect on minority lives.

Very little real research, however, has been done on the Gypsy social situation and culture since my initial work. One reason is the misunderstanding of and consequent uproar caused by certain portions of it (see Grönfors: "From Scientific Social Science to Responsible Research: The Lesson of the Finnish Gypsies," *Acta Sociologica* 25

[1982], 249–257), which made the Gypsies reluctant to participate in research and researchers themselves hesitant to tackle Gypsy issues.

Finally, a note about the use of the word *Gypsy*. I am retaining it in this update of my article for consistency's sake, despite the fact that much has changed as regards its use since the original was written. Although there has been no consensus as yet as to the "correct" word, both *Rom* and *Roma* seem to be the favored terms. My own choice, when writing in English about the Finnish Gypsies, is to use "Rom" for the people and "Romani" both as an adjective and as the name of the language.

NOTE

1. Information acquired by the author while working as a probation officer in New Zealand.

REFERENCES

Bayley, D. H.
1976 *Forces of Order: Police Behavior in Japan and the United States.* Los Angeles: University of California Press.
Becker, H. S.
1963 *Outsiders: Studies in the Sociology of Deviance.* New York: Free Press.
Belson, W. A.
1975 *The Public and the Police.* London: Harper & Row.
Bishton, D., and B. Homer, eds.
1978 *Talking Blues: The Black Community Speaks about Its Relationship with the Police.* Birmingham, England: AFFOR.
Bowden, T.
1978 *Beyond the Limits of the Law: A Comparative Study of the Police in Crisis Politics.* Harmondsworth: Penguin.
Chappell, D., and Wilson, P. R.
1969 *The Police and the Public in Australia and New Zealand.* University of Queensland Press.
Garfinkel, H.
1965 "Conditions of Successful Degradation Ceremonies." *American Journal of Sociology* 61:420–424.

Gove, W. R.
1975 "The Labelling Perspective: An Overview." In *The Labelling of Deviance* (W. R. Gove, ed.). New York: Sage, pp. 3–20.

Grönfors, M.
1977 *Blood Feuding Among Finnish Gypsies*. University of Helsinki Department of Sociology Research Reports 213.
1979 *Ethnic Minorities and Deviance: The Relationship between Finnish Gypsies and the Police*. University of Helsinki Sociology of Law Series 1.

Hall, S., et al.
1978 *Policing the Crisis: Mugging, the State, and Law and Order*. London: Macmillan.

Humphry, D.
1972 *Police Power and Black People*. London: Granada.

Institute of Race Relations
1979 *Police against Black People*. London: Evidence submitted to the Royal Commission on Criminal Procedure by the Institute of Race Relations.

Jakubs, D. L.
1977 "Police Violence in Times of Political Tension: The Case of Brazil 1968–1971." In *Police and Society* (David H. Bayley, ed.). Beverly Hills: Sage.

McNamara, J. H.
1967 "Uncertainties in Police Work." In *The Police* (D. Bordua, ed.). New York: John Wiley, pp. 163–252.

Merton, R. K., and Nisbet, R. A.
1963 *Contemporary Social Problems*. London: Rupert Hart-Davis.

Poliisilaki
1966 §13 and §19 [Police Law].

Redfield, R.
1956 *Peasant Society and Culture: An Anthropological Approach to Civilization*. Chicago: University of Chicago Press.

Skolnick, J. H.
1966 *Justice without Trial: Law Enforcement in Democratic Society*. New York: John Wiley.

Uusitalo, P.
1980 "Kansalaisten palvelija vai pakkovallan virkamies?" [The servant of citizens or an administrator of state force?], *Sosiologia* 1980 (2): 59–102.

Wolf, B. R.
1966 *Peasants*. Englewood Cliffs, New Jersey: Prentice-Hall.

"Mastering the Past": Germans and Gypsies (1982)

Gabrielle Tyrnauer

In the vast body of Holocaust literature, the story of the Gypsy extermination has become an almost forgotten footnote to the history of the Nazi genocide. Under Hitler's rule, approximately half a million European Gypsies were systematically slaughtered. Yet there was no Gypsy witness at the Nuremberg trials and no one was accused of the crime. Neither the scholars who provided the data, nor the officials who formulated the "final solution to the Gypsy problem," nor the bureaucrats and military men who executed it were ever called to account. The Gypsies became the forgotten victims of the Holocaust.

But all this is changing in the Federal Republic of Germany. Thirty-four years after the end of World War II, the victims have at last broken their long silence. In a dramatic reversal, German ministers of state were summoned to the former death camps for negotiations with one-time inmates and their children. A Gypsy civil rights movement has sprung, phoenix-like, out of the ashes of the Holocaust to demand an accounting for the past and to call attention to continued discrimination against Gypsies in Germany. A new chapter in the historical process of *Vergangenheitsbewältigung* (mastery of the past) is under way.

The Legacy of Persecution

Centuries of prejudice and persecution in Germany and elsewhere prepared the ground in which the seeds of genocide were planted. Since the Gypsies' first appearance in Europe in the early fourteenth century, they were regarded with a blend of fear and fascination by the sedentary peoples among whom they moved. Their language and their appearance were strange. They were not farmers or laborers; their women told fortunes, and they all seemed to have a special relationship with the supernatural. They were treated as vagrants, criminals, and spies by the secular powers, often as witches, heretics, and pagans by the church, even when they were nominally Catholic. A sixteenth-century bishop's edict in Sweden, for example, forbade the priests to administer the sacraments to the Gypsies.[1]

Gypsies were imprisoned, expelled, and enslaved by the princes through whose territories they passed. There were also some early attempts to forcibly settle them. The best known of these was that of the eighteenth-century Austro-Hungarian empress, Maria Theresa, who wanted them to become God-fearing peasants and proceeded to forbid them nomadism, the use of their language, and most of their traditional occupations. They were given land and called "New Hungarians," while their children were taken away from them to be raised by more "civilized" foster parents.[2]

At the same time, Gypsies became an important part of the European cultural scene. Individual dancers, musicians, and circus performers acquired legendary reputations among the *gaje* or non-Gypsies. With the advent of the Romantic movement, their unfettered lifestyle became attractive to a restless young generation. There were elements of envy as well as contempt in the composite stereotype. It led to a curious ambivalence in the attitudes of the settled peoples toward the colorful nomads in their midst.[3]

It was in the Nazi concentration camps that this ambivalence assumed its most bizarre forms. The Commandant of Auschwitz, Rudolf Höss, expressed his fondness for the Gypsies in his charge. They were his "best-loved prisoners," "trusting as children." He ordered special rations of salami for them en route to the gas chambers and built a playground for their children a month before their final liquidation.[4] Dr. Mengele never failed to bring the Gypsy children candy before taking them from their parents to perform his deadly experiments. SS officers organized Gypsy orchestras in Auschwitz and other concentration camps.[5] Academic researchers whose work provides the foundation for the system immersed themselves, like good anthropologists, in the language and culture of the people they helped to destroy.

The real *Zigeunerfrage* (Gypsy question) was only formulated, according to one German historian, about the time of German unification in the late nineteenth century. Since then, successive German governments have worked diligently at its solution. Under the monarchy, data collection on the Gypsies began, first with the establishment in 1899 of a "Gypsy Information Service" (*Zigeunernachrichtendienst*). In 1905 the government of Bavaria started a "Gypsy book" (*Zigeunerbuch*) in which acts and edicts related to Gypsies in the years 1816–1903 are compiled as guidelines for the continuing battle against the "Gypsy plague" (*Zigeunerplage*). Matters did not improve for Gypsies under the Weimar Republic, when a variety of legislation aimed at *"Zigeuner, Landfahrer und Arbeitsscheue"* (Gypsies, Travellers, and Malingerers) was passed. In 1926, a "Gypsy conference" was held in Munich to bring some uniformity to the legislation of the different provinces (*Länder*). In fact, anti-Gypsy laws were so harsh during this period that the Nazis continued to use them for their own purposes.[6]

The Third Reich and the "Final Solution"

While the Weimar laws sufficed for the first few years of National Socialist rule, soon new legislation, consistent with Nazi racial ideology, was sought. At the Party's 1935 convention in Nuremberg, the new racial laws were announced. These made Gypsies as well as Jews *"artfremd,"* "alien to the German species." It followed that both could be deprived of their German citizenship.

There began a period of unprecedented government support for research intended to provide the "scientific" underpinnings for future policy. The *Rassenhygienische und Bevölkerungsbiologische Forschungsstelle* was founded in 1936 as a part of the Ministry of Health. By 1942, Dr. Robert Ritter had collected over 30,000 genealogies by means of which he classified almost all the Gypsies of the Reich as either of "pure" or "mixed" race. He designated the "mixed race" Gypsies as *"asozial"* and recommended their sterilization, as did his student, Eva Justin. For those of "pure blood" who—to the embarrassment of Nazi ideology—were closer to the "Aryans" than any other people of Europe, these two scholars recommended a kind of "reservation."[7]

By 1942, Gypsies had been removed from the "normal" criminal procedures and delivered wholly to the jurisdiction of Himmler's SS. The distinctions among them were abandoned as orders were issued for mass deportation to the concentration camps of the "eastern territories." According to a record book hidden by an inmate of the Gypsy camp in Auschwitz, 20,967 Gypsies from all over Europe were transported to the Nazis' most notorious death factory. The first contingents arrived in several cattle cars attached to Jewish transports in February 1943.[8] A year and a half later, about 4,000 remained and these were, on Himmler's orders, exterminated in a single night. Commandant Höss describes the matter routinely in his prison autobiography:

> There remained until August, 1944 ca. 4,000 Gypsies, who must still go to the gas chambers. Up to this time they did not know what awaited them. They only noticed it when they were taken barrack by barrack to Crematorium V. It was not easy to get them into the gas chambers.[9]

The next morning, there were no Gypsies left in Auschwitz.

The Past Becomes Present

On October 27, 1979, a group of German Gypsies, or Sinti, as they call themselves, gathered at the former concentration camp of Bergen-Belsen to honor their Holocaust victims and call attention to the continuing discrimination against them in the Federal Republic. The event was organized by three groups: the *Verband Deutscher Sinti* (Federation of German Sinti), a national organization, the *Romani Union*, an international organization recognized by the United Nations in 1979, and a non-Gypsy support group, *Die Gesellschaft für bedrohte Völker* (The Society for Threatened Peoples). Roma (as the Gypsies are often known internationally)[10] representatives from France, England, Switzerland, the Scandinavian countries, Belgium and the Netherlands, Yugoslavia, Greece, and Italy were there. For the first time German government officials paid homage to the other victims of the "Final Solution." The guest of honor was the president of the Council of Europe, Simone Weil, herself a survivor of Bergen-Belsen, who declared her personal solidarity as well as the support of the Council of

Europe.[11] The wreath was laid by the charismatic young Sinto Romani Rose, who had taken over the leadership of the *Verband Deutscher Sinti* from his uncle, Vinzenz Rose. Thirteen members of Rose's immediate family died in the concentration camps of Hitler's Germany.

The next and still more powerful expression of the Sinti's rendezvous with history was a hunger strike at Dachau—the first concentration camp—on April 4, 1980. In the presence of more than a hundred German and foreign journalists and several television crews, fourteen hunger strikers including one German social worker (the only non-Sinto) began their fast on Good Friday, following an ecumenical service in the chapel. Their objectives included official recognition of the Nazi crimes against the Roma and Sinti, appropriate restitutions,[12] an end to legal discrimination and police harassment, and the establishment of a Sinti cultural center at Dachau. The strike continued for eight days until satisfactory negotiations were initiated with government officials. Members of all three major political parties represented in the Bundestag and representatives of church groups also took part in the negotiations. While Rose proclaimed a "victory" for the Sinti, in fact their demands were met more with supportive rhetoric than real concessions. The city of Dachau vigorously opposed the establishment of the cultural center, expressing the fear that the "unjust" prejudices against the Sinti would be transferred to the city of Dachau, adding to the burden Dachau already carries through its past association with the concentration camp.[13]

Between these two powerfully symbolic events, Sinti, or as they remain more widely known, Zigeuner (Gypsies) burst into the German consciousness with the force of a thirty-five-year time bomb. Within the next year, there was an unprecedented media boom and half a dozen German universities were conducting research on some aspect of past and present Sinti problems.[14] An event which really triggered the explosion, according to many German observers, was the telecasting of the American TV dramatization entitled "Holocaust." For a generation which had little or no knowledge from home or schools of the Nazi period, it became a powerful catalyst to questioning and probing of what remains little more than a common cliché: *"die unbewältigte Vergangenheit,"* "the unmastered past." It was estimated by newspaper surveys that 48 percent of the German population over the age of fourteen saw "Holocaust." Although it contained only fleeting references to the fate of Gypsies, it created an atmosphere in which the Nazi past in all its facets could be reexamined by a new generation. For many Sinti it meant "coming out of the closet" to publicly acknowledge their ethnic identity, past persecution, and hopes for the future. Many could for the first time share their remembered sufferings and individual terrors with members of their own community and outsiders.

In the course of the next two years in almost every city with a concentration of Sinti, an organization came to life. The largest of these are the *Verband Deutscher Sinti* and the *Sinti Union*. In Hamburg there is a unique association of Sinti *and* Roma—the Gypsies from Eastern Europe who play a prominent role in the international organization. Many of the Roma have only recently come to Germany with the waves of immigrant workers or *Gastarbeiter*. They are culturally and linguistically distinct from the Sinti who have been mostly sedentary and partly assimilated to German culture for centuries. The Sinti attitude toward the Roma ranges from indifference to outright hostility, particularly when their sporadic encounters with the police carry over in the popular mind to Sinti.[15] So a joint association, like that in Hamburg, is unusual.

The best-known product of this association is the Duo-Z, two young Gypsy musicians—one Sinto and one Rom—who have developed a repertoire of bitter satirical songs and a national reputation.[16] The duo was among the hunger strikers at Dachau for the first few days, but it was generally decided that their media work was of greater importance to the movement and that their concerts should not be canceled.

Several Gypsy jazz groups in the tradition of the late Django Reinhardt have been popular for years and are increasingly becoming openly engaged in the Sinti as well as the international Roma movement.[17] They are much in demand at universities, festivals, and concerts throughout Germany. They can reach a wider audience than can the political leaders and on a number of musical occasions during the past two years have effectively carried the political message.[18]

The Underlying Factors

The rediscovery of the Holocaust is a historic event for both Germans and Gypsies, which has been made possible by the conjunction of a number of factors. Some of the most important of them are as follows:

1. A postwar generation of Sinti who have grown up in an increasingly, though unintentionally, pluralistic society as waves of foreign workers transformed Germany during the past two decades into an immigrant society.[19] Better educated and more militant than their elders, they are no longer content to choose between assimilation and dissimilation but are proclaiming their ethnic identities and persuading many of their elders to follow suit. These elders, as Romani Rose remarked in explaining his own leadership position, are often broken in spirit as well as in body from their experiences in the Third Reich. "We cannot expect them to carry the burden."[20]

In addition to the social milieu in which the postwar Sinti have grown up, there is a psychological dimension, which has recently acquired a name in the studies of the second-generation Jewish Holocaust survivors. Dr. William B. Niederland, a psychiatrist, claims to have coined the term "survivors' syndrome" after extensive study of Holocaust survivors. The survivors live constantly with their memories and their fears, which are conveyed to their children, who in reaction often exhibit strong tendencies to seek positive action or resistance to compensate for their parents' passivity.[21]

2. Continuing popular prejudice and official discrimination, recently accentuated by the ever-increasing number of immigrants and an economic recession which often makes them competitors for scarce resources. The discrimination, of course, reinforces the Sinti consciousness of minority status and minority rights. This has deepened their historical consciousness (which is absent in the culture of many Gypsy groups in other countries) so that they quickly relate present discrimination to past persecution climaxing in the Holocaust. It also makes them more sensitive than most members of the population (with the exception of Jews) to any stirrings of neo-Nazism. Reactions have ranged from street demonstrations against SS reunions,[22] civil disobedience against exclusion from camping places[23] to the dramatic hunger strike at Dachau which demanded remembrance of the past, just restitution for its victims and the dismantling of institutions, such as special police offices for "Travellers," as well as destruction of data collected by Nazi officials and researchers, still used by police. They maintain (and their claims can be substantiated) that the new wave of xenophobia has led to stricter enforcement of existing laws applying to foreigners, especially to "migrants" or "travelers." Some of these laws

dating back to the Nazi period or still earlier were largely ignored (though in many cases never abolished) in the postwar years. Also, deadlines and legal technicalities related to applications for restitution (*Wiedergutmachung*) and citizenship have been enforced more rigidly, so that there are cases of Sinti whose grandparents were German citizens but who must themselves carry a foreigner's identification (*Fremdenpass*), with restrictions on work and residence.[24] This has led to increasing resentment and fears that "the Nazis are coming back" or, in some cases, never left. One dramatic instance of this is the case of an Auschwitz survivor who drove into a camping place with his trailer and family. When the local official in charge saw the concentration camp number still tattooed on his arm, he said to him, "This place is not for you."[25] Another, even more shocking incident was that of a woman, also an Auschwitz survivor, who was sterilized under Nazi law and when she applied for restitution in the city which had always been her home, found herself, at the required physical examination, face to face with the physician who had performed the sterilization operation.[26] The Sinti's new eagerness to speak publicly about the Nazi past and their experiences in it grow out of their escalating fears of its repetition, perhaps in altered form.[27]

3. The support of key non-Gypsy groups has been an important factor in the whole difficult process—particularly so for a people still largely illiterate and powerless—of remembering the past and organizing for the future. These groups can be divided into religious organizations, ad hoc citizens' groups, social workers, and secular leftist groups, some of which have grown out of the student movement of the late 1960s. There have also been committed unaffiliated individuals in the press and at various universities, some of whom have come together for more effective action. These groups have given moral, financial, and technical support. They have sponsored and helped to organize congresses and issued publications, in almost all of which the Holocaust figures as the central historical experience of Gypsies in Germany.[28]

4. The existence of an international Gypsy organization known as the Romani Union, founded in 1971 and admitted to membership of the Economic and Social Council of the United Nations as a nongovernmental organization in 1979. The third international Congress was held on German soil (in Göttingen, May 1981, cosponsored by the Gesellschaft für bedrohte Völker) and Romani Rose, the German Sinti

leader, was elected vice president of the organization. This suggests the importance of this international connection for German Sinti.

5.   Continuing war crimes trials and the controversy over the statute of limitations. The five-and-a-half-year Maidanek trials, in which one of the defendants was a naturalized American citizen (the only one sentenced to life imprisonment) who was extradited for the trial, was to recent German history what the Eichmann and the Auschwitz trials were to the generation coming to maturity in the early and middle sixties. It was well covered by the German media and remained a constant reminder that the past was not yet "mastered." While it created guilt feelings in some young people who had no personal experience of that past, it raised a wall of anger and hostility in many of the older people who wanted to hear no more about it. In either case, it kept the past in the foreground of the news.

6.   A similar polarized effect resulted from the showing on German television of the American Holocaust dramatization, as mentioned previously. The videotape and the instructional materials which accompanied it were used extensively in the schools, sometimes by teachers who had not wanted or dared to teach their pupils the history of the Third Reich. It also stimulated spontaneous and organized group discussions throughout Germany. The impact on the Sinti, who are avid television watchers, was powerful. Now, they felt, their story too could be told.

Conclusion

All these elements combined to create, in the late 1970s, an awareness and a movement that had been gestating for more than three decades. The elders broke their long silence and spoke publicly about things that had only been whispered in the presence of close family members since the end of World War II. One elder Sinto whose entire family was murdered in Auschwitz, whose wife was sterilized by Dr. Mengele, while her family too was killed, makes a pilgrimage to Auschwitz annually, sometimes twice a year. When asked why, his wife replied simply, "Because my whole family is there. I go there to pray." Her husband has, during the past two years, lectured at clubs, schools, and churches.

Thus, in the twilight of the twentieth century, a new generation of Germans and Gypsies are coming together to wrestle with their still "unmastered" past, trying to assure that the forgotten victims of the Holocaust will be remembered and that their children can live as full and equal citizens of the Federal Republic.

Afterword 1995:

In 1981, when this article was written, no one would have dared to predict the tumultuous changes that were to engulf Central and Eastern Europe by the end of the decade. The fall of Communist governments in country after country, the crumbling of the Berlin Wall, and the unification of the two Germanies had a profound impact on the Roma and Sinti of the whole region.

While there was a brief euphoria in places like Czechoslovakia— where the Gypsies' new organizations and old aspirations received support from the highest levels—those Roma who came proudly "out of the closet" (or out of their ethnic ghettos) soon retreated. They realized that the "new freedom" for the majority meant unleashed hatred directed against many minorities—most especially the two ancient scapegoat peoples of Europe, Jews and Gypsies, as well as the foreigners, who had been welcomed as cheap labor in the expanding economies of postwar Europe.

Old and new popular prejudices combined with carefully manipulated political movements on the newly unchained Right, making life more difficult and dangerous for the "Gypsy" minorities in most European countries than it had been since World War II. In a 1991 visit to Germany, where I videotaped oral history testimony of Sinti Holocaust survivors, I heard horror stories from all of my informants, many of them old friends from my first field experience there ten years earlier. Skinheads, old and new Nazis of all descriptions made many of them sleep with guns under their pillows. "Now when I go into a tavern," my friend the puppeteer told me, "I get hostile stares because my dark skin makes them think I am a Turk. But when I begin to speak an accentless German they know I am a Zigeuner and then the action really starts." A cousin of this man crossed the former border into East Germany to camp with his family on the outskirts of Dresden in his new and well-furnished trailer. That night the skinheads poured a ring of gasoline around it and lit a match. The entire family was incinerated. There were many other incidents of this kind, during which—as I repeatedly was told—the police stood idly by, particularly in areas of former East Germany. In early 1995, a few months after my attendance at a conference entitled "The Other Holocaust," cosponsored by the University of Vienna and an Austrian Romani organization, the past once more became present in an explosion of violence against Zigeuner in Austria's Burgenland, which left four dead. The nation—but especially the Austrian "Gypsies" and other endangered minorities—went into shock. Austria had been relatively free of such incidents in recent years, particularly under the leadership of its moderate socialist premier, Franz Vranitzky, who has made special attempts to master the peculiarly Austrian past—from the jubilant welcome given to Hitler at the time of the Anschluss, or annexation, in 1938, to the election of ex-Nazi Kurt Waldheim as president in 1986. Throughout this period, Austria had escaped all responsibility for its role in the Holocaust against Jews and Gypsies by perpetuating the myth of Austria as a conquered country, as "Hitler's first victim." Now with the fiftieth anniversary of the end of World War II, this history, under Chancellor Vranitzky, is being reconsidered. According to a letter recently issued to surviving Jewish victims of National Socialism, "Austria is no longer suppressing the dark sides of its recent past" and the Austrian parliament passed a federal act on 1 June 1995 setting up, for the first time, a national fund for the victims of National Socialism. In this climate, the terrorist attack in the Burgenland deeply shook the Chancellor and his supporters. I determined that personally in a conversation with him several weeks after it took place.

In Hungary, Romania, Poland, the former Soviet Union—in all the countries in which racism had been officially banned, the old hatreds now seemed unrestrained by either law or ideology. My puppeteer friend commented sadly, "We wish that the Berlin Wall would be rebuilt as quickly as possible." He added that this time, if the Nazis come, he would kill himself and his family. "For us there will never be another Auschwitz."

Thus, in the final decade of the century, the "mastering of the past" has been put on the back burner, as genocide once more becomes a strategy of nationalist aggrandizement, and European armies are again marching under banners made obsolete for several generations by communism and other forms of internationalism. "Ethnic cleansing" is a slogan launched shamelessly by the perpetrators of genocide in the ruins of the multiethnic state of Yugoslavia. The past has again become present—this time not as a subject of reflection and penance but as a model for new configurations of violence. Reading the signals emitted by the "new world order," many Gypsies from the former Communist bloc are again on the move toward any place that will provide them with sanctuary. Hundreds of thousands pour across borders into Western European countries. Many are returned with other unsuccessful asylum seekers or simply as illegals. Sanctuaries are few and far between. And thus, most stay put in their homelands, relying on ancient survival strategies and hoping for better times to come for themselves and their children.

NOTES

1. Donald Kenrick and Grattan Puxon, *Sinti und Roma, Die Vernichtung eines Volkes im NS-Staat* (Göttingen: Die Gesellschaft für bedrohte Volker, 1981), 24. The first edition of this book was in English: *The Destiny of Europe's Gypsies* (London: Chatto-Heinemann-Sussex, 1972).

2. Ibid., 45.

3. The traditional ambivalence springing from the conflict between the Romantic cult of individual freedom and the Protestant ethic of hard work and postponed gratification was reflected in much of the literature which appeared in Europe during the nineteenth century. A recent survey by Roland Schopf of such literature in relation to Gypsies was called "Bürgerfluch und Bürgersehnsucht: Zigeuner im Vorstellungsbild literarische Intelligenz," in Joachim S. Hohmann and Roland Schopf, *Zigeunerleben: Beiträge zur Sozialgeschichte einer Verfolgung* (Darmstadt: ms edition, 1980).

4. Jerzy Ficowski, "Die Vernichtung," in Tilman Zülch, ed., *In Auschwitz vergast, bis heute verfolgt: Zur Situation der Roma (Zigeuner) in Deutschland und Europa*. Reinbek bei Hamburg: Rowohlt, 1979, p. 109.

5. Two particularly shocking stories among the many survivors' accounts of the SS staff's "music appreciation" are recounted by Kenrick and by Streck. The first concerns the Auschwitz Gypsy Orchestra organized by SS Officer Broad. On 25 May 1943 a concert was given for the SS. It was, however, interrupted in the middle, the musicians sent back to the barracks while on

special orders a thousand prisoners were gassed (Donald Kenrick, "Das Schicksal der Zigeuner im NS-Staat" in Donald Kenrick, Grattan Puxon, Tilman Zulch, eds., *Die Zigeuner, Verkannt—Verachtet—Verfolgt* [Hannover: Niedersachsischen Landeszentrale für politische Bildung, 1980], 37–74, 68–69. The second story comes from a death camp in Bosnia, Jasenovac, and was first related by a Franciscan priest who served as chaplain in the German Wehrmacht. "Each twelve-man Gypsy ensemble played one month, from the first day until the last. A month with thirty-one days was luck, a gift for the twelve Gypsies. One day more, twenty-four hours. They played until noon, they played in the evening and on the last day until morning. . . . After dinner the electric light was switched off and only candles were lit . . . now each of the twelve Gypsies prayed that the Kommandant would not become sleepy. When the Kommandant began to grow tired and the night began to glide away, he would point to one of the Gypsy musicians. He would have to lay down his instrument and would walk through the candlelit room to the door of the casino where his escort already waited to take him into the forest. When the shot from the forest came—one could hear it even while the music played in the room—the next one prepared himself. But he continued to play until the Kommandant pointed to him (Bernhard Streck, "Das Ende der Musik: Zigeuner hinterm Stacheldraht" in Georgia A. Rakelmann, *Zigeuner*, Materialien für Unterricht und Bildungsarbeit, Gesellschaft für entwicklungspolitische Bildung, 1980). A grim photograph shows prisoners being led to the gallows accompanied by musicians. The prescribed song for the occasion was "All the little birds are here" (ibid.).

6. Bernhard Streck, "Die Bekämpfung des Zigeunerwesens: Ein Stuck moderner Rechtsgeschichte" in Tilman Zulch, ed., *In Auschwitz Vergast, bis Heute Verfolgt* (Hamburg: Rowohlt Taschenbuch Verlag, 1979), 64–87.

7. Alwin Meyer, "Holocaust der Zigeuner," *Zeichen* (Mitteilungen der Aktion Suhnezeichen/Friedensdienste) 3 (September 1979), 6.

8. Ibid.

9. Ibid.

10. There is considerable ambiguity in the use of this term because it also refers to a subgroup of "Gypsies," now principally stemming from the Balkans. Thus far, no attempts to find an indigenous term to replace the pejorative "Zigeuner" have been successful. "Romani," as in "Romani Union" is sometimes used, but that is also a term used for English Gypsies.

11. Her speech is reproduced in a special publication documenting the occasion, *Sinti und Roma im ehemaligen KZ Bergen Belsen am 27. Oktober 1979* (Göttingen: Verband deutscher Sinti, 1980), 49–57.

12. There has been a long history of controversy over the subject of restitution or "Wiedergutmachung" for European Gypsies who survived the

Holocaust. In the postwar period, the continued fear of official persecution and the lack of required documentation resulted in a situation where few Gypsies exercised their rights and official deadlines for applications passed. Many applications were rejected after a statement by the Minister of the Interior of Baden-Württenberg in 1950, circulated to judges who were concerned with such applications, reminding them that Gypsies were, in the early years of the war, not persecuted on "racial" grounds (which was the legal basis of *Wiedergutmachung*) but on the basis of an "asocial and criminal past" and a security threat. After 1959, when the first *Wiedergutmachung* law expired and was renewed, their situation improved somewhat. Today individual Gypsies can receive DM5 for each day they spent in a concentration camp and some additional money for damage to health. Sterilization was not classified as such a damage (Grattan Puxon, "Verschleppte Wiedergutmachung," in *In Auschwitz Vergast, bis Heute Verfolgt*, 149–157; 168–171).

13. *Dachauer Neueste Nachrichten*, 7 May 1980.

14. Academics, for the most part, approached the subject with extreme caution because of the unhappy past involvement of German scholars with the "Gypsy Question." With the exception of an older scholar, Hermann Arnold, who has become the subject of a storm of controversy, most of the present "Tsiganologues" are young and politically committed and engaging in "action research." Nevertheless, a good deal of suspicion has been expressed by Sinti leaders.

15. A recent example of this was a well-reported incident involving a group of Roma alleged to have been involved in a large number of burglaries. The police rounded them up in their trailers and broadcast an appeal for witnesses. The *Nurnberger Nachrichtern* (1 July 1981) reported that the police rounded up a "hundred-head Sinti clan."

16. The name of the duo was chosen ironically. "Z" for *Zigeuner* was the symbol Gypsies had stamped on their papers—and tattooed on their arms—by the Nazi officials. Their theme song is a grim parody of a traditional German folk song called "Lustig ist das Zigeunerleben" (Merry Is the Gypsy Life), which describes the Gypsies' life in Auschwitz and Buchenwald. The son of a Sinti leader in the Nuremberg area who wanted to perform it for a school festival was prohibited from singing it by his teacher, who explained that it was "too sharp."

17. The names are confusing and reflect the schisms normal among culturally diverse groups attempting to unite politically. Even in the framework of an international congress of the Romani Union, the Sinti have insisted on retaining their name. The outgoing president of the Union, Czech émigré Dr Jan Cibula (himself a Rom in the more restricted sense of the term), now living in Switzerland, urged all Gypsies to adopt the term "Rom" as a generic title

But the Sinti were not persuaded and all posters at the Congress in Göttingen (May 1981) referred to "Roma and Sinti." Thus, today the term "Roma" may designate either a particular ethnic group of mainly Balkan Gypsies or, as used by Romani nationalists, it may refer to all Gypsies. In 1982, the Verband deutscher Sinti was renamed "Zentralrat deutscher Sinti und Roma," reflecting the German umbrella organizations' search for greater inclusiveness as well as its failure to find a simple name that would replace the despised "Zigeuner."

18. Hans'che Weiss, for example, one of the best known of the Gypsy jazz musicians, has popularized a Romanes song entitled "Let Us Demand Our Rights." The program notes for à Gypsy music festival in Darmstadt in 1979 were in fact essays on the past genocide and present persecution of the Gypsy people written by some of the politically engaged young "Tsiganologues" from Giessen University.

19. Friedrich Heckmann, "Socio-Structural Analysis of Immigrant Worker Minorities: The Case of West Germany," *Mid-American Review of Sociology* 5:2 (1980), 13–20.

20. Interview, 29 May 1981.

21. "Das Überlebendensyndrom der Opfer und ihre Kinder," *Zeichen* 3 (September 1979), 14.

22. As an example of this might be cited the demonstration in Würzburg on 18 September 1976, in response to a meeting of former SS men, which escalated into a fight resulting in some minor injuries and prosecution of seven demonstrators, six of whom were Gypsies.

23. Inge Britt, "Zigeunern ist die Benutzung des Campingplatzes untersagt," *Zeichen* 3 (September 1979), 18–20.

24. The Nazis stripped Gypsies, like Jews, of their German citizenship. Some Sinti even served in the armed forces until the order came in 1942 that all Gypsies must be sent to Auschwitz (see Julius Hodost, "Wir werden Euch vertilgen wie die Katzen," *Zeichen* 3 (September 1979), 7. After the war, many of these stateless Gypsies did not have the necessary documentation to regain their citizenship.

25. Personal communication, 5 July 1981, Erlangen Folk Festival.

26. Personal communication, 29 May 1981, Frankfurt.

27. This feared continuity under a changed name is illustrated by a recent cartoon which shows a police official speaking to his two subordinates who are rifling through mountains of disorderly files. "Have you found something on 'Landfahrer' yet?" he asks. "No," one of them replies, "only on Zigeuner, Herr Minister."

28. Some of the most important of the religious groups are the Catholic Caritas, the Evangelischer (Lutheran) Aktion Sühnezeichen, Innere Mission, Diakonisches Werk, Jewish organizations such as the Berlin Jewish congrega-

tion, its leader, Heinz Galinski, and the well-known Jewish Nazi-hunter Simon Wiesenthal; in the last two years, probably the most active group, the liberal secular Gesellschaft für bedrohte Völker; der Verband der Verfolgten des Nazi Regimes, individuals and groups close to the Social Democratic Party, journalists such as Anita Geigges and Bernard Wette, social workers associated with the Deutsche Verein für öffentliche und private Fürsorge, and so forth. Information about the work of a few of these groups can be found in C. Freese, M. Murko, G. Wurzbacher, *Hilfen für Zigeuner und Landfahrer* (Stuttgart: Kohlhammer, 1980).

LANGUAGE

Duty and Beauty, Possession and Truth: "Lexical Impoverishment" as Control (1996)

Ian Hancock

The manipulation by societies in power of the identities of subordinate groups is achieved in many ways. One such way is through discriminatory legislation, such as that enacted against the Romani people in almost every land, including the United States. Another is through media representation, both factual and fictional. This last category, the portrayal of Gypsies in poetry, film, and novels, is the most effective in establishing such negative feelings because they are absorbed subliminally by children and adults.

Apart from descriptions of Romani people and their life, which are legion, the Romani language has also been the target of comment, always worded as fact rather than supposition. In his *Tales of the Real Gypsy*, Paul Kester gives his readers those "real" facts about it (1897:305):

> The Gypsies, like the birds and all wild things, have a language of their own, which is apart from the language of those among whom they dwell. . . the Gypsy['s]. . . language is deep and warm and full of the charm of the out-of-doors world, the scent of the clover and the ripple of streams and the rush of the wind and the storm.

For the Rommany speech is full of all this, and though the Gypsy has few traditions, his rich mother tongue must embalm in each word a thousand associations that thrill in the soul.

Kester was not a linguist, and it is easy to see how he was able to allow his fantasies about the Romani people to shape his preconceptions of the language. Doris Duncan, however, presumably is a linguist, and can claim no such excuse. Writing seventy years later about Romani in a journal of popular linguistics, she made the following observations (1969:42):

All authentic Gypsy communication is, and must be, oral. As they settle for a time in a new country, they acquire some of that country's words and incorporate them into *Roum*, more popularly called Romany. It is believed that the *Roum* language began as a very small one, concerned with the family, the tribe, the horses and herd, words required for a simple existence. It must be very old, for *Roum* is highly idiomatic, and the complication of verbs and genders is endless. There is no way to write it except phonetically, and some sounds of the Gypsy tongue simply defy our twenty-six letter alphabet. . . *Roum* is a disorderly language, and must be learned phrase by phrase. Even the syntax differs from one occasion to another. Verbs are very difficult . . . no one can explain why the verb changes so radically. A major problem is that no Gypsy really knows what a verb is, and it wouldn't matter anyway if he did, because this is the way it must be said. The idiom is paramount in *Roum* and cannot be changed.

Duncan is right in maintaining that Romani has adopted words from those with whom its speakers have come in contact—this is a natural process affecting all languages, and one which has caused English, for example, to lose nearly three-quarters of its original Anglo-Saxon lexicon by dictionary count. But Bayle St. John couldn't simply discuss this phenomenon as lexical adoption when referring to Romani (1853:141), which, he said,

. . . contains traces of an original character, [but which] is encrusted, as it were, with words borrowed—it might be more appropriate to say stolen—from a dozen different dialects.

A number of authors have claimed that, because of our character as a people, Roma lack certain virtues, and that this is reflected in the Romani language which cannot even express them. Those which have been discussed by different writers include *duty, possession, truth, beautiful, read, write, time, danger, warmth,* and *quiet.* How negatively must the non-Gypsy world regard our people, to think that we cannot even express such basic human concepts and skills!*

Over a century ago, Adriano Colocci first introduced a notion which has since become a part of gypsilorist folk wisdom. In his extensive discussion of the Romani people in his 421-page book *The Gypsies,* he maintained that Roma

. . . have no more conception of property than of duty; "I have" is as foreign to them as "I ought." (Colocci 1889:156)

Citing Colocci as his source, Italian criminologist Cesare Lombroso elaborated upon the statement in his widely used book on Gypsies as a

---

*The same kind of prejudice that leads people to claim that these words don't exist in Romani is responsible for the reference in the August 1996 issue of *Disney Adventures: The Magazine for Kids* on page 24 to a condition called "gypsyitis." The symptoms of this affliction include "an urge to run away from it all and dance among the dandelions," and being "footloose and fancy-free," instead of being a normal "buckle-down, rules-and-regulations kinda person," which is to say one for whom "duty" means something. Why this kind of stereotyping is objectionable seems to have escaped the magazine's editor, Phyllis Erhlich, who defended it in a letter to the International Roma Federation as being "on the contrary, a positive portrayal of the Gypsy spirit."

criminal race, and made the jump from concept to actual language by saying that

> the word *ought* does not exist in the Gypsy language. The verb to *have* is almost forgotten by the European Gypsies, and is unknown to the Gypsies of Asia. (Lombroso 1918:41)

In 1928, Konrad Bercovici, probably also using Colocci but not acknowledging any source, repeated this notion on the first page (and again on the third page) of his book *The Story of the Gypsies*, and also interpreted the original observation linguistically, saying

> I am attempting to unravel the story of a people whose vocabulary lacks two words—"duty" and "possession." (Bercovici 1928:1, 3)

He goes on to rationalize this by explaining that "what we own possesses us, jails us." This was then picked up from Bercovici shortly afterwards by Erich von Stroheim who, in his racist Gypsy novel *Paprika*, told his readers that

> the Gypsy mind is timeless. The Gypsy tongue has no words to signify duty or possession, qualities that are like roots, holding civilized people fast in the soil. (von Stroheim 1935:12)

Fifteen years later, the anonymous author of an article in *Coroner* magazine plagiarized and reworded the same statement:

> Even today, there are two important English words for which the Gypsy vocabulary has no known equivalent, and for which the Gypsy people have never exhibited any desire or need. One of them is the word "duty," the other is "possession." (Anonymous 1950:126)

In a 1962 reissue of Leland's *Gypsy Sorcery and Fortune Telling* Margery Silver wrote in her introduction to that edition,

> [In Germany], where they had been chronically subjected to the most relentless and brutal oppression of their European experience

since their first appearance in 1417, five hundred thousand "sons of Egypt"—whose vocabulary a recent writer has described as "lacking two words: 'duty' and 'possession'"—died in the Nazi ovens beside six million sons of Jacob, whose history was founded on just those concepts, duty to God and possession of his law. (Leland 1962:xx)

Five years after that, in perhaps the most invidious way of all, since the plagiarism has been recast in such a way as to suggest an actual verbatim interview, the statement turns up again in an article by Marie Wynn Clarke, predictably entitled "Vanishing Vagabonds":

A young Gypsy wife said "there is no word in our language for 'duty' or 'possession,' but I'm afraid there will be soon." (Clarke 1967:210)

In her introduction to the 1983 edition of Bercovici's *Gypsies: Their Life, Lore and Legends*, Elizabeth Congdon Kovanen repeats this yet again, though adding the suggestion that because of this, Gypsies themselves are responsible for the discrimination against them:

The Gypsy vocabulary lacks the words "duty" and "possession." This reflects their unwillingness to settle down, live in houses, obey the law, educate their children, be employed by others—and helps to explain their almost universal persecution. (Bercovici 1983:viii)

The eighth repetition of this strange idea is found in a novel by Piers Anthony, *Being a Green Mother*. The fact that the words "Gypsies! . . . Beware—they steal children!" appear at the very first mention of the Romani characters when they are introduced on page 18 is an indication of the depiction of Roma throughout the rest of the book. The author describes someone's attempt to learn Romani, but who

. . . discovered that the Gypsy language had no words for what in her own were rendered as "duty" and "possession." This was because these concepts were foreign to the Gypsy nature. (Anthony 1988:39)

The most recent, though no doubt not the last, is found in Roger Moreau's *The Rom*:

> One thing the Romani *chib* never acquired, though, was a future tense. Maybe this was a reflection of their attitude to life? . . . Neither is there the verb "to have" or a word for "possession" in Romanes, which I suppose makes sense if you don't happen to own anything. (Moreau 1995:127–128)

Other words which Romani has been said not to have include "truth," "beautiful," "read," "write," "time," "danger," "warmth," and "quiet." The first was maintained by Jim Phelan, author of many books about Romanichals in which he describes his intimate life with British Travellers, and in which he claims to have been "long ago admitted to the brotherhood." In his book *Wagon Wheels* he says

> there is no word for "truth" in the Romani language. There is the crux of the matter. (1951:81)

The concept "beautiful" is denied to the language in Virginia Woolf's novel *Orlando*:

> One evening, when they were all sitting around the camp fire and the sunset was blazing over the Thessalian hills, Orlando exclaimed "how good to eat!" The gipsies have no word for "beautiful." This is the nearest. (1956:142)

The latest claim to a lack of certain basic human responses or skills is found in Isabel Fonseca's *Bury Me Standing: The Gypsies and Their Journey*, where she maintains that there are no words in Romani for "read" and "write." Elsewhere in the same book she states that there are no words for "time," "danger," "warmth," and "quiet" either, because these are foreign concepts for Roma (1995:98). Even before the book reached the bookstores, reviewers were accepting and repeating these false assumptions:

[the Gypsy's] is a world . . . where there are no words for "time" (or for "danger," "warmth" or "quiet") . . . where no day is different from any other. (Kobak 1995:14)

The assumption that the Romani way of life is evidence of some kind of evolutionary arrested development, which accounts for an inherent disregard for ownership—and by implication a "license to steal," as Marlock and Dowling call (1994) call it—has found its way into at least one standard textbook on anthropology. In words recalling those of Charles Davenport half a century before him (1915:10–11), Cyril Dean Darlington wrote that

the Gipsy communities which eventually wandered into Europe . . . still betray the evidence of their paleolithic ancestry . . . the lack of interest in property or understanding of ownership. For this reason, many of them are regarded by settled societies as criminal tribes or castes (1969:364).

Like Bayle St. John, who saw lexical *thefts* as a more appropriate label than lexical *adoptions* in his discussion of the non-native element in the Romani vocabulary, none of the above writers sufficiently overcame their stereotypical preconceptions of Gypsies or of what they *expected* of the language, to ask a Gypsy himself whether these words existed, or even to consult a Romani dictionary, of which dozens exist. For a people who were enslaved in the Romanian principalities for five and a half centuries, a people whose lives were an interminable succession of duties and obligations and for whom possessions were a precious thing, it should not be surprising that there are in fact many words for these two concepts. For "duty" there are, in the various dialects, the words *musajipé, vója, vužulimós, udžilútno, udžilipé, kandipé, slúžba, kandimós, thoximós,* and *vudžlipé*; for "possession" there are *májtko, aračimáta, sersámo, trjábo, butjí, aparáti, kola, prámi, džéla, džélica, oságo, istarimáta, ičarimós, astarimós,* and *theripé.* The words for "truth" include *tačipén, čačimós, vortimó, siguripé,* and others, while "beautiful" is *šukár, múndro, rínkeno, orčíri, pakváro, jakhaló,* etc., in the various dialects. "Read" is *džin-* or *gin-* or *čit-* or *giláb-* or *drab-*, "write" is *ram-* or *jazd-* or *lekh-* or *pišú-* or *pisát-* or *čet-* or *škur-* or *skrij-* or *čin-*; "time" is variously translated by *vaxt, vákti, vrjámja,* or *čéros,* "danger" by *strážno,* "warmth" by *tatičosimós* or *táblipen* and "quiet" by *míro* or *mirnimós,* although in truth, the fallacy of such a belief, i.e., that such words don't exist in the language, should scarcely need refuting. Many of these words come from the ancient Sanskrit stock of the language, while others, like *prámi* or *míro,* have been adopted from Greek and Slavic. Isabel Fonseca concedes in her book that Romani had to adopt the words for "read" and "write" from other languages but apparently doesn't recognize that English, too, has had to borrow most of its lexicon from other languages (incidentally, the commonest word for "read" is of native Sanskrit origin in Romani). Indeed, a dictionary count of English word origins indicates that only 28 percent of that language is traceable to its original Anglo-Saxon stock; should we assume from that, therefore, that the concepts of "duty," "possession," "beauty," "quiet," "danger," etc., were foreign to the English, since all of these words have been "stolen" from French? Furthermore, English also "lacks" a future tense in the sense meant by Moreau but constructs it, just as Romani does, with a word which expresses the intention or desire to undertake the action ("will" or "shall"; in Romani, *ka/kam*).   There is clearly a double standard operating in the minds of these writers.

The blind repetition of someone's statement without checking the original source for oneself is the mark of shoddy scholarship; perhaps it is felt that less rigor is needed in Romani Studies than in other areas of research. A list of writers who, one after the other, have quoted the Romani proverb about not being able to sit on two horses with one backside, could also be assembled—all traceable without acknowledgment to Jan Yoors's book *The Gypsies*—or the story about the Gypsy in jail who weeps for his jailer who must stay there, or the story of the nails used to crucify Jesus. Victorian writers unashamedly lifted material from each other too. These descriptions of the Gypsy children on the Romanian slave estates are far too similar to be coincidental and appeared in the British and American press at the time that the fictionalized image of the Gypsy was taking shape, though its inspiration seems to be traceable to a German source dating from 1841

> The children are seldom provided with clothing before they are ten years old. This is especially true of the wandering Gypsies . . . the

find every kind of meat good: dogs, cats, rats, mice and even sick
farm animals are eaten by them. (Brockhaus 1841:801)

Thus in British literature just a few years later we find

The children wear no clothes until the age of ten or twelve years;
and resemble imps rather than human beings as they run beside the
carriage of the traveller shrieking for alms, with their long matted
hair flying in the wind, and their black limbs shining in the light.
(Pardoe 1848[i]:168)

The children go naked up to the age of ten or twelve, and whole
swarms of girls and boys may sometimes be seen rolling about
together in the dust or mud in summer, in the water or snow in
winter, like so many black worms. (St. John 1853:140)

The children to the age of ten or twelve, are in a complete state of
nudity, but the men and women, the latter offering frequently the
most symmetrical form and feminine beauty, have a rude clothing.
(Gardner 1857:38)

Another area in which writers have shamelessly appropriated from
each other's work, even to the extent of copying each other's mistakes,
is in Romani lexicography; we find for example the English Romani
word for "hedgehog," *hočiwiči*, turning up in Romanian Romani word
lists such as that by de Kogalnitchan, who lists *hotschauitscha*
(1837:60), or Vaillant, who has *hoc'awiça* (1861:108)—though the
source of the word is in the regional English dialect *urchin* (cf. "sea
urchin") and it exists only in Britain, having first been recorded by
Roberts in 1836, Vaillant's and Kogalnitchan's unacknowledged source.
There is likewise scarcely a dictionary of Caló (Spanish Romani) that
is original, each one copying freely from the one preceding it, mistakes
and all, usually without a word of acknowledgment. Grant has addressed
the particular issue of plagiarism in Romani Studies, calling it the
researcher's "biggest problem" (1995:53).

In its January 8, 1992, issue, *The New York Times* published the
results of a public opinion poll surveying national negative attitudes to
8 different racial and ethnic populations in the United States over a

twenty-five-year period. For the entire quarter century, Gypsies were ranked at the very bottom of the list, the most discriminated-against minority in the eyes of the general population. Since most *gadžé* have no personal or social contact with the Romani American community, such attitudes in this country can only be based upon how we are presented in literature. The persistent, relentless portrayal of Roma as rootless, lawless, immoral, childlike thieves, as a people for whom the basic human concepts of truth and beauty, obligation and ownership do not exist and who are ignorant of danger and never seek warmth or peace or quiet, is attributable to such individuals as Colocci, Lombroso, Bercovici, von Stroheim, Silver, Clarke, Kovanen, Anthony, Woolf, Phelan, Fonseca, Moreau, and others, whose investment in defining our character will ensure that anti-Gypsy prejudice will remain firmly a part of Euro-American racist attitudes.

REFERENCES

Anonymous
1950 "Caravans of Mystery." *Coronet*, August, pp. 17–24.
Anthony, Piers
1988 *Being a Green Mother*. New York: Del Rey Books.
Bercovici, Konrad
1928 *The Story of the Gypsies*. London: Cape.
1983 *Gypsies: Their Life, Lore and Legends*. New York: Crown. [orig. 1929]
Brockhaus, F. A.
1841 *Bilder-Conversations-Lexicon für das deutsche Volk*. Leipzig: Brockhaus.
Clarke, Marie Wynn
1967 "Vanishing Vagabonds: The American Gypsies." *Texas Quarterly* 10:2, 204–210.
Colocci, Adriano
1889 *Gli Zingari*. Turin: Herman Loescher.
Darlington, Cyril D.
1969 *The Evolution of Man and Society*. New York: Simon & Schuster.

Davenport, Charles B.
1915   *The Feebly Inhibited: Nomadism, or the Wandering Impulse, with Special Reference to Heredity*. Washington, D.C.: The Carnegie Institution.

Duncan, Doris
1969   "The Rocky Romany Road." *Quinto Lingo* (December), 42–43.

Fonseca, Isabel
1995   *Bury Me Standing: The Gypsies and Their Journey*. New York: Alfred A. Knopf.

Gardner, Samuel
1857   "Notes on the Condition of the Gypsy Population of Moldavia." *Proceedings of the Royal Geographical Society*, 1, 37–39.

Grant, Anthony
1995   "Plagiarism and Lexical Orphans in the European Romani Lexicon," in Matras 1995:53–68.

Kester, Paul
1897   *Tales of the Real Gypsy*. New York: Doubleday.

Kobak, Annette
1995   "The Gypsy in Our Souls," review of Fonseca 1995, *The New York Times*, October 22.

Kogalnitchan, Michel de
1837   *Esquisse sur l'Histoire, les Mœurs et la Langue des Cigains*. Berlin: Behr.

Kovanen, Elizabeth Congdon
1983   Introduction to Bercovici 1983, pp. i–xi.

Leland, Charles Godfrey
1962   *Gypsy Sorcery and Fortune Telling*. New York: Citadel Press. [1900] Reissued in 1995 by Castle Books.

Lombroso, Cesare
1918   *Crime: Its Causes and Remedies*. The Modern Criminal Science Series. Boston: Little, Brown.

Marlock, Dennis, and John Dowling
1994   *License to Steal: Traveling Con Artists, Their Games, Their Rules, Your Money*. Boulder: Paladin.

Matras, Yaron, ed.
1995   *Romani in Contact: The History, Structure and Sociology of a Language*. Amsterdam & New York: Benjamins.

Moreau, Roger
1995   *The Rom: Walking in the Paths of the Gypsies*. Toronto: Key Porter.

Pardoe, M.
1848   *The City of the Magyar, or, Hungary and Her Institutions*. London:
       Gill & Sons. 2 vols.
Phelan, Jim
1951   *Wagon Wheels*. London: Harrap.
Roberts, Samuel
1836   *The Gypsies*. London: Longman.
St. John, Bayle
1853   "The Gypsy Slaves of Wallachia." *Household Words* 185, 139–142.
Stroheim, Erich von
1935   *Paprika, the Gypsy Trollop*. New York: Universal Publishing.
Vaillant, Jean-Antoine
1861   *Grammaire, Dialogues et Vocabulaire de la Langue Rommanes des
       Cigains*. Paris: Pilloy.
Woolf, Virginia
1956   *Orlando*. New York and London: Harcourt Brace Jovanovich. [orig.
       1928]
Yoors, Jan
1967   *The Gypsies*. London: Allen & Unwin.

EDUCATIONAL PERSPECTIVES

Pictures of Ourselves (1987)

Cathy Kiddle

People arriving at the Plymouth Arts Centre, in Devon, England, for the private view of an exhibition of Josef Koudelka's photographs were surprised to find two exhibitions on show. In the main gallery was Koudelka's work, photographs of Gypsies from all parts of Europe, taken over many years. In the café alongside the gallery were more photographs of Gypsies, but these had all been taken and processed over the previous few months by a group of Gypsy teenagers then living in the city. The novelty of the second exhibition attracted much of the attention of the gallery clientele, and they gave many favorable comments. The reaction I remember most clearly, however, came from a respectably dressed, middle-aged woman, who said, "How can they put those pictures here—those children can't even read. . . ." Then almost as an afterthought she said, "I could do that myself."

The morning following the private viewing, a dozen members of the city's Gypsy community, mothers, fathers, and young children, came into the Arts Centre to see their children's exhibition. It was the first time any of them had been in there. Gypsies in England are treated with great hostility by the housedwelling majority. Living in this climate of prejudice, the Gypsies tend to keep to themselves and do not readily approach our institutions. For them to venture into the gallery was remarkable.

Within moments their unaccustomed and unusual presence dominated the space. For an hour they made the place their own, animating the normally quiet atmosphere of the gallery with their direct comments on the photographs, making comparisons between the two exhibitions, and displaying enormous pride in the children's achievements. The young children took advantage of the novelty of several staircases and open, slippery, polished floors to have a great time, while other visitors to the exhibitions stood by, noticeably culture shocked.

This exhibition had not been planned. The idea grew from a photographic project carried out by a group of teenage Gypsies, mainly girls. Their families were among some Gypsies stopping in the city, on a piece of waste ground, under threat of eviction. They had no legal place to camp, though by law the County Council should have provided an official site for them. They have been campaigning for several years for proper provision to be made for them. Meanwhile they camp without security or proper facilities, in appalling conditions, anywhere they can.

The major obstacle to site provision is the negative stereotype of Gypsies held by housedwellers. Housedwellers are liable to get a distorted view of the Gypsy way of life, if they get one at all. The official campsites which exist tend to be tucked away in isolated or industrial areas, away from other residents, screened from public view. The families strictly maintain their privacy, aware of and keeping away from the housedweller's gaze and hostility wherever possible. Beyond work arrangements there are few opportunities for ordinary social contact between housedwellers and Travellers. The teenage girls are kept under close family control.

The general public sees only the unofficial campsites perched on waste land or roadside verges, on any available space. These tend to be untidy, as there are no sanitary or rubbish disposal facilities. Also, the space outside the trailer is used as a work area, for sorting scrap, clearing metal, and so on. The startling contrast of the inside of the trailers (the only space the families can control), the shining chrome, mirrors, and glass, the scrupulous cleanliness, is not seen by passersby. They form their opinions, reaffirming the stereotypes, from seeing only the outside conditions, which they themselves have forced onto the families by opposing official sites.

I had been working as a teacher with the Gypsy families in the city for several years, trying to ensure that the children have access to education despite the lack of an official campsite. I wanted to work on an educational project of some kind which would focus on the dreadful conditions in which the families were obliged to live. I hoped that, indirectly, this would be a further support to the campaign for a decent site.

At the same time I had been approached by an art student, Sara Hannant, who as part of her course work was expected to initiate an art project in a local community. She was keen to learn more about the Gypsies in order to base her work within this group. She needed an introduction to the families. We discussed the idea of a photographic project and it seemed favorable from various points of view. The teenagers were very interested in photographs, but they had not previously had the chance to learn the process. Sara could come into the group primarily as a technician, an enabler for the project, not an intruder. Photography seemed the ideal vehicle to me for the site statement. So we put the suggestion to the group of teenagers; they were very keen to take some photographs and learn the process of developing and printing. But my idea for the subject matter was rejected straight-away. No one wanted to focus on the mud, the squalor, the broken water tap, the proximity of rubbish dumps, the reminders of what they had to live with day by day. What the girls wanted were pictures of themselves.

All Gypsy Travellers love family photographs and treasure and add to them whenever possible as living, growing family histories. Theirs is an oral culture, each generation passing on the family traditions and lore through conversation and storytelling, accompanied by the photographs they keep. The girls already figured in their family archives of photographs, but now they were being given the opportunity to take control of the process themselves. They could choose where and how to photograph themselves, and they could follow the stages right through to the final prints. They seized the chance to make their own images, to represent themselves.

Much thought was given to the composition and setting of each photograph. Each girl decided how she wanted to present herself, which aspects of her home, her environment, and her lifestyle she wanted to be known to others: how she wanted others to see her. The girls were very conscious of their negative public image. Daily in the media and in personal contacts, they heard themselves scorned and reviled as dirty people, as parasites, as undesirables. They wanted to deny this image, to show themselves as they really were. More important, however, they wanted pictures of themselves for themselves, realizations of a self-image.

Working one day a week, with the encouragement and technical assistance of Sara and myself, the girls gradually produced their portraits. After a disastrous first session in the darkroom, when everything came out black because light was getting into the room and the safelight was faulty, the results were more impressive than any of us had imagined. The girls had captured a sense of themselves and they were delighted. Their achievement went beyond individual prints. Seen as a group of photographs, the pictures gave a positive identity to this small group of Gypsies.

At that stage of the project we discovered that Koudelka's photographs were to be shown in the city later in the year. The coincidence was too good to be ignored, so we approached the Arts Centre with the idea of holding a simultaneous exhibition of the local Gypsy photographs. Our suggestion was taken up and approved. We had just a few weeks to prepare and mount the prints and work on texts to accompany them. The girls decided to write briefly about their daily lives as reflected in their photographs. They described typical days for themselves, their occupations and preoccupations. They wrote of taking and printing the pictures. These texts, extensions and amplifications of the images, stood alongside the photographs.

By now I had realized that the statement the girls had insisted on making for and about themselves was a far more powerful assertion of their right to maintain their own culture and its richness than any I would have contrived. After initial embarrassment that they were on show to whomever might walk into the Arts Centre, publicly presenting their pictures gave the Traveller girls a greater confidence and pride in themselves. They began to take a professional interest in the images by Koudelka. They recognized the quality of his photographs and despaired of ever being able to achieve as much themselves. Yet they also understood that they had been regarded as worthy of displaying their work alongside his. Their community had asserted its right to be given space among other communities, to be seen on its own terms. It was that dignity, a pride in the community, that the parents carried with them when they found the confidence to walk into the Arts Centre to see the exhibitions.

Update 1995:

The "Pictures of Ourselves" exhibition was first shown at the Plymouth Arts Centre in Devon in May 1985 and created a great deal of interest. Since then it has been remounted and is kept as a permanent exhibition by Devon Learning Resources. It is available for loan and has continued to be shown in various venues throughout England.

It has maintained its relevance as the situation for Gypsy families in Britain has not improved. If anything, levels of prejudice have increased.

Though the young people who made the original photographs are now all adult and several of them are married with their own children, there is still no official site in Plymouth. Families continue to live on the derelict land behind the municipal rubbish tip where the photographs were taken in appalling conditions with few facilities.

In the autumn of 1994 the Criminal Justice and Public Order Act came into force in England. This act has repealed the 1968 Caravan Sites Act and so counties no longer have a duty to provide sites for Gypsies. If families stop without permission on any piece of land they are now committing a criminal offense if they refuse to move when asked. Their trailer homes may be confiscated.

Fifty years after the liberation of Auschwitz, where so many Gypsies died, young Gypsies are still trying to generate awareness, understanding, and respect for themselves and their people.

Using the Gypsies' Own Language: Two Contrasting Approaches in Hungarian Schools (1987)

Thomas Acton

The Gypsies of Hungary

In Hungary as everywhere else the government divides its Gypsies into different groups. The majority (60 percent) are called Romungri, but in fact this label, like "Travellers" in the U.K., covers a variety of groups: any Gypsies in fact who do not belong to the other two groups, the Rom (30 percent) and the Beash (10 percent). Unlike the Romungri, whose first language is deemed to be Hungarian (though, like English Gypsies, they know more Romani than they are given credit for), the Rom have as their first language Romanes, and the Beash an archaic Banat dialect of Romanian, adopted in past centuries when they were avoiding slavery by asserting that they were *not* Gypsies.

In Hungary the government has begun to adopt, albeit slowly, a multicultural approach especially in youth work and to encourage experiments in schools. I found one school where there was mother-tongue teaching in Romanes and one where there was utilization of Beash Romanian. The contrast between their approaches is instructive. I will first describe my visit to the school with Beash children.

Pécsszabolcs Elementary School

This school is an ordinary elementary school serving children aged six through fourteen in a working-class suburb of Pécs. Into this suburb in the late 1950s and 1960s numbers of Beash were rehoused from the shantytowns in which they had been living previously. It is clearly a popular school, and the premises are also used for a considerable variety of adult education and other after-school activities. A great deal of the character of the school is given to it by the charismatic figure of its headmaster, Jószef Istvánder, who has served there, first as deputy then as head, since the 1950s. I was there one day from 11:00 a.m. to 3:30 p.m., having the school lunch, and was able to observe both the formal school classes in the morning and after-school activities in the afternoon. (Hungarian schools follow the continental pattern of a long school morning, with no school afternoon.)

The school now contains around eighty Beash children, who form around 20 percent of the whole. The school is proud that Gypsies now also form around 20 percent of their final year; that is to say that Beash scholastic achievement has reached parity with Hungarian achievement. One can in fact trace this in the portraits of graduating years dotted around the school. These are a peculiarly Hungarian folk-art form, which can be found in many institutions. They are not group photos as in the U.K. but rather an assemblage of individual portrait photos about four times passport size artistically arranged in a pattern on a large piece of card decorated or illustrated in some way, the whole glazed and framed in wood, around three feet by two feet in size. At this school the design, illustration, and framing are usually done by some of the parents of the graduating class, and each one is different. Together they illustrate the development of popular taste: in the 50s a mixture of traditional decoration and socialist realism; from the mid-60s a burst of enthusiasm for sputniks and space travel; more recently a geometric modernism; but always radiating a sense of achievement. There are no dark faces in the early graduating classes; from the mid-70s on there are at first a sprinkling, then a solid proportion of dark faces, looking down from the school corridors on the Gypsy and Hungarian children who walk (but do not run) along them. Gypsy children are also equally represented among the red-scarved young Pioneers who act as monitors at break periods. And on the corridor walls also there are examples of children's work—limited, it is true, to certain areas of noticeboard, rather than all over the place as in an English school, but still again representing the achievement of the child rather than the mere dominance of an externally imposed culture, like the commercial prints on the walls of some other Hungarian schools. This has not been achieved either by lowering standards or by pressure to monocultural assimilation. The school library, for example, lends an average of fourteen books per annum per child for home reading, as opposed to an average of eight for schools in the county. (The school has a staff member who apart from a very few Hungarian classes acts as librarian full-time.) The school has a Commodore 64 computer with disk drive (I promised to try to send some software) plus some Commodore 16s. These appear to be the only microcomputer widely available in Hungary.

Recognition of Beash and other Gypsy language and culture is not segregated to separate classes of Gypsies. I observed a Hungarian class in which Hungarian translations of foreign Gypsies were recited by children, including Leksa Manush and Frantishek Demeter (in the case of the latter, the very poem, "Kin ka mange gitarika," that I had used for a children's book in England). In 1979 with a previous visiting party I had been entertained by songs in Beash. Now there are voluntary afternoon classes in Beash for children taught by a Beash social worker, Orsós Lajos. I also attended an afternoon drama class which included Beash songs and dialogue as well as Hungarian. The Hungarian children in this class either kept silence during the Beash bits—or else joined in where they knew the words. In other words, the linguistic traffic was not one-way only; practice here is on its way to the genuinely multilingual school, not as a peculiarity (or worse, a problem) of the Gypsy children.

Other voluntary afternoon activities include a folk dance club (which I attended), sports, gardening (I was shown over large green-houses all provided by voluntary work), and cookery classes for Gypsy mothers. A doctor attends every Thursday. Since both the parents of many of the children work, activities and supervision are provided for the whole length of the normal working day. There are three sittings for dinner with all food cooked in the school's own kitchens.

A great deal of what has been achieved depends on the personality of the headmaster, who possesses in abundant measure the most important gift that a headmaster can possess, the ability to inspire and liberate the energies of staff and pupils. As we walked about the school it was possible to see pupils hoping to be noticed by him, and whenever he did stop to speak to a child, the child seemed to glow under the attention. He seemed to be the kind of teacher that children are lucky to meet once in a lifetime. He seemed to overflow with energy, continually taking us on to see new activities (and also to answer questions from staff during the pupils' midday break), dashing away to carry on the administration, and to host a small party of local notables, councilors, and party officials for his name day but never being too busy to deal with queries either from me or from everybody else who came to him in the course of the day.

Ráckeve Elementary School

Ráckeve is a small town some 30 kilometers south of Budapest at the end of a light railway line. In addition to having the normal population of a rural town, it has Serbian and Romani communities and is a popular resort for weekend fishermen, whose huts line the banks of the Danube which passes to one side of the town.

With my interpreter I was taken to the new elementary school, to meet the headmaster and a regional Ministry of Education and Culture inspector. The inspector's role was approximately equal to that of one of Her Majesty's Inspectors of Schools in the U.K. before the Inspection service was privatized. There it was explained to me how the start of mother-tongue teaching had greatly increased the attainment of Gypsy children. Because the Gypsy children often came to school not speaking Hungarian, special classes had had to be held for them for some time, and some old school buildings on the other side of town had been utilized for this. Teachers of those classes had to be forced to learn some Romanes, so the introduction of formal mother-tongue teaching in 1984 had been a natural progression. It had owed a great deal to the drive of a Romani teacher, Karsai Ervin, who had prepared the materials with a Rom, Rostás Farkas. Mr. Karsai now taught grades 1–4 in the school, at some sacrifice to himself, since his qualifications could command a much higher salary elsewhere. The special materials for the mother-tongue teaching are only formally in use in the school in Ráckeve, though they have been circulated fairly widely for extra-curricular use.

We were then taken in an official car, with driver, to the "old school" five minutes' drive away on the other, and poorer, side of town.

The old school consisted of a two-room building in a tree-shaded yard, with outside sanitation, near to a nursery school of the same age, which took both Gypsies and non-Gypsies. The two classes took Grades 1–4 (that is, ages six through ten) and 5–8 (ages eleven through fourteen). Children could, however, be held down in the lower class if they were unsuccessful. It seemed to me that there were more younger children than older children present. In each class each grade was represented by a block of eight or ten desks, and there were more empty desks in the older grades. We went first into the younger class where Karsai Ervin was teaching. The children were engaged in writing followed by drawing, using the Romani books specially prepared for this experimental work. Some of the children, however, were just drawing. On their request, I addressed the children in Romanes and told them about English Gypsies living in caravans and their struggles to get schooling, Karsai standing alongside and glossing or adding to what I said whenever I departed from what the children would understand. This seemed to go down well, and afterwards I answered questions from about half the children who gathered around me, while the other half returned to their work. One little boy insisted on addressing me in Hungarian, and when the others told him he must speak in Romanes, he finally asked me why I didn't speak Hungarian. I told him I came from England where most people didn't speak Hungarian. "Sostar?" (Why?) he asked wonderingly. I told him that Romanes would be more use to him in England than Hungarian.

I made it into the older class just before a break time, so I was speaking to them over into their break time. I seemed to come in at the end of a geography lesson in Hungarian. The teacher was a middle-aged Hungarian man, and like Ervin, he seemed responsible for teaching all subjects to the class, except that Ervin did any mother-tongue teaching required. He again stood next to me while I spoke to the children. After that I was taken to the nursery school which was on break for the middle of the day. Some of the children were sleeping on little beds, while others were being given their meals. I was taken to various tots said to be Gypsies, but they were all very shy, and neither they, nor any of the white-coated staff, attempted to speak Romani with me. After this and some general discussion I and the interpreter were taken back directly to the station.

One thing noticeable to me about the nursery, the old school, and those parts of the new school that I saw that compares strongly against schools in England (and with the other Hungarian school I saw in Pécsszabolcs) is that there was no work by pupils pinned up on the walls—only a few dowdy prints.

Mr. Karsai, the Romani teacher, is a very committed and scholarly man, who has collaborated with those, like Donald Kenrick, engaged on similar work in other countries. His abundant enthusiasm and dedication was impressive and had obviously had an effect on the rest of the school staff.

Obviously, a segregated situation in which the Gypsy children are being taught something interesting and relevant and use their mother tongue with a teacher who is dedicated and enthusiastic is preferable to what existed prior to 1984, which was segregation with no success or special provision for the Gypsy children. It must, however, be pointed out that this is still a situation in which the Gypsy children are segregated into an old and crumbling building, away from the facilities of the new and modern school, and with four grades crammed into a single class, and still with much less chance of completing the curriculum than Hungarian children in the town. Worse, one suspects that this segregation is one of the main reasons why the mother school supports the mother-tongue teaching. One hopes (a) that this is a transitional situation and (b) that mother-tongue teaching does not come to be equated with "withdrawal" or segregation.

In my view the "multiculturalism" of the Pécsszabolcs school must be ultimately a better model than the "withdrawal" of Ráckeve. A number of qualifications must be made to this view, however. First, whether it can be achieved or not depends more on the attitude of the school than of either the Gypsies or those most directly involved in teaching them. Secondly, since Romanian is after all the language of a friendly neighboring state, and Beash can be presented as Romanian, or at least as a dialect of it, it starts off with more status than Romanes even though (correctly in my view) the Beash work in Pécsszabolcs starts from the dialect of the children rather than an externally imposed standard dialect. Thirdly, despite (or perhaps because of) this, considerably more progress has been made in creating appropriate printed teaching materials for Lovari Romanes than for Beash.

Afterword 1996 (by Nidhi Trehan):

Roma in the Hungarian Educational System: Still the Invisible Minority

"If Hungarian children didn't hear about Hungarian history and culture in school, how would they learn it? Similarly, Romani students don't know their history and culture because the schools have never taught it" —Angéla Kóczé, a Romani student at the Sociology Faculty at Eötvös Loránd University (Budapest).

Thomas Acton's essay contrasting two approaches to Romani education in Hungary was written when educational reform was beginning to warrant serious attention by the state. The Ráckeve and Pécsszabolcs schools are two cases where Romani students are being taught in a culturally sensitive manner; the question remains whether these schools are representative of Hungarian schools as a whole. For example, both have actively utilized the students' mother tongue in the classroom, while the average Hungarian school would not.

In 1985, the Act of Education paved the way for alternative schooling and curricula, and in 1988 the nation's first private school (a high school for the study of economics) was founded. Today, in 1996, several positive changes have taken place in the educational system of Hungary, including initiatives to improve the educational success of Roma, the largest minority in the country.

The 1993 law on Ethnic and National Minorities allows for mother-tongue instruction in the Romani and Beash languages for Romani communities in Hungary. Thus far, however, no school has been created which would use Romani or Beash as the language of instruction, since it is not clear whether this would be the best option for Romani children if integration is a primary goal.[1] Another major development has been the change in the funding system of schools. As school administration became more decentralized in the early 1990s, funds no longer came exclusively from the central government, and the local governments became responsible for a significant share of the funding. While this gives more autonomy to local-level officials, it also means facing budget crises, particularly at the village level. The structure of the school system has also changed with the replacement of the "special schools," or *kisegitőiskolák*, with remedial classes within the regular school (*általános iskola*) system. In the 1993–1994 school year, there were 35,503 children in Hungarian remedial educational programs, an estimated 40 percent from the Romani community.[2] For these remedial classes, the old curriculum continues to be the norm, though children in these classes now have the opportunity to interact socially with children from regular classes. In 1996, there was a new initiative to provide ethnic schools with more per capita funding from the Ministry of Education. Despite these positive steps, most of the changes since 1989 have affected primarily the children of elite Hungarians, not the majority of ethnic Hungarian or Romani children. Nonetheless, the Ministry of Education has also been actively involved in developing alternative schools (for example, Gandhi School) and programs, some of which are described below.

Gandhi School. Located in southern Hungary, in Pécs, this fully accredited *gimnázium* serves as the first free college preparatory school for economically disadvantaged children.[3] The ethnic makeup is primarily Beash Romani, though a small number of Vlax Romani and ethnic Hungarian children are also represented. There are currently about 110 children between the ages of twelve and seventeen, and the majority are boarders from small towns and villages in the trans-Danubia region. There are also a few students from Budapest and other counties. The school is seen as a model institution for Hungarian Roma because of its emphasis on Romani and Beash culture, its high academic standard, as well as its emphasis on the humanities and social sciences (mythology, foreign languages, sociology, etc.). The language of instruction is Hungarian, though Romanes and Beash language classes are also compulsory. Students have the freedom to express themselves through art, drama, dance, and creative writing. The Hungarian government has the explicit goal of fostering the development of a Romani intelligentsia through the establishment of the Gandhi Gimnázium.

Romani Dormitory System. One program which the Hungarian government hopes to implement through the Gandhi Foundation umbrella is a nationwide Romani students' dormitory system in approximately five cities. The idea is to support, both financially and morally, Romani students who wish to pursue advanced study but have no opportunity to do so at their home village or town. A system of tutors and mentors who are knowledgeable about and sensitive to diversity within Romani culture is envisioned to aid the students in their educational development. The children will attend regular Hungarian high schools but will benefit from counseling and tutoring at the dormitory. At this stage, this program is still at the preparatory phase and has to be discussed further by the Board of the Gandhi Foundation.

Kalyi Jag Romani National Academy. Supported by the Hungarian state, as well as private donors, this school is primarily a vocational school which offers courses in subject areas such as mathematics, history, languages (including Romanes and English), computers, and so forth. It fosters the development of Romani identity through its emphasis on Romani traditions, history, language, culture, and art forms. It also seeks to strengthen the links, both culturally and historically, with India.

Zsámbek Romani Studies. Funded by the Hungarian state, this is an initiative begun by the teachers and administrators at the Zsámbek Catholic Teachers' Training College. There are approximately five courses offered to teachers who wish to specialize in the education of Romani students or who simply wish to learn more about Romani culture and language. Students can get a special concentration in Romology upon the completion of coursework. Not surprisingly, the majority of students at this department are ethnic Hungarians. In 1995, approximately 25 students were registered for courses in Romology.

Csenyéte Schools Project. Funded by the Csenyéte Foundation, this project has successfully built two schools (one elementary school and one kindergarten) in one of the poorest and most isolated settlements in Hungary. Nearly every adult in Csenyéte is unemployed and nonliterate, and economic opportunities for the future are scarce.

Local Initiatives. There are many privately funded and government-funded local level initiatives throughout Hungary like the project above, including the Kiskunhalas project (funded by the County Pedagogical

Institute in Kecskemét), Nyírtelek project (supported by the local government), and many others which work toward bettering educational standards for Romani children.

The Hungarian government is taking steps to address the problem of the invisibility of Roma in the educational system, especially at the higher grade levels. However, it is clearly not enough. The majority society continues to be ignorant of Romani culture and history. Ethnic Hungarian children, the classmates of young Roma, continue to be raised with inexcusable anti-Romani prejudices and negative stereotypes, which are at times condoned by teachers as well. It is time for the Hungarian government to take seriously the educational status of its largest minority and to foster a positive image for all of the nation's children, including Romani children.

NOTES

1. There is still considerable debate in the country between the "segregationists," those who claim that separate teaching is more beneficial, and the "integrationists," who claim that mixed schools are better. In 1994, a study by István Kemény, Gábor Havas, and Gábor Kertesi revealed that approximately 57 percent of Hungarian Roma finish the first eight years of school, and out of this number only 35 percent continue their education, mostly attending vocational schools.

2. Information obtained from Művelődési Közöktátasi Miniszterium *oktátasi statisztikaiévkönyv* and the Ministry of Culture and Education. Out of 35,503 children in special schools in 1993–1994, the majority (28,616) were listed in the category of minor disability (*enyhén fogyatékos*), which indicates a sizable number of borderline children (children who are considered mildly disabled).

3. The cost per child for attending Gandhi Gimnázium is covered by the Hungarian state as well as donations from private foundations and individuals. There has been discussion about parents contributing a small portion of the fees toward their child's education.

PERFORMING ARTS

Roma (Gypsies) in the Soviet Union and the Moscow Teatr "Romen" (1991)

Alaina Lemon

The Moscow Teatr "Romen," dating back to 1931, is famous throughout the Soviet Union, and its performers have been some of the country's best known. The Teatr draws Roma to audition from all over the country; however, many who work there are related: three generations of a family may appear on the stage at one time. These "dynasties," along with Roma working as professionals, make up an elite within the Romani community in Moscow. They are the most outwardly assimilated (wearing European dress, and so forth),[1] most fluent and literate in Russian as well as Romani. These families usually move in different social spheres than do Roma who live in villages around Moscow, who work in cooperatives or as independent merchants.[2] This is because the performers generally belong to a group of Roma who have been in Russia much longer than the others. While some "dynasties" include Roma of other groups, such as the Vlach, most performing families are "Russka" or "Ukrainska" Roma ("Khaldytka" and "Servitska").

Most studies of Gypsies[3] (including those of non-Roma, such as Irish Travellers in the United Kingdom) assume a certain uniformity of social life:

> The refusal to acknowledge Gypsy upward mobility in the context of a dominant society has also prevented research of class dif-

ference within Gypsy groups and created a sense of marginalized homogeneity that does not reflect reality.[4]

The Teatr "Romen" is a case that demands such acknowledgment. In a sense, these elites are doubly marginal, both as performers[5] who represent "Gypsy culture" to non-Roma and as ethnic outsiders who "threaten the rhetoric and narratives of nationalism."[6] Currently in the USSR, such narratives are in flux, as many "national minorities" demand greater cultural and political autonomy. Roma, however, are not demanding their own republic, and they often temper requests for schools and radio shows with the assertion that "this country has been kind to Gypsies." Romani elites are in a peculiar position: charged with representing folkloric and spectacular images of Gypsiness to outsiders, they are also concerned about maintaining the integrity of their own self-identity as "real Roma."

The first performance of the Teatr "Romen" was in 1931; however, Gypsy music had long been popular with Russians, and there was already a settled community of Romani performers in Moscow well before the 1917 revolution. In the nineteenth and early twentieth centuries, Russian poets and writers haunted the taverns and restaurants where Gypsy choirs performed, and their impressions of the Gypsy singers are now canonized.[7] These visits literally seeded the social worlds of both Russian and Romani elites; it became quite prestigious for Russian aristocrats and poets to acquire Gypsy wives from the choirs, as did Leo Tolstoi's brother.

Performance is not only a stage or an arena where images are displayed, but is also a nexus of social, political, and cultural relationships. This essay looks "backstage,"[8] that is, it assumes that theater is a social world in itself, as actors and directors argue over interpretation and presentation, and performers relearn appropriate modes of behavior. The world backstage is also part of the whole social world that surrounds and defines the moment of performance.[9] I thus combine consideration of the political and social conditions surrounding the establishment of the theater, and affecting Roma in general, with ethnographic observation of Romani performers and performance in Moscow in the autumn of 1990 and the winter of 1991.

On October 4, 1930, at the meeting of the Active Section on National Art of the People's Commissariat of the Enlightenmen

(*Narkompros*), the Studio of the Indo-Romen Theater was established. Officially, the Teatr "Romen" was created both to "preserve a national culture" and to "aid the assimilation, sedentarization and education of nomadic peoples."[10] At first glance it seems that the Teatr was mandated from the top down. Indeed, the Soviet state, like the tsarist one before it (and like other states), certainly attempted to control the cultural activities of the various nationalities within its borders. Still, such "assimilation" cannot be reduced to coercion nor considered as one-sided.

Ivan Rom-Lebedev, playwright and actor from a Romani family of settled musicians, recalls that the Teatr was the idea of literate Bolshevik activists, Roma who had been working in Romani literacy campaigns and in setting up Romani cultural centers. Their hope was that the Teatr would help raise standards of living through political literacy and information about opportunities for Roma. It was with this hope in mind that Rom-Lebedev first appealed to the head of Narkompros, Anatolii Lunacharskii, for support in establishing such a theater.

He quotes Lunacharskii as saying, "Gypsies?! Does this mean that the word of Lenin has reached even them?"[11] This statement of course indexed the "distance" of Roma from the new Soviet state, as well as it lauded the saving power of Lenin's tongue (and of "the word"[12]) and of socialist proselytizing.

Romani "activists" were enthusiastic about using the Teatr to reach other Roma with the good news. In the warm months, troupes from the Teatr traveled throughout the countryside presenting didactic plays to Romani audiences. The plays urged them to settle and join collectives, if they had not already, to become literate, to learn about socialism, to give up fortune-telling, and so on. The performers now describe Roma as having interpreted the plays according to their own categories: Marx, for instance, was a good man—after all, he was a Rom, for it was clear from his picture that "he had a Gypsy's beard."[13] Despite any identification they might have aroused with Marx, these missionary visits mainly failed; most Roma refused to accept the free huts and land offered by the government, nor would they submit to learn to drive tractors.

When the Teatr was young, many Roma spoke of it as the center of a cultural renaissance and hoped that the Teatr would outshine other

Gypsy performers who were seen as ersatz. Rom-Lebedev writes of the rise in popularity of "inauthentic" performances by certain Romani choirs and non-Gypsy imitators—termed *tsyganshchina* or *psevdotsyganshchina*[14]—during the time of the New Economic Policy (NEP) in the 1920s. The Teatr, as he saw it, was to offer an antidote to *tsyganshchina* by competing with it, supporting instead the "folk art of Gypsies born in the camps, villages, and *Kolkhozy* [collective farms]."[15] The Teatr did recruit performing artists from the countryside, though more of them—and all of the stars—were actually veterans of the long-established Gypsy choirs in Moscow. Roma from the country were valued not for their individual skill but for how they might infuse the Teatr with "real camp songs" that would give it authenticity. City-raised performers would make trips to the country to steep themselves in this "wandering" lifestyle and to cull details and anecdotes from their interactions that they could play on the stage. It was thus intended, at least at first, that the Teatr "Romen" would provide a realistic view of "Gypsy life"; the Teatr's premiere production in 1931 was a documentary tableau of camp life titled *"Etnograficheskii Eskiz"* (An Ethnographic Sketch).

Despite the dream that the Teatr would open a window onto Romani life and provide a place for Romani culture to "develop," there were important ways that Teatr directors altered Romani performance to fit within both Euro-Russian theatrical expectations and the bounds of socialist realism. Then and today, the dancers study classical ballet; young actors learn to recite Russian classical poetry and study the method of Stanislavskii. Urban, choir Roma who were long accustomed to performing for Russians filled the leading roles since they already knew stage conventions. Performers enlisted from the country, however, had to learn to move and sing anew. Even backstage, conventions were different: for instance, women who had always kept their legs modestly covered according to Romani practices were now expected to wear exercise pants to rehearsals.[16]

The Teatr "Romen" was, after all, an institution at first meant to encourage assimilation and political literacy. The plays performed then were part of a small genre of Soviet stories in which a Gypsy hero comes to see the socialist light. In Mikhailov's *"Tsyganskaia Zaria"* (Gypsy Dawn),[17] for one, a previously ineducable Gypsy becomes an *aktivist* and testifies onstage to the glory of the Red Army, shouting in

Romani, "Proletarians of the world, unite!" Other stories and plays explored the conflicts that were ostensibly involved in convincing entire families to settle and farm, as in *"Zhizn' na Kolesakh,"* in which the patriarchal leader of the camp tries to prevent other Gypsies from joining the nearby collective.

These political and didactic works, published in Romani only until 1937, were written by several Roma. It appears that these people were quite sincere and believed that their stories and plays were worthy arguments and examples for social change for Roma and that the programs and offers of the Bolsheviks were an improvement over tsarist policies: Roma were after all being offered land and schools and could publish for the first time in Romani. Under the tsars, it was only Russian literacy that counted. After the October revolution, the terms of literacy changed; "bourgeois imperialism" was denounced, and the state decided that "national minorities" should become politically literate in socialism through their mother tongue (the slogan being "nationalist in form, socialist in content"). A Cyrillic alphabet was devised for Romani;[18] after 1926, Romani authors began to publish poetry, fiction, and translations, and at least four schools were opened to teach literacy in Romani. For the first three years of the Teatr's existence, most of its plays were performed in Romani, the better to reach and to educate rural Roma. By the late thirties, however, all the plays were performed in Russian, and today the Teatr serves to entertain Russians and tourists with images of Gypsies.

At any rate, during the late twenties and early thirties, there was a boom in publishing for a handful of Romani writers who had never published before. Their literary activism was, however, double-edged. On the one hand, Roma could finally be active in Romani in a public, political realm, but, on the other hand, non-Roma already defined the terms. The aims of political literacy (rather than those of literacy in the language itself) circumscribed the writers' themes and subjects. *Nevo Drom,* for example, a Romani journal published from 1930 to 1936, included articles explaining the new land tenure system, the five-year plan, how to work in collectives, how to be an atheist, live in houses, and go to school. One of the alphabet books and grammars, co-authored in Romani by Dudarova and Pankov, tells the parable of a family who starves because their only means of subsistence is fortune-telling until they change their ways and go to work in the factory. A lesson accompanies each letter of the alphabet: B is for "*buti*" (Romani) or "work" and the lesson continues: "our work," "Masha works," "Our Romani women don't work but tell fortunes," "I want to work. . . ."[19]

Hundreds of books and plays had been published in Romani between 1928 and 1937,[20] when the state abruptly terminated all publishing and education in Romani.[21] This was a casualty to the general swing of state nationalities' policy from "Leninist" *korenizatsiia* ("going to the roots," i.e., Sovietization via ethnic cultural forms) to Stalinist *sliianie* ("drawing together"), which entailed Russification. Many languages that had been latinized after the Revolution were once again cyrillicized, as they had been under the tsars. Romani, already in a Cyrillic alphabet, was simply eliminated in written form. Already in 1936, the Romani language schools were closed, and after 1937 nothing was published in Romani until once in the 1970s and then again only in the late 1980s. Romani children, if they went to school, studied only Russian; Romani was confined to home and kin.

The absence of Romani from public spheres was not absolute, however: one could still find Romani phrases in the songs and plays performed at the Teatr and in small restaurants with Gypsy ensembles. Still, despite the occasional Romani song or line, Teatr performances were primarily in Russian and structured in terms of Russian convention. Actors there perform today almost entirely in Russian, peppering only a few standard Romani phrases throughout: *"Ekh, dui, trin, shtar!"* (One, two, three, four!) or *"Romale!"* (Hey, Roma!) To Russian audiences these words mean little, save that they are standard phrases signifying "counting" or "calling." Heard from the other side of the proscenium, they merely emphasize that the play concerns "mysterious people" who sometimes speak a foreign tongue.[22] Song lyrics are likewise scenery for the melodies the audience admires. That the lyrics are incomprehensible to them is unimportant—the meaning of Gypsy music to the outsider is elemental emotion which "needs no words."[23] But to the Romani listener familiar with the words, perhaps even known by heart, the lyrics remain important.

Romani actors and singers are perfectly aware of the gap in communication. Rom-Lebedev describes his experience at the 1931 premiere of the Teatr:

"Romale shunen'te tume man!" (Roma, listen to me!), I vainly called out to the audience in someone else's voice . . . there were no Gypsies, and there was no one to understand.[24]

Rom-Lebedev feels his voice fall into an empty space of incomprehension—it even renders his own voice foreign to himself. Yet the show went on, he reports in his memoirs, with great success (though many scenes did not arouse the intended effect, he reports), and the audience left entertained yet unaware of the disjuncture of meanings.

Romani performers and non-Romani audiences are politically unequal participants in such events of performance; the Teatr performs for outsiders and is dependent upon their approval. This means that the plots have to converge with official or "classic" (canonical) versions of history and understandings of society. For instance, Rom-Lebedev's "Daughter of the Tents" narrates Balkan Gypsies' resistance against the "faschisty" ("the fascists," or axis powers, especially in reference to "the Germans") during World War II. This play did depart from romantic stereotypes—the Gypsy is a Red Army hero instead of a horse thief or fortune-teller—but it did so within the proper socialist frame. More recently, the repertoire of the Teatr is comprised of "classics"—that is, plays based on the work of Pushkin, Tolstoi, Lorca, or Hugo. The images in such plays are ones with which the audience is familiar and which reflect Russian fantasies about the freedom and mystery of Gypsies.

There are, of course, differences in what Roma produce for the Russian (and tourist) public in Russian and what they perform for Roma in Romani. The epic plots of the *Lunzhe Gilia* (Vlach Romani dialect: Long Songs), for instance, have no place on the stage, and are neither adapted as plays themselves nor encapsulated as songs within other plays. Nor do the Teatr's plays address the themes of such songs. This is partly because there are very few Kalderash ("*Keldelari*") Roma performing in the Teatr's floodlights—recall that the "dynasties" of actors belong to families of other dialect groups, such as the Servi or Khaldytko Roma. However, even seasoned actors of these groups speak of a difference between performance "for others" and "for our own."

"Everyday songs," more likely to be sung "for our own," may speak, for instance, to the ambivalence of living in the *gazhekani* (non-

Romani) world, where one must depend on the good will of *gazhe* (non-Roma):

Ake tuke mas thulo,	Here, have some meat fat,
Ake vi manxro kalo,	Take some black bread, too,
Ake tuke tsyrra thud,	Here's a little milk for you,
Chi dine l'gazhe mai bud.	The *gazhe* didn't give [us] any more.[25]

Russian audiences usually hear songs with romantic themes of love, and if Roma sometimes perform more ironic or penetrating lyrics for non-Roma, the ambivalence and references are, of course, lost: to the audience the songs are a musical interlude, or an "expression" of elemental feeling. Romani performers are aware of this, and most are glad to keep such meanings in reserve. Roma appreciate and may find amusing the irony that arises when watching a fellow performer sing for Russians. Romani performers work deftly with elements marked as belonging to both Romani and Russian (or Soviet) culture and, in the process, also create forms with more than one intended meaning, depending on the audience. This sort of bricolage is more than a mode of synthesis, and though ironic, it is not detached, but can also be a form of social commentary.[26]

Returning to the social context of such performance, when speaking of the social mobility of performers who master Russian and Soviet standard forms, it might be helpful to take the "up" out of any discussion of their "upward" mobility, and to speak instead of how people calibrate their actions to an "official center" of discourse.[27] In the case of Romani performers, this center was not only that set by the state, but by a state comprised of "outsiders," "non-Roma," that is, *gazhe*.

This need not mean that Romani performers gave up Romani language and culture, as many in Russia assert, but that they learned to "cross the dialect frontier" when called upon to.[28] Because these elite Romani performers had to succeed in terms of the system *and* strive to maintain their integrity as "real Roma," the identity that they have constructed for themselves is interstitial. Ideally, they want to be both "civilized" and "authentic," able to move among all social worlds—from Kremlin balls to village Romani weddings.[29] In reality, of course, their social scope is more limited, yet their position requires great agility in understanding the requirements of diverse situations and institutional settings—in terms of behavior, language, and so forth. Still, the practice of theatrical art has had real effects on the social practice of Romani performers, especially those enacted in movement, speech, and dress. Roma refer to these more visible changes to mark differences between Romani groups. Performers remark that they have little to talk about with the others, that their own neckties stigmatize them as "like the *gazhe*" to Roma in villages (although in fact many non-elite Roma also favor neckties for celebrations). Some actors, having accepted the notion that their urban lifestyle is led intolerably *gazhekanes* (*gazhe* style), compete to be more "genuine" than others. As theatrical art is embedded in political life, discourse about performance concentrates on issues of genuineness in identity: actors speak of anger at Gypsy impersonators, pride in modes of singing that "only Gypsies do well," and recount narratives that express the problems of living with the *gazhe*.

The question "What does it mean to be a 'real Gypsy'?" has too often been answered by non-Roma; performers draw their criteria of "genuineness" from the same categories of familiar stereotypy that informed official Soviet reckoning of policy and demographic divisions. Stereotypes about Gypsies have deep roots in the century before the revolution. In the nineteenth century, Russian poets painted Gypsies romantically as closer to the chaotic forces of nature; at the same time, they are also figured as a source of cultural rejuvenation. Pushkin's classic poem, *Tsygany* (The Gypsies), portrays them as people who value freedom above all; transcending the laws of society, they are also somehow better, more peaceful. This wildness and otherworldliness, especially in women, takes on exotic sensuality: in Derzhavin's "*Tsyganskaia Pliaska*" (Gypsy Dance), the twirling of a Gypsy woman is hypnotically sensual precisely because she is from another world.[30] Yet, just as Gypsies are admired as romantic musicians[31] and passionate wanderers with "smoldering eyes,"[32] they are also feared as "robbers, beggars and fortune-tellers."[33] Both sets of images construct each other and arise in the same conditions of marginality: "Gypsiness" figures in the Russian national identity—as its wild alter, or as part of the Russian landscape—but Roma themselves are outsiders to Russia's "imagined" nation.[34]

Roma, aware of these categories and images, transform them from "symbolic capital" to economic capital in making a living.[35]

Thus the issue of authenticity is not just an academic question; performing Roma must accept and enact images of "real Gypsiness" as Russians define them in order to subsist. Yet, in using this symbolic capital, they undermine their own status as "real." As early as 1931, Barranikov, a scholar of Romani culture and language, wrote that performing, "urban Gypsies have no special culture," and that there was "nothing of the Gypsy left in their songs save the tunes."[36] Despite the fact that with different criteria one might perceive Romani culture as vital and particular, such statements tap real insecurities about cultural validity.

The vitality of the Teatr—or rather, its current loss of vitality—is also explained by actors and Russians in terms of "authenticity." In recent years, the popularity of the Teatr "Romen" has declined, and community pride in it is ebbing. Talent has also drained away from the Teatr, as performers says they can make better money in the more lucrative ensembles that play in expensive restaurants for *biznismeny* and foreigners. Some Roma say that performers are leaving because of a decline in the quality of direction and acting—and they blame this decline on an urban existence that has made third-generation performers too "professional," too removed from the folkloric life they should portray on the stage. Indeed, it is rare to find plays that depict urban, "modern" Romani families, but this is not seen as the problem. Rather, performers worry that they are no longer *nastoiashchie* (genuine) and that their children are losing the Romani language.[37]

Although the Teatr "Romen" is no longer primarily a platform for socialist agitation among Roma, there remains a sense among actors and Romani elites in Moscow that besides being representatives of Romani culture, they are its caretakers. Although they may be concerned about losing their "genuineness," they certainly see themselves as "more civilized" than rural or traveling Roma, and speak of their responsibility to educate the others, to "raise the cultural level." At the same time, however, they distance themselves from the "bad Gypsies" who do beg on the streets in the center of Moscow, or who market at the train stations, or who do tell fortunes—"it's a sin!" *"Oni zhe dikie!"* ("They are wild!")

Performers and other Romani elite reinforce this distance when they speak of "becoming civilized" with reference to changes in social practices through time. "In the olden days, if a fork was dropped on the floor, we threw it away, as *marime* (polluted, unclean), but now we just wash it with soap."[38] Many scholars of Roma have argued that concepts of pollution (moral and physical) are central to Romani culture.[39] However, not only do the practices vary while Roma maintain their sense of Romaniness, the ways they vary and are described as changing in Romani discourses reflect specific political and social relationships and conditions.

Genealogies likewise do more than define Romani kinship terminology or map social structures "particular to" Roma. Stories about recent ancestors may be mythic accounts of how the family became urban, as when the well-traveled Keldelari great-grandfather of one prominent elite family married a Romani woman from a different Romani group than his own (from the settled Russka Roma who populated the choirs in St. Petersburg and Moscow). She influenced him to change his way of dressing and to become literate—well before the revolution. In Russian terms, these are stories of an initial separation from a natural world, but they are also accounts of cultural politics. Many performing Roma trace genealogies (some real, some mythic) to Russian aristocrats: "My great-aunt's mother married Tolstoi's brother," or "Lialia Chiornaia's [a famous Romani actress, and the first female star of the Teatr] mother married a Golitsyn." In part, such talk aligns with larger narratives of history—like many Soviets, Roma speak differently of the October revolution than they did a few years ago, when that event was touted as marking the beginning of civil rights for Roma in the USSR. Now many recall—or imagine—the time of the tsars as one of elegance, beauty, and freedom. In this context, old family ties with aristocracy gain fresh currency.

In the USSR, there are at least ten groups classified as Tsygane who differ—or see themselves as differing—in dialect, language, and culture. Roma, for instance, see no similarities between themselves and the Central Asian Liuli, though both are classified as Tsygane.[40] Vlach Roma,[41] who resided mostly in Moldavia and Romania until the mid-1800s (when they were emancipated from slavery),[42] do not always consider non-Vlach Roma "like us," although non-Vlach generally consider Vlach to be "more strict," that is, more "traditional." Vlach

Lovari take pride in being neither "like the *gazhe*," as performers are classified, nor "uncivilized," as they consider the Keldelari. Thus while Roma participate in Russian, European, or Soviet definitions of civilization and ethnicity, many do sustain other discourses on identity, equally important to their experience of the social world, though usually invisible to Russians. Such divisions and definitions are meaningful to Roma; through reference to them, status, kinship, and group identity are constructed.

Roma from several different groups work at the Teatr "Romen"— though, of course, the Russka are by far the most predominant, and Vlach Roma are very rare. This had made at times for volatile internal and favoritist politics, although officially providing all Roma with a center for unified cultural activity. On the stage, interestingly enough, dramatic plots do not mark these "ethnic" differences among groups: conflicts are played out in terms of "modern"/"traditional" or "worker"/"anti-socialist," as if (not surprisingly) all differences among Roma could be traced to categories of class.

The Teatr thus also elides the diverse historical narratives told by families of different groups. In most plays, the Teatr portrays European accounts of Gypsy history, that is, it portrays them as "without history." Gypsy movement over the map is the only image that counts; it is the master image, rather than the deeds of ancestors and heroic individuals, as in European histories. The play *My Tsygane* (We Are Gypsies—note that the title is in Russian, not in Romani, and not even using the ethnonym) is such a script. The musical play, through a series of vignettes, traces the movement of Roma from India to Iran, across the Balkans, up through Europe and finally back east to Russia. A scene from *Carmen* represents Gypsies' "time" in Spain (although many Roma settled there centuries ago). The beckoning voices of a Russian women's folk choir herald the arrival to Russia. The play uses European political boundaries, and in the end deploys Gypsies as emblems of various nation-states, rather than dealing with actual Romani histories in the various sites of their diaspora. *My Tsygane* defines the Gypsy self only through its passage through other places, with scant reference to Romani categories. As one former actor commented, mimicking the voice of the play's narrator which one hears over the Teatr's speakers between scenes: "'They went, they went, they went!!!' Where is the conflict? Where are the heroes?"[43]

Roma remember their stars, heroes, and ancestors. Many even remember the thirties fondly as a time of opportunity for Romani performers and intellectuals. They speak of the Nazi massacre of entire Romani collectives in Smolensk and Ukraine, as does the Soviet press. But there is nothing, of course, in the plays of the deportations of Roma to Siberia or the "liquidations" of Romani clubs and collective farms.[44] The Teatr "Romen," because of the constraints upon it, imposed by directors, censors, and budget managers (nearly all Russian, incidentally), can only present a partial reflection of the conflicts and experiences of Roma. With recent political transformations in the Soviet Union, elite Roma have begun to reassert their interests in press conferences, articles, and radio interviews. They have formed a Romani National Union and established contact with the International Romani Union. Romani delegates from Russia were finally permitted to attend the World Romani Union Congress in 1990.[45] Literacy drives are emerging, led once again by the urban Romani intelligentsia, who published a bilingual collection of Romani (Keldelari dialect) stories and songs in 1988 and a dictionary in the same dialect in 1990.[46] Roma in Ukraine are setting up new cultural centers. If such movements gain momentum, the Teatr "Romen" may see a rebirth, and be able to create an entire repertoire bound neither by the demands of socialist realism nor by those of the Russian "classics."

Afterword 1995:

Even with the changes in government since 1991, the Teatr repertoire remains the same as before. My optimistic projections that the Teatr would see a rebirth seem unfounded. The main concern of the Teatr remains the entertainment of Russians and foreign tour groups. Performers express the hope not that the Teatr will become a base for the development of Romani themes for Romani audiences but that Gypsy performance will regain the kinds of audiences it once had among the elite and aristocracy before the revolution—only this time, the desired audience would be wealthy foreign and Russian business people.

Performers continue to leave the Teatr to work as musicians in restaurant ensembles or to act in films shot by Russian directors. In these film productions, artistic control remains the privilege of the

Russian directors; even where Romani may be incorporated, the director determines when, how much, and which Romani words are uttered. Likewise with costume and the portrayal of tradition. While actors may grumble among themselves at moments they feel their culture is misrepresented, they give way to the constraints of the conditions of their employment and attend to their future ability to be hired as performers.

A film studio, Romfilm, was recently formed by Teatr members, who seek funding and projects. Some of the Romani intelligentsia began to make connections with international Romani organizations and to lay plans for publishing newsletters, but these have proven difficult to organize and fund in the current climate. Others have emigrated to Europe to work there with Romani political organizations. A Sunday school, Romano Drom (Romani Road), was established in 1992, nominally under the wing of UNESCO. However, children of other Romani groups besides those of Romani performers do not attend, and only a few of those who do may become eligible for a UNESCO-sponsored academic exchange to the United States.

In 1994, part of the Teatr toured large cities in America, performing for nostalgic audiences of Russian émigrés, though for the most part these appearances went unnoticed by the American press. Several performers and their relatives have emigrated to America and appear occasionally in restaurants in New York or Los Angeles. Such opportunities are unavailable to the majority of the Romani population in Russia and the former Soviet Union. These people have not, of course, had the chance to meet with those who might organize trips abroad. They remain marginal not only to Russian society but to the elite community of performers.

Meanwhile racism toward Roma in Russia has worsened. Although most of Russian disdain for and fear of "blacks" is focused against groups such as Chechen and Azeri traders, Gypsies are also seen as criminal, Mafia-like, and mercenary. Those Roma who have done well in commerce find their prosperity precarious as Russians envy what they see as unjust earnings in the hands of "blacks." Although pogroms and anti-Gypsy movements are not as concentrated as in the countries of Eastern Europe, there have been violent incidents, and Roma worry that they will be caught in the middle of battles not their own. Their concern lies more in assuring the safety and livelihood of their own families than in achieving pan-Romani cultural autonomy through state institutions such as the Teatr "Romen."

NOTES

1. In other Romani groups, "European" dress is either modified or worn more selectively by the women, or, in some groups, only worn by the men. Female performers, though, wear even pants in public.

2. "Elite" urban Roma work in the health professions—there are several dentists and nurses and one surgeon—in academic positions, and as performers. Others work as grocery store managers, factory workers, and gardeners in the cities, as well as running several small cooperatives that make shirts and jewelry (from interviews and field observations, March 1991; see also V. I. Ivashchenko, "Tsyganskoe Shchaste," in *Komsomolets* [July 6, 1990], 2). Some also work in the informal markets, selling chocolate, vodka, cigarettes, and gold, or telling fortunes. In tsarist Russia, rural Roma repaired cooking vessels, worked as blacksmiths and jewelers, and were also merchants, horsetraders, and entertainers (A. P. Barranikov, *Tsygane SSSR: Kratki Istorikoetnograficheskii Ocherk* [Tsentrizdat: Moscow, 1931], 145). Some of these were settled well before the revolution of 1917 (A. Danilken, "The First Gypsy Collective in Ukraine," unpublished manuscript, 1990). After the revolution, some groups took up farming and factory work (I. M. Andronikova, "Evolutsia Zhilischa Russkikh Tsygan," *Sovetskaia Etnografiia*, 1970:4, 31–45; A. Germano, "Tsygane," *Bezbozhnik*, 1928:1, 11–13).

3. Roma sometimes use names given by outsiders, such as "Gypsies," even among themselves. The people I worked with usually use such terms ironically or ambivalently, or to cater to non-Roma audiences. I try to preserve this sense in my own writing by using "Gypsy" to indicate a view that is either Russian (as in "Gypsy music") or, if it is a Romani view, an ironic one. I use "Roma" to indicate a more "serious," Romani-centered mode of indexing identity. Of course, either term could be used otherwise, but this distinction will help clarify my own analytic position without doing too much violence to local discourses.

4. Sam Beck, review of *Gypsies and the Holocaust: A Bibliography and Introductory Essay,* by Gabrielle Tyrnauer (1989), in *Anthropology of East Europe Review*, 1990:8(1), 44–47.

5. Richard Bauman, among others, notes that "the association between performance and disreputability has often been marked" (*Verbal Art as Performance* [Rowley, MA: Newbury, 1978], 29). Because the performer is both feared and admired for [her or] his skill, [she or] he is marginalized. Cf.

also Steven Mullaney, *The Place of the Stage: License, Play and Power in Renaissance England* (Chicago: University of Chicago Press, 1988), 9.

6. Katherine Maria Trumpener, "Goddam Gipsy: People Without History and the Narratives of Nationalism," *The Voice of the Past. Anxieties of Cultural Transmission in Post-Enlightenment Europe: Tradition, Folklore, Textuality, History* (Ph.D. dissertation, Stanford University, 1990), 2–59.

7. See especially Pushkin's *Tsygany* and Leskov's *The Enchanted Wanderer.*

8. Cf. Johannes Fabian, *Power and Performance: Ethnographic Explorations Through Proverbial Wisdom and Theater in Shaba Zaire* (Madison, WI: University of Wisconsin Press, 1990).

9. See Bauman, *Verbal Art as Performance,* 28. The challenge, as Bauman puts it, is to establish "the continuity between the noticeable and public performance of cultural performances and the spontaneous, unscheduled, optional performance contexts of everyday life."

10. The *Bolshaia Sovetskaia Entsiklopedia* of 1974 asserts that the Teatr "Romen" was to facilitate policies such as the Order of the Supreme Soviet of 1926, which provided land to those Gypsies wishing to settle. (On these policies as reported by the Soviet press, see, for instance, in *Bednota,* "Nadelenie Zemlei Tsygan, Perekhodiashchikh k Trudovoi Zhizni," July 13, 1928; "Obo Vsem," June 17, 1928, "Tsyganski Kolxozy," July 18, 1929.) The order of 1956 was more strict and forbade wandering completely. Nadia Demeter claims that it is the "only Soviet law that defines a crime on the basis of nationality" (V. Zenkovich, "Tsyganskoe Schaste," *Nedelia,* September 4–10, 1989, 12).

11. Ivan Rom-Lebedev, *Ot Tsyganskogo Khora k Teatru "Romen."* (Moscow: Isskustvo, 1990), 165.

12. On the relation of language forms and the "words of Lenin" to Soviet nation building, see Alaina Lemon, "Maiakovskii and the 'Language of Lenin,'" *Chicago Anthropology Exchange,* 19 (Winter 1990), 1–25.

13. Rom-Lebedev, 164.

14. For more on *tsyganshchina* in the context of general criticism of Soviet popular music, see Robert Rothstein, "The Quiet Rehabilitation of the Brick Factory: Early Soviet Popular Music and Its Critics" in *Slavic Review,* 1980:39/3, 373–388.

15. Rom-Lebedev, 164.

16. Ibid.

17. Semion Mikhailov, *Tsyganskaia Zaria* (Moscow, Literatura I Voina, 1932).

18. "Pervyi Obrazets Tsyganskoi Pis'mennosti," in *Izvestiia,* August 11, 1928. See also N. G. Demeter, *Semeinaia Obriadnost' Tsygan v Kontse XIX-*

XXV. (Na Primere Etnicheskoi Gruppy Keldelari) Moscow: Dissertation of the ANSSR Institute of Ethnography, 1987.

19. N. Dudarovo and N. Pankov, *Nevo Drom—Bukvario vash Bare Manushenge* (Moscow: Tsentrizdat, 1928).

20. These are cataloged in the *Biblioteka im. Lenina*. Up to 1930 they are recorded in Germano's *Bibliografiia Tsygan*.

21. For retrospective commentary by Romani intellectuals, see Elena Bernaskoni, interview with N. G. Demeter, "Narod Vetra i Ognia" (People of Wind and Fire) in *Ekho Planety* 7, February 10–16, 1990, 26–34.

22. Indeed, Romani is a low-status language, considered a "forbidden gibberish" or "secret idiom." (See Diane Tong, "Romani as Symbol: Sociolinguistic Strategies of the Gypsies of Thessaloniki" in *Papers from the Fourth and Fifth Annual Meetings*, Gypsy Lore Society, North American Chapter. New York: GLS, Publication No. 2 [1985], 179–187.)

23. Interviews with audience members.

24. Rom-Lebedev, 174.

25. This particular song I heard only in the homes of urban Keldelari-Servi Roma. Yet, many other songs speak to the relationship to the *gazhe* in similar ways, some more humorously, some more bitterly. On another way that song speaks to and is shaped by relations with the *gazhe*, see Michael Stewart, "'True Speech': Song and the Moral Order of a Hungarian Vlach Gypsy Community." *Man* 24:1 (March 1989), 79–102.

26. On critical bricolage that has "accompanied capitalist penetration into the Third World," see Jean Comaroff, *Body of Power, Spirit of Resistance* (Chicago: University of Chicago Press, 1985). Such critical modes are also present, of course, under socialism.

27. On standards and centers in discourse, see Michael Silverstein, "Language Structure and Linguistic Ideology," in *The Elements: A Parasession on Linguistic Units and Levels*, ed. Paul Kline et al., Chicago Linguistic Society, April 20–21, 1979, and "Are Cultures Texts All the Way Down?" University of Chicago Departmental Seminar, Department of Anthropology, February 5, 1990.

28. See chapter two of Allette Olin Hill, *Mother Tongue, Father Time* (Bloomington: Indiana University Press, 1986).

29. On ways Soviet citizens actually did adopt particular modes of speaking and behaving in order to project a proletarian identity, for instance, in Soviet institutional settings, see Sheila Fitzpatrick, "The Problem of Class Identity in NEP Society," in *Russia in the Era of NEP*, eds. Sheila Fitzpatrick, Alexander Rabinowitch, and Richard Stites (Bloomington: Indiana University Press, 1991), 1–33. In general, see Erving Goffman, *The Presentation of Self in Everyday Life* (New York: Overlook Press, 1973).

30.   For more detailed analysis of Gypsy women as an image in Russian poetry, see Alaina Lemon, "Pride in Shame: 'Gypsy Temperament,' 'Romani daughters,' and 'Russian Sluts,'" ms, n.d.

31.   Leksa Manush writes that Gypsies are "innately musical," disregarding how Roma were historically limited to certain kinds of labor ("K Probleme Muzykal'nogo Folk'lora Tsygan [Istoki Muzyki v Evrope]," *Sovetskaia Etnografiia,* 5 [September/October 1985], 46–56.) See also Franz Liszt, *The Gipsy in Music,* trans. Edwin Evans (London: William Reeves, 1926).

32.   "Ochi chiornie, ochi strastnie, ochi zhguchie i prekrasnie . . . !" (Black eyes, impassioned eyes, smoldering and beautiful eyes . . . !) From a line of the famous Gypsy romance (a genre of Russian love song associated with Gypsy performance) *Ochi Chiornie.*

33.   Gypsies are often assumed a priori to be criminals; police surveillance and identification of Gypsies (including children) as "potential criminals" is a common practice. (See, for instance, Morten-Gotthold's review of *Polizei und "Zigeuner": Strategien, Handlungsmuster und Alltagstheorien im polizeilichen Umgang mit Sinti und Roma,* by Wolfgang Feuerhelm, in the newsletter of the Gypsy Lore Society [13:4 (1990), 4–5].) Besides making constructivist arguments that Gypsy activities are defined as crimes because of xenophobia (Cf. Ian Hancock, *The Pariah Syndrome: An Account of Gypsy Slavery and Persecution* [Ann Arbor: Karoma, 1987]), it can be empirically shown that many accusations were unfounded. See, for instance, Sheila Salo, "'Stolen by Gypsies': The Kidnap Accusation in the United States" in *Papers from the Eighth and Ninth Annual Meetings* (New York: Gypsy Lore Society, North American Chapter, Publication No. 4, 1988), 25–41, and also articles listed by A. V. Germano in *Bibliografiia o Tsyganakh Tsentrizdat,* Moscow, 1930.

34.   See also Benedict Anderson, *Imagined Communities: Reflections on the Origin and Spread of Nationalism* (London: Verso, 1983). I borrow the phrase in its broadest sense, without intending here any specific reference to national language standards or the rise of print capitalism.

35.   On symbolic capital, see Pierre Bourdieu, *Outline of a Theory of Practice,* trans. Richard Nice (Cambridge: Cambridge University Press, 1977), 171–183.

36.   A. P. Barranikov, 47.

37.   These concerns seem to distress performers much more than they do Roma of other groups, who speak much more Romani at home, and do not worry about the effect of owning VCRs on their Romaniness—in fact, these non-performers see such toys of modernity as aids to preserving custom.

38.   Interview, 1990.

39.   For detailed structural analyses of *Magripe/Marimos* in North America see Anne Sutherland, "The Body as a Social Symbol Among the Rom" in *The*

Anthropology of the Body, ed. J. Blacking (New York: Academic Press, 1977), 375–390, and Carol Miller, *Machwaya Gypsy Marime* (master's thesis, University of Washington, 1968).

40. Terms such as "Gypsies" or "Tsygane" are used to describe almost any traveling people, such as Irish Travellers, who are also not Roma. "Tsygane" in turn are lumped together with other non-Russians such as Tatars or Azeris as "Blacks." (On a similar process of lumping groups "targeted for assimilation" in West Germany, see Ruth Mandel, "Ethnicity and Identity among Migrant Guestworkers in West Berlin," in *Conflict, Migration and the Expression of Identity*, ed. Nancy L. Gonzalez [Boulder, CO: Westview Press, 1989].) Attempts to define the "pure" Gypsy is another analytic error, based on pseudo-biological characteristics. Those classified under Third Reich policy as "pure Gypsies" were set aside at first in "cultural preserves," while "mixed" Gypsies went straight to the camps. (For a detailed account, see Thomas A. Acton, *Gypsy Politics and Social Change: The Development of Ethnic Ideology and Pressure Politics Among British Gypsies from Victorian Reformism to Romany Nationalism* [London and Boston: Routledge and Kegan Paul, 1974].) The stigma and danger of these modes of classification explain why it is so difficult to determine how many Roma live in the USSR. Officially the number (as of the 1987 census) is 209,000. However, this number includes only those willing to write *Tsygan* in their passports—most Roma who I encountered prefer to call themselves "Moldavian" or "Bessarabian" on paper. See also Grattan Puxon, *Rom: Europe's Gypsies* (London: Minority Rights Group, 1979), 14–15.

41. Including Lovari, Keldelari (Kalderash), Machvani, Ungri, and others.

42. See Ian Hancock, *The Pariah Syndrome: An Account of Gypsy Slavery and Persecution* (Ann Arbor: Karoma Publishers, 1987).

43. Interview, 1990, Kiev.

44. Interviews, 1990, and A. Danilken, "The First Gypsy Collective in Ukraine," unpublished manuscript, 1990.

45. Interview, 1990. See also Ivashchenko, "Tsyganskoe Shchaste," in *Komsomolets* (July 6, 1990), 2.

46. R. S. and P. S. Demeter, *Obraztsy Folklora Tsygan Keldelara*, Glavnaia Redaktsiia Vostochnoi Literatury, Moscow, 1981, and *Tsygansko-Russkii, Russko-Tsyganskii Slovar' (Kelderarskii Dialekt)* (Moscow: Russkii Iazik, 1990).

"The Duende Roams Freely This Night": An Analysis of an Interethnic Event in Granada, Spain (1985)

Bertha B. Quintana

This essay describes and analyzes an event involving interaction between *gitanos* of Granada and approximately three hundred representatives of the city's majority population, for example, writers, artists, government officials, educators, flamenco aficionados. The historic union took place in June 1982 to celebrate the "presentation" of a book by Ángel Carmona, *Romi: Sacro-Monte 1880–1980,* published under the auspices of the Provincial Ministry of Culture. Guests of honor included the heads of *gitano flamenco* dynasties whose reactions to the occasion, and to nascent proposals made by program speakers for restoring the Sacro-Monte, and improving interpersonal relationships, I recorded both during and after the event. While a single event is used for ethnographic focus, data reported are reflective of the historical and contextual relationship of Granada's Sacro-Monte Gypsy population to segments of the city's majority population as well as to one another. Conceptually, then, the approach used is neither fully "holistic," nor is it as narrowly limited as the title might imply. Rather, the attempt is made to study *gitano* role segmentation and the effects of contacts with outsiders in terms outlined in Irwin Press's paradigm of urban organization (1979:9–12), and in Hsu's concept of psychosocial homeostasis (1971). The author's twenty-four years of continuous association with Sacro-Monte *gitanos* facilitated the collection of new and sensitive data and provided a long-term basis for demonstrating the role subjective standards continue to play in guiding *gitano* behavior and reactions to proposed change.

In order to understand factors which led to the well-intentioned staging of the event, on the one hand, and its failure, as perceived by *gitanos*, to achieve significant goals on the other, it is necessary to examine major contemporary forces which have affected the famed *zambras* (*gitano* festivals, with music and dancing) of the Sacro-Monte, and the artists who mount them. This article is concerned primarily with this occupational segment and with the effect of touristic manipulation of its artistic and economic enterprises. Similarly, the interethnic event it details involved the same minority, albeit Carmona's book refers also to other traditional occupations pursued by Sacro-Monteños.

As reported in earlier works (Quintana and Floyd 1972 [1986], 1976), the growth of tourism in Spain was a mixed blessing for Granada's Gypsies.[1] Regarded by many as the embodiment of the "romantic image" of Spain, a visit to the caves of the Sacro-Monte to witness a *zambra* was and remains part of every package tour to Granada. In the sixties, such tours, which were smaller and more numerous than today's, yielded a modest but reasonable income to *gitanos* who mounted the seven principal Sacro-Monte *zambras*. Most had a least one major salon for performances and one or two smaller caves for overflow audiences. Some of Spain's finest dancers, singers, and *tocadores*, who were born and taught in the Sacro-Monte, participated in them between tours and hotel and nightclub engagements. While the quality of performance was often uneven, many still communicated some of the vitality of the legendary private *zambras* of the past.

By the early seventies, however, excess commercialism, crass exploitation by growing tour agencies, and the inability of *gitanos* to organize effectively to protect their *zambra* interests resulted in the almost total deterioration of what little artistic merit remained. The best of the flamenco artists left the Sacro-Monte to perform in larger cities and in other countries (for example, Japan, Mexico, Caribbean resort areas) where higher wages have enabled them to improve their standard of living and to achieve steadier, if often short-term, employment. Left behind was the aging population of some of the most venerable of

Granada's *zambra* dynasties, dependent on less-gifted guitarists, old women, transient *gitanas*, and children to satiate tourist demands for "pure" Gypsy folk art. By the summer of 1982, only two of the famous flamenco seven continue to mount *zambras* regularly, the only ones willing to accept as little as 10 percent of what tour guides charge to "see" them. Visitors are warned of the "dangers" of going to the Sacro-Monte in private parties and are prevented even from buying castanets, small copper wares, and so forth, from *gitanos* who watch from cave entrances as bus groups are prodded up the hill to their prearranged destination. One of the authentic bars bears the subtitle "Discotheque" in bold red and black letters on its white wall. Even *gitanos* who work for the agencies must depend on extra income from the sale of castanets and fortune-telling fees, and as performances are commercial parodies only of flamenco art forms, visitors leave complaining of having been "taken in" by the Gypsies! Tour agencies and their guides, who present themselves as protectors of the tourists, are the only ones who profit significantly from these enterprises and who strengthen racist stereotypes of Gypsies as "dangerous" in order to (1) monopolize Sacro-Monte tours, and 2) capitalize on tourist demands for the "exotic."

All of these abuses have culminated in a declining interest in the Sacro-Monte, its indigenous peoples, their history, culture, and rich artistic heritage. Except for one or two bus tours in the late afternoon and/or evening, a famed *gitana* notes, "Not even a bird passes by." Today most of the *cuevas* are silent. Empty chairs are lined neatly against the walls, copper artifacts are kept gleaming—*"si por acaso"*—and costumes hang limply in dark recesses. The old *patronas* wait half hoping for the return of past successes but living mainly with memories only of cheering aficionados at private *zambras*, nights at the house of Falla, performances at the Alhambra Palace Hotel. In large measure, these are the consequences of refusing to *"cooperate"* with the highly organized tour agencies, pay "kickbacks," or mount *zambras* of increasingly inferior quality. They are the consequences also of intercave *gitano* rivalries, failure to recognize the need to unite against the inroads made by outside interests, and inability to counteract forces which attracted the best of the performers away from the Sacro-Monte.

These problems are compounded today by shifting patterns of tourism in Spain, high employment and inflation, and escalating social problems—crime, poverty, and so forth. Gypsies with whom I have worked for nearly a quarter of a century warned continuously against wearing jewelry in "town," carrying a camera or purse, or walking alone. While they feared Gypsy "fights" more than anything else, one result of transient *gitanos* moving in and out of the city, they were fully aware that street muggings and robberies are crimes committed primarily by members of the *payo* (non-Gypsy) majority.

As for Gypsy coping mechanisms under economic stress, they were highly reminiscent in 1982 of those of 1959. Peddling and illegal street vending are on the increase. Shoe shining, taxi driving for the more affluent, traveling with fairs and market caravans, and scrap collecting all provide varying degrees of income. Some activities, such as begging and the very small, but highly visible, number of *gitano* pimps loitering at hotels and other tourist stops, confirm to the stranger the stereotypic images perpetuated by their guides and guidebooks. Less visible is the terrible poverty of most *gitanos,* some of whom cull the hot sierra during the summer for berries and other seasonal wild produce.

Not all signs are bleak, however. A nascent activist movement, the Association of Gypsies of Granada, has helped increase *gitano* awareness of various medical, social, and pension plans available to them. The highly publicized examples of Juan de Dios Ramírez Heredia, the first Gypsy elected to the Spanish Parliament, and that of José Heredia Maya, head of the Andalusian activist movement, professor of Spanish literature, poet, and author of the award-winning drama and film *Camelamos Naquerar* (We Want to Speak), provide some help and hope. While Heredia commented that "our work goes slowly," their advocacy of education, restoration of the Sacro-Monte, and revitalization of the artistic heritage of Granada's Gypsy population already had attracted the attention of liberal government and local officials. A number of them were among the guests who attended the interethnic event of 30 June 1982, held in the beautiful patio of the Corral del Carbón, built by the Moors in the first half of the fourteenth century. The union, historic in terms of both people and place, did more than celebrate the publication of Carmona's work, being in fact "a call to save the Sacro-Monte from its present degradation." Speakers also emphasize the sociopolitical nature of the problems faced by its inhabitants, the need to "humanize" living conditions and interpersonal relationships, and the value to Granada and to Spain of restoring "this universal barrio." As for the *gitano* "presence," it added excitement and color in the form of a lively *zambra* improvised at the conclusion of the program by the flamenco artists among them. "The duende," stated Vicente Gonzales Barberán of the Ministry of Culture, "roams freely this night through Granada."

Gitano *Reactions*

To begin with, attendance at the event was viewed by the *gitanos* it honored with diverse feelings. While all had had contacts with Carmona, a native of Granada, during the several years it took him to gather the materials presented in *Romi*, some were unsure about participating. Most frequently expressed was the belief that the occasion was a *payo* not a *gitano* affair. Those *gitanos* who did attend either perceived an advantage in being involved for an evening with members of the "operative" society upon which they were dependent for continued recognition and income or feared that special advantage might accrue to rival groups in attendance. Others felt pressure to respond to demands originating from people they viewed as "power wielders." A few were just curious. *Gitanos* with whom the author of this article had worked for more than two decades went "mainly because we knew you wanted to go." The temptation of being picked up in "limousines" (actually taxis), "dressing up" to go "downtown," and the promise of catered refreshments served as additional inducements. Carmona himself was referred to with varying degrees of good nature closely correlated with the number of pictures of particular *gitanos* included in his book. As gift copies had been distributed to them prior to the event, jealousies about overattention to one versus another were already at peak level, as were criticisms about inaccuracies in reporting family relationships, relative merit of rival artists, and so forth.

The actual arrival of the *gitanos* (mainly *gitanas*) at the Corral del Carbón was greeted with enthusiasm by those already there (*¡Aquí vienen los gitanos!*), to which they responded with characteristic "style." As all had been or were famous professional performers, they accepted applause, being seated in a reserved section, and presentations of large floral bouquets as "natural" but interacted only with other family members or people they knew intimately. As spectators, they subsequently became impatient with speeches which they regarded as "too many and too long" and punctuated several of them with loud comments about the hardness of their chairs. Finally all of the *gitano* "guests" were asked up onto the stage, something many of them did not expect, and about which some of the older *gitanas* expressed concern. Once there, each was presented to what now had become an audience, and flamenco music, both live and recorded, blared forth. The group sat silently facing the audience, bewildered about what to do until one famed *gitana* started marking the rhythms with *palmas*. (Later she commented, "I could not just sit there on display.") This triggered the spontaneous and boisterous *zambra* to which reference already has been made, and in which traditional rivals found themselves reluctantly sharing the same stage. In short, the honored "guests" ultimately did the only thing they could, revert to their traditional roles as entertainers of the "outsiders." The fact that the knowledgeable Granadine audience reacted with cheers, laughter, calls for particular artists, and so forth, reinforced the impression of some that the interethnic event had turned into "business as usual."

In reviewing the event during the days that followed it, several major reasons emerged for its failure to achieve intended goals. For *gitanos*, contacts based on "role" (usefulness) run contrary to the emphasis on affect (feeling) in the intimate society and culture of the Sacro-Monte. Consequently, appeals made by speakers to shared identities and loyalties ("We are one!") ignored the heterogeneity both outside and within the *gitano* community and are antithetical to the *gitano* insistence upon boundary maintenance. On the other hand, Press's observation that ". . . cities sustain and create a number of socio-economic role types" (1979:11) was evidenced in both audience expectation and *gitano* reactions to them. The shift from honored spectators to performers was bewildering, but facilitated by *gitano* familiarity with the latter.

Promises made and broken in the past about restoring the Sacro-Monte ("this universal barrio") were cited as justifying *gitano* suspicion about bureaucratic interference in Sacro-Monte affairs—"Even if kept," they asked, "for whose benefit?" Similarly, references to the new liberalization of Spain's political process left *gitanos* uneasy and worried. "*They* will only charge *us* higher prices and taxes." Finally, in spite of the tendency to blame contemporary Sacro-Monte problems on the "bust" qualities of overdependence on tourism, *gitanos* both like and thrive on tourism and view it as an important economic resource for many of their number. What they most desire is *reform* in the system, a remote possibility given their reluctance to unite with one another in its pursuit. As for Granada's majority population, only a small elite segment of it is active in efforts to improve the quality of life in the Sacro-Monte. *Gitano* relationships with even the most trusted among them are predominantly dyadic and offer, in Press's words, "little feedback to significant others for purposes of sanction" (1979:9).

Summary

In the case of the interethnic event of June 1982, *gitanos* participated as spectators and traditional role players only. They responded to outside pressure to attend an event intended to honor them but remained unconvinced about its future outcomes. To them, the event itself was just that, an event at which they performed. They heard that there was a newspaper article about it, but a number of them did not want copies. For one thing they disliked being photographed with rival flamenco artists, a fact overlooked in the original planning by the organizers. For another, it was an evening, like hundreds before it, when the duende "walked"—but followed a familiar and well-worn path.

Afterword 1995:

Data collected five years later revealed that Gypsy coping mechanisms had remained relatively unchanged (Quintana 1990). While greater awareness of social, health, and educational programs was servicing some essential *gitano* needs in Granada, their full potential remained unrealized especially by the poorest, the neediest. For the majority, changes had not significantly improved the quality of their lives, nor of local interpersonal relationships. The heterogeneity that characterizes Granada's *gitano* population still played a major role in acceptance or rejection patterns, as did limited exchanges and feedback between diverse and rival constituencies. Progress that had been made in these areas was due largely to the efforts of the Association of Gypsies of Granada, an activist organization which includes prominent Gyspies, liberal government officials and, as in the time of García Lorca, writers, intellectuals, and artists. Optimistic talk of restoring the Sacro-Monte and of artistic revitalization of its famed flamenco *zambras* had not, as *gitanos* had predicted earlier, resulted in any tangible improvements. Will these hopes ever be realized? Perhaps not, but *gitano* cultural and artistic tenacity has been written off before only to resurface in renewed form.

NOTE

1. Of Granada's total population of more than 250,000 inhabitants, its sedentary Gypsy population is estimated at between 5,000 and 6,000 people, approximately 1,500 of whom continue to live in the Sacro-Monte in cave dwellings ranging from comparatively lavish (mainly those of flamenco artists) to wretched (those of poor residents of the upper regions).

REFERENCES

Carmona, Ángel
1982   *Romi: Sacro-Monte 1880-1980*. Granada: Maracena.
Hsu, Francis L. K.
1971   "Psychosocial Homeostasis and Jen: Conceptual Tools for Advancing Psychological Anthropology." *American Anthropologist* 73(1): 23–44.
Press, Irwin
1979   *The City as Context: Urbanism and Behavioral Constraints in Seville*. Urbana: University of Illinois Press.
Quintana, Bertha B., and Lois Gray Floyd
1976   "Gypsies, Tourism, and the New Spanish Economy." In *Economic Transformation and Steady-State Values: Essays in the Ethnography of Spain* (Joseph B. Aceves, Edward C. Hansen, and Gloria Levitas, eds.). New York: Queens College Press, 9–13.
1986   *¡Qué Gitano! Gypsies of Southern Spain*. Prospect Heights, Illinois: Waveland Press. (Original publication 1972. New York: Holt, Rinehart and Winston.)
Quintana, Bertha B.
1990   "Only the Dogs Bark at Night: A Retrospective of Granada's Sacro-Monte Zambras." In *100 Years of Gypsy Studies* (Matt Salo, ed.). Cheverly, Maryland: The Gypsy Lore Society.

Andalusian, Gypsy, and Class Identity in the Contemporary Flamenco Complex (1989)

Peter Manuel

For over a century flamenco has comprised a continuum of styles, from the spontaneous music of the informal Gypsy *juerga* (spree) to the commercialized and adulterated fare performed in cabarets by professional musicians for non-Gypsy audiences. Since the early 1960s, the unprecedented vogue of flamenco, together with a set of broader extramusical factors, has rendered the flamenco complex even more heterogeneous, generating a host of innovative, eclectic, and popular substyles that now coexist with traditional "pure" flamenco. While the flamenco scholarship (*flamencología*) that has mushroomed in the same period has produced dozens of informative books, these have tended to focus on traditional *flamenco puro* rather than on the contemporary status of the art and its related derivatives.

A holistic perspective of modern flamenco—including the traditional styles—must comprehend the panoply of flamenco-related hybrids that have flourished in recent decades and now form an intrinsic part of Spanish culture; moreover, such a perspective must situate these musics in the context of the social, economic, and political currents that have reshaped Spanish society in the last half-century.

Ideally, such a study should be the subject of a book, or several books; until these have been undertaken, however, this essay may serve as an introductory attempt to contextualize the modern flamenco aggregate of styles in its sociocultural background. These styles include traditional flamenco, recent fusions of flamenco with Arab musics, *nueva canción andaluza* (Andalusian new song), and the variety of related commercial popular musics which have emerged in recent decades. This continuum of styles must be understood in the context of Andalusia's unique culture and history, its present crisis of underdevelopment and mass emigration, the rise of political mobilization and regional pride, and the special role played by Andalusian Gypsies in the flamenco complex.

For modern Andalusians, the goal of revitalizing regional culture has become linked with the movements for political autonomy, socialism, and Gypsy identity. Flamenco and its derivatives have come to play an important role in this cultural ferment, both through the deliberate efforts of socially conscious musicians as well as through the enthusiasm of intellectuals and audiences. In this article, after summarizing the region's current sociohistorical background, I will endeavor to illustrate the important role played by flamenco and related subgenres in expressing and, to a considerable extent, helping to shape modern Andalusian identity. In this way I will attempt to demonstrate how musical style as well as text content can function not merely as passive reflections of broader sociocultural phenomena that shape them but also as active contributors to the processes of cultural change.

The Andalusian Legacy:
Cultural Wealth, Material Poverty, and Regional Identity

It has been commonplace for Spanish authors to describe flamenco—both in terms of vocal style and text content—as a "cry of pain"—pain, most specifically of the persecuted Gypsies, but in a more general sense of Andalusians as a whole, whose post-reconquest history of poverty and exploitation has only been aggravated by the memory of their former glory under the Moors. The sense of Andalusian oppression has been a central theme in flamenco, and the present political freedom and crisis of mass emigration have, if anything, intensified the use of flamenco as a vehicle for social commentary—both through text content and, less overtly, through stylistic innovations. Flamenco, whether traditional or contemporary, cannot be understood in isolation from its historical context—aspects of which are briefly summarized here.

The last centuries of Moorish rule bestowed upon Andalusia a period of cultural and economic prominence in many ways unsurpassed since the Castilian Christian *reconquista*, which culminated with the fall of Granada in 1492. Moorish Andalusia was the wealthiest and most populous region of Spain, its economy buoyed by commerce, intensive canal-based agriculture, and textile production. Its cultural life was arguably the most cosmopolitan in Europe, synthesizing the learning and arts of the Arab, Christian, and Jewish communities, which coexisted in relative harmony (see Comin 1985:25–27).

The *reconquista* put an end to this golden age. The Castilian crown replaced Moorish tolerance with the Inquisition, expelling Jews and Muslims, and persecuting and even massacring many of the remaining converts (see, for example, Grande 1979, 1:59–64, 127). The imperial Madrid government treated Andalusia as a conquered and occupied territory rather than as a region of economic value to be developed. Hence, under Spanish rule, irrigation networks collapsed, trade withered, and land ownership became concentrated in the hands of a tiny absentee *latifundista* elite. Ruinous imperials wars, mass emigration to America, and internal stagnation and repression further devastated Andalusia, causing recurrent famines which persisted through the nineteenth century (see Molina 1985:35ff.). While the development of mining around Linares and Murcia in the mid-1800s provided employment for many landless laborers, it also intensified emigration and condemned countless workers to blindness, lung disease, and early deaths. Even this, however, was preferable to the fate of the thousands of indigent Andalusian draftees who perished in the colonial nineteenth-century wars in America.

Such conditions generated two interrelated attitudes among Andalusians, which have intensified in this century and constituted basic animating themes of flamenco. The first of these is a sense of Andalusian solidarity, coupled with a hostility to Madrid authority. The immediate and disastrous effects of the *reconquista* on Andalusian culture and economy made contempt for central rule proverbial by the seventeenth century; this enmity was expressed in many Andalusian popular verses (*coplas*; see Comin 1985:29–30) and, more indirectly, in widespread smuggling and banditry (*bandolerismo*—also celebrated in innumerable *coplas*).

Linked to this animosity toward Madrid was the emergence, among the Andalusian poor, of an acute class consciousness, itself a product of the extreme inequalities of wealth and the progressive currents of thought entering the region via the port of Cádiz. During the course of the nineteenth century, the inchoate antimonarchism and social discontent so widespread in Andalusia found new shape in Fourier-influenced proto-socialism, in anarchism, and, ultimately, in Marxism. The militant unionization of mine workers at Linares was a crucial development. By mid-century the civic discontent once expressed in *bandolerismo* and fatalism was generating strikes, unions, leftist publications, open revolts (for example, in 1868), and explicit social commentary in flamenco *coplas* (see Grande 1979, 2:402–416; Ortiz Nuevo 1985:78–143; Comin 1985: 32–40).

Although the conditions that formerly precipitated recurrent famines were ameliorated during the twentieth century, Andalusians still found little reason to temper their resentment of central authority and *latifundista* landlordism. The socialist mobilization that had abounded under the Republic was brutally quashed by Franco, who recognized Andalusia as a hotbed of discontent. Subsequently, while central and northern Spain became increasingly industrialized and prosperous, neglect from the center and from the insouciant absentee landlords effectively inhibited development of Andalusia's rich agricultural, fishing, and industrial potential. Thus, throughout the century, Andalusia and neighboring Extremadura—long ago, the commercial and demographic centers of Spain—have remained the poorest regions of the country.

Urbanization has been one inevitable consequence of rural unemployment and underdevelopment, but the Andalusian cities—now quaint provincial towns with negligible industry or commerce—have been able to absorb only a tiny percentage of the indigent unemployed. Rather, it is the industrial centers to the north—Madrid, French and German cities, and above all, Barcelona—to which the unemployed have been obliged to migrate in search of work. The mass migration of Andalusians—now measured in the millions—has become such a central feature of Spanish economic and cultural life that it has become commonplace to note that Andalusia must now be sought in the suburbs and slums of Barcelona and Madrid (see, for example, Comin 1985:105–126). Because the Andalusian "guest workers" do not, on the whole, assimilate to their host cities, the diaspora appears to have heightened rather than diluted Andalusian autonomist sentiment as well as cultural solidarity.

Since the restoration of democracy in 1977, the autonomist and socialist movements have become basic and open features of Andalusian sociopolitical life, and further, they have become important influences on and themes of regional music, including flamenco and its commercial hybrids which have emerged among the proletarian emigrant communities.

Before turning at last to music, I must briefly complete my summary of flamenco's sociohistorical background with some mention of the ethnic subculture which has played such a crucial role in its evolution.

Gypsy Subculture in Modern Spain

A holistic view of the contemporary flamenco complex must include some discussion of the Gypsy community, whose members continue to dominate not only flamenco itself but also its commercial pop derivatives.

Since first arriving in Spain via France in the fifteenth century, the many thousands of Gypsies who settled in Andalusia came to share the poverty of their compatriots while bearing an added burden of persecution (see, for example, Grande 1979). Inquisitional intolerance, the need for scapegoats for imperial decline, and popular resentment of parasitic begging and thievery (real or imaginary) led to a history of repression and harassment. Such conditions, however, appear traditionally to have reinforced rather than to have broken the defensive ethnic pride, endogamy, and isolation of the Gypsy community; accordingly, the freedom-cherishing Gypsies have tended to prefer self-employment in marginal, albeit functional sectors of the economy (for example, skinning mules, trading horses, smuggling, basket-weaving, repainting kitchen utensils, and hawking cigarettes).

Nevertheless, from the late 1700s, when Romantic literature began to idealize nomadic Gypsies (Grande 1979, 1:277–285), substantial communities of settled, assimilated Gypsies (including many blacksmiths) arose in the cities and towns of Seville and Cádiz provinces. It was primarily these *casero* (house-owning) Gypsies, as opposed to their nomadic *andarrío* and *canastero* kin, that nurtured and developed flamenco in a complex process of syncretic, dialectic interaction with non-Gypsy audiences and musics.

The mid-twentieth century was a period of adjustment and dislocation for most Gypsies, especially since almost all of the traditional Gypsy occupations became obsolete. In the period of adaptation, several *casero* Gypsies (including many from former blacksmith families) were able to capitalize upon and further promote the spread of flamenco by becoming professional musicians (see Pérez de Guzmán 1982:105–113). Many more, including the tiny percent that remain nomadic, have been able to eke out humble livings in new marginal roles (recycling trash, shining shoes, selling lottery tickets, and so forth). Perhaps the largest group, like Andalusians in general, have simply become proletarianized, in many cases emigrating to the barrios of Barcelona and Madrid. In the "miracle" decades of the 1950s and 1960s, many thousands of Gypsies found decent jobs in the booming industrial centers, but the unemployment, inflation, and recession of subsequent years have once again marginalized the urban Gypsies and constituted a new sort of threat to their cultural and economic survival (see San Román 1986:201ff.). It is the subculture of these urban Gypsies that has generated the new popular music hybrids of flamenco, Cuban *rumba*, and rock, to which we shall return below.

On the whole, Gypsies occupy the lowest rungs in the Spanish economy, with the Andalusian Gypsies as the poorest of the poor (again, see Grande 1979, 2:575–622). Since the 1970s, significant attempts to organize and aid the Gypsy communities have emerged. Nevertheless, probably the most important and effective vehicle for the emerging Gypsy consciousness has been music—specifically, flamenco and its contemporary offshoots which have emerged recently as products of socioeconomic changes, external musical influences (especially rock and Cuban music), political and cultural freedom, and the flamenco boom itself.

Flamenco

Flamenco, regardless of its ever-growing acceptance by foreign as well as Spanish middle classes, has evolved as a product of the Andalusian urban lower classes and, in particular, the settled Gypsies of Seville and Cádiz provinces. Since its coalescence in the mid-1800s, diluted and commercialized forms of the genre (for example, flamenco opera) have flourished and perished in accordance with the changes in bourgeois taste, but a current of traditional flamenco, however inherently syncretic it may be, has always remained at the inspirational and stylistic core of the genre.

Flamenco texts have tended to reflect their social origins in more concrete terms than flamenco style per se, and, indeed, Andalusian song lyrics in general (*coplas, seguidillas*, and so forth) constitute a rich repository of oral history. A large number of flamenco lyrics focus on (unrequited) love, in a more or less ahistorical manner. In contexts where flamenco has served as light entertainment for bourgeois patrons (i.e., the *café-cantante* cabarets, flamenco opera, and the current tourist-oriented *tablaos*), singers have tended to trivialize their verses, eschewing any content which might disturb or displease their audiences (see, for example, Grande 1979, 2:427; Urbano Pérez 1980:13, 95; and Ortiz Nuevo 1985:10). Moreover, one function of flamenco—and particularly of the festive, lighter, dance-oriented *cantes chicos*—has always been to divert and entertain rather than to confront social woes. Nevertheless, even the amatory lyrics tend to display the values of machismo, fatalism, pride, and male self-pity which, although not unique to Andalusian society, are certainly characteristic of it. Further, most flamenco texts, regardless of the topic, express an intense sorrow which is regarded as basic to the Andalusian aesthetic. Just as Gypsy flamenco style has always coexisted with and nourished commercial-oriented substyles, so have flamenco lyrics—especially in their private or lower-class milieus—served as persistent and ever-effective vehicles for expression of the anxieties and vicissitudes of Andalusian and Gypsy daily life.

Many traditional flamenco texts clearly reflect their Gypsy origin. In this category, for example, are those celebrating Gypsy-style freedom from authority, and, more poignantly, the innumerable verses narrating persecution and prison life. Often cited is the following *copla*, in Spanish mixed with Gypsy Caló (allegedly from Triana, Seville, ca. 800):

> Los jeray por las esquinas con velones y farol
> en voz alta se decían: ¡Mararlo que es calorró!

> The horsemen on the corners, with lanterns and torches
> Were shouting "Kill him, he's a Gypsy!"

Like most surviving traditional *coplas*, this one does not argue a case, make abstract sociopolitical generalizations, or rely on an extended narrative plot; rather, it is like a snapshot, a vignette of a specific, immediate personal event. At the same time, given the abundance of traditional couplets like this one, it would be foolish to argue, as some have, that the "political" perspective in flamenco is somehow new and artificial. Whether this *copla* argues a stance or not, it remains a terse and eloquent portrayal of the sociopolitical experience of its author.

Many Gypsy *coplas* portraying indigence and contempt for civil authority were clearly perceived as expressing experiences and sentiments shared by Andalusians as a whole. In this sense such *coplas* merge with the mass of song texts, whether of Gypsy or non-Gypsy origin, which convey the hardships of Andalusian life in general. Like the *copla* above, these tend to present personal, specific vignettes—of hunger, of languishing in fetid hospitals, or of abominable work conditions in the mines. By the mid-1800s, however, *coplas* were expressing a more generalized and explicit class consciousness; such a perspective first surfaces in those songs originating among the increasingly mobilized and radical mining unions (see Grande 1979, 2:369–397).

Minero, ¿pa[ra] qué trabajas si pa[ra] ti no es el producto?
Pa[ra] el patrón son las alhojas, para tu familia el luto,
Y para ti la mortaja.[1]

Miner, why do you work, if the profits aren't for you?
For the boss are the jewels, for your family, mourning,
And for you, the funeral shroud.

Such overt politicization of flamenco lyrics increased in the twentieth century, as Marxist thought swept through Andalusia and indigent workers discarded their traditional fatalism for radical mobilization (see, for example, Ortiz Nuevo 1985; Urbano Pérez 1980). At the same time that imported radical political philosophies were spreading, flamenco singers' use of sophisticated lyrics became commonplace, and many respected poets were happy to write verse specifically designed for flamenco performance. García Lorca was the most prominent modern poet to bridge the gap between rustic, often nonliterate Gypsy singers and the literary intellectual world. In his wake, singer-poet collaborations have proliferated, with a corresponding enrichment and broadening of flamenco lyrics.

Explicitly progressive or leftist lyrics were, of course, prohibited under fascist rule, although they evidently circulated in private. However, as Franco's grip loosened and, later, with the advent of democracy, such texts have again come to occupy an important place in flamenco expression. Particularly worthy of mention in this respect are the singers José Menese, Enrique Morente, Pepe Taranto, Manuel Gerena, and José Domínguez ("El Cabrero"). Morente, a dynamic Gypsy vocalist, has recorded several eloquent verses of the late radical poet Miguel Hernández; Gerena, less popular a singer but no less outspoken, was imprisoned in the early 1970s for his views. Domínguez, in the mid-1980s, was clearly, along with Camarón de la Isla, the most popular flamenco singer on the scene. Born to a family of goatherds (*cabreros*), he continues to practice his hereditary profession alongside his successful musical career. His song texts generally extol rural life and the rights of the poor and downtrodden; these verses elicit such roars of approval from his audiences that his concerts often assume the character of political rallies. It is clear that much of Domínguez's popularity derives from his image as a "man of the people" who, together with his rustic lifestyle, has an acute sociopolitical consciousness.

Also noteworthy here is the theatrical production "Quejío" (Lament), which enjoyed considerable success in Spain (despite being censored) and in greater European and Latin American tours in 1972–1973. "Quejío" consisted of a series of loosely narrative vignettes structured around flamenco *cantes*, focusing on themes of poverty, separation, and, above all, social injustice (see Drillon et al. 1975).

Overt politicization of flamenco lyrics does not, however, elicit unanimous approval—especially since most of the top singers continue to favor more personal or amatory themes. I may mention, for example, the views of *flamencólogo* Félix Grande; Grande, although having devoted three books to the task of situating flamenco in its historical context of social injustice, observes that many of the committed texts employed by politically minded singers are not entirely successful as song texts. He further notes that, for instance, a traditional *taranta* relating the plight of miners sung by Camarón, may convey a sense of social iniquity much more effectively than the prosaic pontifications of less gifted vocalists (Grande 1979, 2:639–641). For his own part, Camarón avoided explicit sociopolitical commentary, while not hesitating to give a benefit concert for the Socialist Party (PSOE) in 1987. Insofar as Gypsies still constitute the majority of leading flamenco singers, the genre continues to be an important focus and inspiration for the Gypsy community. Gypsy vocalists appear to be sensitive to their value and significance to their community, recognizing that they, along with Gypsy rock stars, are the most visible and even influential representatives of their people.

As I have noted, *gitanismo* (Gypsy ethos) pervades many flamenco texts in the form of themes of freedom, persecution, Gypsy lore, and references to other Gypsies. Since the mid-1970s, musicians have self-consciously used flamenco as an explicit and concentrated vehicle of Gypsy identity. The music of Camarón de la Isla is particularly noteworthy for its redolent *gitanismo*, without needing recourse to blunt sociopolitical sloganeering. Among leading Gypsy vocalists, however, the most ardent and committed spokesperson of Gypsy identity has been Juan Peña, "El Lebrijano," who has devoted much, if not most, of his recent musical output to promoting the cause of his people. Aside from his *flamenco árabe* excursions to be considered below, particularly noteworthy has been his 1976 LP "Persecución," which consists of a series of poems (by Félix Grande) recited or set to flamenco *cantes*, dramatizing the plight of the Andalusian Gypsies over the centuries; the songs adhere to traditional forms, such as a *romance* regarding the royal edicts against Gypsies, and a *galeras* and *tarantas* depicting, respectively, the woe of Gypsies sent to row and perish in the galleons and of those suffering in the nineteenth-century mines.

Also worthy of special mention is "Camelamos Naquerar" (Caló: We Want to Speak), a 1976 theatrical production of Gypsy activist and intellectual José Heredia Maya. This opus was roughly similar to "Quejío" in form, but was devoted specially to Gypsy identity, calling attention to the Gypsies' past and present misfortune and persecution and attacking the romantic myth that Gypsies have always been carefree, wild, and lazy sybarites, merrily drinking and dancing their way through life.[2]

Our discussion of flamenco thus far has concentrated on text and dramatic content, as it is within these parameters that social identity is most explicitly expressed. Nevertheless, style may also function as an important symbol of identity, and indeed, traditional flamenco style can be seen to proclaim its class, regional, and ethnic orientation fairly unambiguously. The specifically Andalusian character of flamenco is clear in its Arab-influenced modal melodies and melismatic vocal style, and in its combination, or juxtaposition, of European common-practice I-IV-V harmonies with progressions and chords that have evolved from modal origins (most notably, the familiar progression Am-G-F-E, in E Phrygian/major).[3] Within this framework, flamenco includes *cantes* (song-types) specifically associated with Gypsy origins (for example, *soleares, bulerías, siguiriyas*) and others derived from Andalusian non-Gypsy folk music (especially the *fandango* family). The Gypsy *cantes* are markedly more modal in flavor than the non-Gypsy ones, and thus modality per se is strongly associated with Gypsy identity. Also valued in flamenco are stylistic features specifically associated with Gypsies, such as raspy vocal timbre, sobbing-like falsetto breaks, and a generally strenuous, impassioned, and histrionic vocal style. The latter features have been interpreted as reflecting the sense of struggle and adversity so central to the Andalusian aesthetic and identity (Mercado 1982:91). Finally, in terms of its class character, it should be obvious that some of the most basic aspects of the flamenco aesthetic are antithetical to those of Western classical music, the music of the Spanish elite.

Flamenco style has changed dramatically over the last century, and its transformation can also be seen to reflect broader developments within Andalusian society in general. I have mentioned above that flamenco evolved as a product of the dialectic confrontation and interaction between Andalusian Gypsy and non-Gypsy societies. While private Gypsy fiestas have been an important context for flamenco since its inception, so have professional formats in which Gypsies earned money by performing flamenco for non-Gypsy patrons. Thus, professionalization has always constituted an important trend within flamenco, and one that has reached unprecedented heights in the twentieth century. Concomitant with this development has been the successive broadening of flamenco in image, audience, performer background, and style, from a purely Gypsy genre, to a regional, national, and finally, an international music. These developments have involved not only enhanced professionalization, but also what Brook Zern (personal communication) has referred to as the self-conscious "dignification" of flamenco by several of its performers. Nineteenth-century manifestations of this trend would include the introduction of a more polished and professional flamenco by Silverio Franconetti into bourgeois cabarets, and the adoption of the honorific "Don" by vocalist Antonio Chacón. In this century, the most renowned exponent of "dignification" has been vocalist Antonio Mairena (1909–1983), who, in his writings, lectures, performances, and general demeanor sought to refute the negative associations of flamenco as the debauched music of lazy and uncouth Gypsies (see esp. Mairena 1976). Meanwhile, the professional contexts of flamenco performance—large festivals, tourist-oriented *tablaos*, and formal concerts—have come to dominate the genre, which was once commonly heard informally in cafés and homes throughout urban Andalusia.

The professionalization and dignification of flamenco have dramatically affected flamenco style. While raspy vocal timbre continues to be appreciated, the flexible intonation standards evident in many older singers and recordings have tightened considerably; modern audiences, accustomed to other musics and to close scrutiny of recordings, appear to be less tolerant of vocalists who sing out of tune. Another development particularly prominent in the tourist-oriented *tablaos*, which employ the greatest number of flamenco artists, is the emphasis on dance. Knowing that tourists prefer dance to flamenco singing, *tablao* performers stress the former at the expense of the latter and include choreographed solo and group dance to *cantes* like *siguiriyas* which traditionally never accompanied dance.

A third stylistic change is the emergence of solo flamenco guitar as a concert art. While short guitar solos were not entirely unheard of in nineteenth-century *cafés-cantantes*, on the whole, the guitar in this period was used only for accompaniment, and guitar technique was relatively rudimentary, limited largely to strumming (*rasgueo*) and plucking with the thumb (*alzapua*). In the first half of the twentieth century, however, Ramón Montoya (d. 1949) popularized solo guitar performances and inspired many imitators; subsequent artists like Sabicas and Mario Escudero further formalized and "dignified" the art by playing precomposed, poetically named pieces rather than loose sequences of *falsetas* ("riffs" normally played between sung verses). A the same time, flamenco guitar technique became incomparably more complex and virtuosic, incorporating *picado* (single-note runs), tremolo, arpeggio, and a greatly enriched harmonic vocabulary. These trends have since culminated in the music of guitarist Paco de Lucía, who is generally described as having "revolutionized" a guitar idiom already in transition.

The rising standards of intonation and guitar virtuosity can be seen, on the one hand, as natural products of a maturing and dynamic art form. At the same time, however, they, and the unprecedented prominence of dance in the *tablaos*, reflect broader developments within Andalusian society. Flamenco's professionalization, which has brought the genre from the Gypsy and landlord *juerga* to the public stage, can be attributed in part to the extension of the market economy into previously informal sectors of Andalusian society. The advent of the mass media has also contributed to rising technical standards, as musicians since the 1930s have been accustomed to studying and imitating recordings. Finally, as we have suggested, flamenco's professionalization and stylistic advances can be seen to some extent as the products of a self-conscious desire to dignify the art and thereby enhance the image of Andalusia and its Gypsies. Andalusians, whether personally fond of flamenco or not, are highly conscious of the genre's national and international renown, and as such it forms a particularly important symbol of their identity.

Of course, there are many critics and aficionados who prefer the older, rougher, and allegedly more soulful styles of singing. Such traditionalists (including several guitarists) also tend to regard the solo concert guitar style as a sterile and dull idiom, on the grounds, first, that it lacks the spontaneity of traditional flamenco guitar accompaniment, and second, that the essence of flamenco is singing, with or without guitar backup. Hence, flamenco's supposed dignification is opposed by those who regard the genre not as an international abstract art form to be cultivated at will by Japanese and American enthusiasts, but as the expression of uniquely Andalusian conditions and sentiments. It is ironic, and yet not surprising, that "dignified" concert flamenco, in reaching out to a bourgeois and international audience, loses some of the characteristics which were most cherished and symbolically expressive to its native patrons. Musical development, like socioeconomic development, inevitably engenders new contradictions and controversies.

Flamenco Árabe

We may now turn to a particularly unusual, if not extraordinary musical phenomenon, that is, the various fusions of flamenco with Arab and Moroccan musics which a handful of flamenco artists have generated in the last decade. Since Spaniards do not speak Arabic and have shown no special interest in Arab music or culture for several centuries, the emergence of such hybrids (under the rubric *flamenco árabe*) would seem an unlikely event. In fact, as should be increasingly clear to the reader, attempts by flamenco musicians to reunite Andalusian and Arab cultures are quite natural in view of the contemporary sociocultural climate of southern Spain.

The first *flamenco árabe* excursions were those of Gypsy vocalists Lole Montoya and her mother, La Negra, who was born in Tetuán, formerly in Spanish Morocco. By the early 1970s these two became known for their settings of Arab songs to flamenco-style *cantes*. Lole, as part of the now disbanded duo Lole y Manuel, has pursued her Arab interest by performing, alongside her flamenco singing, contemporary Arab songs à la Umm Kulthum with Arab-style or flamenco accompaniment (for example, "Sangre gitana y mora"); her eclecticism reached new extremes in June 1987, when she included in her major concert a blues, sung in Arabic, accompanied by drums, bass, and flamenco-rock guitarists.

In the late 1970s, the Arab connection was pursued in another theatrical production of José Heredia Maya entitled "Macama Jonda." A musical narrating the marriage of a Gypsy and a Moor, "Macama [*maqāma*] Jonda" similarly matched flamenco singers and guitarists with a Moroccan Andalusian ensemble. (Moroccan art music derives from the Moorish court music which was transplanted to North Africa during and after the *reconquista*.) "Macama Jonda" adroitly juxtaposed and combined the two musics with a fairly even balance of emphasis. The blending is regarded by many as quite successful, in spite of the fact that the two musical systems do not really have much in common. Moroccan art music, unlike flamenco, is mostly precomposed, ensemble oriented, reserved in temperament, and strictly monophonic and modal (*maqām*-based).

In the wake of "Macama Jonda," during the mid-1980s there followed a derivative and soon-forgotten imitation ("Diquela de la Alhambra") and, more important, a set of recordings and concerts by Juan Peña, also fusing flamenco with a Moroccan Andalusian ensemble from Tangiers. Like Heredia Maya's production, Peña's show both juxtaposed and synthesized the two musics, the combinations consisting of flamenco singing over Moroccan background music, or flamenco *cantes* accompanied by guitars and Moroccan-style percussion and violin; song texts (for example, "Dáme la libertad"—Give Me Freedom) were oriented toward Gypsy themes and reality.

One might think that such hybrids could never constitute more than a marginal curiosity on the Andalusian music scene, especially considering that Moroccan art music can barely be regarded as commercially viable in its own homeland. Time will tell, of course, whether these musical excursions will have any lasting impact, but at present, the commercial success of these ventures, however marginal they may be, has been considerable. In particular, the recordings of Peña and Lole y Manuel (which also contain traditional flamenco) have been among the best-selling Andalusian flamenco-based cassettes in recent years.

Part of the explanation for their popularity, if the author may hazard a subjective value judgment, is that Peña's and Heredia Maya's experiments are quite tasteful and enjoyable as music. It is clear, however, that much of the appeal of *flamenco árabe* rests on the extramusical significance of the subgenre. *Flamenco árabe* represents a reaffirmation of Andalusia's distinct cultural heritage in the form of a celebration of its Moorish ties. At the same time it may be seen as a willful renunciation of the economic and political domination imposed over the centuries by Madrid, whose monarchs traditionally regarded Arabs as heathen enemies and Andalusians as suspect by virtue of their Moorish past. It seems that autonomous Andalusia, free at last from repression imposed by despotic kings and dictators, is finally able to attempt to reclaim aspects of its erstwhile cosmopolitan cultural richness. *Flamenco árabe*, in a word, represents much more than an eccentric musical experiment. The appeal of the subgenre also illustrates how musical *style* can function as an important symbol and vehicle of social identity, for the celebration of Andalusia's distinct heritage in *flamenco árabe*'s form as well as its text content.

Flamenco Pop

Despite the wealth of scholarly and journalistic attention focused in recent decades on flamenco, the genre cannot claim mass popularity; the extent and, in some ways, the character of its appeal are perhaps comparable to those of jazz in the United States, with Andalusian folk music and blues constituting comparably broader traditional sources. Hence, flamenco is better classified as an urban folk music rather than a true popular music, if we define the latter as music whose evolution is inextricably associated with the mass media and its production on a mass basis for sale as a commodity.

Commercialized pop forms of flamenco, however, have existed since the 1930s, and record companies often insisted that their flamenco singers record such lighter, more accessible pieces (see, for example, Mairena 1976:106–107). It was not until the early 1960s, however, that a flamenco-related popular music emerged that has gained a truly mass audience and, at the same time, come to serve as a vehicle for the expression of some of the same ideologies which animate traditional and modern flamenco.

The development of pop flamenco can be seen as a product of the social, cultural, political, and economic factors which have shaped contemporary flamenco in general. The flamenco boom of recent decades has been one obvious stimulant, engendering in its wake a variety of derivative subgenres. The expansion of the mass media—particularly cassettes and radio—has further promoted the flowering of syncretic musics.[4] Political freedom has also removed a substantial impediment to the spread of popular youth musics; for example, while the Franco regime was hardly able to ban rock, it regarded such music as degenerate and corrupting and strictly circumscribed its transmission on the mass media. Indeed, such was the insularity of the *dictadura* that it banned the Mexican *corrido* "La Cucaracha" because of its whimsical reference to marijuana.

More important catalysts in the development of flamenco pop have been the related phenomena of urbanization and the mass migration of proletarianized Andalusians to Barcelona and Madrid. In Spain, as throughout the world, the process of urbanization has generated new social classes with new social, cultural, and aesthetic needs and outlooks. A natural product of such situations is the rise of syncretic popular musics which fuse tradition and modernity, and local and imported elements. In the case of Andalusian society, as we have seen, the urbanization process has been accompanied by an economically induced diaspora, leading to the growth of a substantial urban subculture of transplanted southerners in the lower-class barrios of Barcelona, Madrid, and elsewhere. It is this subculture that has given birth to the various hybrids of flamenco, rock, and Cuban music which have become among the most vital components of the Spanish musical scene.

In purely musical terms, the influence of Cuban popular music has also constituted an important stimulus of modern flamenco pop. The Cuban *rumba* (or, more properly, the *son*), had been incorporated, in stylized form, as a light flamenco *cante chico* in the early twentieth century, and it enjoyed particular popularity, along with the *fandango*, in flamenco's lean decades of the 1940s and 1950s. Spanish *rumba* as a commercial entity first emerged in the 1960s, when a Catalonian Gypsy, Peret (Pedro Pubill Calaf) popularized a rather crude fusion of rock rhythm and instrumentation, Cuban refrain patterns, and, occasionally, flamenco-like harmonies and guitar backing. By the early 1970s, the *rumba catalán* had assumed a more definitive shape in the music of groups like Las Grecas, Los Chunguitos, and Los Chichos, whose members consisted mostly of first- or second-generation Gypsy migrants from the south.

While the *rumba catalán* germinated in the barrios of Barcelona, it has nothing to do with Catalonian music. Further, it is much closer in rhythm and instrumentation to rock than to *rumba*. It does, however, bear some affinities to the flamenco-style *rumba* in its Andalusian harmonic progressions, simple instrumental arrangements, and, occasionally, vocal style. In most cases, however, songs are rendered by two voices, in unison, in a more or less straightforward and dispassionate style.

In the early 1970s the flamenco pop scene diversified somewhat. Particularly influential have been the eclectic experiments of the brilliant guitarist Paco de Lucía, often in collaboration with star Gypsy vocalist Camarón de la Isla. Lucía's pop-flavored instrumental *rumbas* (for example, "Entre dos aguas") and *tangos* (which he records alongside more traditional flamenco) have inspired many imitators and have come to constitute a sui generis pop substyle.

In Paco de Lucía's wake has flowered a variety of eclectic fusions of flamenco with more commercial rock, disco, and *canción* (sentimental ballad). Perhaps the most popular exponent of flamenco rock since the early 1980s has been Malagan vocalist Tijeritas, whose music reflects a greater influence of disco and, at the same time, a closer orientation with flamenco in its harmonic vocabulary and intense, impassioned vocal style.

In accordance with the flamenco associations of such music, much flamenco pop remains rooted in Gypsy society, both in terms of performers and the core audience. This association is often made explicit in song texts through references to Gypsies—hence the terms *rock gitano* (Gypsy rock) and *poder gitano* (Gypsy power) to denote such musics. More indirectly, many songs celebrate Gypsy values of freedom and hostility to authority; others relate the alienation and marginalization which have beset Gypsy society as never before in recent decades, when unemployment has erased many of the gains made by assimilating working-class Gypsies in the 1950s and 1960s. As such conditions increasingly extend to lower-class non-Gypsies, so does the audience of this music spread to non-Gypsy Andalusians throughout the country.

While most songs deal with sentimental love, commentators tend to recognize as particularly significant and representative the songs relating the harsh realities of barrio life, i.e., unemployment, drug addiction, delinquency, and a general sense of alienation and marginalization.[5] The mid-1980s hit of Los Chichos, "Vagando por ahí," is typical:

Tienes diez y ocho años y estás cansado de vivir
Porque el mundo en el que vives no te puede hacer feliz . . .
Por un poco de dinero con qualquiera tú te vas
De noche y de día vagando por ahí
No sabes lo que hacer, no tienes donde ir
El mundo te olvidó, ¿qué va a ser de ti?

You're eighteen years old and tired of living
Because the world in which you live can't make you happy . . .

For a little money you'll hang out with anyone
Wandering about night and day
You don't know what to do or where to go
The world has forgotten you—what will become of you?

Such song texts should not be seen simply as passive expressions of social reality but as active participants in the formation of a new urban identity. Via mass dissemination, pop flamenco has become an important symbol of the new urban Andalusian consciousness; amid the complexities of modern barrio life, it serves as an arena of contention, a field of negotiation and mediation for the interlocking dialectics of tradition and modernity, corporate control and grassroots culture, indigenous roots and imported trends, proletarian and elite societies, and Gypsy and non-Gypsy identities.

In a more abstract, but no less effective sense does pop flamenco *style* serve to embody and mediate these dialects of modern Andalusian society. Regardless of one's verdict on the merit of such music, its fusions, whether felicitous or artificial, of old and new, of Andalusian and foreign elements, and of commercial formulae and spontaneous populist elements serve to influence and articulate aspects of modern urban social identity; in its own way, flamenco pop style, like that of music in general, can constitute a symbol whose effectiveness derives from its very indirectness, its ability to convey meaning through abstract suggestions rather than prosaic argument.

Nueva Canción Andaluza

The musical genre which addresses most explicitly Andalusia's current ideological ferment is *nueva canción andaluza* (Andalusian new song). This music, like its counterpart in Latin America, Catalonia, and elsewhere, is specifically committed to the expression of sociopolitical sentiments through the medium of song. While a leftist perspective underlies much *nueva canción andaluza*, its main themes are the specific problems of southern Spain which have been discussed above. Such themes as emigration, unemployment, and urban alienation have, of course, become common in flamenco and pop flamenco, as well as other genres like *sevillanas* and the folk *tangos* and *pasodobles* of the Cádiz carnival. *Nueva canción* differs from these genres in its core audience—a relatively small group of students and activists—and in the styles that it encompasses. Despite the genre's anticommercial ethos, much of it may be said to resemble mainstream Western commercial soft rock or even sentimental pop ballads in style. Indeed, like much Latin American *nueva canción*, Andalusian new song may be said to be essentially bourgeois in style—as well as in the constitution of its audience. However, a specifically Andalusian or flamenco flavor does enliven some *nueva canción andaluza* (especially, for example, the music of Miguel López); the use of such stylistic elements is clearly self-conscious and intended to express regional solidarity. Leading exponents of the genre (López, Carlos Cano, Pepe Suero, and others) tend to sing relatively highbrow poetry, generally at relatively small concerts, but occasionally at larger events such as the 1978 "Festival of Andalusian Emigration" in Madrid.[6] While the genre cannot claim mass popularity, it appears to be generally respected, and it does reflect the politicization of the Andalusian intelligentsia.

Conclusions

It may seem anomalous to hear and read of an Andalusian "crisis" at a time when the region's level of autonomy and standard of living are dramatically higher than they have been for several centuries. But more important than such factors in terms of the nature and coalescence of regional identity are the heritage of prolonged poverty and oppression, the state's unfulfilled economic *potential*, and above all, the *perception* that Andalusia is exploited and neglected and that its culture is being debilitated by emigration, political impotence, and marginalization. For many Andalusian intellectuals, the cultural and socioeconomic predicaments are closely linked, as are the autonomy and socialist movements. Envisioned both as a tool and as a crucial goal in itself is the development of new, revitalized forms of Andalusian culture—forms which are at once nonelite and distinct from those of northern and central Spain (see, for example, Vázquez Medel 1980:332–333) and which reclaim the region's rich cultural heritage while at the same time adapting to the realities of a modern, predominantly urban society.

Since music, and particularly flamenco, have traditionally been the most renowned of Andalusian arts, it is not surprising that the course of modern flamenco and its derivatives should be of special visibility and importance in the region and that flamenco should play a particularly prominent part in the promulgation of a heightened Andalusian identity. This importance is reflected on literary and bureaucratic levels by the profusion of recent literature (much of it published by the state government) that is devoted to flamenco, regional identity, and, often, the relation between the two; the special role and contribution of Gypsies in Andalusian society, and particularly in flamenco, are important subsidiary themes in these discussions.

For their part, flamenco singers, now as always, have used their music as a vehicle for the expression of social reality as well as of more conventional romantic themes. Thus, both the work of flamencologists like Félix Grande and the music of artists like José Domínguez can be said to be aimed at reestablishing flamenco's legacy as a mouthpiece of the full spectrum of Andalusian sentiments—including but going well beyond the romantic love which dominated the distorted flamenco of the opera and, to some extent, the cabarets.

Meanwhile, a different sort of visibility and importance is enjoyed by the varieties of flamenco-related popular musics that have arisen in recent decades with the advent of political freedom, the mass media, regional autonomy, and external musical influences. All these musics at once influence and have been shaped by the cluster of interlocking ideologies—especially autonomy, socialism, and Gypsy identity—that address the problems of Andalusian underdevelopment, emigration, and alienation. In some cases, as in *nueva canción*, the conveyance of sociopolitical messages is deliberate and explicit in song texts; in other cases, as in *flamenco árabe* and most *rock gitano*, it is the general nature and style of the music in question that reflect its social context and, by extension, the dialectical forces shaping contemporary identity.

While all music can be said to reflect social identity in one way or another, the relation between Andalusian identity and the flamenco complex of musics should be particularly intimate and visible. The task of articulating this relationship acquires special importance because of previous and pervasive efforts to obfuscate or deny it. The widespread traditional misconception of Gypsies as merry and carefree hedonists has been one unfortunate product of the popular misunderstanding of flamenco. A more deliberate and cynical misrepresentation was the prolonged attempt by Franco to use a sterilized image of flamenco to present, for foreigners as well as Spaniards themselves, as picture of an idyllic Spain engrossed in joyous music and dance (see Heredia Maya 1977). Ortega y Gasset's warped idealization of Andalusian life was equally obscurantist in this regard (see Comin 1985:41–42). Finally, formalistic studies by bourgeois musicologists have often distorted the social significance of music by implying that the musical meaning resides primarily, or even solely, in its internal structure. A study of contemporary flamenco and its derivatives should well illustrate how music can be at once a product of and an active influence upon the formation of social identity in general.

NOTES

1. From Ortiz Nuevo 1985:137.
2. See introduction by J. Heredia Maya to the LP by the same name (EDX 73308).
3. For further discussion of flamenco harmony, see Manuel 1986.
4. Only since the advent of democracy have a few private radio stations (in Barcelona) been officially tolerated by the state. While records are still widely marketed, they are now by far outnumbered by cassettes, whether of multinational subsidiaries or smaller local firms.
5. For further discussion of these themes, and of contemporary Spanish popular music in general, see Ordovás 1986:298–309, and Manuel 1988, chapter 4.
6. See Claudín 1981:272–279 for further discussion of *nueva canción andaluza*.

REFERENCES

Claudín, Victor
    1981 *Canción de autor en España*. N.p.: Jucar.
Comin, Alfonso
    1985 *Noticia de Andalucía*. Seville: Biblioteca de la Cultura Andaluza.
Drillon, Lilyane, et al.
    1975 *Quejío: Informe*. Barcelona: Ediciones Demofilo.
Grande, Félix
    1979 *Memoria del flamenco*. 2 vols. Madrid: Espasa-Calpe.
Heredia Maya, José
    1977 *Camelamos Naquerar*. Disc and notes. EDX 73308.

Mairena, Antonio
1976   *Las Confesiones de Antonio Mairena*. Seville: University of Seville.
Manuel, Peter
1986   "Evolution and Structure in Flamenco Harmony." *Current Musicology* 42:46–57.
1988   *Popular Musics of the Non-Western World: An Introductory Survey*. New York: Oxford University Press.
Mercado, José
1982   *La seguidilla gitana*. Madrid: Taurus Ediciones.
Molina, Ricardo
1985   *Misterios del arte flamenco*. Seville: Biblioteca de la Cultura Andaluza.
Ordovás, Jesús
1986   *Historia de la música pop española*. Madrid: Alianza Universidad.
Ortiz Nuevo, José Luis
1985   *Pensamiento político en el cante flamenco*. Seville: Biblioteca de la Cultura Andaluza.
Pérez de Guzmán, Torcuato
1982   *Los gitanos herreros de Sevilla*. Seville: Biblioteca de la Cultura Andaluza.
San Román, Teresa, ed.
1986   *Entre la marginación y el racismo: reflexiones sobre la vida de los gitanos*. Madrid: Alianza Universidad.
Urbano Pérez, Manuel
1980   *Pueblo y política en el cante jondo*. Seville: Servicio de Publicaciones de Ayuntamiento de Sevilla.
Vázquez Medel, Manuel
1980   "Una cultura y un pueblo reclaman las riendas de su futuro," in *Hacia una Andalucía libre*, 331–334. Seville: Edisur.

SOCIAL ORGANIZATION

American Roma and the Ideology of Defilement (1975)

Carol Miller

The ideology of defilement, or *marime* as defilement is called in Romani, pervades the most important categories of belief and thought among the Roma. It extends to all areas of life in some way, underwriting a hygienic attitude toward the world, themselves, and others. Pollution ideas work on the life of society, especially in the sense of symbolizing certain dangers and expressing a general view of the social order. Lines are drawn between the Gypsy and the non-Gypsy, the clean and the unclean, health and disease, the good and the bad, which are made obvious and visible through the offices of ritual avoidance.

The map upon which these lines are portrayed is the human body itself, certain areas of which are designated as sanctified and pure, notably the head and mouth and, in somewhat lesser degree, the entire upper body region. Rites of purification and separation protect the auspicious power associated with the upper region and, the Roma believe, the health and well-being of the person performing them. Items that come into contact with these areas are separately maintained, washed in running water or special basins and stored apart from ordinary items; items like soaps, towels, razors and combs,[1] clothes, pillows, furniture like the backs of chairs, the tops of tables, tablecloths, aprons, sinks, food utensils and, of course, food itself, which is prepared, served, and eaten with the greatest consideration for ritual quality. Body orifices that give access to the inner body are defensively guarded, some from further pollution and some from any pollution at all. Because the process of ingestion breaches the margins of the inviolate body area, eating is a delicate and closely regulated matter. Numerous rituals of avoidance dramatize the different character and what the Roma understand to be the naturally disparate and opposing functions of the two body areas. Any contact between the lower half of the body, particularly the genitals, which are conceptually the ultimate source of *marime*, and the upper body is forbidden. The inward character of the genitals, especially the female genitalia which are associated with the mysteries of blood and birth, makes them consummately impure.[2] Items and surfaces that have contact with this area are carefully segregated because they contain a dangerous potential to the status of pure items and surfaces. The most dreadful contact, of course, would be between the genitals and the oral cavity.[3] Every precaution is taken to increase spatial and temporal distance between these.

Under normal circumstances, the status of the adult body areas is conceptualized as relatively permanent and stable. Ritual separation is assumed to maintain the purity of one, by containing the impurity of the other. The transitional status of the hands, whose qualities can be improved by rinsing under running water and washing with "face" soaps and towels, permits the hands the necessary task of ministering to both body regions. In order to bring the hands into consonance with the goodness of the upper body and to avoid injury to this goodness, washing ritual is performed with regularity after contaminating contact with the lower body[4] and before preparing food or handling the religious icons.

During certain progressive periods of the life cycle, the ratio of purity/impurity is automatically altered. At birth, the infant is regarded as *marime* upon the entire body surface because of the polluting nature of the site of recent origin. The mother, owing to her intensive contact with the infant, is also thought to be dangerously impure. Both are isolated for a period of time that varies from the three days of post-partum hospitalization to several weeks if there are other family members to assume the household duties of washing and cooking. Subsequent to this period, the infant, and later the child, is not *marime* at all[5] although, as much of the child's contact is with the floor and other polluting surfaces, the Roma recognize the logical inconsistency of this singular condition by admitting that "he [or she] should be." Children are believed to be blameless to sin, including defilement, because they are new and innocent, and not yet fully aware of the consequences of their deeds. Their purity tends to ameliorate defiling contacts; they are usually forgiven if they come to the table without washing and are permitted many freedoms of speech and movement that the adults of the family are denied.[6]

Innocence ends with marriage, which properly activates the full capacity for pollution. At the same time, these powers are contained by the complementary structure of marital roles and responsibilities. Marriage is the *rite de passage* to adulthood. A girl becomes a Romni with marriage, a woman and a wife; a boy becomes a Rom, a man and husband.[7]

For one group of Roma, the Machvaia of California, an important aspect of their adult responsibilities involves segregating the two sexes as well as the two body areas. The etiquette of respect-avoidance restrains and minimizes cross-sex contact between Machvaia of adult status and gives additional opportunity for expression of belief in the superior qualities of ritual purity by "putting a face on things." Even the married couple are respectful and decorous in approaching one another; they are not allowed to touch or display affection overtly, either in public or at home in front of their children. Among the many proscriptions upon association, they were, until recently, prevented from eating together; to remark the difference in purity, privilege, and authority, men ate first and were served by their wives, their daughters, or their daughters-in-law.[8]

Innocence is gradually regained, in some measure, with old age, a stage in the life cycle considered as spiritually elevated. The *phurotem*, the elders, are close to the gods and the ancestors, a condition of great gravity and potential danger to the living. Avoidance is publicly augmented in order to show the *phurotem* a respect consistent with their advancing years. As the powers of purity increase, the powers of impurity would seem to be in decline. Because they do not bear children or menstruate, old women no longer have the power to defile men by "tossing the skirt" (see note 18). The *phurotem* themselves are not criticized for slighting avoidance. Old men of decent reputation can flirt with young women without being chastised.

Under normal circumstances adult men and women, as well as children and *phurotem*, are assumed to be reasonably clean, the latter because of their innocence and presumed lack of interest in heterosexual contact,[9] the former because they are careful to confine their contact to the appropriate connubial time and place. The burden of avoidance obligation rests with adult Roma, who are at the most dangerous and most endangered stage of life. It is apparent from the changing intensities of power and danger at various stages, infant, child, adult, and elder, that the ritual separation of the body areas, upper from lower, inner from outer, and male from female, has a primary function to the control of sexual behavior and that sexual desires are conceptualized as potentially threatening. Improper sexual contacts spread shame and defilement through the kin group. They are frequently contacts that Roma regard as bordering upon the incestuous because they involve couples whose status is inappropriate to sexual contact, for example, a Rom and his daughter-in-law (see Appendix, Case 5) or a couple related in *chivrimos* (co-godparenthood), a sacred relationship that is protective to the health and well-being of the godchild.

Relationships between a Rom or Romni and a non-Gypsy also join what should not be joined and offend ideas regarding appropriate sexual union (see Appendix, Cases 2 and 3). Sanction is applied discriminately to males and females. Upon occasion a Rom marries a non-Gypsy woman, has children and, over a period of years, is permitted to return to public life and public favor as a married man. His wife may even be treated with tolerance. The Machvaia, however, don't permit marriage to non-Gypsies. Among traditional Roma, the Romni is never allowed this privilege. A Romni has the burden of responsibility for the purity of the race, and is vulnerable to irreparable damage by contact of such kind. Parents are said to forget the name of a daughter who marries a non-Gypsy.

A girl who marries "outside" is described as running away. Runaways are theoretically ruined "forever." They lose their rights as Rom citizens and are denied access to their families. Their parents, however, are normally too softhearted to conform to the letter of the law, and daughters are gradually reinstated after they have left their non-Gypsy husbands, presented medical evidence clearing them of any trace of venereal infection, and demonstrated remorse.[10] The punishment is likely to encourage their remorse. The girl is often married off at a low price to the first family that asks for her, a family that may be poor and lower class.

The *gaje*, as the Roma call non-Gypsies, are conceived as a different race and kind of being whose main value is economic and whose raison d'être is to trouble the Roma. The major offense of the *gaje*, the one offense that the Roma can never forgive, is their propensity to defilement. *Gaje* confuse the critical distinction between the pure and the impure. They are observed in various situations which the Roma regard as compromising: forgetting to wash in public bathrooms; eating with the fork that they rescued from the floor of the restaurant; washing face towels and tablecloths with underwear at the local self-service laundry; relaxing with their feet resting upon the top surface of the table. Because they do not protect the upper half, the head and mouth, from damage, the *gaje* are construed as *marime* all over, head to foot. This condition, according to belief, invites and spreads contagious disease. Roma tend to think of all illness and physical disability as communicable and to treat them accordingly. The classic disease that the *gaje* convey is venereal disease. This is not limited to sexual contact. The Rom that eats with *gaje* or works for them is usually libeled as *marime* by some segment of the community. Theories of disease dictate a castelike separation of the two kinds of people, Gypsy and *gaje*, along a spectrum of opposition that is analogous to the distinction that is made between upper and lower. In either case, the danger of one must be contained to protect the power of the other. Consequently, with the exception of the most expedient and profane of circumstances, making money or by reason of economic necessity, the *gaje* are forbidden contact or association.[11]

Categories of thought that rank the *gaje* as inferior in the many attributes associated with purity and health have an obvious advantage to the bolstering of pride and self-respect.[12] By believing in the protection of a power that is equivalent, or greater, the Roma make symbolic defense against the inroads of the larger and politically more powerful society. Centuries of persecution and abuse, including a long period of enslavement, have been documented. In most European countries, Gypsies are historically the lowest-status group. Beliefs about defilement promote feelings of self-worth. As a result, despite a sometimes demeaning life situation, morale is maintained at a favorable level. When a Romni is arrested for telling fortunes or a family is forced to move because the landlord has discovered that ten children, instead of the two or three expected, are living in one house, the aggravation can be lessened by a counteroffensive of verbal abuse in Romani concerning the appearance of the skin, the odor, moral character, and personal habits of the *gaje*.

For a variety of reasons, business and social, the majority of Roma prefer to live in the context of the city or in towns that approximate to large urban centers.[13] The urban world is perceived as pervasively *marime*, filled with items and surfaces that are subject to use and reuse by careless *gaje*, polluted, diseased, and therefore dangerous. In making their way through this unfavorable environment, they are forced by their circumstances to rely much upon the appearance of surfaces in gauging their merit. Roma prefer to shop in stores, rent houses, and travel in cars that "look clean," because, hopefully, they are. Ritual precaution and proscriptions serve as perpetual reminder to the rules of dissociation, however. A Rom who is working away from his home washes his face and hands whenever he feels his luck leaving him during the day; he washes again upon returning from his work. Children are normally not allowed to play with *gaje* children; they are even less likely to be allowed to bring a *gajo* child into their home. Animal, vegetable, or mineral, whatever crosses the doorstep is carefully scrutinized. Only articles that are newly manufactured or freshly grown are considered entirely safe. Even so, those things that can be washed are subject to thorough cleansing; food, including meat, is most notable in this regard.

The home is the final bastion of defense against defilement and the only place that the Roma feel entirely at ease. For the religious holidays that relate to the *slava* feast of southeastern Europe, a section of the house is transformed into a church. The saints, who are "up," are supplicated for the good health and well-being, *sastimos*, and good luck, *baxt*, that forms the simple central theme of ritual and doctrine. On these occasions the appropriate condition of the house, the inhabitants, and the table, is as close to an immaculate condition as is attainable by measures that the people know, namely, washing and scrubbing, sewing new covers for furniture and beds, replacing draperies, rugs, and dishes, painting. In a degree depending upon the family's social standing or social aspirations, ordinary household maintenance will also require similar improvement efforts. Purchase and replacement is laborious and costly if the family is particularly mobile; only the wealthy are able to move often and present an estimable household appearance; usually the wealthy, for some of these same reasons, fall high on the scale of purity and respect.[14] The moral worth of the Romni is supposedly incremented in proportion to her efforts to fight dirt and decay, and she makes a good public impression if she appears continually engaged in these sanitary activities. She makes an even better impression if she can sit and talk with guests while food and beverage are served, and the house is impeccably maintained by a bevy of unobtrusive and obedient daughters-in-law.

The household is open to hospitality visits from other Roma; at any time of the day or night neighbors or travelers may drop in and, in this sense, the home and its occupants are always on display. A place that looks new and fresh is associated with people who look healthy and good. These are ranked as more prestigious on the scale of purity and social value than people and houses that appear neglected or disordered. For reasons of contagion, the latter are avoided by upper-class Rom who express their distaste by complaining of feeling unlucky, upset, or nauseated after visiting them. Complaints of this kind are also frequent when Roma eat with *gaje* in restaurants.

Wherever food is served, at home or in public, the delicacy of feelings toward the process of ingestion is indicated by ease of insult. It is important that commensal conditions be favorable. Food in *gaje* restaurants will go untouched or be thrown away if the atmosphere is strange, the room is crowded, or the food is suspect. Well-lighted restaurants where the food preparation can be easily observed are preferred. Among Machvaia, coffee is somewhat of a fetish: if the cup and saucer, the taste, the cream, and so forth, are inadequate in any way, the people refuse to drink it. These same beliefs and feelings are closely associated with customs of hospitality. With fellow Rom, the eating situation is *ideally* relaxed and unstrained because the kitchen is presumably maintained according to standards for purity and the company is ritually correct.

In addition to everyday hospitality events, the Roma come together for socio-ceremonial occasions which involve feasting and special foods. The *pomana* offers a table for the dead and invites them to eat in heaven, even as the company assembled eats at the same table. The *slava* feast is preceded by coffee and prayer; a candle coaxes the saint in the direction of the commensal table. The *slava* foods include the auspicious foods, *sarmaa* (cabbage rolls), *gushvada* (cheese strudel), as well as one of the following: a ritually sacrificed lamb, a young pig, or a large baked fish. At ceremonial events, the eating is less important than an ample presentation for all attending to see. Machvaia believe generosity brings luck. A stingy feast is expected to please no one, including the supernatural guests.

Good food in generous amounts is congruent with good health. Until recently, when a number of the fat Machvaia died from heart attacks in their prime, the size of a man was the measure of his strength, power, and wealth. The word for "big man," *baro* (or "big woman," *bari*) suggests corporeal size as well as political importance. Just as they are in most societies, nurturance and affection are expressed through gifts of food. When greeting an intimate, the most popular inquiry is to ask whether or not she or he ate that day, and what. The expression has a practical basis. Those middle-aged and older have memories of many days when food was unobtainable. They report that nothing is harder for parents to endure than the sound of children crying from hunger. Lack of food is associated with bad living, bad luck, poverty, and disease; if people lose weight, even if the weight loss is reasonable from the standpoint of Western medical norms, the presumption is that they have been sick. It is entirely appropriate at such times for the public to express concern about what is considered lack of appetite or a shortage of food, either of which may portend failing health. Food is recognized as the most basic human need. Hunger is feared and ungratified appetite is dangerous. Supernatural sanctions are associated with these concerns. People who don't get what they want to eat become *postarniko*, obsessed by their need to taste a particular food that they have recently seen and have in their mind. *Postarniko* people can get sick, die, and become the ghosts that will haunt the living. The dream of a dead relative asking for food is especially fearful and requires heroic appeasement with food offerings and fasting.

Commensality makes an important statement concerning altruistic attitudes toward other Roma, as well as the purity and equivalent respect of those who eat together. These are linked to the good health and vitality of the community-at-large as is particularly apparent upon socio-ceremonial occasions. Rituals of commensality work upon the body politic through the symbolic medium of the physical body. The act of eating together conjoins communion with the Romani public, with generations that are gone and generations yet unborn. The living are reminded of their common destiny and their obligation to guard the strength, unity, and goodness of the corporate unit from damage. The work is done by the women but the ritual of commensality is primarily the business of males. Men represent their families at all public affairs and are responsible for their families' protection as well as being answerable to the public for their offenses. The men meet at the table as equals in respect and privilege, none with more power than the other except by reason of the increased spirituality associated with age. As has been indicated, food is a primary medium of *marime* and disease. It is consumed with equanimity in the company of responsible and congenial Roma. Eating together denotes trust. The presence of one disgraced or sickly Rom at the commensal table is believed to be polluting to the rest. Each Rom has the same potential for damage to the others in these regards. On the other hand, the proper sensibility for custom is demonstrated by always accepting food that is offered by those people in good repute.[15]

In addition, commensality makes important statements about the distinction between the Rom and the *gaje*, the inner and the outer group, by emphasizing commensal separation. The minority standing and vulnerability of the smaller society in the context of the larger, the need for protection and for unity, is reflected in exaggerated concern with the exits and entrances of the human body. Proscriptions on contact provide focus to fears of political absorption; behaviors most apt to betrayal—eating and making love with the *gaje*—are subject to penalty by law. To remark the difference, Rom do not eat in *gaje* homes; they offer *gaje* hospitality in their own homes by service from china and eating utensils that are specially washed and segregated from other household items.

As is typical with many small-scale societies, gossip and scandal are a main source of social control, and public opinion is continually engaged in sifting reputations through the exacting sieve of Gypsy norms and values. A Rom, fallen into disrepute for any reason, for example, if his daughter has run away, is liable to commensal isolation. He may learn of his disgraced condition when his hostess presents him old coffee in a cracked cup or fails to serve him when everyone else is served. Worse, he may suspect that he has been drinking coffee from the cup reserved for the *gaje*. Treatment like the *gaje* indicates that the Rom is graded low on the scale of purity and respect, that he is dirty, disreputable, diseased, in fact *marime*.[16]

The crimes of *marime* are moral crimes, or "shames." These damage the cherished image of the body politic, even as they threaten the carefully enlisted powers of *sastimos*. According to belief, the attributes of a good life, health, wealth, and happiness are locked into clean and moral family living.[17] Shames join what should not be joined and upset the recognized order of events, so that calamity visits the family in a form of *sastimos* reversed, illness, loss of money, bad luck, unhappiness, insanity, even death. Most vulnerable to these supernatural sanctions are the children of the extended family. For these reasons, whenever shames of any size become public knowledge, in order to protect the family and to stem the tide of unpropitious events, the agent of the shame is labeled as *marime* and dangerous.

In this context, the stigma of *marime* is understood by the Roma as an official state of social disgrace. The stigma serves social ends as a kind of impersonal punishment for wrongdoing. Because they have a public status that women lack and because of their superior ritual purity, men are the primary focus of *marime* sanction. The Rom *marime* is outcast from social and political affairs. To remove the stigma and restore respect, the Rom is compelled to face his accusers—the women are invariably represented by men—and make public denial or public redress. In cases of *marime*, pollution taboos buttress and supplement a serious shortage of punitive sanctions. The court, which otherwise would be limited to an advisory and counseling capacity, is provided the means for redress of moral crimes through the offices of ritual avoidance.

Beliefs about purity/defilement are associated with standards of morality/immorality, but not in a one-to-one relationship. Moral situations are not always easy to define, whereas pollution rules are unequivocal. An interesting example of how these can work together to social purpose when ordinary means have failed is the sanction of skirt-tossing, a power for penalty by pollution afforded to women. Skirt-tossing creates a scandal that focuses public gossip upon disputes and inequities. The method is simple. Anything having contact with the lower female body, traditionally the underskirt, is deliberately juxtaposed upon the upper and saintly extremity of the Rom.[18] When news of the event reaches the community, the Rom is ostracized. It is traditionally his responsibility to call the court together that will help him clear his name. If the Rom is found guilty, the court recommends public apology, the payment of a fine, or a period of isolation. If the Rom complies with the court's decision, the Romni forgives him by admitting that the skirt-tossing story was fictional. This admission is essential to the peaceful settlement of the case. The Roma do not know any purifying ritual that will cleanse a man's head, the nexus of respect and honor, of such impurity. In fact, skirt-toss *marime* "never happens . . . it's a lie [because] if she really did it, he's out . . . no one could eat with that family forever . . . generations."

In keeping with Romani ideology, social isolation is expressed, in large part, by commensal isolation. *Marime* status extends to the household and, if the Rom is suspected of having eaten with them, the extended family. Even distant relatives become somewhat apprehensive about commensal refusal and hesitate to visit other households. Until the slander is forgotten or publicly forgiven, any uncertainty about the legitimacy of respect status in the community is apt to result, according to the relationship with the Rom *marime*, in a variable degree of withdrawal from public life. Because kinsmen are affected, they will encourage the Rom to a quick settlement of the case.

Processes of ingestion have been described as portraying political incorporation. The ritual of reinstatement is, appropriately, the ritual of commensality. The decision of the court is expressed in a similar manner; those voting for the defendant will drink coffee with him: those voting against will not. The subsequent gossip that circulates through the community is tailored, and retailored, to agree with various viewpoints about the proceedings and the temper of personal relationships with the defendant. The important piece of information, for those not participating in the trial, is whether or not the Roma ate or drank with the defendant before they left the courtroom.

According to the best reports available, the sanction of *marime* has been applied locally in the following situations and with the following kinds of results during the past eight years (see Appendix). The relevant population of approximately 1,000 encompasses four of the major cities in the northwest United States. In four of the cases mentioned (2, 3, 5,

6), the elders were involved in the decision-making process, either in a proper *kris romani*, with the members of several families represented, or as a smaller, more informal discussion group. In only one instance did the court agree upon a finite period of isolation (6). Two of the defendants have chosen to live elsewhere (1, 5). Half of the cases involved *gaje*, or problems with outsiders; the other half related to internal affairs exclusively. Of the former, cases involving outsiders, isolation continued in two until the defendants desired reinstatement and made conciliatory overtures to the public. (2, 3).[19]

The cases studied are few (only six). The record clearly indicates that the inflexibility of pollution beliefs is easily adapted to a variable punishment that fits court and community decisions regarding the nature of the crime and possibilities for settlement and reconciliation. The sanction's clear intention in the context of "keeping Gypsies good to other Gypsies" is to modify behavior, not to outcast indefinitely.

The formality of isolation is, of course, only a small part of the penalty. Most humiliating is that lower-status Roma and despised enemies gain ascendancy over the *marime* family and that the extended family is subject to slights and contemptuous treatment by other Roma. Further, the period of isolation that the court specifies only begins the penalty. The shame lasts as long as the memories of the living, to follow the family wherever they travel. Even unsubstantiated rumors, if they become popular and are repeated often, can have a sinister effect upon a family's reputation.

The standards for propriety are high, and the reputation of the family is, in large part, the history of their scandals. But families are also ranked along parameters of a more immediate kind—the clean appearance of the household, the skill with which hospitality ritual is performed, food generosity, the rectitude of women, their gifts for making money telling fortunes, the family's appearance and decorum at public events. Gossip keeps the Roma under constant scrutiny. Any changes in appearance and deportment are evaluated according to ideas about the pure and good. Much stress is placed upon the ability to command respect by conveying a positive impression of health and prosperity. Efforts of such kind are part of a larger system of congruent beliefs and actions and are instrumental in ordering, framing, and focusing experience to agree with ideas about the superior purity and superior morals of Roma.

Postscript 1995:

Nowadays, the Machvaia say "*marime* is out." What they are referring to is the act of public defilement by a woman which results in public rejection and can only be cleared by Romani court proceedings. Sometime in the 1970s, probably about the time this article was first published, the California Machvaia met and abolished the traditional penalty of *marime*. As the men explained, "Too many women were doing it. *Marime* was getting ridiculous."

In actuality, the procedure didn't seem to be working and probably hadn't for some time. I know of one woman who, during the previous decade and most likely at her husband's urging, had publicly defiled two different men on separate occasions. In neither case were her efforts effective, however. In fact, when she called her sister-in-law, Luludji, to announce the news (she threw an undergarment at the man's head), Luludji responded in dismay: "Hush. Don't tell anyone. How could you do that? I'd be so embarrassed. I'm embarrassed for you now."

At present, the culprit can be brought to justice without recourse to defilement. Gentleman Joe says, "We get the men together. If the defendant doesn't come, he's automatically blackballed. It's like three strikes and you're out; he can have two excuses, like his wife was sick and he couldn't make it. After that, he's blackballed. If he does come and we find him guilty, he gets a fine or a period of rejection. Yes, that includes everyone in his family.

"So that's what happens. We used to call it *marime*. But now we call it *ballo* [blackball]. It usually works after a while. Sometimes people don't think they will care. But they find out they do."

APPENDIX

Marime Cases, 1965–1973

Case 1
Offense: Rape of the *gaji* wife of a Rom.
Result: No official court because defendant left the area to live elsewhere.

Case 2

Offense: Married a *gaji* and lived with her part of the time, returning to his wife upon occasion.

Result: Court threatened *marime* unless the Rom left his *gaji* wife. When he failed to comply, the community began the process of commensal isolation. During his five years of isolation, his brothers received him in private. Marriage to another Romni began reinstatement process.

Case 3

Offense: Married a *gaji*, but stayed with his Romni wife most of the time.

Result: Court decision split because defendant denied *gaji* relationship and his Romni backed him up. Three years of isolation from the segment of the community that refused clearance followed. Household involved.

Case 4

Offense: Cursed a Romni during an argument; Romni said that she defiled him.

Result: No court. Public refused to acknowledge *marime*, largely because the offense was insufficient to justify isolation.

Case 5

Offense: Stole son's young Romni bride after the wedding.

Result: When couple found, girl's family reclaimed her without returning brideprice ($5,000). The defendant's household subsequently moved to another area.

Case 6

Offense: Beat up the wife of another Rom; Romni said she defiled her attacker.

Result: Court decision for isolation of one month which included the four households of the defendant's brothers.

Author's note: Although Roma of Machvaia affiliation were the major source for the preceding information, the six cases of *marime* sanction include both Machvaia and Kalderasha.

NOTES

1.   The following conveys something of the feeling state associated with *marime* rituals of separation:

The one thing I always do . . . I'm strict . . . is to wash my face and take care of my razor right. If there isn't a face towel, I use my children's T-shirt. Sometimes when the soap falls out on the floor and I don't have any more, I look at it and it's hard, but like the razor falling on the floor or being used for something else, I can always tell if it's *marime*. I break out in a rash. (Carol J. Miller, *Mačwaya Gypsy Marimé*. M.A. Thesis, University of Washington, [Seattle], 1968, 12.)

2. Any reference, by word or by gesture, to the genitals, to defecation, or sexual intercourse, is a shame, particularly in cross-sex situations or between Roma in different age categories. Taboos extend to such matters as yawning or looking sleepy at the table, because "it means you're thinking about going to bed." Beds and bathrooms are impolite topics of conversation, as are childbearing and babies. Daughters are not likely to mention pregnancy to their mothers, largely because of the relation of pregnancy to intercourse. When the baby is born, it is better for someone of the same age and sex to report the news rather than either the girl or her husband. "Where were you found?" is preferred to the question "Where were you born?" according to Jan Tompkins, a social worker who has spent many years with Gypsy clients in both business and social situations.

3. The fellatio-cunnilingus contact. Needless to say, the article is dealing with a discussion of Rom cognitive structures, beliefs, and rituals. It may well be that in private life these taboos simply increase the titillation of such contact.

4. For some examples, washing the hands is recommended after touching the belt, putting on shoes, or making a bed. See Thomas William Thompson, "The Uncleanness of Women among English Gypsies," *Journal of the Gypsy Lore Society* 1:1 (1922), 15–43, for an appreciation of more elaborated rituals of separation among the English Gypsies.

5. Some few families still use separate tubs for adults and children to protect the children's purity from contamination and separate portable toilets for the same reason.

6. Other people's children are criticized in private for their bad manners, dirty appearance, and foul language, however. Similar mistakes by their own children are likely to be tolerated. The Roma are generally very indulgent with their children. They try to please them and give them everything they want because love is largely expressed through being "unable to refuse anything." There is little teaching or disciplining by verbal direction. Children are expected to learn indirectly and by mimicry.

7. The transition may be dramatic for the boy who marries young. One fourteen-year-old husband, small for his age, dresses in a suit, tie, and hat, and drives a late-model Cadillac to conduct business transactions with the *gaje* used-

car dealers. The older Kalderash Roma are careful to treat him as an equal, and he is given a man's respect by adult Rom women.

8.   Eugene Hammel has kindly pointed out that the tradition for modesty of demeanor toward the opposite sex, particularly the modesty of women, is pervasive in areas around the Mediterranean and the Middle East and most marked in the formal avoidance characteristic of upper-caste Hindus.

9.   The Roma like to believe that their elders have no interest in sexual relationships. The marriage of widowers over forty years old or couples with grandchildren is explained charitably: "They just need a little company because they get lonesome now that the children are big."

10.   The family of the runaway girl is automatically isolated from public commensal association when she returns.

11.   An outspoken Kalderash Rom describes the *gaje* as follows:

> You know what we think of Americans? We think they're stupid, crazy, ignorant, filthy, and no good. Why? Because Americans always have syphilis and clap. They go down on each other. We throw the glass they drink out of away. They're filthy. It's not the same as clean and dirty. It's a lot worse. Americans wash their face with the same towel they wash feet with. Ugh! The old folks didn't have anything to do with *gaje*, but now we have to work with them in the car business.

12.   Jean-Paul Clébert, *The Gypsies*, trans. Charles Duff (Harmondsworth: Penguin Books, 1966).

13.   Gropper's ethnography of the Bigby family describes the transition and adjustment to an urban and semi-nomadic lifestyle. (Rena C. Gropper, "Urban Nomads—The Gypsies of New York City," *Transactions,* New York Academy of Sciences, series II, 29 [1967], 1050–1056.)

14.   Nothing succeeds like success in the eyes of the Rom, and a healthy, wealthy, and "lucky" appearance is considered as visible confirmation of merit. Nowhere is this more tangibly apparent than at the large public events that attract hundreds of Roma, the men in expensive, well-tailored suits and diamond rings, the women wearing voluminous dresses of sparkling fabrics and dazzling jewels. (For reasons relating to defilement custom, the dresses cover the legs but bare the bosom.) The ability of the Machvaia to display to better advantage than any other group is, in part, connected to their superior status in terms of ritual purity.

15.   To refuse to eat with other Roma insults their ritual habits and defames their character. "Everyone always tries to take a little food anyway. If you turn somebody down altogether, it's not a good idea . . . makes you feel like you

think their food is *marime*." Conversely, to be asked to leave a Gypsy's house implies rejection for reprehensible reasons.

16. The Roma also say "reject," "blackball," or "he's out."

17. Health is often a good indicator of the condition of household affairs. If her husband, son, or daughter ignores her admonitions and disobeys moral precepts, the Romni is apt to experience health affliction. She is well within the limits of her role to cry hysterically for days, behave erratically, lose interest in making money or paying bills, forget to eat, lose weight, and become sickly. If the problem continues for any period of time, the entire family may suffer a general decline in health and living conditions. As one elderly Romni explains, "That's their belief. If you live in the home right, everything goes together. If the man chases women, spends money, the family gets sick, loses business and happiness. All goes together. That's the way it happens."

18. Skirt-tossing pollution was probably more effective before the days of sanitary pads. Shoe-tossing seems equally common these days, and the exposure of the female genitalia, although less lethal, is also popular. A pubic hair, applied to the face of a Rom, is also a very strong sanction at present and indicates "real hate." (Jan Yoors [*The Gypsies* (New York: Simon and Schuster, 1967)], who spent the large part of his youth with the Lowara Roma of Europe, is of the opinion that their uncleanliness "assured Gypsy women an absolute sense both of privacy and of protection among their own kind anywhere at large" [p. 150].) He describes an incident involving a young man whose brutal beating is ended abruptly when the young man's wife began flailing the attackers with her skirt. Similar incidents are reported in the States. One young girl stopped a fight by disrobing and yelling for the combatants' attention. The men, she said, ran in all directions. The woman's power to reject is complementary to her husband's susceptibility to rejection. A Rom will take his wife along when he visits stranger Roma, not only to make the proper public impression but also to be assured that, in the event of hostilities, he is armed and can retaliate in kind.

19. Cotten found court verdicts involving *marime* of two types: a finite period of isolation and permanent excommunication which required another trial to remand the verdict. She had the impression that verdicts were becoming less severe with the breakdown of some of the traditional lines of authority (Rena Maxine Cotten [Gropper], "The Fork in the Road: A Study of Acculturation Among the Kalderaš Gypsies," Diss., Columbia University, 1950, pp. 164–165). The experiences of my informants support this impression; only the eldest could remember a permanent *marime*. They also noted that court action on brideprice payment or brideprice return, which used to be the most frequent type of case involving skirt-tossing, had declined, and suggested that problems of such kind were being settled out of court.

Sex Dichotomy Among the American Kalderaš Gypsies (1951)

Rena M. Cotten (Gropper)

The sexual division of labor is an old phenomenon to anthropologists, but it has never been studied in detail with reference to cultures in a state of flux. A study of American Kalderaš Gypsies has revealed that this Gypsy culture has carried the division of life's activities between the sexes to a high degree of development and that the resultant dichotomy has influenced the process of acculturation. I shall first explore the reasons for the extreme distinction between male and female and the consequent difference in functions in a pre-acculturation situation, and then the changes under acculturation will be discussed. Although the presentation is purely factual, the data will be seen to justify me in offering Kalderaš culture as an exception to the generalization that women are the more conservative element in a society.

The Kalderaš, or Coppersmith, Gypsies form one tribe within the Gypsy ethnic group by virtue of a common dialect of Romani, similar customs and beliefs, and a sense of group identity. Kalderaš in large migration-waves began to settle in the New World in the 1890s; today, about one-half of the 50,000 to 100,000 Gypsies in the United States are of Kalderaš extraction. The Kalderaš themselves claim that all Coppersmith Gypsies have the same basic institutions, regardless of the European country from which they migrated, and a cursory comparison of Russian, Serbian, and Greek-Argentine Kalderaš in New York City revealed that the groups had almost identical behavior patterns. Since any European acculturation that may have occurred seems not to have differentiated the Kalderaš groups according to country of origin, one may treat the culture brought to the United States as the stable Kalderaš culture and consider the deviations brought about by contacts with North American culture as the changes caused by acculturative influences.

The Bases for Kalderaš Sex Dichotomy

The Kalderaš Gypsies are organized into patrilineal bands (*vitsa*s) under a "king"[1] and a council of elders made up of the heads of the component extended families. Except in the very large *vitsa*s, wives must be bought from other Kalderaš bands, since these Gypsies are forbidden to marry relatives as close as first cousins. Until after the birth of the first child, the bride and groom live in the same dwelling as the boy's parents and unmarried siblings; after the woman becomes a mother, she may either continue to reside with her mother-in-law or she may decide to set up her own establishment. In either event, however, the couple remains in the man's *vitsa* and under the control of his extended family. This, of course, means that the women in any *vitsa* are strangers both to the men, who belong to the *vitsa* by birth, and to the other women, who come from a number of different *vitsa*s. There is always a distrust of strangers in Gypsy society, and, although the men are united by ties of kinship and common interests, the women are alienated from each other. A woman must get along with her mother- and sisters-in-law because the extended family functions as a single unit, but her relationships with the other women of the *vitsa* are her own affair. Consequently, Kalderaš society may be viewed as a number of *vitsa*s, each of which has a solid core of males surrounded by a periphery of females.

The second factor of major importance in discussing the status and role of women in Kalderaš society is the concept of defilement.[2] During menstruation and for six weeks after the birth of a child, a woman is *maxrime* (unclean), and she is barred from all contact with men. The status of *maxrime* is contagious, and any man who speaks to, touches or sleeps with a menstruating woman becomes defiled. Even inadverten contact with objects that have been touched by a *maχrime* woman will be sufficient to ruin the purity of a man. If a man breaks one of these *maχrime* taboos, the Gypsies hold a court trial, presided over by the "king" or one of the elders and attended by the male members of the *vitsa*. A formal verdict of "*maχrime*" is declared, and the offender is banned from Gypsy society. Any individual who associates with the culprit will also become *maχrime*; hence, his own biological family will refuse to speak to him, and he may neither sleep in any Gypsy household nor eat with the Kalderaš. Reinstatement is possible only through nullification of the original verdict in another trial. This is a lengthy, arduous, and expensive procedure because: (1) it involves much scheming on the part of the outcast to make contact with an elder who must then be convinced that reacceptance is desirable and feasible before he will consent to call another trial; (2) the entire history of the case must be reviewed and new arguments presented and weighed; (3) the defendant must pay for food for the entire *vitsa*—food which he will be invited to eat if and when he is declared *bimaχrime* (not unclean); and (4) there is always the possibility that his petition will be refused, and the entire chain of events will have to be repeated. Obviously, it is much simpler to avoid close contact with women who are not relatives.

The Sex Dichotomy in Action

In terms of Kalderaš culture, political life may be defined as that behavior instituted by members of different extended families acting together; in this way, social behavior[3] is made to equate with the feast-complex which is called into action and controlled by one extended family, who act as hosts and invite other Kalderaš families to attend the celebration. The political life has a legislative, an executive, and a judicial form. *Vitsa* policies[4] are determined by the "big men" (the patriarchs)[5] in meetings of the council of elders.[6] If the *vitsa* is faced with a problem of unusual importance, all the men will be summoned to attend a preliminary meeting in which individual opinions are presented and discussed. The "king" fulfills the role of chief executive; each elder is responsible to him for the obedience of the male members of their extended family, and each man supervises his wife and children. Judicial matters are the jurisdiction of the court system; one of the big men acts as arbiter and judge, and the other men act as advocates and jury after the prosecutor and defendant have presented their cases. Women do not attend council meetings, *vitsa* sessions to discuss matters of interest to the group as a whole, or court trials. The political sphere of life belongs exclusively to the men, both because the presence of women might defile and also because the women do not belong to the *vitsa* by birth and hence are not the proper people to be entrusted with its affairs. A woman is always an alien tied to her conjugal *vitsa* only through the children to whom she has given birth.

Strictly speaking, economic activities are performed by both sexes, but the man's intermittent coppersmithing and the woman's daily fortune-telling are not equated in Kalderaš thought. The women are the main source of income, and their clairvoyance provides the wherewithal for food, rent, and clothing. When the men get any money, it is given to their wives for safekeeping and/or disposal.

Because of the different occupations, the sexes also vary in their rates of interaction with non-Gypsies. Metalworking commissions were solicited by the heads of the extended families, and the work was brought home to be done by the men as a group. This meant that most of the men were relatively isolated from the outside world. The woman's life has accustomed her to taking the initiative in talking with customers and in dealing with tradespeople; within the *vitsa*, however, she must be retiring and deferential when in the company of adult men.

The care of the home is woman's work. The wife sweeps the rugs, scrubs the floors, puts the feather beds away in the morning, washes the clothes, and does the shopping. The daily cooking (except when *maxrime*) is carried on by the women, but cooking done for festivals to celebrate religious holidays and the life-crises ceremonies of baptism, marriage, and death is the province of the men, for then the entire *vitsa* convenes, and there would be too much danger of defilement if the women handled the food.

The dates of these feasts are determined by the occurrence of the events being honored. Each extended family prepares for the Russian Orthodox holy days; friends visit each other to eat, drink, and dance and then go off to the next house. The life-crisis rites differ by their own nature, but the invitations are sent to the same group of families with whom they spend the religious festivals. The choice of their guests rests upon factors besides the desires of the men or women: close relatives have a right to attend; families of the same socioeconomic rank would be insulted if they were not asked; social-climbing aspirations motivate the family to request the presence of the big men. The men have the final veto power in social life since they can refuse to mingle with unwanted guests and because they have the right to forbid their wives to visit other households.

Since the women are occupied in fortune-telling during most of the day, they cannot be expected to give the children too much attention. Even if the men are at home, they are considered too important to be bothered with the petty affairs of children, and they are overly quick to resort to physical chastisement. For these reasons, the children must be self-reliant, and older siblings are supposed to care for and train their younger sisters and brothers. Gypsy culture reinforces this behavior by instilling the belief that no child learns well who learns by having adults tell [her or] him what to do; the correct educational method is to furnish a model the child can imitate, and these models are members of the family play group. The mother interferes in this children's world only when the youngsters demand attention, or become too noisy, or when there has been a gross infringement of Kalderaš rules and regulations.

Thus far we have seen that the woman is most active in those facets of life necessary for biological survival, but cultural survival is in male hands since the men are the initiators and major participants of group institutions. To phrase it another way: the focal point of interest for the men is the *vitsa* and its component extended families; the center of concern for the woman is her own conjugal biological family. It is this difference which results in the fact that sorcerers are always old women and never old men. At least in America, the witch is nothing but a perpetual danger to the *vitsa*. She is very free in using her ability to curse people, and these curses fall upon the members of the *vitsa* into which she has married. The witch is the symbol of feminine antisocial behavior and thinking—she is thought to be motivated by a desire to help herself, her husband, and her children without regard for the fate of the rest of the *vitsa*. But the old women gain a certain amount of power in the *vitsa* since the only way of dealing with witches is to do everything they wish.[7]

Repercussions for the Individual

Every time a wedding is held, a new vulnerability is introduced into the *vitsa*. As a young bride, the girl is an unknown quantity that must be explored and tested by her husband, her mother-in-law,[8] and her sisters-in-law; the other members of the *vitsa* avoid her until, by the birth of a child, they are assured that she is to be a permanent member of their group. As a matron, the woman is a potential danger because she comes from another *vitsa* which may harbor feelings of animosity toward some members of the husband's band. Therefore, any friendship the other wives can give must be earned by the newcomer, and the women who are closest to her are the ones who are least apt to treat her kindly. This is based on rivalry and competition for masculine affection and respect, since the position of a woman is dependent on the support she may expect from the men in the event of quarrels. A mother is afraid that her sons will forsake her and focus their attentions on their wives. The woman's sisters-in-law are anxious to show their husband's mother that they will help her fight the intruder, and they also fear that the bride will excel them in fecundity, cooking, moneymaking, sewing, dancing, and other feminine accomplishments.

If the men find themselves drawn into an argument between the women of the household, they punish their wives for bothering them and leave the house to seek male company and sympathy. But the only tranquillity the wife experiences is during the monthly seclusion. In this manner, the sexes are conditioned to want different social situations. To the man, pleasure comes from his association with his *vitsa* kinsmen; the woman seeks isolation from the *vitsa*. The success of this conditioning is evident in general social gatherings, for the men sit together and talk between dances, whereas the women sit near each other in silence.

The young woman can expect no allies from the group of other women, and her contacts with the men are hampered because of the masculine fear of the unclean stranger and because she must observe varying degrees of respect-avoidance toward her husband's relatives. Her husband is a constant reminder of the "trauma" experienced in getting married: for the first time, she is left completely alone with a group of strangers, and she must begin to assume responsibilities she has never had before. She must provide her husband with sexual gratification, service, and children in exchange for the bride-price paid by his parents, and she must do her work without expectations of gratitude from the others and regardless of her treatment at the hands of her spouse. Without friends and relatives in whom she can confide, her only avenue for the release of frustrations is in her contacts with non-Gypsies, and in that situation her aggressive impulses must be tempered by the knowledge that she is supposed to make money and may not show her real feelings toward the stupid clients.

The destructive energy generated by the woman's unresolved conflicts is used to foment trouble within the *vitsa*, and she sometimes tries to gain ascendance over the other women and, if possible, over the men and to effect a separation from the other families.

Changes Under Acculturation

The Kalderaš Gypsies have been exposed to contacts with non-Gypsies ever since they have been in existence as a cultural group. From the time they appeared in Western Europe in the early fifteenth century, they have lived among people who were not of their kind, and their very occupations required the patronage of these strangers. Yet, until recently, the Kalderaš were able to continue their own way of life almost untouched by foreign influences. This resistance to acculturation was due to many different factors both within and without Gypsy culture and society, but one of these mechanisms has been mentioned in this article, namely, the point that the relatively intensive contacts with non-Gypsies were experienced by the women, who had no important role in determining *vitsa* policies. The men were kept comparatively ignorant of non-Gypsy culture, and they were made to feel that the real business of life was that section of behavior in which Gypsy met with Gypsy.

After 1933 the ability of the Gypsies to separate themselves was progressively diminished. Mass production of utensils fashioned from iron and steel ruined the market for handmade copper articles, and the cheapness of these factory-produced goods made it inadvisable to repair broken objects.[9] Prejudice against the Gypsies increased with the decrease in their economic utility to Americans, and the women were unable to obtain fortune-telling concessions in carnivals and fairs; the owners preferred to lease to Americans who would masquerade as

Gypsies. In addition, the women could not cater to customers in their stores because the practice had been declared illegal. The Kalderaš were unable to support themselves, and they applied for relief. In order to receive the benefits of the Relief Act, they had to remain in the large cities where they were subject to much more intensive contacts with non-Gypsies and to invasions of their privacy in the form of the police, welfare workers, landlords, tradespeople, and neighbors. Male cohesiveness began to disintegrate because of the disappearance of the smithery and the substitution of fender- and furnace-repairing (occupations which were best handled by one individual craftsman without assistance) and because of the need for separate housing of the biological families of the same extended family unit. This change in economic behavior had three effects: in the first place, each Kalderaš man began to associate with non-Gypsies, first in the course of his work, and later in the pursuit of amusement; second, the man had to travel all over the city and so absented himself from his family and *vitsa* for the major part of each day; this in turn made for the disappearance of band solidarity, which had been in the hands of the group of adult males in constant and close interaction with one another, and for the consequent attenuation of political and social life.

With the disappearance of the *vitsa* and extended family as the active units in the society, the importance of the man also diminished. The biological family came to the foreground, and in this heretofore insignificant unit the man and woman had been of equivalent worth. The man, in his role as husband and father and as the link with the larger Kalderaš coteries, was supposed to be the head of the unit, but it was recognized that the woman had the lion's share of the work and responsibilities.

In the meantime, the children also came under the influence of non-Gypsy youngsters encountered in the streets. Initiative learning was extended to include copying these new models, and the play group changed in composition. The parents were asked for toys and clothing "like other children have," and the weekly movie became a part of the child's schedule.[10] The effects of this intermingling have recently become more serious with the attainment to adulthood of the first generation of children thus exposed to foreign influence. The young girls are less acquiescent about their uncertain position in their husbands' *vitsa*s, the despotic role of the men, and the need to try to support their households without male assistance. Some of them have voiced hopes of using birth control and intentions of breaking with the conjugal *vitsa* as soon as they become mothers.[11]

The young men have similarly come to see the difference between the Gypsy and non-Gypsy marriage customs, but, inasmuch as the role of husband devised by Kalderaš culture is less demanding than the one assigned by non-Gypsy patterns, their rebellion is directed only to attempts to choose their own wives. Since the custom of bride-price remains in full force, they must accept the girls chosen by their parents, and the burden of their discontent is vented upon the wives so selected. Formerly, it was extremely rare for marriages to be dissolved after the birth of children, but today wives have been known to run away after they have given as many as four children to their husbands' *vitsa*s. This change in divorce pattern is alarming since it vitiates the security that used to be felt once the wife became a mother—the *vitsa* can no longer be sure that any woman will remain in the band.

Conclusion

Kalderaš sex dichotomy worked efficiently as long as the culture was in a state of equilibrium. The dominant position of the man was justified in the existence of such institutions as the *vitsa* council, the court trials, and the extended family—institutions which were exclusively masculine pursuits. The women remained within the confines of the biological family; they could not join together against the men because of the *maxrime* restrictions and because they distrusted one another as much as they distrusted the men. The culture had been blocked out into large chunks which were assigned to either the men or the women. Those behavioral patterns which had been the province of the men disappeared, and the women, whose training and attitudes remained much the same as in the pre-acculturation situation, were left in control of the rest of the cultural institutions.

Vitsa solidarity was dependent on male cohesion, a cohesion strong enough to overcome the segregational tendencies of the women. Without this cohesiveness, the biological families tend to isolate themselves and to become engulfed in the non-Gypsy community.

Update 1995:

Culture change is to be expected, of course, and one should not be surprised that gender roles have altered among the Roma. I had argued in this article that, while the men had no reason to complain about masculine status and role assignments, feminine status and roles were affected considerably by the individual's age. Once a woman obtained a secure and influential position in the group into which she had married, she was beginning to derive personal benefit from the lowly status of younger women, some of whom were her daughters-in-law. So the older women upheld the gender roles.

Many factors began to reduce the power enjoyed by the older women and to ameliorate the lowly conditions of recently married ones, as Carol Miller (1988) has documented so tellingly. In the cities extended families could not share housing, and nuclear families became independent households situated blocks or even boroughs apart in New York City. This means the older women were unable to exercise close supervision over daily routines. In addition, television programs reinforced the knowledge of non-Gypsy gender roles the women were obtaining from their customers. The customers themselves felt less constrained in talking freely with the advisers in the fortune-telling stores than they had when the Gypsy women traveled to the non-Gypsy households where other family members could eavesdrop on the consultation. (Viewing motion picture films had been less effective as a source of information not only because attendance was limited in frequency but also because the films themselves often depicted other historic periods and varying geographic locales.)

Living in cities also diminished the importance of the men as chauffeurs. Taxicabs were readily available, at first because hacks cruised the streets in search of potential fares and later through the initiation of radio-dispatched cars sent as a result of telephoning a central location. In addition, young women began to drive automobiles, obtaining a driver's license as readily as their brothers and husbands and owning cars themselves.

Regular contact with their parents and other relatives was as easy as the closest telephone, especially when the Roma installed telephones in their *ofisa*s (stores). Pay telephones were replaced by private ones in the late fifties. Today telephones are ubiquitous and include cellular models.

Frequent visits by the women to their relatives occur thanks to modern jet airplanes, cross-country travel requiring a time expenditure of mere hours. Some women (and men) confess to fear of flying, but generous libations en route dull the trepidation satisfactorily for most.

Feminine gender markers have decreased the emphasis on the mother role, which now requires no more than one child to legitimate a woman's claim to adult status. Family size has decreased, probably through the use of contraceptive devices. Knowledge of contraception is available through private consultations with health professionals, and husbands and in-laws are not aware of a visit. Pills can be prescribed and purchased without involving the mother-in-law and/or husband. Intrauterine devices can be inserted with equal lack of fanfare.

Reduction in number of births buttressed a change in attitude toward pregnancy and parturition. When I first began fieldwork, middle-aged women regarded pregnancy as the normal physiological state for young married women and birth as a process as unremarkable as menstruation. The need for seclusion during birth and for the following six weeks (because of pollution avoidance) presented difficulties once the Roma accepted city living as their preferred residential pattern. They solved that problem by sending the parturient to a hospital for birthing. However, Rom distrust and fear of hospitals as dangerous places, to be used only in critically life-threatening circumstances, cast a shadow of vulnerability over childbearing itself. The young women were quick to appreciate the psychological advantage this gave them in gaining control over their husbands. Pregnant women admitted to numerous aches and pains, especially when their desires were thwarted by their mothers-in-law. Expectant fathers began to side with their wives and demanded that their mothers treat the young women more considerately.

A woman only needs to raise a child or two to establish her claim to adulthood, as I have said. A man's status is tied more closely to the number of sons he has fathered since sons (and sometimes sons-in-law) supply a cadre of political supporters. Hence, men still want large families and uphold the custom of claiming the weaned children in cases of divorce. A contented wife who will remain married to him and produce at least a handful of healthy children is a goal most men desire, even if they must argue with their mothers to achieve it.

Being a daughter-in-law is no longer as arduous as it had been and being a mother-in-law is less enjoyable. The older woman is left with her husband or is a widow. Since today's Gypsy women can support themselves and move around on their own, there is no practical benefit to be derived from financing the presence of a man (and the Roma still feel that individuals who are grandparents should cease sexual activities). So there is a strong temptation to get divorced (or at least separated), especially if the man spends a great deal of money without contributing any. One influence that discourages such behavior is the acceptance of the Christian evangelical movement with its condemnation of fortune-telling. A woman who cannot tell fortunes or obtain welfare payments for many dependents cannot take care of her financial needs. Thus, older women do not embrace the born-again sects in large numbers. What remains to be seen is whether their voice will be heard strongly in the next several years.

NOTES

1. The average *vitsa* has from 200 to 300 people; a large *vitsa* may have as many as 600 members. The term "king" is used to describe the leader of the entire *vitsa*: the word "chief" occurs not at all. Indeed many of the Gypsy groups in America state that kings are a thing of the past and that "all Gypsies are the same now." The Kalderaš I studied were only beginning to follow this line of thought toward the end of my two years' work with them. It is my belief: (1) that the Gypsies feel that kingship is not in the same high regard as formerly, and they fear that the *gaje* would seize upon the existence of an institution of kingship as an excuse for further persecutions; and (2) that they have come to regard the word "king" as meaning an absolute monarch and hence unsuitable as a descriptive term for their *vitsa*-heads. From the anthropological viewpoint it is infinitely preferable to employ "chief," but I follow the custom of my friends when I write "king." One must remember, however, that the leadership among the Gypsies is often more like the "chieftainship" of certain American Indian tribes in that the head is an adviser and persuader.

2. See also Thompson 1929:33–38; Brown 1929:164–165; Yates 1942:101; Myers 1943:88–90; Myers 1945:92–93.

3. See also Thompson 1923:116–121.

4. These policies refer to such questions as relations with other *vitsas* and tribes, relations with municipal authorities, time and place for moving, resolution of conflicts between different traditional usages, and similar topics.

5. The "king" acts as the head of his extended family.

6. The council meeting and court trial are two slightly different phenomena among the American Kalderaš I have studied, and the term *kris* applies only to the latter. See also Brown 1929:162–165.

7. Among the Kalderaš all old women are suspected of being witches.

8. See also McFarlane 1949:136.

9. See also Victor Weybright (1945:2–8) on Steve Kaslov.

10. Today all Kalderaš children over two years speak a colloquial English indistinguishable from that of their non-Gypsy contemporaries.

11. This is seemingly inconsistent with the statement that the women have long been familiar with non-Gypsies. Actually, adolescent girls did very little fortune-telling until after marriage. Today they are exposed to romantic films, and they supplement this information in their conversations with young non-Gypsies.

REFERENCES

Brown, Irving
  1929 "The Gypsies in America." *Journal of the Gypsy Lore Society* 8:4, 145–176.
McFarlane, Andrew
  1949 "Supplementary Notes on the Social Customs of the Rudari." *Journal of the Gypsy Lore Society* 28:3–4 (July–October), 134–137.
Miller, Carol
  1988 "Girls Go Home: The Changing Status of the Machvanka Daughter-in-Law." In *Papers from the Eighth and Ninth Annual Meetings, Gypsy Lore Society, North American Chapter* (Cara DeSilva, Joanne Grumet, and David J. Nemeth, eds.). New York: Gypsy Lore Society, North American Chapter, Publication No. 4, 95–104.
Myers, John
  1943 "The 'Greek' Nomad Gypsies in South Wales, during August 1942." *Journal of the Gypsy Lore Society* 22:3–4 (July–October), 88–94.
  1945 "Supplementary Jottings on the Customs of the 'Greek' Nomad Gypsies." *Journal of the Gypsy Lore Society* 24:3–4 (July–October), 88–94.

Thompson, T. W.
1923 "Social Polity of the English Gypsies," *Journal of the Gypsy Lore Society*, 113–139.
1929 "Additional Notes on English Gypsy Uncleanness Taboos," *Journal of the Gypsy Lore Society*, 33–39.
Weybright, Victor
1945 "A Nomad Gypsy Coppersmith in New York." *Journal of the Gypsy Lore Society* 24:1–2 (January–April), 2–8.
Yates, D. S.
1942 "The 'Greek' Nomad Gypsies in Britain 1929–1940. Part I. Compiled from the Note-books of Professor Walter Starkie, Andrew McFarlane, John Myers, and E. O. Winstedt." *Journal of the Gypsy Lore Society* 21:3–4 (July–October), 88–110.

Economic Stratification and Interaction: Roma, an Ethnic Jati in East Slovakia (1984)

Milena Hübschmannová

This essay is based on data which I have been collecting since 1970 among Gypsy groups (Rom)[1] in East Slovakia and will describe the changing social position of Roma in rural East Slovakia. Economic interaction between the minority group and mainstream society and thus, traditional Rom occupations, will be analyzed.

Slovak Roma (rough estimate: 80 percent), along with Hungarian Roma (10–15 percent) and Vlachi, who were itinerant until the antinomadism law was passed in 1959 (5–10 percent), now represent the three major Rom groups in Czechoslovakia. The Rom population of the Czech lands (the present Czech Socialist Republic = ČSR) was exterminated by the Nazis during the Second World War. In Slovakia (the present Slovak Socialist Republic = SSR), which between 1939 and 1945 was a formally independent State not directly governed by the Germans, Roma survived in spite of racial persecution. At present, two-thirds of Rom live in the SSR, while one-third inhabit the ČSR. Roma in the ČSR are postwar immigrants from Slovakia, and 45 percent of them are concentrated in East Slovakia (Census of 1970), which until not long ago was the most backward rural area in the whole country. In some districts of East Slovakia (Rožnava, Poprad) Roma constitute more than 10 percent of the total population.

Slovak and Hungarian Roms started to sedentarize as early as in the seventeenth century. For instance, according to the Liptov register, 96 families were entirely settled in this area in 1651, living from smithery, basket weaving, trough-carving, and brush making (Horváthová

1963:104). In other regions (*župa*) too, Rom artisan groups, especially blacksmiths, were allowed to settle at the peripheries and suburbs of towns and villages (see also Guy 1975). All these groups had been till then itinerant within their respective localities. While "our Gypsies" were allowed to settle, "foreign Gypsies," those who came from other districts or countries and those whose subsistence activities were unproductive (for example, palmistry) were effectively kept out of the district by strict local edicts. Thus, the official approach to Roma differed from district to district on the one hand, and according to various attributes of discrete Rom-jatis ("domestic" vs. "foreign," "productive" vs. "unproductive" occupations) on the other hand. This differentiated official attitude might also have enhanced the mutual social distance between distinct Rom-jatis, a point which will be discussed later. In periods of general social insecurity or tension, Roma were persecuted on the whole, irrespective of the occupational group they belonged to.

Ethnic Jati: A Unique Social Formation of the Roma

As late as the first half of this century, Roma in Eastern Slovakia constituted a cluster of low-status jatis. They used their own language, Romani, in inter-Rom communication and because of their indigenous Indian culture and community structure, were alien to Slovak society. They could thus be called an ethnic jati.

The concept of an ethnic jati has already been discussed elsewhere (Hübschmannová 1972; 1976), but I shall recapitulate it here briefly, as I consider it very important for the understanding of Rom society. Jati is a group which interacts with the rest of society (in India, with other jatis) on the basis of economic complementarity: distinct jatis exchange products and services, deriving from their specific jati-profession(s). While there is indispensable exchange in the economic sphere, other conceptually delimited spheres of social reproduction and communication (compare Lévi-Strauss 1967:413) are limited within the jati boundaries, which are fortified by status barriers and regulations of social distance. Thus, kinship does not cut across jati-boundaries and many habits, customs, skills, ideas, beliefs, and values are shared only among jati members. Jati as a social formation manifests a double character: being fully economically dependent on other jatis, it is a social group; being isolated and self-contained in other spheres of social life, it has many features of a complex society.

How then did the Rom ethnic jatis live and interact with the local population in East Slovakia? East Slovakia was a rural area. The mainstream society was a peasant society, and people were bound to one place by landownership and land-cultivating obligations. In contrast to this, Roma—with rare exceptions—never owned land. Yet the majority of them lived in villages,[2] as they provided the Slovak farmers with products and services necessitated by agriculture and rural life. Rom jatis in East Slovakia were artisan, service, and trading jatis. A striking and immediately visible ecological manifestation of the pariya status of Roma were "Gypsy settlements" at the very edge of Slovak villages, some of them even 1 to 3 kilometers away from the village.

The general attitude toward Roma is reflected in Slovak proverbs: "There will never be bacon from a wolf, there will never be a human being from a Gypsy." Or, "Not even the cap of a Gypsy is any good; wherever you find it, beat it up."[3] An eighty-six-year-old Slovak villager from Rakúsy (district Poprad) once told me: "We played with the Gypsy children, but only because we were the poorest whites in the whole village. Still, when Mother saw me running around with Gypsy boys, she would shout, 'What a shame.'" Ruda Dzurko, a Rom painter, corroborated this attitude toward the Roma: "My father used to say that for the non-Roma, a Rom was a human being only when he was far away. As soon as he came nearer, he was only a Gypsy."[4] The social distance between non-Roma (*gadže*) and Roma is also expressed by a Rom proverb: "Rom Romeha, gadžo gadžeha," that is, "Rom with Rom, non-Rom with non-Rom." Just as the gadže threatened their misbehaving children with "Don't be naughty or the Gypsy will carry you away," so also the Roma threatened their children with the image of the *gadžo*. Once, while I watched TV in a family of Rom friends in Rakúsy, the mother said to a noisy child, "Don't make noise, or a *gadžo* will take you away."[5]

To marry a Gypsy was something unimaginable among decent *gadže*. But in many Rom families a *gadžo* ancestor does crop up now and then. Such *gadže* were usually the poorest of the poor, themselves outcasts from the wider society. All those I happened to meet knew Romani as well as native Romani speakers and in fact were assimilated in the Rom community. I encountered one such case in the settlement

Rakúsy, where I lived for several months in 1968–1969. Four brothers, two of whom lived "down" in the village, were well to do, decent, respected, and one even had a political job. The fifth brother, however, did not succeed in finding a prosperous job, nor did he succeed in building a new house, an important symbol of prestige in Slovak villages. Moreover, he was sent to jail for theft and drank more than the publicly accepted norm allows. His four brothers rejected him; thus, he moved into the "Gypsy settlement" and started living with a nice, deaf, divorced Rom woman with whom he had three children. He hardly ever came "down" to the village (2.5 kilometers away from the "Gypsy settlement") and the _gadže_ avoided him. Roma treated him with sympathy and compassion; they made use of his ability to read and write (many inhabitants of Rakúsy were illiterate in 1969), but his social status in the "Gypsy settlement" was very low. It was said of him: _"Ňiko na phučel leskero lav"_ ("Nobody asks for his 'word'").

In spite of their low status, Roma were in a way integrated in the traditional, semifeudal village society by virtue of their economic roles (see table 1). A Rom proverb says: _"Gadžo Romes paťiv na del, ale buťi lestar mangel,"_ that is, "The _gadžo_ does not pay any respect to the Rom, but he demands work from him." There was no economic exchange between Roma and poor _gadže_. However, I have come across several cases where a rich and well-established Rom blacksmith employed a _čoro gadžo_, a poor _gadžo_, as the egalitarian pressure typical for intra-jati relations would not allow a Rom to employ another Rom.

The following description of traditional Rom occupations is based on interviews with Rom informants; statements of some non-Roma are included as well. The period analyzed is roughly the time span between the two world wars. Although the social situation of Roma was essentially the same all over East Slovakia, there was naturally a certain range of regional variance, depending on, among other things, the overall character and prosperity of the respective region.

Smithery[6]

The most traditional and in the past probably the predominant jati profession of the Slovak Roma was smithery. The Slovak saying "Not every Gypsy is a blacksmith"[7] shows, in fact, that the majority of Roma

Table 1. Goods and Services Exchanged Between Roma and Non-Roma

Rom to Non-Roma	Gadže Peasants to Roma
Traditional handicrafts	Food or money
Music	Money
Miscellaneous services	
(e.g., firewood chopping)	Food
Seasonal work in the fields	Food or money
Store-bought small wares	Money

Jews (Čhinde) to Roma

Miscellaneous services	Salt, tobacco, kerosene, or money
Music (occasionally)	Money

Gadže Landowners (Chulaj) to Roma

Seasonal work in the fields	Food or money
Music	Money
Miscellaneous services	Food

Gadže Intelligentsia (Raj) to Roma

Miscellaneous services	Money
Produce of gathering	
(e.g., wild berries, mushrooms)	Money
Music	Money

Gadže Priest (Rašaj) to Roma and Municipal Authorities

Miscellaneous services	Food
Postal worker, messenger, drummer,	
servant of the local municipal council	Food
Traditional handicrafts	Religious service at Rom rites of passage

must have once been blacksmiths and that the *gadže* in general did not stop thinking of them as such even after the situation had gradually changed. Allusions to Rom blacksmiths are embedded in Slovak folklore, proverbs, and sayings, and some Roma claim that the first blacksmith ever was a Rom.[8] In many villages only Rom blacksmiths provided the peasants with goods such as horseshoes, nails, shoes, chains, and so forth. One of my informants also narrated the "pro-Rom" version of the widely known legend about the Rom blacksmith and the crucifixion of Christ: A Rom was asked to forge four nails; only when three of the nails were ready did he come to know that they were intended to crucify Jesus. He now refused to make the fourth one and as a punishment was condemned to the fate of a wanderer.[9] According to the "anti-Rom" version, also generally known among Roma and *gadže*, only a Rom blacksmith was willing to forge the nail for the crucifixion and the same punishment followed.[10] The belief in the superiority and exclusiveness of the Rom blacksmith, shared by so many Rom informants, is supported by several historically true instances as well as by Rom legends and folk narrations. In some localities, a Rom blacksmith was accorded a little more respect than other Gypsies, and when somebody wanted to get married and there was no priest at hand, he would perform the ceremony for the Rom as well as for the *gadže*. Some of the blacksmiths were even a little better off than the rest of the Rom population and some kept cows and horses with which they rendered the *gadže* carting services. But the "Gypsy" label, with all its stereotypic markers—such as eating carrion—stuck fast to even well-to-do blacksmiths.

Some blacksmiths who were better liked by the *gadže* tried to "sanskritize" by getting rid of their Gypsyhood and passing into the prestigious *gadžo* society and cutting off relations with other Roma.

In some villages, in addition to a Rom blacksmith there was also a *gadžo* blacksmith. Usually, there was no rivalry between them, as the Rom did *romaňi buťi*, Gypsy work for which even in Slovakian there is a special term, *cigánská práca*, that is, special articles produced by special technology—and above all cheaper than the products of a *gadžo* blacksmith. "A Gypsy was a Gypsy; he did not dare to ask much for his job, he was content when the white man gave him some milk, potatoes and a piece of bacon, or some small change for tobacco. A white blacksmith knew his rights, he demanded money."[11] Later, when smiths were less in demand, the authorities were strict and demanded the apprentice certificate as a condition for a blacksmith's trade license and the Roma were at a disadvantage. They learned smithery (*chart'iko but'i*) from their fathers, in the family and within the jati, and so the institutionally qualified white blacksmith took over the blacksmith's trade. In smithery—as in all other Rom occupations—all members of the extended family (*familia*) took part and performed their specific role according to their sex and age.

Three phases can be distinguished in smithery:

1. the preparatory phase consisting of burning charcoal and procuring raw material;
2. the phase of technical production;
3. the phase of commercialization.

The father was the one who went to the forest to burn charcoal and the children would usually go along to help him. To obtain scrap iron was often the duty of the children. As Vasil Demeter put it, "We, the children, collected scrap iron. Sometimes we saw pieces of scrap iron in a farmer's yard and if he did not need them, we took them."[12] But sometimes, the father himself had to procure scrap iron: "Sometimes iron was nowhere to be found, so Father went to a Jew—since usually only Jews were shopkeepers in our place and they also liked us more than the *gadže* did—and so the Jew gave him some. Not free; Father had to work for him in return."

The phase of technical production was directed by the father. He mastered the technology and was the most skillful person in giving shape to various iron articles. But he was assisted by his wife and/or children. The wife and girls would blow the bellows, the boys would hold the glowing iron in the tongs while the father hammered. Gradually, the boys were allowed to hammer themselves. Zuzana Surmajová, who comes from a family with six daughters and no son, had to do the work of a boy: "Our father woke us at four o'clock in the morning. 'Get up, we have to earn our living.' And so, we got up; one of us blew the bellows, another hammered on the horseshoes, de!, and Father said, 'Blow, my girls, blow!' 'Oh, Daddy, I won't blow, I'm hungry!' Father wanted to beat me, but did not. He was kind. 'You will eat, wait; as soon as Mother comes home from the village she will bring food.' And so we struck with the hammer slowly on the holes in the horseshoes. From ten years old on, I started to work with the hammer."[13]

The smith's wife was responsible for the sale of the blacksmith's products. She would pack the horseshoes, nails, hoes, and so forth, into her *zajda* (an old cover folded in a big bundle carried on the back) and go from village to village (*pal o gava*). Andrej Giňa states that his mother walked about 30 kilometers every day, carrying 20 to 30 kilograms of ironware in her *zajda*. In return for these products she obtained food. Zuzana Surmajová described it as follows: "Mother brought milk in a jar, potatoes in her *zajda*, and bread in her apron. She came home and Father would make one horseshoe more. 'Take it, go to the Jew and sell it for money so that we can buy salt and tobacco,' he would say."[14]

The period I am dealing with was a period of gradual decline of Rom smithery. One of the reasons for this was a major increase in the Rom population, leading to a surplus in blacksmiths, since the demand for them did not grow so quickly. The jati-craft was passed on from father to son. But what if there were five or six sons in the family? And that was the usual rather than the exceptional case with the Roma. In the past, this problem had been solved by a specific kind of spatial movement, which I will call *generational dispersion*. According to Veselovský, a retired archivist from Kežmarok, whom I interviewed, "One son took over his father's trade in the native village, while other sons moved to places which did not have their Gypsy smiths yet." This way a new Gypsy settlement was often founded in a locality where no Rom had lived until then. Thus for instance arose the settlement in Rakúsy: in 1880 two Rom brothers came here from Ždiar which already had its Gypsy blacksmith, while in Rakúsy a smith was needed. But in the course of time even the generational dispersion could not solve the problem of unwanted blacksmiths, and so Rom blacksmiths had to explore other ways of procuring their livelihood. Many of them were attracted by music making because musicians (*lavutara*) had an even higher status than the blacksmiths. Besides, they were paid in cash. Josef Mirga, one of my informants, expressed it as follows: "Once, our Slovak Roma did not know how to play music, only the Hungarian Roma knew how to. But our Roma learned it from them, in order to make an easier living."[15]

The musicians considered themselves something better, because they played and did not work (*bašavnas a na kerenas buťi*). In fact, before I realized that *te kerel buťi* (literally, to do work) implies doing something physical, hard, and usually dirty, I upset several musicians by asking them, "What sort of work did you do when you were young?" They would retort, "I did not work, I played music!" (*Me na keravas buťi, me bašavavas!*), often adding, "Only silly people who did not know anything worked!" (*Ča diline kernas buťi, so na džanenas nič!*). The ancestors of my Rom friends did both smithery and played music. Thus, according to Jan Horváth, "My father hammered horseshoes during the week and on Saturdays and Sundays he went to play."[16] Those who did not know how to play music, or who were not so good at it, crushed stones at the road construction sites, assisted bricklayers as unskilled laborers, cleaned wells, helped the farmers in the fields, and so forth. As most of these jobs had lower prestige than smithery, men often refused to do them and stayed home doing nothing (*sas khere, na kernas nič*). The burden of "bringing bread" (*te anel maro*) thus rested more and more on the women and children. They picked wild berries, medicinal plants, mushrooms, collected wastepaper and old rugs; women used to smear the ovens of the villagers with adobe and in some places they used to weave linen (*pochtan*) for sale. Children grazed the farmer's cattle, sheep, and so forth. Most often women went from village to village; in one place they chopped firewood, in another they cleaned the farmer's yard, or just begged. Sons of the blacksmiths gradually stopped learning the craft of their fathers, and the decline of the craft meant for many Roma pauperization and further fall in status.

Music

Playing music at the weddings (*bijav*) and baptism (*boňa*) of the *gadže*, at village fairs and village entertainments, was a monopoly of Rom *avutara*. "Wherever you would have looked, nobody could ever play; only the Roma could," said Jano Andrej, and this was confirmed by Jano Laco: "Never should anyone but a Rom play music. At least so it was in my father's and grandfather's time. Today even *gadže* hunt for the music-making skill, but they play like barbarians, two, three chords in one song. I get bad nerves hearing that! The Rom plays like a cultured man, difficult chords, six, seven, eight in one song. But the *gadžo*, never! The *gadžo* will never learn what the Rom knows."[17] Interestingly enough, I recorded a very similar statement from a Bulgarian musician (*lavutaris*) in Straldza, in 1980.

While smithery gradually declined, music making (*bašaviben*) brings some extra money to Roma even today, and it flourished in times when *charťiko buťi* was already a thing of the past. "Those Roma who knew how to play would eat; those who did not know would not eat,"[18] said František Giňa. Rom musicians were paid in cash and not in kind (for example, food). For a wedding the basic fee was agreed upon with the bridegroom (*terno*) and paid to the bandmaster (*primašis*), who distributed the money equally among all members of the band. Besides that, the musicians earned extra money for each song which the wedding guests requested them to play. This money was stuck in the hair of the violin bow or into the double bass.

Paradoxically, wives of many musicians—of those who were not the best and most popular—went begging. For one thing, the weddings and village dances were not regular sources of income; secondly, the status of a *lavutaris* had to be demonstrated. The musician was obliged to stand other Roma drinks to show that he could afford it. Besides, progeny in musician families were as numerous as in other Rom families, and the fee was not high enough to provide so many people with food. Mr. and Mrs. Horváth narrated their experiences to me as follows:

Jan Horváth: "When I went to play at a wedding, I bargained nine hundred, or a thousand, or eight hundred crowns with the bridegroom. Besides, the village boys paid me extra for every song. We earned five or six thousand crowns for five people. We were five in our band—the bandmaster, that was me, the second violin, viola, cimbalom, and also a double bass player. I was the first in the whole district! When the judge met me in town, he said, 'Oh, hello, Mr. Horváth!' and he even shook my hand. I did not recognize him, but he recognized me."[19] And then, Anna Horváthova, his wife, said, "And I went begging in the villages. Every single Rom woman went and when I got a piece of bread, I broke it into seven pieces because I had seven children. He went to play, he got money, but what of that since he spent it in drinking with the men! He had to, he could not have helped it, he had to show what a big spender he was. And when he brought money, we put some aside to buy clothes for the children. And the main thing was he needed a good suit—he was a musician, wasn't he! A white shirt, a hat on his head!"[20]

A special class of musicians were the *foroskere lavutara*, the town musicians who played in cafés, restaurants, and nightclubs for a salary. Many of them were from Hungary, because it was a fashion to have a Hungarian Gypsy band playing in a wine restaurant (*vinárna*). The dream of every village musician (*gavutno lavutaris*) was to play in the towns, but of course, few succeeded. The town musicians represented a sort of Gypsy aristocracy; they went around in showy dresses, living in showy houses, and because of them the status of a *lavutaris* was something to be envied or longed for. Jan Brehár described the situation vividly in the following account: "Until my sixteenth year I worked as a shepherd, since I had no mother and no father. But as soon as I became a little cleverer, I learned to play music—because I wanted to live better, easier, to walk like a gentleman, dressed nicely. I wanted the people to respect me more. Whenever I heard that there was music somewhere—be it in the fifth village away—I went there in the evening. I watched how the musician fingered his violin and as soon as he put it down, I took it up in my hand. 'Uncle,' I said, 'you won't be upset, may I try?' 'Just play, my boy, play,' he would say. For one whole year I wandered from Rom to Rom and I learned to play music from foreign Roma, because I had no relatives of my own. When I was twenty-one years old, they accepted me in a music band. I wanted to play in the town, but that was just a dream."[21]

When a young man came to court a girl from a "good" family, her father would accept him as a son-in-law only if he knew how to play music, or at least to do smithery. Thus, Zuzana Surmajová told me, "One boy ran after me and my father told him this: 'Well, my boy, take a hammer, go to the smithery, and work. If you are as good as I am, I will give you my daughter. If you are not, go home.' And the boy said, 'I know how to play music.' 'That's even better, my boy,' said my father. 'Take a violin in your hand and let us hear how you play.' The boy took up the violin and then my father said, 'My boy, go home. You don't know anything! Girl, do you want him? If you want him, take him by the hand and go away with him. But I won't let you stay in my house, because he does not know how to do either the blacksmith's job or how to play music. If you get together with him you'll die of hunger!'"[22]

The music bands were constituted by the male members of the extended family (*familia*). "They did not take foreign Roma into the bands, only their own people, so that they could make a living with that," said František Giňa.[23] While in blacksmith families the working group consisted of the members of the nuclear family, members of one music band could have been either brothers or cousins, brothers-in-law, fathers and sons, uncles and nephews, fathers-in-law and sons-in-law, and so forth. Women never went to play: it was not considered decent for them to be exposed to the sights of drunken men at weddings and to have the chance to commit adultery.

In the course of time fewer and fewer musicians were able to survive from music making (*bašaviben*) alone. What was the reason? Musicians were not so much endangered by gramophones or radio sets—even today, in East Slovakia it is more prestigious to have a music band playing at a wedding than a tape recorder or a gramophone. Neither could the changing musical taste of the public adversely affect the Rom musicians, as they are famous for their flexibility and ability to play anything that is demanded of them: "Only once the village boy sang his song to you, and you had to play it immediately after him. If you were not able to play it, he would crush your violin on your head,"[24] said an informant nicknamed Partyzán. Jano Laco's statement corroborates this: "We play whatever people want. When somebody wants jazz, we play jazz for him. If somebody likes old, slow songs, we play for him in an old-fashioned way."[25] The reason that fewer and fewer families could make a living out of music alone was rather, once again, the number of musicians, which was out of proportion to the demand. To be a musician was so attractive that everybody wanted to become one. Not only did the four or five sons of one musician become musicians as well, but even Roma of other professions tried to play music; thus the chances for all of them were more and more reduced. Musicians had thus to seek other jobs to sustain their families. The case of Andrej Jožko's father was an example: "My father played music and he also worked. He was a *primašis* number one! He played the violin. But then, there were few chances for music making, since there were as many musicians as there are hairs on the head. So my father had to go to work at a railway construction site."[26]

Women and children of course contributed to the family food-income just as in all other Rom families. Here now are some examples of supplementary jobs which the fathers of some of my informants and some other members of their families had to do (see table 2). This model of subsistence activities reoccurred with slight variations, again and again. Some types of work were seasonal: spring to autumn—work in the fields, picking wild berries, and so forth; winter—weaving, feather stripping. Some jobs, such as crushing stones and making bricks, were occasional. Some jobs were done along with music playing, while others supported the family when there were no chances for playing music.

Other Crafts

It is interesting that while there are special terms in Romani for a musician (*lavutaris*) and a blacksmith (*chart'as*), a professional denomination for other craftsmen is expressed by a predicative construction: X weaves wicker baskets (*chuvel opalki*) or X makes baskets (*kerel košara*) or, again, X makes brooms (*kerel metli*). It could be that these crafts were usually subsidiary occupations, while the main jati professions were smithery or music. Recently, discussing Rom occupations with the French anthropologist Philippe de Marne, I realized how much sedentarization had influenced the sociocultural system of Slovak Roma, including the jati-profession structure. In Romania, for instance, where Roma are still itinerant or semi-itinerant, there are innumerable groups who denote themselves—and are denoted by others—according to their profession. As in a jati system, the professional and kinship boundaries overlap. If a new occupation crops up which a certain kinship group can adopt as its new, main profession, a new jati comes into existence. I observed this phenomenon in Romania in 1969 among a group of *collectori* (bottle collectors), who traveled in the region of Arad, Sibiu, and so on. The *collectori* collected used milk bottles from people, paid them one lei for each bottle, and got two lei when they deposited these bottles in the store. *Collectori* split away from the *calderari* (cauldron makers), whose profession was dying out due to increasing industrialization. While the status of *calderari* was very high, the *collectori*, because forced to perform a less qualified and less financially rewarding service, descended a lot in social status. The new jati profession, new jati name, and changed jati status also brought in its wake another phenomenon typical for the jati system: jati-distance, expressed among others through endogamy. The previous jati-brethren the *calderari* hesitated to marry their daughter or son to a *collectori*.

Table 2. Subsistence of 5 Rom families according to the age and sex of their members.*

Household	FATHER	MOTHER	SONS	DAUGHTERS
JG	*lavutaris** basket-weaving crushing stones for road constructions	*pal o gava** picking wild berries	*(4)lavutaris** (2) basket-weaving	picking wild berries
	. . . seasonal work in the farmers' fields (harvesting, potato picking)			
LK	*lavutaris**	*pal o gava**	*(3)lavutaris**	
	. . . work in the farmers' vineyards and seasonal work in the fields			
	. . . adobe brick making			
	. . . . collecting healing plants			
ZS	*chartas-lavutaris**	*pal o gava** weaving picking wild berries stripping feathers	help in the smithy	weaving picking wild berries
LH	*lavutaris**	*pal o gava**	*(2) lavutaris*	care for gadžes' cattle
	. . . . occasional work in the brick kiln			
RD	*lavutaris** broom making	*pal o gava** picking wild berries smearing ovens with adobe	. . . . care for gadžes' cattle . . . . . broom making basket weaving	picking wild berries

---

*An * indicates the primary resources. Number in brackets denote number of sons performing the respective subsistence activity.

With itinerant groups monoprofessionality is more possible than with sedentary groups, as the demand for a certain service or product is obviously higher in a broad locality than in a limited one. Thus Slovak Roma tended somewhat to add subsidiary professions and ways of living to their primary or main traditional jati-profession. Subsequently, the process of inner jati-differentiation was not so intense. It has often been noted that among Slovak Roma there are few professional groups, few jati names, and also little endogamy among their various subgroups. This could perhaps be explained by their early sedentarization, which led to polyprofessionalization—for an individual as well as within the family. Thus, only the traditional names such as *chartas* and *lavutaris* were preserved as jati denominations. A family, living much more from fruit picking, adobe-brick making, stone crushing, and the like would still denote itself as *charťiko fajta* or *lavutariko fajta*—a blacksmith or musician descent group by virtue of their father having once been a blacksmith or musician, at least occasionally. As will be analyzed later, a blacksmith who had to give up his profession or his family members learned new skills such as wicker basket weaving or broom making from Roma in other Rom settlements on their daily trips or migrations. One of my informants, Jan Blado, said, "My father knew how to play, but not so very perfectly. So he learned to weave wicker baskets. Wicker baskets, that is where the *gadže* put their potatoes—they pick the potatoes and throw them in the *opalki*. Roma learned it from one another; they went, they looked, they learned. If you are in need, you will learn everything."[27] Families, the fathers of which could neither play music nor do blacksmith work and could only weave baskets or make brooms, were less respected and their economic position was usually worse. Somewhat more respected was trough making, but none of my informants was from a trough-making family. There are, however, several families of Romanian Roma who were trough makers; they do not speak Romanes anymore, their mother tongue being Romanian, and a lot of them deny their Gypsy origins.

Buťi

Buťi means the work of a hired laborer, who worked for wages. Most frequently mentioned kinds of *buťi* were: work at a railway construction site, work at the construction at some public building like a town hall, a cinema, and so on, felling trees in the forest, work in a quarry or in some small local factory (for example, transport of potatoes to a distillery, filling bottles with soda water in a soda water factory, etc.). Work in the farmers' fields was not denoted by the word *buťi* but by a predicative construction, *kernas pal o mali*, that is, "they worked in the fields." Occasional help or service rendered in the *gadžes'* yards (for example, chopping firewood, cleaning the stables, and so forth) was described as *kernas pal o gadže*, that is, "they worked at the *gadžes'*." The term for a hired laborer is *buťakero* (from *buťi*), but a person who works in the farmers' fields is not a *buťakero*.

Though *buťi* had a lower status than crafts, let alone music, more and more Roma had to resort to it. The trouble was that there was unemployment (*buťa na sas*). Nearly every elderly man and woman I asked how the Roma once lived, started off with the following sentence: *"Darekana buťa na sas"* ("Once there were no jobs"). Thus, Aladár Kurej said, "If work cropped up somewhere—if for instance they built a railway or constructed a town hall, as they did in our place—a hundred people would rush there, but only one would be employed. And they would not take the best worker, but the man who agreed for least money."[28] According to Jozef Andrej, "They would employ only a person who brought eggs, hens, geese. But the Roma had nothing like that; how then could a Rom be employed?"[29] Anna Bogárová's statement was in the same tone: "They did not employ even poor *gadže* and a Rom was the most despised among all. How then could he have been given a job?"[30] Still, there were Roma who were lucky enough to get *buťi*. Maybe because they were willing to work for less than others. The regular wages and the low status which did not force them to spend money on entertaining others and wearing fashionable clothes, as the musicians had to, gave rise to a new jati trade—peddling.

Peddling

Peddling (*pal o gava*) was usually done by women, very rarely by men. Wives of those Roma who brought in wages from their *buťi* bought all sorts of small wares in town shops and went from village to village offering them to the peasants' wives for cash or, sometimes, for kind. "My man worked, didn't he, so he got money. And I bought those candles, cups, plates, or needles or thread. I bought these sorts of things in a shop in Michalovce. I took these small wares and I went peddling from village to village,"[31] said Anna Bogárová. Some years before the Second World War, Roma from some localities "discovered" Prague and went peddling there with coat hangers, mousetraps, and the like. This subsistence activity was interrupted by the war.

Communal Services

Gradual increase in the Rom population resulted in the growth of "Gypsy colonies." Traditional Roma settlements, consisting of no more than five, six, or seven huts, were inhabited by relatives who lived from one main jati occupation and several supplementary subsistence activities. The size of a settlement was regulated by reasonable balance between *gadžo* demand for and the Rom offer of products and services. If the offer greatly exceeded the demand, generational dispersion solved the problem. But in time there was no village which did not have Gypsies of its own, and thus, Gypsy colonies with five to six hundred and even a thousand or more Roma inhabitants arose. Such huge settlements were, for instance, Podskalka near the town of Humenné, Pavlovce nad Uhom, Rakúsy, and the like. These big communities were much more heterogeneous in all respects than the small settlements. Also, subsidiary practices of subsistence were much more varied here. The Roma had to grasp any job opportunities that presented themselves. Thus some of them agreed to perform communal services which were despised and which other people were not willing to do, for example, the job of a cesspool cleaner (*god'aris*), a knacker or man who destroys dogs (*hinclikos*), and scrap collector. These communal services were considered so dirty among other Roma that "*god'aris*" and "*hinclikos*" were used as swear words. In normative terms, other Roma kept their distance from the *familia* (extended family) of a *god'aris*, but the reality was less rigid. "The Roma hated cesspool cleaners. 'Oh, you're a cesspool cleaner; I won't talk to you,'"[32] said Vojtěch Fabian. In this context I will now quote part of an interesting interview I once recorded in Podskalka with Ludvík Tokár and his wife, Julie Tokárová. Tokár: "It is a great shame, my girl! My father—they were four brothers—they had a cart and the four of them went through the town and—excuse me, that I talk this way in the presence of your dear, golden face—they went from one lavatory to another." Tokárová, his wife: "It is a shame!

Why do you talk this way! They will mock you!" Tokár: "Let her know how people used to live once. They cleaned it, threw it in a barrel, and carried it to the river Laborec, disposed of it there and went back; and the town hall paid them 6 or 7 crowns a day. My father was their boss, because he was the oldest. They did this for eight years."[33] The grandfather of one of my friends was also a *god'aris*. As he had the monopoly in this job, he got so rich that he started dealing in pigs. Some of his sons learned to play music to enhance their group status. They claimed to have musician ancestors and gradually they became not only the richest, but also the most respected *fajta* (patrilineal descent group) in the whole region.

Pig Dealing

Several Roma settlements (Lučka, Kapušany, Sebeš, for example) near the towns of Prešov and Bardejov were famous for pig dealing, and as Vojtěch Fabian said, "Pig dealers, along with some of the most well established and popular musicians, were the richest Roma."[34]

The pig trade between Slovakia and the Czech lands started on a large scale after the Austrian empire collapsed in 1918 and the new state of Czechoslovakia was formed. Two enterprising contractors started to purchase pigs in rural East Slovakia and transport them to Czech towns for sale. Two main transport centers were the East Slovak towns of Prešov and Bardejov. It was necessary to find an intermediary, or dealer, who would go from farmer to farmer, buy the pigs from him, and then drive all the pigs to a railway station from which they could be transported to Czech lands.

As various social sections of *gadžo* society were involved either in agriculture (land ownership being the most frequent case) or in some other steady profession, it was the Roma who were free to grasp at the new trade and at the chances of profit making. Thanks to specific laws and regulations resulting from Rom kinship structure, brothers, cousins, uncles, brothers-in-law, and so forth always managed to gather enough money to buy the trading license and constitute some initial entrepreneurial resources. Soon, the pig trade was in the hands of several Rom kin groups. "The pig dealers were such families—brothers-in-law, brothers, cousins, all together. There were four brothers and they married four sisters. It was such a dynasty, you see!"[35] said Vojtěch

Fabian. In fact, an interview with this informant yielded the following valuable information on pig dealing: "The pig dealers went from one farmer to another and bought the pigs, one, two, three, as many as the farmer was willing to sell. On Wednesdays, wagons came to take the pigs away and the dealers got the pigs together on Saturdays and Sundays. They took them home and fed them a lot, so that they got fat. They gave them potatoes, bran, and antimony to become fat. On Wednesdays, Priputin from Prague would come, and one more, one Mareš would also come; they were two of them who bought pigs. In Prešov and Bardejov there was a pen where all the pigs were driven together before being loaded into wagons. The men brought them in motor cars, as the dealers had lorries of their own. Each of them would make a sign on his pigs. And then they would weigh the pigs. The price was, let us say, 6.50 crowns per kilo. But all of a sudden the price would rise: 7 crowns, 9 crowns. But the pig dealer would not tell the *gadže*, never! He would go to a *gadžo* and ask, 'Have you a pig?' 'I have. How much?' 'Five crowns.' 'I won't give it away!' '5.50.' 'Okay.' He would then buy it from the farmer at 5.50 per kilo and sell it to Mareš for 9. They made 150 to 200 crowns' profit on each pig. But Priputin and Mareš profited even more. They all robbed one another. Roma robbed the *gadže* and Priputin and Mareš robbed the Roma."[36]

In a pig-dealing family the working unit consisted of all the family members who fulfilled specific duties according to their sex and age. Men purchased and sold the pigs, while women and children fed them and cultivated a piece of land, on which they grew potatoes and some corn for the pigs. Pig dealers' wives were perhaps the only Rom women who had to give up going *pal o gava*, as this would not have been compatible with their status. As the pig-dealing profession was something new and nontraditional, a proper and visible manifestation had also to be found for the status of a rich pig dealer. One of the immediately visible markers was dress. As Margita Miková told me, "My father would never put on an ordinary suit. Only leather trousers, a leather coat, and leather boots."[37] It is interesting that I did not find much intermarriage with *gadže* in the pig dealers' families. I think that this is because while poor Roma would accept a poor white outcast and vice versa a *čoro gadžo* would not mind getting assimilated to Gypsies, the rich pig dealer considered himself superior to a *čoro gadžo*, and a well-to-do, decent *gadžo* would not like to marry a Gypsy.

The pig-dealing profession, however, flourished for only a very short time and came to an end by the Second World War when racist Nazi laws prohibited Roma from processing trading licenses.

Other Occupations and Ways of Subsistence Acquisition

Some ancestors of my Rom friends had several other minor occupations. These jobs, as most other Rom occupations, were of an occasional character, bringing in no regular revenue. They also demanded a sort of itinerancy or spatial movement within a specific area. Umbrella repairing was one such job often done by Roma. Umbrella repairers (*ambrelara*) would go from village to village and repair umbrellas in the houses of their customers. Their daily itinerary was quite extensive, and often they had to stay overnight with foreign Roma (*pal o cudza Roma*). Some Roma women sewed and sold *duchni* (sg. *duchna*)—bulky sacks stuffed with feathers or down and used as a sleeping cover. They would go to Jewish households (*pal o Čhinde*), pluck the feathers of their geese and ducks, and get the feathers from them for some small service. At home, the Roma women would wash the feathers and stuff them in a *duchna* which they then sold in the town market.

Some Roma lived from the carting trade. The articles which they transported were determined by the economic character of the region. Where there was a limestone quarry, for example, a Rom carter would transport lime from the quarry to individual customers. In southeast Slovakia lots of vegetables were grown; there the Rom carter bought red peppers, watermelons, tomatoes, and the like from the farmers and transported them to the town market for sale. Often the cart and horse were used for collecting scrap material. Some Rom carters became rich, but even their trade was destroyed by the racist laws of the fascist Slovak state.

As already stated, Roma seldom owned land. Only the pig dealers had to have a piece of land which they bought from some *gadže*, to grow food for their pigs. However, in some places *gadže* farmers hired out a small field to a Rom family, which had to cultivate and fertilize it. In return, the Rom family could take home every fifth, seventh, or tenth sheaf, depending on the specific oral agreement entered into with the farmer.

In the last quarter of the nineteenth century, large-scale migration started from poor, rural East Slovakia to the U.S. Many *gadže* migrated to America for good and so did some Rom families. But as the Roma had perhaps closer ties with their vast kin group, they went to the U.S. on temporary contracts, leaving their wives and children behind. When they had earned some money they would return. According to Vojtěch Fabian there were "manpower dealers" who hired men, arranged the working contracts for them, and paid their ship fares. Then these men would cash their wages, leaving only a small part to the Rom workers. Still, some of the Roma who worked in America for some time (*Hamericana*) succeeded in saving up enough money to become pig dealers after their return to Slovakia.

Gypsies are generally believed to live from theft, which is considered to be their main source of subsistence. This was not true of the sedentary Slovak Roma. As Veselovský said, "Our Gypsies did not steal. Would a villager invite a Gypsy music band to play at his son's wedding if he knew that half his poultry would disappear?" The following statement by Lájoš Horváth is a fine example of ethnic prejudice carried over from the majority to the minority: "Only those Vlachi who went around in caravans would steal. They were here one day and the next day nobody knew where they got lost. But we lived in one place all the time and our *gadže* knew us. If we had stolen, they would have turned us out, away! And for whom would I then have been the farrier?"[38] The Slovak Roma who were under the control of the permanent *gadžo* neighborhood would at the most steal a small amount of potatoes from the *gadžes'* fields, and the children would pluck fruits from the trees in the *gadžes'* gardens.

Spatial Mobility of Slovak Roma

Though Slovak Roma have been sedentary for roughly three centuries, various sorts of spatial movement were an inherent feature of their economic and social life. In fact, all the jati-professions were connected with or even conditioned by some kind of spatial mobility. There was, nevertheless, a difference between the spatial mobility of the Slovak Roma and that of the Vlachi.

While Slovak Roma inhabited permanent huts, Vlachi lodged in _verdana_ (caravans); while Slovak Roma were settled in permanent colonies, Vlachi were constantly changing their _rito_ (camping ground); while Slovak Roma dwelled in villages surrounded by a stable _gadžo_ neighborhood, Vlachi passed through various towns and villages constantly changing their _gadžo_ environment. While Vlachi, much more isolated from mainstream _gadžo_ society, preserved many indigenous habits in the form of integral functioning systems, Slovak Roma, due to daily economic contacts with the same _gadžo_ neighborhood and embedded in the social structure of one village and one locality, surrendered much more to the sociocultural influence of the _gadže_. Of course, the Slovak Roma preserved the Romani language; they preserved the specific creative forms of their culture; they also preserved some ancient beliefs; they had and still have a set of ethical norms resulting from a specific socioeconomic structure, which in fact is their kinship structure, but they have forgotten and lost many institutions which still regulate the everyday life of the Vlachi. The Vlachi, for instance, have a judicial system of their own; the Slovak Roma, however, were absorbed by—and have themselves adopted—the legal system of the _gadže_. Thus, the institution of _kris_—an elected court analogous to the _panchayat_ in Indian villages—does not exist anymore among Slovak Roma, and neither does the concept of _marime_ (a set of complex beliefs and taboos connected with purity and pollution), so important in the Vlachi community. Excommunication as a punishment for transgression of Rom law is now unknown among Slovak Roma. What in Vlachi communities functions as an integral system, strictly and ceremoniously observed, has in Slovak Roma communities been transformed into a set of ideas, the remains of ancient Rom norms, not so strictly followed in real life.

Sedentarism and itinerancy of Slovak and Vlachi Roma respectively have influenced relations between the Roma as well as Roma-_gadže_ relations. Thus, while the Vlachi who changed their _gadžo_ environment frequently could perhaps have made theft a part of their subsistence activities, Slovak Roma, as I have mentioned before, could not afford to steal without risking the chances of losing their _gadže_ customers. Thus, the antagonism of the _gadže_ toward the itinerant Vlachi was much more aggressive and punitive than the patronizingly disdainful ethnosocial discrimination toward the sedentary Roma, "our Gypsies."

Still, *gadžo* society on the whole did not differentiate between distinct Roma groups: *"cikán jako cikán"* ("Gypsy is the same as Gypsy," that is, all Gypsies are the same) and thus even the sedentary Slovak Roma suffered from *gadžo* aggression, in turn provoked by the behavior of the Vlachi. In an attempt to protect themselves, to be accepted by *gadžo* society, the Slovak Roma—in addition to the traditional jati distance—therefore adopted the negative attitudes of the *gadže* toward the Vlachi and tried at all costs to differentiate themselves from the Vlachi. I once witnessed two Roma children playing teasing games. One boy said to the other, *"Phen prachos"* ("Say ashes"). His playmate repeated the sentence and then the first boy added a teasing rhyme to it: *"Tiro dad Vlachos"* ("Your father is a Vlach Rom")—and at that the other boy, feeling very offended, fell on him and a fight started. The Vlachi are disdained because they allegedly *čoren* (steal) and *phiren verdonenca, nane len khera* (go around in caravans, don't have houses). But the attitude of Slovak Roma toward Vlachi is actually rather ambivalent. On the one hand, influenced by the *gadže*, they hold them in contempt, but on the other hand they express highest admiration and envy for the Vlachi "because they steal and thus are rich and have a lot of gold" and then, because they are *"buter Roma sar amen"* ("they are more Rom than we") and *"džanen te likeren lengere romipen"* ("they know how to preserve their Rom identity"). The positive attitude toward Vlachi is really an indirectly expressed wish to preserve their own identity; it is a sort of defense against "gadžikanization," a sort of strategy aimed at "boundary maintenance."

To come back to the spatial mobility of the sedentary Slovak Roma: though in comparison to the itinerant Vlachi, the Slovak Roma were sedentary, there was a great difference between their sedentarism and the settled life of the *gadže* villagers. The spatial movement of *gadžo* peasants was limited to their daily walk from their house to their fields, to a weekly journey from their house to the town market; at solemn occasions they would attend an annual feast, or a wedding, or some dance in another village. Of course, there were poor *gadže* who emigrated to America; there were also well-known itinerant Slovak tinkers and young Slovak girls who went to Czech towns to work as servants. But the peasant *gadže* with whom Roma had economic relations lived in the safety of their houses, their fields, and their church. While discussing Rom professions, I have already mentioned various kinds of spatial movement. There was first of all the specific intergenerational mobility, the generational dispersion. Emigration was another type of mobility. There were some Rom families who migrated to America early in this century and until the Second World War, but they were numerically insignificant. Most often, only Rom men went to America, with the intention of earning quick money and coming back as soon as possible usually to start the pig-dealing trade. Emigration as a permanent shift of the entire family was not a typical form of spatial movement for the Slovak Roma in the first half of this century, but it appeared on a large scale after 1945 when Roma from Slovakia went in large numbers to the Czech lands. Similar to the working expeditions to the U.S. were the peddling expeditions of Rom men to Prague, which started in the early 1930s and were over by the Second World War. Rom men came to Prague to sell mousetraps, clothes hangers, candles, and so forth; they stayed several months, lodged in emergency shelters where fifty people crammed into one room slept on the floor. Having earned some money, they would return to their families. Temporary stays in America and in Prague transgressed the borders of *amaro krajos* (our region) and differed only in their respective distance from home and thus in their length. Otherwise, both were a sort of emergency, an attempt to find new sources of subsistence, when the traditional jati products or services could not ensure a reasonable income anymore.

Each society, however socially homogeneous and egalitarian it may be—and this was the case of the Slovak Roma—has its *čore* (poor, miserable, beggars). Among Slovak Roma also there were people who, for one reason or another—economic crisis, poor professional skills, disintegration of the family, repudiation by the Rom community for transgressing Rom law, and so forth—were or became *čore* or *čorarde* (pauperized). These people found it easier or necessary to leave their own settlement or locality and to *phirel pal o cudza Roma* (to go from one "foreign" Rom to another). The traditional laws of hospitality obliged Roma to offer them shelter for several days and even weeks. Vasil Demeter, son of a well-established blacksmith, told me, "My father was very good. When poor Roma came, he would take them to sleep at our place; they would stay two weeks, three weeks, even a month. He gave them food. He prepared a tub for them so that they could take a bath, sometimes he himself washed them, he shaved them, and he even gave them a clean shirt. And when they were about to leave, he showed them the way and told them where they could find work. . . . (In our house) they would do some work or other. They would fetch water or chop firewood; they would even clean the house, they would sweep—it was women's work, but they were poor, so they did whatever was necessary." Lájoš Horváth told me, "My father liked these vagrants, as we always came to know from them what was happening where, what all the news under the sun was."

On the margin between spatial movements connected with economically stable professions and those which were a consequence of economic or social disintegration was the itinerancy of various *repairers*, most often umbrella repairers (*ambrelara*). They would repair umbrellas for *gadže* in the whole region; they would sleep in the huts of *cudza Roma* (foreign Roma), and they would pay for their hospitality by telling the news of the rest of the world. All *ambrelara* I came to know were single people: a man who became a little odd because his wife ran away from him, an elderly lesbian, an elderly bachelor.

All other types of spatial mobility were an integral part of distinct *jati* professions and were indispensable for their performance and accomplishment; or—to put it the other way around—there were hardly any Roma professions which did not necessitate one type of spatial movement or the other.

Families who lived—only partially—from adobe-brick making may be classified as semi-itinerant. They lived in huts, but from spring to autumn when farmers in the locality went in for building, the whole family would leave the settlement and stay at the working place till the adobe bricks were ready. Even children of four or five years helped in the process. The family slept outside when the weather was fine and in the farmer's barn when it rained. After finishing the work in one place in a week or two, the family would move on to another place. When no more adobe bricks were required in the locality, the family would return home.

The carter's and scrap collector's trade also required a semi-itinerant way of life. Still, neither the carters selling vegetables, fruits, or lime in the towns of their region nor the scrap collectors stayed away for more than a few nights at a time. Besides, the whole family did not participate in the profession. It was either the father with some sons or a couple with their youngest child who went *kheral pal o maro* (away from home to get bread). The carters would stay overnight in their carts or with some relative who lived in the locality, for it would have been improper for those who did not share the status of the *čore Roma* (poor Roma) to sleep in the houses of *cudza Roma* (foreign Roma).

Spatial movement was indispensable for accomplishing even those professions which did not force any family member to stay outside their hut and settlement overnight. A specific type of mobility was the daily *phiriben pal o gava* (going from village to village) of the Rom woman. As I said before, the blacksmiths' wives went *pal o gava* to sell their husbands' ironware products; wives of the *lavutara* (musicians) went *pal o gava* to sell some service in the farmers' yards or to beg; wives of the *butakere* (workers) went *pal o gava* to peddle; some women went *pal o gava* to smear ovens with adobe or whitewash houses, and so forth. Each woman visited two to five villages daily and covered twenty to thirty kilometers.

Among the men, the musicians went to various villages of their locality two or three times a week to play at *bijava* (weddings), *zabavi* (dances), or *boňa* (baptisms). A high degree of spatial mobility was necessary, because in one village Roma did not find sufficient demand for their jati products or services. The *charťi* (blacksmiths) also had to leave their homes and stay away for several days when they went to burn charcoal.

Thanks to these different types of spatial mobility, the Roma themselves could develop a broad system of information exchange. While wandering (*phirindos*), Rom women and men received information on eventual professional opportunities. Entering other Roma settlements on their trips, they saw *pal soste aver Roma dživen* (what other Roma live from), and sometimes they learned their skills from them: wicker basket weaving, music making, and so on. Apart from economic information, Roma acquired very important social information: for example, where a good bride for their son or a good bridegroom for their daughter could be found. Everybody was on the lookout for a *lačhi familia* (a good family), for *žuže Roma* (clean Roma, that is, those who did not eat the flesh of horses and dogs, which, in turn, presupposed a good economic position). They were looking for a family where there were musicians or blacksmiths (*kaj lavutara vaj charťi*), which implied economic well-being, and where there were many male members in case of a fight (*kaj but murša, te perel-mariben*), which meant political power or at least security within the kinship structure of the community. Spatial mobility also enabled the Slovak Roma to acquire and pass over information of a general nature, "all the news under the sun," as Lájoš Horváth put it. I often heard various *gadže* admiring the promptness of the Rom information system: in the morning a baby is born, an unfaithful wife is murdered, or a youngster elopes with a girl—in the evening Roma from the entire area know about the event. It is spatial mobility which helped to spread every important bit of news quickly. Trips made for professional as well as social reasons, such as visiting numerous relatives, also enabled the transmission of creative forms of traditional culture (songs, tales) and strengthened the ethical norms and values of the Slovak Rom community as a whole. This happened especially in popular, public discussions which took place whenever visitors came from some other village; people condemned things which were to be condemned and praised things which were to be praised, and thus it became clearer to all what was good and what was bad.

It would be interesting to analyze the itinerancy of the basically sedentary Slovak Roma from the psychological point of view. I daresay that the ability to stand hardship, the flexibility and adaptability to inevitable situations without loss of identity—*romano kokal na phagela ňiko*, nobody can break the Rom bone—are all very much conditioned by their spatial mobility. Aware of the significance mobility had for them, the Roma often quote the proverb *Ko but phirel, but džanel* (the person who wanders a lot knows a lot).

Conclusion

What can be said about the Rom economy as a whole? It seems that the time span described by my Rom friends was a period of inter- as well as intragenerational occupational shift. The traditional and lifelong jati professions—namely smithery and music—were no longer able to provide a Rom family with sufficient livelihood. Thus, all family members, including the children above six years, had to do all sorts of supplementary jobs, render occasional services, and perform subsidiary crafts or small trade to procure enough for subsistence. Most women and men earned their livelihood successively and/or simultaneously in various ways; they also went through several periods of exploring new avenues of work and learning new skills. On the other hand the range of occupations accessible to the Roma was limited by their jati determination and pariya status. First of all, in more and more professions institutional education was required. But Roma children acquired their education and professional qualifications in their own families, within their jati. A blacksmith's sons, for example, would help their father from the age of six onward, and the musician's sons learned to play from early childhood. "At the age of three I was pulling a small violin behind me. When I was ten years old, I already went to play with my father. He put a stool under me, because I was small, and I played,"[39] said Partyzán.

Girls either went *pal o gava* with their mothers or stayed home and took care of their younger brothers and sisters, learning thus to fulfill their future role of mother and housewife. Children learned by helping the adults, by looking at what their fathers and mothers showed them. "To show" in Romani is expressed by the verb *te sikhavel*, which also means "to learn." Though school attendance became compulsory even for Rom children—sometimes policemen would come to take children to school—in fact nobody made any serious and consistent effort to formally educate the Rom population. The 69.9 percent of illiteracy (Census of 1970) is a proof of this. On the one hand, *gadžo* society was not especially interested in having Gypsies at school; on the other hand, Rom parents did not see any advantage in institutional education for their children. Dudi Kot'o, for example, told me, "My father used to say, 'You will not sit at a writing desk, will you! You won't become a studied gentleman. Have you ever seen a Rom doctor or a notary? Something like that has never existed in the whole world! Why do you need school then? Go and take the violin in your hand.'"[40]

There were, in addition, two other important factors which restricted the choice of occupations: payment in kind (that is, in food instead of cash) and a specific, traditional expenditure stereotype influenced by status duties and egalitarian pressures within the Rom community. Most Roma got, in exchange for their craft products and services, foodstuffs which one family would consume in one day. This type of earning contributed to a stereotype of day-to-day life, which required little planning or long-term perspectives; it also ruled out the possibility of saving money for potential investment or business of any kind. Those Roma who were paid in money had to spend a lot on their status manifestation, which required *te del paťiv*—entertaining others; and of course they were obliged to help their whole kin group unless they wanted to be slandered: *izdrano sar gadžo*, "stingy like a *gadžo*." If people became too rich, there was the danger that they would try to get rid of their despised Gypsyhood, that they would stop knowing their people, and that they would no longer observe the laws of kinship and group solidarity. Thus, egalitarian pressures, like envious gossip on the one hand and high praise of generosity and extravagance on the other, hindered those who had access to money from putting aside a lot of savings and eventually taking up some *gadžo* profession. When a family grew too rich, it had to leave the Rom settlement. Such a case was recorded as late as 1969 in the settlement where I lived. A father and his four sons earned a lot of money at the subway construction site in Prague. They bought a car but were not willing to spend their money with others. A fight (*mariben*) finally drove them away from the settlement, and they settled in a town where they got a flat.

When the pig trade suddenly emerged, entire kin groups—dynasties, as Vojtěch Fabian put it—took up this profession and thus constituted a new jati. But such rich Roma (*barvale Roma*) founded settlements of their own, each known as a *barvaľi vatra*, a rich community or settlement. Fifteen or twenty years ago, when there was still a Gypsy settlement behind most East Slovak villages, one could at once see which one was a *čori vatra* (poor community) and which a *barvaľi vatra* (rich community). Within one single settlement, however, the differences between *barvale* and *čore Roma* were not so conspicuous.

Social development, which was bringing along occupational, economic, and to a certain extent even class differentiation among the Slovak Roma and which was restructuring the traditional jatis, was abruptly interrupted by the Second World War.

Today, we are going through a period of overall, basic social change in Slovakia. These changes are unobtrusively linked to many old habits and stereotypes of *gadžo* society, but a connecting link between the present social order and the past social situation of Roma is totally missing. Thus, a Rom boy who used to be fully economically independent at the age of fifteen or sixteen and so, according to an old proverb *ko kamel romňa, mi thoval peske piri* ("he who wants to have a wife, let him provide his own pot") was not hindered by anything in founding a family of his own, will today be considered abhorrent if he married at this "immature" age. A musician who formerly need not have known about the existence of musical notes because he could play without them will today not have the chance of making a living from music unless he passes exams in music theory. Youths who go scrap-collecting instead of attending to their jobs in a factory—just because scrap-collecting may bring in more money, or because at scrap-collecting they are with their brothers, cousins, and Rom friends, while in the factory they are surrounded by *gadže*—will be threatened by legal paragraphs and courts. Children who fail at school because their mother tongue is not being respected or young girls and boys who refuse to enter the apprentice schools because they want to earn money quickly, either to contribute to the family revenue or to buy fashionable suits to be better than *gadže*, will be labeled as "incorrigible" or "unreeducable" or by some other nice, official term. Families who travel in search of better earning opportunities will be referred to in despair as "typical Gypsy nomads"—though Slovak Roma have not been nomadic for the past three centuries! People who spend money on entertaining other Roma instead of saving up to buy flats or other material goods will be regularly discussed by social workers in the Gypsy commissions. A man who cannot stand working eight hours a day for eight years at one conveyor belt because formerly he used to do different jobs in winter and in summer, or because he used to work out of doors, or because he used to decide for himself when and where to strike with the hammer, while now it is decided for him by the conveyor belt, will be qualified as an "inadaptable person without proper working habits."

By this I do not mean to say that Roma should remain "gypsies." Social and economic integration of Roma into the society is indispensable for Roma as well as for *gadže*. But in every society the major social group should, by virtue of being the majority—which usually implies that it is also the decision-making element, directing and having laws at its disposal—understand the social and historical background of the minority which it endeavors to integrate. An old Rom proverb says, *Manuš šaj sikhľol savoro lačho the nalačho*, that is, "People are able to learn everything, good as well as bad." It would be good if the mainstream society gave Roma a chance to learn the *lačho* rather than the *nalačho*, by respecting their ethnocultural uniqueness.

Afterword 1995:

Since the dismantling of the communist regimes in Eastern Europe, there have been many changes in former Czechoslovakia. First, there has been an explosion of anti-Gypsyism and racism: skinhead attacks, discrimination on the labor market, anti-Gypsy graffiti ("gas all Gypsies"), barring of Roma from restaurants, police aggression, and the pauperization of the Roma. There have also been changes within Romani society. There has been a rise in Gypsy criminality as a consequence of the type of anti-Gypsy acts listed above and also as a consequence of the disintegration of traditional Romani community and extended family. There has also arisen a Romani ethno-emancipation effort as reflected in a renaissance of literature, journalism, and theater; an increase in the number of university graduates; and the rise of a very thin but important layer of extremely rich entrepreneurs.

NOTES

1. I have used the spelling of Romani developed by the linguistic commission of the Union of Gypsies–Roma (Svaz Cikánů–Romů) which was active in the years 1969–1973: č to be read as ch (in English); j to be read as y (in English); dž to be read as j (in English); ch to be read as x (in Greek); h denotes aspiration in čh, kh, ph, and th. Romani (adv. Romanes) is the language of the Roma. I use the ethnonym Rom (pl. Roma), which the Roma themselves prefer to the derogatory appellative "Gypsy." [The quotes from Roma have been translated into English in the body of the essay. The original Romani is given in footnotes. Ed.]

2. According to the Census of 1970, 72 percent of Roma in the SSR were village dwellers.

3. "Z vlka nebude slanina, z cigána nebude človek"; "Z cigána ani, čiapka nedobrá, keď ju nejdeš, tak ju bij."

4. "Miro dad phenelas, hoj gadže likernas Romes ča akor manušeske, kana sas dur. Sar avlă pašeder, ta sas ča cigán."

5. "Ma ker vika, lela tut o gadžo."

6. *charťas* (Greek) or *kováčis* (Slovak) = the smith.

7.   "Cigánove deti neboja sa isiker." "... Cigáni mi klince kujú v hlave."
8.   Darekana pre Slovensko jekhfeder odborňikos pre charťiko buťi sas
Rom. Gadžo na džanelas te kerel oda so Rom. Le Romes sas talentos pre
charťiko buťi. . . . O Roma sikhade le gadžen oja buťi. O gadže kamenas te
sikhľol, kaj pem kole Romestar te na mušinen te mangel. Avelas o goro sig
tosara, phenďa pre miro dad "Janku, ušti!" Ušťaďa mire dades. "Kampel mange
petalos te kerel!" A sar o dad kerlas, o gadžo dikhelas, sar jov kerel. Jekhvar
dikhenas, masovar dikhenas, ta the jon dosikhľonas oja charťiko buťi. O dad
peske lelas tiž terne rakles te sikhľol. Ale hjaba, pre oja charťiko buťi ča o Rom
sas jekh.
9.   K'amende ča romano charťas sas andro gav. Oda sas ajsi sar životno
buťi. Ke leste o gadže avnas a mangenas pes leske. Jou sas jekhašundeder.
Varese charťi solacharnas. Kamelas vareko romňa te lel a na sas rašaj, ta
solarcharas ou, o charťas romano, the le romanen the le gadžikanen.
10.   Amen bokh na merahas sar aver Roma, bo o dad sas lengero, le
gadžengero kovačis. K'amende varekana o bale kavka murdaľonas, andre gruľa
tašlonas, vareso les kavka pre čang, phageripen, barvale gadže murdarnas les.
Oda pervo avnas pal mro dad. Has odoj kovačis, rado les dikhenas. "Av tuke
vaš o balo." Dzekana anenas leske avka topanki purane vaš o čhave, choľovori.
11.   K'amende sas charťas, ale maškar amende na bešelas, bešelas avrether,
maškar o barvale, ou sas imar feder, imar pes na vičinlas, hoj hino "cigán,"
imar pes na stikinlas amenca. Čoro sas tiž, ale imar sar pes chudňa andr'oda
remeslos, ta le Romenca na vakerlas, sas barikano.
12.   Amen o čhave anahas trasta. Darekana dikhľam le gadženge pre dvora
ajse cikne purane trastora, te na kamľahas iľam len.
13.   O dad amen uštavlas štare orendar tosara. "Ušťen čhajale!" "No uštav
dado, bo šil!" "Ušti, te chal kampel!" A imar uštahas, savi phurdelas o pišot,
savi de! le svirindeha pro petala, de! O dad: "Phurden, mre čhajora, phurden!"
"Jaj dado, na phurdhav, bo bokhaľi!" O dad man kamelas te marel, ale na
marlas, ča šukaribnaha: "Maj chana, sar e daj avla pal o gava khere, anla te
chan." Ta marahas polokores, lemás pro cheva andro petala. Deše beršendar
kerás le čokanoha.
14.   E daj anlas thudoro andro knoro, andre zajda bandurki, andre leketa
maroro. Avlas khere, o dad kerlas mek petalicis. "Dža ko Čhindo, biken
lovenge, kaj amen pro lon pro dohanos t'avel."
15.   Darekana amare slovaňika Roma na džanenas te bašavel, oda ča ungrika
Roma džanenas. Ale amare Roma sikhľonas lendar, kaj feder peske te dživen.
16.   Miro dad tel o kurko petalunlas, sombatone kurke phirelas te bašavel.
17.   Oda na existinlas, kaj aver te bašaďahas sar Rom. Mek paš miro dad,
paš miro papus avka sas. Adaďives tho'o gadže chuden pes andro bašaviben, ale
bašaven sar dziva manuša: duj, trin hangi thoven andre jekh giľi, man nervi

olestar! Rom te bašavel, ta sar kulturno manuš, phare hangi, šov, efta, ochto andre jakh giľi. Ale gadžo? Kaj o gadžo sikhľola oda so o Rom!

18. Save Roma džanenas te bašavel, chanas, save na džanenas, na chanas.

19. Me te džas bijaveste, ta eňa šel, ezeros, ochto šel—sar kana—man sas pojedňíman le ternestar. A so o rakle sas, ta vaš jekh giľi poťinenas mange avrether. Zakerahas pandž ezera, šov ezera vaš o pandždžne samas andre banda: jekh primašis, me, jekh kontra, brača, cymbalma, mek o bugošis. Pre celo okresis somas peršo me. O sudcas mange maškar o foros: "Pan Horváth servus!" Až o vast mange diňa. Me les na prindžarďom a jov man prindžarďa.

20. A me phiravas te žobrinel pal o gava. Dojekh Romňi džalas, a te chudás maro, ta rozphagás maroro pro efta kotorora, bo man sas efta čhave. Džalas jov te bašavel, chudelas love, ale so, te le muršenca prepijelas! Mušinda, so šaj kerďa, mušinlas te sikhavel, savo hino frajeris! A te anďa love, ta thoďom vareso pre sera, kaj le čhavenge pro gadora. Ale hlavno veca, leske kampelas gada, na, sar lavutariske! Parno gad, kalapa pro šero.

21. Dži dešušov berš me sogalinavas ko pastiris, bo man na sas daj aňi dad. Ale sar imar chudňom goďi, ta sikhľiľom te bašavkerel. Bo kamás feder te dživel, lokeder, kamás rajkanes te phirel, šukarel urdo Kamás, kaj the man ťavel feder paťiv maškar o manuša! Kaj šunás, že bašaven, the pro pandžto gav, me džás raťi, dikhás, kaj thovel o angušta—a sar thovlas tele e lavuta, me lás andro vast: "Ujcu, na rušena tumen? Šaj probalinav?" "Ča bašav mro čho!" Jekh berš phirás Rom Romendar, pal cudza Roma, bo miri famelija man na sas. No imar bišthajjekh berš, ile man andre banda. Kamás andro foros te bašavel, ale oda imar ča suno sas.

22. Avľa pal ma jekh čhavo, o dad leske avka phenďa: "No mro čho, le o čokanos, dža ker andre šmikňa buťi. Te džaneha avka sar me, ta tut dá mira čha. Te na džaneha, dža tuke khere. A ou phenlas: 'me džanav te bašaven.' 'Mek sa feder, mro čno! Le lavuta andro vast, mi šunav, sar bašaves!' Lelas o čhavo e lavuta, o dad. 'Mro čho, dža tuke khere! Na džanes ňič! Čhaje, kames les? Te les kames, chude les vastestar a dža tuke leha! Ale adaj n'aveha mang' andro kher! Bo na džanel aňi te bašavel. Te tu leha zjejďineha, mereha bokhate."

23. Na lenas cudzonen andre banda, ča peskeren, hoj kolestar te dživen.

24. Ča jekhvar tuke zagiľavlas o raklo leskeri giľi, takoj mušinehas te bašavel pal leste. Te na džanľalas, ta tuke phagerďahas e lavuta pal o šero.

25. Amen bašavas ko so kamel. Te kamel džaz—kola terne—prosím, bašavas leske džaz. Te kamel phurikane halgatovi, bašavas leske phurikanes.

26. Miro dad džanelas te bašavel, he kerlas buťi. Angluno primašis sas miro dad. Pre lavuta bašavlas. Palis imar sas le bašavibnastar bida, bo sas lavutara sar bala pro šero, ta gejľas te kerel pre štreka.

27. Miro dad džanelas te bašaven, ale na až kavka. Ta sikhľiľa opalki te chuven, kajse buťa, košara pletinlas. Opalki, kaj bandurki kiden pro maľio o gadže, chanen, čhiven andro opalki. O Roma sikhľile jekh avrestar, džanas, dikhenas, sikhľonas. Andre bida sa sikhľoha.

28. Te pes arakhelas buťi—kernas štreka, abo budinlas pes, phenas, foroskero kher, sar k'amende, ta ispidenas pes šeldžene a lelas jekhes. Na lelas savo jekhfeder buťakero, ale savo tuňeder džalas.

29. Lenas ča kajses, so anelas jandre, kachňen, papiňen. A le Romen ajso vareso na sas, ta sar iľahas Romes andre buťi?

30. Aňi čore gadžen na lenas andre buťi a Rom sas jekhgoreder podceňimen maškar savore, ta sar iľahas?

31. Sem o rom kerlas buťi, ta kidelas love. Ta cinás me ola momeľora, kučora, taňirici, vaj suva, thava, kajse kova, cinás me Mihajate andre sklepa, lás me odi pramaťi a phirás pal o gava te bikenavel.

32. Le goďaristar o Roma igen džungľonas. Jaj, tu sal goďaris, tuha duma na dav!

33. Oda hin bari ladž, mri rakľori! Miro dad—sas štar phrala—sas len verdan ajso odala štar phrala phirenas pal o foros a so paťiphenav angle tiro mujoro somnakuno, phirnas pal o budara. /Tokárová/ Oda ladž! So des ajsi duma! Lena tut pro asaben! /Tokár/ Ta mi džanel, sar dživahas čirla! On koda kidenas, čnivkernas andre bočka a ledžanas pre Laborca, mukhenas avri, džanas pale a oda foroskero kher lenge poťinelas 6–7 koruni ďivesekero. Miro dad sas majstros pre lende, bo sas jekhphureder. Jon oda kernas ochtor berš.

34. Handľara the ajse viychvalna, ašunde lavutara, ola sas jekhbarvaleder Roma.

35. O handľara sas ajse fameliji—šougora, phrala, brantanci, savore jekhetane. Jon sas štardžene phrala a ile štaredžene pheňen. Ajsi dinastija sas. No dikhes!

36. Ola handľara phirenas pal o gadže, cinavenas baličen, po jekh, po duj, po trin, keci ko kamelas te bikenel. Štredone avnas o vagoni, a jon sombatone, kurke stradenas le baličen. Anenas len khere, karminenas, denas but te chal, kaj but te važinen. Bandurki denas, šeľa a kodi antimonija denas, kaj te thuľon. Stredone avnas o Priputin a mek jekh, o Mareš, Prahatar, jon sas duj, so cinenas baličen. Preješiste, Bartvate sas ajsi ohrada, kodoj savore baliče sas, medig len na ispidne andro vagoni. O Roma len lenas kodoj pro motora, bo le handľaren sas lengere nakladno motora. Sako peske značinlas peskere baličes. No akana le baličen važinenas. O baliče monas phenas 6,50 koruni kilos. Ale jekhvar avľa e cena opre. Šidzen koruni, eňa. A oda handľaris na phenďa le gadžeske, ta kaj! Avľas ko gadžo: 'Máš praše?' 'Ano. Keľo?' 'Pec koruni.' 'Nedám.' 'Tumáš pec pedzešát.' 'Dobre.' Lelas le gadžestar pro 5,50 a le Marešiske bikenlas po eňa.

Zakernas 150–200 pre jekh baličo. Ale o Mareš o Priputin zakernas mek buter. O Roma le gadžen občorkernas, o Priputin, Mareš le Romen občorkernas.
37. Miro dad šoha na urlas ča ajse gada. Ča morčuňi cirach, morčuňi cholov, morčuno gerekos.
38. Ča ola Vlachi, so phirenas verdonenca, ta on čornas. Jekh ďives sas adaj, aver ďives ňiko na džanelas, kaj našľile. Amen bešahas furt pre jekh than, ta ola amare gadže imar džanenas amen. Te čorďamas, ta amen tradňahas het. Ta vaš kaske petalunďomas palis le grajen?
39. Trine beršendar cirdavas pal mande e lavutica. Kana mange sas deš berš, imar phiravas te bašavel le dadeha. O dad mange thoďa stolkos, bo somas cikno mek, a bašavás.
40. Miro dad phenlas: "Th'avka pal o skamind na bešeha, raj tutar n'ela. Dikhľal Romes doktoris abo notaris? Na existinel pro svetos! Dža, chude lavuta andro vast."

REFERENCES

Census 1970
1971 *Cikánské obyavatelstvo podle scitani lidu, domu a bytu 1.1.2.1970.* Praha; FSÚ. Zprávy a rozbory, c. 23.
Guy, Willy
1975 "Ways of Looking at Roms: The Case of Czechoslovakia," in *Gypsies, Tinkers and other Travellers,* ed. Farnham Rehfisch (London: Academic Press), pp. 201–229. (Reprinted here, with changes and an afterword, on pages 13–68.)
Horváthová, Emilia
1963 *Cigáni na Slovensku.* Bratislava: SAV.
Hübschmannová, Milena
1972 "What Can Sociology Suggest about the Origin of Roms[?]," *Archiv Orientálni* 40:51–64.
1976 "Romové ve svete," *Demografie* 18:226–232.
Lévi-Strauss, Claude
1967 *Structural Anthropology.* New York: Doubleday Anchor.

IMAGES OF GYPSIES

Black·Quadroon·Gypsy: Women in the Art of George Fuller (1985)

Sarah Burns

Quite recently, the work of American painter George Fuller (1822–1884) has begun to receive new attention and appreciation after several decades of critical and scholarly neglect. This native of Deerfield, in western Massachusetts, is now on the way to being reestablished as a significant creator of romantically dreamy images in the poetic tonalist style of the later nineteenth century.[1] His subjects ranged from tranquil scenes of farm life to mysterious visions of witchcraft in colonial New England and images of Yankee women and girls. While he was best known for his evocative treatments of the latter themes, Fuller also drew and painted women who were outsiders: the southern black woman, the quadroon, and the Gypsy.

During the first phases of his career Fuller (whose artistic education, characteristically for one of his generation in America, was somewhat sporadic) worked mainly as a portrait painter in New England, New York, and in several towns in the South. In 1860 his professional development was severely interrupted by the obligation to return to Deerfield after his father's death to take over the management of his family's farm, "The Bars." For more than fifteen years, marriage, fatherhood, and agriculture claimed his energies, and he contented himself with Sunday painting in an outbuilding fitted up as studio.

Fuller's drudgery on the farm ended with the financial panic of 1873 and the disastrous agricultural depression that followed in its wake. By 1875, "The Bars" was perilously close to bankruptcy, and Fuller, with nothing to lose, decided to take a selection of his paintings into Boston to test them on the art market. This venture was a considerable success. Critics bestowed praise; patrons came forth; Boston painters, including the influential and charismatic William Morris Hunt, welcomed this Rip Van Winkle of art into their circle, and William Dean Howells befriended him as well. Within two years, Fuller was exhibiting his paintings regularly both in Boston and New York. By the time of his death in 1884 many critics considered him one of America's greatest artists.

During his farming years, Fuller had developed and transformed his style, in spite of the fact that he was all but completely cut off from the stimulus of the metropolitan art scene. The paintings in his initial 1876 exhibition bore little resemblance to his tightly worked, slick-surfaced portraits of the 1850s. He had been affected by slowly fermenting memories of old master paintings seen in Europe in 1860 (his only trip abroad, taken before returning to the farm at Deerfield) and by the romantic, bucolic landscape and figure paintings of contemporary French Barbizon artists such as Jean-François Millet, Camille Corot, Narcisse Díaz, and others. In response to these lingering impressions, Fuller rejected literal realism and gradually created the style that launched his reputation. The landscapes and the figure paintings of his last decade become progressively more nebulous. They are rendered in dim, muffled tones of amber, green, or tannic brown. Details are suppressed and outlines blurred; veils of dimmed atmosphere shroud the compositions. In the 1870s and 1880s critical consensus was that such shadowy vagueness was the quintessence of pictorial poetry.

Fuller was perhaps best known and most appreciated for his paintings of young, pensive country women, such as *Winifred Dysart* (1881; Worcester Art Museum). In these imaginary figures of budding adolescents, critics again and again claimed to perceive materializations of spirit, portraits of unsullied girlhood's very soul. Fuller in fact did intend such images to be pictorial equivalents of some higher ideal, evoking a response similar to his own (during his 1860 European tour) on beholding the portrait of a young Renaissance princess, of which he wrote, "You could not forget her sweet sad face. . . . How many inspired to nobler life by her beauty! How many to feel (like myself) in the presence of those beautiful eyes raised from the littleness of ordinary life!"[2] Fuller's reverent attitude toward womanly inspirational power and purity was thoroughly in harmony with prevalent sentiments, so perfectly epitomized in English author Coventry Patmore's domestic epic *The Angel in the House* (1854–1856), not to mention hundreds of other English and American works of prose and poetry devoted to the spotless, celestial heroine.

The sometimes cloying goodness of the soulful white maiden is counterbalanced in Fuller's work by a company of darker women, types often perceived by the racist orientation of the society as sexually dangerous and lawlessly passionate. Broadly speaking, Fuller's black, quadroon, and Gypsy women correspond to threatening "dark ladies," conventional in nineteenth-century fiction.[3] Fuller's women are not stereotyped in this way, however. In a series of sketches (all now in the Memorial Hall Museum, Deerfield, Massachusetts) drawn from life during his 1857–1858 winter in Montgomery, Alabama, and in several later paintings, Fuller sought to depict the black woman, and in particular the oppressed black female slave, as an American equivalent to the toiling, elemental, timeless French peasant celebrated by Millet and the other French genre painters Fuller admired. In *The Quadroon* (Fig. 2), he portrayed a woman of mixed race as a soulful, melancholic heroine. Most alien of all were his Gypsies, *The Romany Girl* (Fig. 3) and *Fedalma* (Fig. 4), symbols of exotic energies, of all that nineteenth-century middle-class culture was not: free, wild, natural, and savage. In varying degrees, all of these types embody Fuller's interweaving of his early antislavery ideals along with romance, realism, literary ideas, French prototypes, and his own pensive, dreamlike sensibility.

The desire to record selected aspects of black slave life arose strongly only during the third and last of Fuller's portrait-painting tours of the South, the winter of 1857–1858 in Montgomery. He had spent the winter and summer of 1849–1850 in Augusta, Georgia, and in the winter of 1856–1857 he settled and worked in Mobile, Alabama. As his diaries and letters reveal, Fuller had ample occasion to observe scenes of slavery. He held the slave system to be "a very bad cause" and lamented the plight of slaves sold like cattle at auction. His resolute social criticism was combined with his feeling for black woman submerged into slavery. Fuller beheld the blacks as a rich source of subject matter: "There is with them always such a free motion and unstudied attitude and their costume is so appropriate as to make them real prizes in an artistic way."

This quite sudden growth of interest in drawing the slaves was the result of Fuller's response to new tendencies in contemporary French painting, examples of which he had opportunities to study in Boston and New York in the 1850s, when he was very much in the midst of the art world. Works by the Barbizon painters, and by related rural genre specialists such as Edouard Frère, inspired Fuller to emulation. In the Barbizon world, nature was tenderly poetic, not sublime; intimate rather than awesome; familiar and rustic, rather than remote and savage. The peasant inhabitants of this usually serene bucolic terrain were simple, humble, pious creatures whose lives were regulated by the cycles of nature. When Fuller looked about him in the American South—his mind still teeming with recent impressions of French rural landscapes and peasant paintings seen in New York—certain stylistic and thematic elements were suggested to him as he began his exploration of the black American "peasant."

Fuller was especially fascinated by black women: in the sketchbook, drawings of female slaves far outnumber those in which black men appear in prominent roles. It must be noted that these sketches depicting women engaged in domestic occupations such as cooking and washing, or more taxing outdoors labors are all critically real, without any ambiguous Barbizon haze. One drawing, inscribed with the model's name, "Grace" (1857), is an intensely believable portrait that reflects this northern artist's wholehearted response to the features of this sunbonneted slave woman. In the wash drawing of Mariah (Fig. 1), a young black mother carries her child in Madonna-like fashion. We are aware of what continually interested Fuller: slaves as mothers, in nurturing roles, and performing humble, housewifely tasks in the manner of the archetypal goodwives of preindustrial agricultural societies.

In one of several cabin interiors, a woman sits close to her hearth as she tends the fire and prepares a meal for her children glimpsed as they peek out around the frame of the door leading to an interior room. In another (1858) a woman in a rocking chair mends a shirt. A drawing of a cabin doorstep (1858) shows similarly tranquil activity: a plump, older black woman winds a ball of yarn from a skein held by a girl in head scarf and apron. A baby sits in the shelter of the yarn-winder's skirts; a boy sits on the doorstep; a woman does laundry behind them. In these sketches there is little to suggest the roughness and meanness

Figure 1: *Mariah*

Figure 2: *The Quadroon*

Figure 3: *The Romany Girl*

Figure 4: *Fedalma*

of slave housekeeping, the often brutal reality of their lives and surroundings. The drawings depict the dignity of the slaves' lives, however meager their material comfort. These sketchbooks are among the few memorable depictions of slave life in the South before the Civil War.

Fuller produced one fully realized painting on the theme of black domesticity: the *Negro Nurse and Child* (private collection, 1859), which, unlike the sketches, depicts a black woman in the nurturing yet subservient role to her owner's small blond daughter. Although Fuller probably hoped to exhibit and sell the painting, which he completed shortly before leaving for Europe, the subsequent agricultural detour seems to have ruined that plan, and the *Negro Nurse* remained in the family.

The finery displayed by the Nurse is in sharp contrast to the simple garb of the black women who toil outdoors in Fuller's sketches and paintings; these women are hardy, earthy laborers. His laundresses are strong women capable of performing the Herculean feats of cleaning implied by the huge kettles and tubs that furnish their laundry yards. One of the Montgomery sketches ("Cotton Gin," 1858) depicts a female slave plowing behind a mule in a field dominated by a cotton press; another ("Slave Women Digging," 1858) shows several black women clustered around a wagon and engaged in the strenuous task of breaking up soil with pickax and shovels; behind them, the dome of the state capitol looms over the trees. Except in German farm communities in Pennsylvania free white women seldom if ever did heavy field work. Indeed, among other factors, it was the exemption of women from such labor that demonstrated the superiority of the Yankee farmer to the European peasant, whose women were put to work like beasts of burden. Yet what could be more peasant-like, in the South, than this very phenomenon, observed and noted by Fuller, of strong black women tilling the soil, seeming to him, perhaps, like true, natural, unrefined children of the earth?

Too much should not be read into these slight drawings, they are essentially notations—aides-mémoire—and offer little either of detailed description or sentiment. It was only much later that Fuller created an exhibition oil painting, *Turkey Pasture in Kentucky* (1878; Chrysler Museum at Norfolk), in which he fully explored and defined the idea of the black pastorale. By that time Fuller was much more deeply familiar with the Barbizon painters. He had seen works by Millet, Corot, Troyon, and others from time to time during the 1860s, and once he had returned to the art world he could steep himself in Barbizon pictures through his friendship with the lively Barbizon promoter, the painter William Morris Hunt; through contact with such Boston collectors as Quincy Adams Shaw, and through institutional and commercial exhibitions. A recurrent theme of the French peasant painters was that of the young female herder: shepherdess, cowherd, goose girl, and the like. Fuller's *Turkey Pasture* is a localized, American version of this subject. It is likely that he based the idea of the turkey herder on examples of Barbizon painting. Millet had painted a melancholy *Autumn Landscape with a Flock of Turkeys* (ca. 1870–1874; Metropolitan Museum of Art, New York), and Fuller had in his possession a lithograph after Constant Troyon's painting *La Gardeuse des dindons* (Louvre), depicting a French peasant girl in the midst of her clustering turkeys. In Fuller's painting the young black woman in the foreground exemplifies that spirit of rural tranquillity so important to the Barbizon sensibility. Brown, barefoot, garbed in head scarf and a simple, shapeless dress untouched by fashion, this figure symbolizes at once the humble, the elemental, and the timeless dimensions of rustic life. Like her French peasant cousins, she is a child of nature, one with the earth, in perfect harmony with her fellow herders, her flock, and the landscape. Fuller's broad technique and his use of a unifying, greenish atmospheric tone enhance the almost meditational effect of this scene. The circumstance of the turkey girl's race seems almost beside the point; indeed, one of Fuller's last paintings reiterates the theme and replaces the black herder with a white counterpart. In the earlier painting, however, the figures surely contribute a regional flavor. Commentators on *Turkey Pasture* read the painting as a rustic idyll rather than a commentary on southern rural life. The *Worcester Daily Spy* noted the work was memorable for its "intense poetic rendering."

Poetic in intent but infused with pathos is Fuller's *The Quadroon* (1880; Fig. 2) which while it also depicts a southern scene—this time a cotton harvest—shifts the emphasis from bucolic tranquillity to personal and racial tragedy. It is a work in which the artist's own dim memory images converged with a midcentury literary genre and, once more, with French Barbizon types to produce the pensive image of a tragic, romantic heroine.

The autobiographic source of *The Quadroon* was a slave auction attended by Fuller during his first southern season, the winter of 1850 in Augusta, Georgia. Among the lots to be sold was a young, beautiful quadroon whose heartbreaking plight deeply moved the artist. As he wrote in a letter home:

> Who is the girl with eyes large and black? The blood of the white and dark races is at enmity in her veins—the former predominated. About 3/4 white says one dealer. Three fourths blessed, a fraction accursed. She is under thy feet, white man. . . .Is she not your sister? . . . She impresses me with sadness! The pensive expression of her finely formed mouth and her drooping eyes seemed to ask for sympathy. . . . Now she looks up, now her eyes fall before the rude gaze of those who are but calculating her charms or serviceable qualities. . . . Oh, is beauty so cheap!

While Fuller's sentiment is undoubtedly heartfelt, his language, interestingly, clearly echoes the elaborate prose of midcentury fiction, and analogs may be discovered in the antislavery novels of the 1840s and 1850s. It is perhaps not entirely fortuitous that Fuller's uncle by marriage was the historian Richard Hildreth, who produced in 1836 one of the first such novels, *The Slave: or, Memoirs of Archy Moore*, reissued in 1840 and 1852 under the new title, *The White Slave: or Memoirs of a Fugitive*. Fuller read this book sometime in the early 1840s. Although the chief figure is a male quadroon—son of a mulatto mother and Colonel Moore, a planter—the plot involves the cruelties and lovers' separations that characterize other, later examples of the genre, such as Lydia Maria Child's short story "The Quadroons" (1849) and Mayne Reid's *The Quadroon: or, A Lover's Adventure in Louisiana* (1856).

The racially mixed heroines of the antislavery novels were generally little more than duskier and more passionate versions of their free white sisters. Like well-brought-up white girls, they were educated, genteel, and pure. It was obviously easier for a white reading audience to identify and sympathize with near-whiteness than with unadulterated blackness, to weep over the dilemma of graceful, helpless innocence doomed to bondage by a few drops of African blood. Xarifa, the quadroon heroine of Lydia Child's story, has a complexion "rich and glowing as an autumnal leaf. The iris of her large, dark eye had the melting, mezzotinto outline, which remains the last vestige of African ancestry, and gives that plaintive expression, so often observed, and so appropriate to that docile and injured race." Aurore, Mayne Reid's heroine, has "masses of glossy black hair, waving along the brows and falling over the shoulders in curling clusters. Within this ebon framework were features to mock the sculptor's chisel." Aurore's eye is "like a gorgeous gem," with smoldering light in its depths.[4] Each of these tales includes an auction scene, in which the sad quadroon maiden must endure lustful stares from the gross men who compete to possess her. Child's Xarifa, who has been raised as a white, is suddenly plunged into bondage when it is discovered that she is the granddaughter of a slave. She is then "ruthlessly seized by a sheriff and placed on the public auction-stand in Savannah. There she stood, trembling, blushing, and weeping: compelled to listen to the grossest language and shrinking from the rude hands that examined the graceful proportions of her beautiful frame."[5] While a quadroon heroine was occasionally permitted to find happiness, she was more likely to be destined for a miserable end. Xarifa, for example, becomes a raving maniac after her lover has been killed during an attempt to help her escape from her new owner.

Fuller's *Quadroon* is a belated branch of this family of dark, sad heroines. She is an outsider, imprisoned in a racial limbo somewhere between the black and the white world. Instead of creating a storytelling picture featuring all the trappings and drama of the antebellum slave auction, Fuller with characteristic understatement paraphrased the motif, so frequently used in French peasant painting, of the pensive shepherdess or the weary gleaner. The heavy limpness of the quadroon's arms and the exhausted slouch of her posture are the pictorial equivalents of her spiritual heaviness and hopelessness. Fuller's quadroon has the burning dark eyes and the luxuriant raven locks of the midcentury heroines; she is an exotic, melancholy exile whose beauty can never save her from a life of no expectations.

Fuller was an artist more interested in communicating essential ideas and feelings than in describing the facts of the visible world. In *The Quadroon* he was not only constructing a meditative image based on past experiences but was also discovering a symbol for despair and alienation, a symbol which might easily be comprehended by viewers of the time. In 1880, the year *The Quadroon* was exhibited at the

National Academy of Design in New York, a critic for the *Springfield Republican* wrote: "The face . . . is like that of a hopeless Undine, whose tricksy graces and happy spirits have been clouded but not sanctioned by the love that has come to her. The woman is awakened and exalted, but the slave is lower than ever. . . . It is the history and burden of a race that this beautiful creature bears. . . . This is a true historical painting, and must survive the age in which it is painted."

The Quadroon is based on experience and seems to some extent to have been inspired by literature without in the least being a literary painting. Fuller's pictures of Gypsy women are no more "literary" in presentation than *The Quadroon*. Yet Fuller's interest in Gypsies, and his knowledge of them, probably came almost entirely from reading; there is no evidence that he had any firsthand acquaintance with Gypsies as he did with southern blacks. As one of Fuller's sons observed to William Dean Howells, to the very end of his career the painter "trusted as much in the cultivation of his art to the books he read as to the pictures he saw."[6] A number of literary sources, encountered over a long span of years, contributed to Fuller's concept of Gypsy women as romantic outsiders, differing from the Quadroon in their ability freely to choose nomadic exile in preference to the physical and spiritual imprisonment represented by conventional society.

Goethe's *Wilhelm Meister*, which in 1854 Fuller read in Thomas Carlyle's translation, evokes a world of wandering performers and bohemian aristocrats. One of the characters in this novel is the Gypsy-like girl Mignon, who can dance the fandango blindfolded without breaking the eggs scattered at her feet and who is fascinatingly dark, melancholy, and mysterious. In the 1858 Alabama sketchbook a drawing gives evidence that Fuller had recently read and appreciated George Borrow's *Romany Rye* (1857), a popular picaresque narrative of Gypsy life, romantically based on this Englishman's own experiences. Dated March 28, and inscribed with the title *Romany Rye*, Fuller's sketch depicts a forest scene with wagons, a tent, and figures resting under the trees. Borrow's colorful book, whose title in translation means "The Gypsy Gentleman," was the final installment of his richly embroidered autobiography and is not so much a novel as a magpie gathering of characters, events, customs, and languages among the Gypsies of Spain and England. Borrow offers in these books the vision of a society of free men and women who live in forest dingles, survive by tinkering and wily thievery, and marry outside the law. They speak a strange tongue and hold lavish celebrations of feasting and song. The women have black, lustrous braids and wear long, golden earrings.

Broadly speaking, the nineteenth-century cult of exoticism, expressed in the figure of the Gypsy, was romantic escapism at its most fantastic. It expressed a yearning after the primitive, the wild, the natural, the strange as would-be antidote or smoke screen against the manifold and ever-ramifying political, economic, and social consequences of the industrial revolution. European painting of this era abounds in subjects drawn from southern and Oriental cultures: the Spanish dance; the vividly anachronistic Italian peasant; the heated, languid mysteries of the harem. Fuller's awareness of such tendencies in French painting, especially among the Barbizon group he admired, may well have reinforced the inspiration of his reading. In particular, Narcisse Díaz was drawn to the glamour of Gypsy life, and he sometimes populated his forest landscapes with richly embellished bohemians, the gleam of their golden trinkets and the warm tints of their garments giving strange light to the forest gloom. Adolphe Monticelli, a Marseilles painter whom Fuller deeply admired in his later years, created similar works in which fantastically dressed, theatrical figures make music and romance in dimly illuminated, dreamlike parks.

Fuller's first Gypsy, *The Romany Girl* (1877–1879; Fig. 3) was given its title after the painting had been finished. This was in fact the case with most of his later works. As W. D. Howells recalled: "It was so much a feeling with him, so purely emotional a thing, that he had usually completed one of those divine figures or touching histories before his thought had crystallized a name for it. Then he turned to his friends for help, and in one such extremity I had the honor of suggesting The Romany Girl to him."[7] Howells went on to say that this title was taken from the poem of the same name by Ralph Waldo Emerson. Fuller's initial vague concept revolved around wildness, freedom, nature; these abstractions coalesced in his imagination in the form of a Gypsy woman—denizen of an alien universe. Howells's choice of title was felicitous. Establishing a metaphorical opposition between the Gypsy and the Yankee girl, Emerson in his poem "The Romany Girl" summed up the pervasive, deep-rooted nineteenth-century tensions between well-behaved, artificial civilization and outlaw, elemental nature.[8]

> The sun goes down, and with him takes
> The coarseness of my poor attire;
> The fair moon mounts, and aye the flame
> Of Gypsy beauty blazes higher.
>
> Pale Northern Girls! you scorn our race;
> You captives of your air-tight halls,
> Wear out indoors your sickly days,
> But leaves us the horizon walls.
> ...
> Go, keep your cheek's rose from the rain,
> For teeth and hair with shopmen deal;
> My swarthy tint is in the grain.
> The rocks and forest know it real.

With her tilted black eyes and brows and her tangle of dark hair waving down to her shoulders, Fuller's *Romany Girl*, like Emerson's, is meant to appear as savage and wild as the shadowed forest primeval from which she peers out at the beholder. Around her head is wrapped a kind of turban, decorated with sprigs of greenery. Her simple garb, with its archaic cut and touches of embroidery, further emphasizes the theme of exotic otherness.[9]

Contemporary critics writing about this painting responded appropriately to its subject and content. A *Scribner's* reviewer, commenting on the National Academy of Design exhibition, observed: "the spirit of the painting is Gypsy-like . . . the face is wild enough and shrewd enough to suit the name, while the surroundings are not without a good share of the mysterious." Another writer almost rapturously described the "vaguely thrilling" experience of meeting the "deep meaning of her weirdly glancing eyes," which seemed to weave "a mystic spell over our fancy." One went so far as to claim nationality for Fuller's creation: "His *Romany Girl* is an American Gypsy—a wild creature of our own woods and not of any other."[10]

Although the Romany girl was in essence a creature of Fuller's imagination—a figure in his mental landscape—it is also true that as far back as colonial times, there had been a modest Gypsy presence in North America. Living in clans, they were often squatters, pursuing such livelihoods as tinkering, peddling, horse dealing, and fortune-telling. Whether Fuller intended to represent a local, American Gypsy is impossible to say. With reference to this tawny, smoldering female type, however, there is an interesting contemporary document that sharpens our perception of the kind of spirit Fuller desired to evoke. In a contemporary magazine article, several speakers carry on a lively debate about just what constitutes the spirit and character of the New England woman. In refutation of the prevalent notion that New England women are cold, puritanical, pale, bloodless intellectuals, one man argues:

> Not at all; not at all; not bloodless beauties! . . . Just as beautiful as Italians, Spaniards. . . . Why, I have in my mind now a valley in New England where the dark-haired, red-lipped, high-instepped, full-figured women seem to me to have come from Andalusia, instead of from Vermont. . . . They were of the passionate type, too: long black lashes, black eyes, rich complexions. . . . Had they been at home, in Spain, what guitar tinklings, what madrigals, what fans! Ten duennas apiece would not have protected these dashing creatures from insidious love-letters. . . .[11]

It is mere coincidence that *The Romany Girl* resembles the "Andalusians" of Vermont. The point resides in one key phrase here: "passionate type" (or, as it may seem to us, stereotype). The attributes of Fuller's Gypsy are those of the dark, romantic, emotional soul, that part of the human spirit which feels rather than thinks: loves the mysteries of the nocturnal and the lunar rather than the rational clarities of day and sunlight. Given the cultural climate of nineteenth-century America, it is perhaps not surprising to read, in the words of William Crary Brownell that in his judgment both *The Quadroon* and *The Romany Girl* are on "a distinctly lower plane" than Fuller's more ideal pictures such as *And She Was a Witch* (1877–1883; Metropolitan Museum of Art, New York), the subject here being the arrest of an accused witch in a murky New England forest in the seventeenth century.[12]

In contrast to *The Romany Girl*, Fuller's *Fedalma* (1883–1884; Fig. 4) represents a much more elevated and nobly tragic passionate type. It also represents one of the rare instances in Fuller's work where the title was not an afterthought. The subject was directly inspired by a literary source: George Eliot's long dramatic poem *The Spanish Gypsy*, first published in 1868. The plot concerns the maiden Fedalma, who despite mysterious origins has been brought up by the mother of the Duke, Don Silva. Having matured into sultry, statuesque beauty and grace, she is betrothed to marry this young nobleman. The happiness of the engagement is destroyed by the military campaign which the Duke is pressing against the infidel Moors and their allies the Gypsies. A band of the latter has recently been captured by the Duke's forces and brought to his stronghold.

Fuller chose to depict the quiet, introspective, yet pivotal episode in which the truth of her ancestry begins to dawn upon Fedalma. The necklace that droops from her hand is part of a glittering treasure trove bestowed by her lover. On picking up his heavy rope of gold, Fedalma has fallen into a mystical trance. The glowing strand has induced strange, subconscious thoughts that tease and tantalize her. Nebulous impressions of dim, forgotten dreams and emotions begin to stir at the bottom of her mind, which she feels is like "an eye that stares/into the darkness painfully."[13] The necklace is indeed her fate: it is booty from the captured Gypsy chief, who somehow contrives to steal into Fedalma's presence to reveal that he is her father and to appeal to her to renounce her false affiliations, abandon her duke, and join with her father to become leader and savior of the Spanish Gypsies. The rest of the poem follows Fedalma as she bows to the imperatives of blood and becomes a splendid dagger-bearing Gypsy queen, raven hair in plaits and hung about with golden ornaments. No trivial tinker or fortune-teller, Fedalma represents the heights of tragic self-denial, brave renunciation, and noble obedience to duty. Swarthy she may be, but she behaves like the most conscientious of Victorians in her devotion to a worthy cause. Thus may inborn passion be elevated from transitory gratification to transcendent act.

So somber and pensive is Fuller's painting that it recalls certain moods in the work of Rembrandt, one of the masters he most reverently admired. His conception of Fedalma's fateful moment is veiled in brooding shadow. The figure of Fedalma, painted in rich, golden tones, stands motionless, her expression one of deep introspection and melancholy, which a viewer can comprehend without knowing much if anything of Eliot's story. Every element in this painting represents

Fuller's struggle to go beyond description and to evoke the spiritual state of his exotic sufferer, to create the pictorial equivalent of her bemused and vaguely foreboding intuitions. In this, one of his last paintings, Fuller offers his vision of the dusky heroine in a most romantically tragic embodiment. Whereas *The Romany Girl* signifies the freedom of the natural outlaw, *Fedalma* symbolizes a natural nobility of soul.

From his vision of the black woman as peasant and slave to his solemn evocation of the Gypsy as a tragedy queen, Fuller unfolded a rich spectrum of dark, allegedly exotic womanhood, the stuff of nineteenth-century white romantic dreams, though in real social terms the women were peripheral, alienated, and outcast. This artist's portrayals, whether of a directly observed slave plowing behind a mule, or of an imagined soul like the forlorn quadroon, are invariably dignified and sympathetic. There is very little in these figures to suggest the erotic attractions that so often were the major ingredients—overt or covert—in representations of the supposedly passionate dark lady. A painter of perhaps uncommon earnestness and simple straightforwardness, whose sweet good humor was often remarked by acquaintances, Fuller seems to have been interested in his dark ladies as personages, as bodies possessing souls, worthy to be put into paintings for their own sake. It cannot be denied that there is an element of romantic fantasy in these works. Ultimately, though, Fuller's exotics must be perceived as individuals, and it is this emphasis that makes them still worth looking at and thinking about today.

Afterword 1995:

Were I writing this article today, I would tend to be more critical of its assumptions. Even though George Fuller may have seemed to be an earnest and straightforward painter, full of sympathy for his outsider subjects, he was still a middle-class Yankee whose simple sincerity cannot be so easily taken for granted. Today, I would probably try to reconfigure the argument to suggest that Fuller's images of blacks and Gypsies represented the appropriation of these marginal figures for the purposes of white spectatorship, which enjoyed privileged access to the romantic, sexual, or nostalgic fantasies such "exotic" types evoked. This might not cancel out Fuller's sympathetic attitude, of course. It would, however, point to the power relations in force between the dominant white culture and the African American and Gypsy communities.

NOTES

1.   Recent publications include Suzanne L. Flynt, *George Fuller: At Home*, exhibition catalog, Deerfield Memorial Hall Museum, 1984; three articles by Sarah Burns, "A Study of the Life and Poetic Vision of George Fuller (1822–1884)," *The American Art Journal* 13 (Autumn 1981), 11–37; "Images of Slavery: George Fuller's Depictions of the Antebellum South," *The American Art Journal* 15 (Summer 1983), 35–60; and "George Fuller: The Hawthorne of Our Art," *Winterthur Portfolio* 17 (Summer/Autumn 1983), 125–145. Also valuable for information and thoughts on Fuller's life and career is David M. Robb, Jr., "George Fuller, American Barbizon Painters: A Study of His Life, Work, and Times" (B.A. thesis, Princeton University, 1959). The best older source is the memorial volume, edited by Josiah B. Millet, *George Fuller, His Life and Works* (Boston: Houghton, Mifflin and Co., 1886), which contains a biography of the artist by William Dean Howells and contributions by F. D. Millet, Thomas Ball, William J. Stillman, J. J. Enneking, and William Closson; the volume ends with a sonnet, dedicated to the painter, by John Greenleaf Whittier.

2.   Unless otherwise indicated, all the citations from Fuller's diaries and correspondence and all the press clippings excerpted in this article, are from the most essential Fuller documents: the Fuller-Higginson Papers, deposited in The Memorial Libraries (Pocumtuck Valley Memorial Association Library and Henry N. Flynt Library), Deerfield, Massachusetts.

3.   On the subject of these dark ladies in romantic American literature, see Ralph P. Boas, "The Romantic Lady" in George Boas, ed., *Romanticism in America* (Baltimore: Johns Hopkins Press, 1940), pp. 63–88.

4.   Lydia Maria Child, "The Quadroons" (1849) in *The Children of Mount Ida and Other Stories* (New York: Charles S. Francis, 1871), p. 63; Mayne Reid, *The Quadroon: or, A Lover's Adventures in Louisiana* (New York: Robert M. De Witt, 1856), p. 70.

5.   Child, "The Quadroons," p. 74.

6.   Cited by William Dean Howells, "Sketch of Fuller's Life" in Millet, ed., *George Fuller, His Life and Works*, p. 5.

7.   Howells, "Sketch of Fuller's Life," p. 49.

8. Ralph Waldo Emerson, "The Romany Girl" (1857), *Complete Poems*, ed. Edward W. Emerson (Boston: Houghton, Mifflin, and Co., 1911), pp. 227–228.

9. The painting discussed here is the sketch for the work that was actually exhibited. The latter is now in a private collection.

10. "The Academy of Design," *Scribner's Monthly Magazine* 18 (September 1879), p. 313; Samuel Greene Wheeler Benjamin, *Art in America. A Critical and Historical Sketch* (New York: Harper and Brothers, 1880), p. 117; Mariana Griswold van Rensselaer, "George Fuller," *Century Illustrated Magazine* 27 (1883–1884), p. 234.

11. M. E. W. Sherwood, "New England Women," *Atlantic Monthly* 42 (August 1878), p. 232.

12. William Crary Brownell, "The Younger Painters of America," *Scribner's Monthly Magazine* 20 (July 1880), p. 326.

13. George Eliot, *The Spanish Gypsy* (Boston: Ticknor and Fields, 1878), p. 88.

The Church of Knowledge: Representations of Gypsies in Dutch Encyclopedias and Their Sources (1724–1984) (1990)

Wim Willems and Leo Lucassen

This essay will deal with the Dutch but also the West European image of Gypsies during the last two hundred and fifty years. In order to grasp that view, we have used oral, iconographic, and written sources at our disposal: surveys, sculpture, literature, magazines, and newspapers which can tell us much about the norms, values, and impressions of a society. These sources contain a wealth of information about people's ideas, their behavior towards others, and their internal relations.

The analysis will be focused on one written source in particular: encyclopedias.[1] We assume that they contain summaries of current information on Gypsies and that they are written in more or less the same way. Because encyclopedic information has always been seen as authoritative, we can use it to trace the prevailing opinions on Gypsies through time. The assumption is that encyclopedias have played an important role in spreading a certain view of Gypsies, particularly among the upper classes. The fact that the people who decided on the policies concerning them came from those ranks justifies the choice of encyclopedias as a main source.

Because of the derived character of the entries in encyclopedias, a study of the representation of Gypsies should also be concerned with the sources which have been used by the editors.[2] After all, the encyclopedias function only as a "channel" for the existing knowledge about Gypsies: they show what is considered the objective opinion of the moment. A critical examination of the sources is often left out by the editors. Consequently, both the prejudiced and unprejudiced views belonging to a certain period can be deduced from the entries.[3]

The aim of this essay is to set up a "genealogy of ideas" about Gypsies and to make a contribution to demythologize the stereotypes concerning them. It has been impossible to eradicate certain stereotypic views from encyclopedias and scholarly works over time, while other views change at a certain point. We will try to provide an explanation for both phenomena. A number of recurring themes in the sources, such as physical appearance, national character, morals and customs, religion, occupations, and art have been chosen as guidelines for the discussion.

The Physical Appearance of the Gypsies

The ideas about the physical appearance of Gypsies and the way these ideas have been put into words have hardly changed over the past two and a half centuries. In other words, a general feeling about the physical characteristics of the category "Gypsies" exists, and what stands out is that the descriptions commonly used are fairly positive.[4] The physical appearance of Gypsies induces admiration in many people; the features which can be distinguished are all exemplary. According to many authors, depravity is a distinctive characteristic of the Gypsies, but there is no hint of this in the encyclopedia descriptions of Gypsy physiognomy. This is particularly remarkable when we consider that certain branches of anthropology (namely phrenology and physiognomy) always emphasized the connection between humankind's inner self and physical appearance (Mosse 1978:17–34; Poliakov 1979:156–184). By means of scientific measurements and comparisons of skulls and faces, people tried to make a reasonable case for gaining insights into the characters of nations and races. Anthropological sources were often used to support statements about the nature and the morals of Gypsies. Comparative linguistics was also used as a source, and this discipline, in its quest to discover the nature of language, was tempted into the kind of speculation which proved to be grist for the mill of later racists.[5]

The description of the physical appearance of Gypsies does not appear to be influenced by these ideas. The fascination with their exotic facial and physical characteristics created a portrait which in some of its details is reminiscent of the Greek ideal of beauty. However, we do not come across such positive descriptions in the sixteenth or seventeenth century. In those times, Gypsies were often described as frightening and hideous. A good example is provided by Münster's *Cosmographia universalis* (1550). In the eighteenth century, the Gypsies' physical appearance is interpreted more positively, as in the Viennese journal *Anzeigen aus der sämmtlichen Kaiserl. Königl. Erbländern* (1770–1776), which Grellmann often used as a source. From this journal the author distilled a type of standard description (1787:36) which has been adopted and in some points expanded upon by many writers.

The encyclopedias emulate their sources carefully, and this has resulted in the following image of Gypsies: mesocephalic skull (the normal "European type"),[6] raven hair, dark complexion, a high forehead, coal-black, lively eyes, a somewhat bent nose, a fine mouth with snow-white teeth, slender and flexible, olive skin (also dark or yellowish brown). One or two people mention a "bronze-like" skin; others think that the glow of the Gypsies' skin originates from the East. The girls have a somewhat lighter skin color and are generally found to be very attractive. However, it is often noted that their beauty is doomed to fade quickly. The idea that their dark skin color is the result of their Eastern heritage has not always dominated. For instance, Grellmann (1787:40) posits that the Gypsies' skin color, like that of the Laplanders, has to do with their way of life. Supposedly they do not wash themselves, and they constantly sit in the smoke from their fires: *"längst würde er aufgehört haben, negerartig zu sein, wenn er aufgehört hätte, zigeunerisch zu leben"* (He would have stopped resembling a Negro long ago, if he had stopped living in a Gypsy way) is his conclusion. He does not connect skin color with race but with living conditions.

According to several nineteenth-century editors, the fact that Gypsies are well formed has also to do with their nomadic existence. The pure mountain air and the smell of herbs which they breathe in supposedly give them the ability to survive all hardships and to reach, quite often, the ripe old age of one hundred. According to the same editors, there are no fat-bellied, hunchbacked, blind, or lame Gypsies, and they are never ill.

National Character

Judging by the ideal sculptured features of the Gypsies, one would never expect that their nature has been described in the most negative terms from the very beginning. They might be physically attractive, with characteristics reminiscent of Greek aesthetics, but according to the views of the time, they do not have the appropriate harmony of soul which belongs to their physical appearance. The eighteenth- and nineteenth-century editors provide a good example of how science managed, by way of language studies, to trace the origins of both the Gypsies and the West Europeans to India, only to argue, in an incredible manner amounting to wishful thinking, that the Gypsies have a pernicious nature, while the "Aryans" have a noble nature. Before Rüdiger and Grellmann pointed out this Indian heritage, others had also tried to establish a relationship between the national character of the Gypsies and their supposed place of origin. For instance, in part of the scholarly writings in the eighteenth century, it was supposed that Egypt was their place of origin. People tried to make this hypothesis acceptable by pointing out similar (usually negative) characteristics of the Egyptians. In this way, Swinburne (1779:30) suggested that Gypsies originated from the worshipers of Isis, who distinguished themselves by fortune-telling, nomadic existence, and thievery. Twiss (1776:204–205) saw a resemblance to Egyptian sorcerers, while Salmon (1733:472), whose work has been translated into Dutch, lumped the Gypsies together with contemporary Egyptians. Apparently, the latter were stereotyped for their mendacity, their lazy nature, and for being thieves.

    In 1724, when the first Dutch encyclopedia appears, people are already convinced that Gypsies are thieves who proved to be a great nuisance to the indigenous populations, and for this reason their persecution has been justified by different governments. However, the editors went no further than to present bits of superficial information. Once one is led toward India, as mentioned before, via language studies (Grellmann is often quoted in this respect), a scientific rationalization comes into being which functions as a source of negative views of Gypsies for more than two centuries. Grellmann based his notion of the Gypsy's Indian heritage on two factors: the first comprised comparative language studies which, according to Grellmann, indicated a strong affinity between the Romani language of the Gypsies and the Indic languages. The second factor originated from the travelers' journals[7] which Grellmann read and where he learned about the existence of the caste of the Pariahs, or Suders, whose color, shape, character, morals, and customs showed many similarities with the image he had of Gypsies and their way of life.

Besides the caste of these pariahs, another group supposedly lived in India. These people were hard-working, agrarian Aryans who were noted for their steadfast character (all the middle-class capitalistic virtues of the nineteenth century are included in this image). They left India at a time when Sanskrit was still spoken there, distinguishing themselves positively from the Indians who stayed behind and finally settling in Western Europe (see, for example, Mosse 1980:41–42). The Gypsies, however, supposedly left India (for reasons which, similar to the case of the Aryans, will probably always remain unknown) and retained their national character, which was to be found in its purest form among the caste of the pariahs. Only the Gypsies changed from a sedentary to a nomadic people (which is also true for some of the Suders). It is generally conceded that this nomadic way of life gradually took root in the Gypsies; until recently, most people agreed that traveling was "in their blood."

This analogy between the national character of the Gypsies and that of the Indian pariahs determined the way most Gypsiologists thought until the twentieth century. This development probably contributed to the fact that in various encyclopedias, the character of the Gypsies has been described in terms which are suspiciously similar. A number of characteristics stand out in the impression promulgated by the encyclopedias and their sources:

(a) They show a predilection for a life without ties, prefer the *dolce far niente* (the sweetness of doing nothing) and they are prepared to put up with the worst consequences of their own attitude. This characteristic, along with many others, is, according to many authors, not only inherent in Gypsies but also in the Eastern and Slavic nations. Popp Serboianu (1930:25) wrote that they are sly by nature and like all Orientals supposedly live from day to day and are not interested in the future.

(b) Thus, as a matter of course, they are lazy and work-shy. They will work only when forced by the utmost necessity. The work-shy character of the Gypsies comprises one of the many constants in scholarly writings from the eighteenth century onward. Almost every book mentions this characteristic, and a number of authors go into great detail on this issue. Once again, Grellmann (1787:80) is the great popularizer. According to him, Gypsies detest work, particularly when it requires an effort. They would rather submit to hunger and misery than improve their lot by working. Kogalnitchan (1840:30) completely agrees with that point of view. According to this author, Gypsies like doing nothing at all, and they prefer stealing to working. More than a century after Grellmann's work, Wlislocki (1890:196), who presents himself as the protector of Gypsy culture, fails to change this view. Although this "Gypsy expert" insists that he has no prejudices, because, unlike other observers, he has intensely involved himself in the Gypsy world, it is remarkable that many of his descriptions are taken word for word from earlier authors (for example, Liebich 1863 and Schwicker 1883).

(c) They do not lack cleverness but, because of their upbringing and low morality, this characteristic usually develops into slyness. And this, in particular, should help them in stealing and committing fraud. They are trained from a very early age, and they subsequently develop a great dexterity in these "skills." According to many authors, they usually operate on a small scale. This "limitation" is often explained by a reference to their cowardice. We can already observe this supposed characteristic in Grellmann's work. This author claims that Gypsies are afraid to commit robberies at night. Kogalnitchan (1840:33) explains this by referring to the centuries of Gypsy serfdom in the Balkans: *"Muth und Tapferkeit sind niemals das Erbtheil eines zum Sklaven herabgewürdigten Menschen"* (Courage and bravery have never been characteristics of people who were degraded to slavery; see also Block 1936:101, who takes over this view unquestioningly). The "fact" that Gypsies limit themselves mainly to small burglaries is seldom appreciated as a positive point. It is always the negative characteristics (cowardice, inability to think) which prevent them from committing larger crimes (see, among others, Borrow 1841:45–50; Paspati 1870:22; Liebich 1863:3).

(d) Because Gypsies (generally) lack notions of morality, they allow their instincts to rule them more easily, they have no sense of honor, they are greedy, wasteful, intemperate with food and drink, lecherous, and frivolous. However, the opinions concerning their "loose" morals vary considerably. For some these opinions are beyond questioning (for example, for Grellmann 1787:94 and Twiss 1776:204–205). For instance, Twiss claims that all Spanish female Gypsies practice prostitution. Borrow (1841:30, 331ff.), however, emphasizes the chastity of the Spanish Gypsies. Then again, Popp Serboianu (1930:74) claims that Gypsies have absolutely no sexual control; according to him, the Gypsies love life constitutes nothing more than an indulgence in sensuality. Block (1936:171) does not support this claim. He argues that while Gypsy women may look sensual, this says nothing of their inner nature. Because they are a primitive people, the outward appearance and behavior (dancing) of the women apparently do not excite them the way civilized men would be excited. It is only when modern anthropological research starts to develop that the supposed licentiousness of the Gypsies is proved to be a fable (see Okely 1983:201ff.; Liégeois 1983:98).

(e) Further, they are rough and uncivilized, which leads to the following standard description in nineteenth-century encyclopedias: "Although they have lived among Christian people for centuries, they have not cast off their heathendom, and they have remained rude and uncivilized, attached to a nomadic existence, making do with plain and sometimes disgusting food in miserable huts" (*Encyclopedia of Nieuwhuis* 1856–H:262; *Algemene Nederlandsche Encyclopedie* 1866–VII:281; *Sijthof Encyclopedia* 1890–IV:475).

(f) A number of characteristics which are inferred from these sources are mendacity, disloyalty, and cruelty toward animals. Moreover, the Gypsies supposedly lack courage and bravery, and they are faint-hearted.[8] This supposed cruelty of the Gypsies, which is also directed at people, has generated prolific writings. What particularly encourages this view is the fact that from the fifteenth century onward Gypsies were hired as executioners in Romania and Hungary. Borrow (1841:355) later adds a horrible story which enforces this particular image. An old man is tortured by Gypsies; they rub fresh peppers into his eyes in order to find out where he has hidden his money. Even the

French professor Bloch (1953:39) repeats this story without comment, though he pleads for more understanding for the group.

* * *

The attributed thievish nature of Gypsies, which only disappears from the Dutch encyclopedias after the Second World War but even then not completely, raises fears of moral degeneration in late-nineteenth-century thinking as well as in the first half of the twentieth century. Inspired by the work of antirevolutionary statesman A. Kuyper, *Om de oude wereldzee* (1907–1908), the Christian encyclopedias in particular emphasized that the heathenish and amoral behavior of the Gypsies was dangerously contagious. "Their influence on several nations in Europe manifested itself in the cultivation of banditry, in the encouragement of superstition and fortune-telling, and in a spirit of cunning and guile."[9] Even though this passage indicates religious intolerance only, the idea of "degeneration" has far-reaching consequences for the concept of race, which is first worked out by physical anthropologists and later shamelessly exploited by the Nazis. In actual practice it becomes clear that authors obsessed by purity are at the same time fixated on the lack of it. That is definitely the case with the anthropological research on the "Gypsy race." At the end of the nineteenth century, the physical anthropologists begin to distinguish between the naturally "pure" Gypsies and the mixed forms. In this respect, it is remarkable that before the breakthrough of the idea of race (in the second half of the nineteenth century), people were convinced that nothing would be more preferable than to mix Gypsies with Europeans (Borrow 1841:274). According to this line of thought, the nomadic character of the Gypsies would then disappear of its own accord. Taking away children from their parents must also be seen in this light. Upbringing was seen as a determining factor rather than race or heredity (Grellmann 1787:190).

It is only in the second half of the nineteenth century that the concept of race, which was introduced in the eighteenth century, is further developed. Anthropometrical research, which concerns the measurements and proportions of the human body, is one of the factors which particularly influences this development. Pittard had been studying Gypsies in the Balkan countries and in Hungary because they were supposedly the purest race of European Gypsies. In his report in

1908, he noted that the Gypsies had mingled with all kinds of people. Supposedly, the Scandinavian and north Germanic Gypsies in particular originated partly from native drifters. In several countries Gypsies could be found among the "normal" traveling folk. He therefore concluded that the Gypsies did not belong to the "Hindu type" and that a mixed heritage (from the "original population" in India) should be assumed. The dichotomy between "original" and "mixed," which is often related to nomadism and a sedentary life, prevailed until the 1940s. The reference to a mixed heritage and the Aryan race does not disappear from the Dutch entries concerning Gypsies until 1953.

Morals and Customs

It is almost inevitable that the extended description of the Gypsy character, which is already marked by a complete lack of values, does not relate the morals and customs of the Gypsies in the most positive terms. Even after the Second World War, the encyclopedias propagate ideas such as "once a thief, always a thief" and state that those who live off society like parasites cannot, by definition, have enviable manners or cultural traditions. The fact that the Gypsies are "different" is emphasized again and again, and the opinion which plays underneath is that they are a peculiar people. No stone is left unturned when it comes to proving that they are barbarians. According to the most contemporary views, they may have been unjustly persecuted and oppressed, but that does not take away from the fact that they are deviants whose function, particularly in modern society, is unclear.

If we examine the way people perceived the social organization of the Gypsies through the centuries, we can see that the eighteenth-century ideas on the subject were fairly "romantic." Later, it is continually pointed out that they travel in bands of two to three hundred people. Each tribe is headed by a chosen leader, called the "raj." He is the highest judge; he represents the tribe to the outside world; he decides the direction in which the tribe travels, and he relegates a traveling area to each extended family. The editors have always been fascinated by Gypsy titles. For instance, the *Volkenkundige* (Ethnographical) *Encyclopedie* of 1962 points out that more or less related groups have a "queen," an idea which became popular in the nineteenth century. It is not until 1976 that the *Grote Winkler Prins* indicates that while the outside world refers to a "king" or "queen," the Gypsies themselves in all probability reject these titles as incorrect. Jan Yoors, an artist who grew up in Antwerp, traveled with a Gypsy group, Lowara, for more than ten years from the time he was twelve years old. In his books, he describes "the other side," based on his own experiences, and he rejects those titles as well. He does write that the Gypsy communities do present certain members as "kings," but he also mentions that these kings mainly function as lightning rods during conflicts with the *gaje* (non-Gypsies).

The dietary habits of Gypsies are seldom left out. Most editors feel that they must first point out that Gypsy cooking is disgusting. They apparently enjoy vegetables like onions and garlic the most. Usually it is added that this habit is "in accordance with Eastern customs." Although they usually live on bread and water (according to the 1912 *Winkler Prins*), they do not scorn fat meat, game, or pork. One editor mentions that the hedgehog is a national dish for the Gypsies, while another notes that they even eat dogs, cats, rats, and mice. Moreover, even some twentieth-century works claim that Gypsies particularly like the meat of dead animals. Some, like Borrow, go even further and are convinced that Gypsies use their knowledge of medicine in order to deliberately cause cattle diseases and even poison animals; subsequently, they visit the farmers in order to pick up the cadavers. Borrow admits that this allegation is based largely on rumor, but in view of the Gypsies' nature, he thinks there is a high probability that it is true (Borrow 1841:19). Others claim that Gypsies dig up dead animals in order to eat them later. For example, Schwicker (1883:113) was informed that Gypsies in Temesvar had to be kept away from a dead horse by soldiers, but *"die Zigeuner gruben es später dennoch heraus und verzehrten es"* (Nevertheless, the Gypsies dug it up later and ate it). Leland (1893:124) pointed out that the Indian pariahs were no stranger to this custom.

Oftentimes, a direct connection between eating cadavers and cannibalism is implied. The most notorious accusation of Gypsy cannibalism occurred in 1782, when two hundred of them were suspected of it. After being tortured by the villagers, some of them confessed, and forty-nine Gypsies had already been executed (partially beheaded, partially hanged, then put on the rack and quartered) when an official investigations committee arrived, sent there by Kaiser Joseph II. The committee soon discovered that the confessions must have been false, because the supposed victims were still alive (De Chalmot 1789XI:2910–2911); *Grote Spectrum Encyclopedie* 1979XX:374). However, the fascination with this type of excess remains so intense that it overshadows any notion of disbelief. Although the accusation of cannibalism is first heard of around 1629 in Spain, little attention is paid to the matter outside this country. Only after Borrow (1841:102–104) quotes the Spanish source on cannibalism, Quinones (1632), do we find it in other works. For central and northwest Europe, the allegation probably starts at an earlier date. Most Gypsiologists refer to the famous Hungarian trial in 1782. Grellmann (1787:50–51), the first author to mention this trial, even writes that he has no knowledge of older accusations. The nineteenth and twentieth centuries witness sporadic accusations of cannibalism, but only a few authors really believe them. In recent Gypsiology, as far as we know, only Popp Serboianu is convinced that Gypsies are indeed cannibals. Block (1936:6, 66), who refers to the same trial, dismisses the allegations as a fable.

Child-stealing is often mentioned in one and the same breath with the allegation of cannibalism. The idea proves to be a tenacious one, for even in Oosthoek's 1940 encyclopedia (Z-885) the following is found: "Accusations of child-stealing and even (mutual) cannibalism repeatedly led to persecution in the nineteenth and twentieth century; however, these accusations were *seldom* substantiated" (emphasis added). This standard phrase changes only in later editions, after the Second World War, and then it becomes "The child-stealing allegations continually proved to be mere insinuations." It is remarkable that Grellmann, who did not reject the most negative interpretation possible of other points, rejected both the allegation of child-stealing and of cannibalism. Influenced by the ideas of the Enlightenment, he considered these "absurd" allegations as signs of superstition and irrational thinking (Grellmann 1787:48–59). The opinions of Borrow (1841:82, 83) and Popp Serboianu (1930:68) are directly opposed to this. The former claims that Gypsies stole children in order to sell them, and Popp Serboianu thought that these children were mutilated in order to turn them into beggars. Block's view of the matter differs completely. According to this author, Gypsies stole "white children" because of a *"Selbsterhaltungstrieb der Zigeuner als Rasse"* (the drive to preserve the Gypsy race) (Block 1936:64–65). In this way, "degeneration" of the Gypsy race would be prevented. The marital traditions of the Gypsies have also generated the wildest speculations. To many, the abduction of the bride, the incestuous conduct and unchristian marriage ritual which are attributed to Gypsies, are a thorn in the side. It would definitely be interesting to find out when accusations of incest started to be projected on Gypsy societies and what arguments were used. For the imagination of many a scholar has been richly stimulated by this subject.

We need not go into the Indian origins of Romani, the generic term for all Gypsy dialects. This consideration is not important to the image of the Gypsy. What we wish to consider summarily is a claim which is first made in the 1938 *Winkler Prins* encyclopedia that besides their colloquial language, the Gypsies have developed a sign language which they use on the road in order to inform the groups following them about the best route, the behavior of the police, the economic status of the inhabitants, and so on. As far as we know, Avé-Lallemant[10] was the first to note the supposed influence of the Gypsy language on secret sign languages (German *Zinken*). In his influential work about the German *Gaunerthum*, the Gypsies are equated with thieves without the slightest mitigating nuance. Because of this, the author thinks that there is a connection between the German word for scoundrel (*Gauner*) and the word *Zigeuner* (Gypsy). The latter term is supposedly a collocation of *Zieh* ("roam" or "wander") and *Gauner* (1858:11). In the second half of the century the secret sign language of the Gypsies becomes an increasingly popular theme particularly in German criminology. Liebich (1863:95–97) goes into great detail on the subject of *Zinken*, and the authoritative criminologist Lombroso (1894:138ff.; 1887:317; 1902:34ff.), who maintains a very negative view of the Gypsies in his works, also refers to their secret sign language (1887:398). Later, the work of these authors on the subject is worked out in great detail by Gross (1904:318–345). According to him, the *Zigeunergesindel* uses the signs mainly to facilitate their criminal activities such as theft, murder, and so on.

This negative interpretation does not diminish until long after the Second World War. In the *Grote Spectrum Encyclopedie* of 1979 (XX:374) we read the following on this subject: "The wandering, illiterate families used a system of signs: *patrinya* or *patteran*, which means 'messages.' These signs were used to inform the Gypsy groups which followed where there were potential customers, whether they could find food or a place to stay, and if they would be received in a friendly way." Furthermore, the mixed character of the Gypsy language is mentioned; apparently, the Gypsies adopted many elements (and thieves' jargon) from the languages of the people they met on their journeys. However, the opposite has also been claimed. In 1932, Moormann published a dissertation which mainly concerned Dutch secret languages used by nomadic groups. In this dissertation he tries to analyze the influence of Gypsy language on the secret languages of the Dutch (1932:354–426). He counted a total of 104 Gypsy words in contrast to the Dutch Arabist De Goeje, who did not get any further than 13 Gypsy words in 1903.[11] Although his conclusion points out that the influence of the Gypsy language on secret languages has been minimal, his work is still used to keep alive the image of the Gypsy as a thief (particularly in encyclopedias), an image which is based on Grellmann, Dirks, and Popp Serboianu.

Religion

From the eighteenth century up to today, encyclopedias have insisted that Gypsies are not religious, at least not in the true sense of the word. They might appear to follow the way of Christ in Christian countries and to be Mohammedans in Islamic countries, but, according to the editors, they do this only for opportunistic reasons, such as gaining access to a particular country. In addition, it is noted that they have never bothered about religious concepts, religious education, or customs,[12] except for—and no encyclopedia fails to emphasize this—their "custom" of having a newborn child baptized as often as possible in order to get a fair number of christening gifts from the various godparents. Taking into account the negative view of the Gypsies, it is not surprising that baptism for money and presents has always been interpreted as proof of begging and fraud.

Besides the question of how widespread this custom actually was, a critical remark is especially justified here, particularly because this supposed custom is often mentioned in order to illustrate how undesirable Gypsies apparently were in early times (as well as today). We can find a good example of such a negative interpretation in Van

Kappen's dissertation on the early history of Gypsies in the Netherlands (1965:136–137). He is convinced that Gypsies had their children baptized mainly for the sake of the presents from the godparents. He bases his conclusion on the decision of various synods of the Dutch Reformed church at the beginning of the seventeenth century. These synods imposed injunctions which were not against baptizing Gypsy children but against petitions for godfathers and godmothers. Van Kappen sees this as proof that multiple baptisms did occur and that society found this objectionable. At the same time, he shows that such injunctions did not prevent the rural population from giving the Gypsies money after a baptism ceremony (1965:272). If we also take into account that the injunctions against godparenthood were circumvented, one can conclude just as easily that the Gypsies were not as unwanted as was supposed earlier, particularly where the rural population was concerned. This contradiction definitely merits further study.

Around the middle of the nineteenth century, the opinions concerning the Gypsies' official beliefs change in scholarly writings; they might be religious in a superficial way, but it cannot be denied that they have religious feelings. Kogalnitchan (1840:27) is the first who presents us with this idea. Later, the same idea is worked out in much greater detail by Liebich, Schwicker, and Wlislocki (1891). Wlislocki in particular has closely examined all kinds of creation myths, fairy tales, superstitions, magic, and such. In the twentieth century this theme is elaborated upon in many and various ways (see, for example, Derlon 1981). Around this time the realization that Gypsy communities have certain ideas and customs with a religious character slowly starts to penetrate within the encyclopedias. Nevertheless, the Christian encyclopedias are always quick to note that the fundamental principles of the Gypsies are inspired by heathendom and atheism. The *Oosthoek* mentions that Gypsy customs concerning their oldest woman are indicative of ancient religious ideas. The fact that some foods are forbidden (horse flesh in particular), that there are declarations of impurity (of their midwives, among others) and that certain trees and animals are worshiped, point toward the same conclusion. According to the *Oosthoek*, the Gypsies' ancestor worship originates from fear of the dead. It is not until 1976 that the *Grote Winkler Prins* encyclopedia reports that this type of worship has a central function in the religious experience of the Gypsies. During this century, the emphasis has been more and more on those beliefs of the Gypsies which were thought to be superstitions. The recent editions of the *Oosthoek* mention that the Gypsies still believe in magic. For instance, it is said that one woman from the tribe performs all the magic ceremonies. Before she dies, she passes on her knowledge of herbs and songs to another woman. According to *Oosthoek*, we cannot label palm reading or crystal ball reading as magical activities, because the Gypsies themselves consider these only as sources of income.

Occupations

For the researcher whose aim is to demythologize the stereotypes concerning Gypsies, the representation of their professions forms one of the most rewarding subjects. In many studies about Gypsies and also in encyclopedias, two contradictory views can be found: (1) because of their specialized professions, Gypsies have always played a unique role in the labor market, for instance, as tinkers or sieve makers; (2) Gypsies are extremely work-shy, they hardly ever work. Most authors do not seem to be aware of this contradiction. Nevertheless, logically one of the views must be untenable. After all, it is impossible to master a manual profession to the finest detail without long-term training and instruction.

Already in the eighteenth century, people seemed to be convinced that Gypsies prefer to do jobs which require little effort,[13] and above all, no permanent residence (see the 1940 *Oosthoek*). In view of the prevailing impression of the Gypsy character, this interpretation is hardly surprising. In addition, attempts have been made to categorize Gypsies according to group or tribe, on the basis of descent and according to their way of life. However, the Gypsies have been categorized mainly according to their professions. For example, *Nieuwenhuis* in 1844 divides the so-called *Kroon-Ciganen* into four groups: a) Rudari, mainly goldwashers; b) Ursari, who are well known as bearleaders; c) Lingurari, who make wooden utensils (especially spoons); d) Laïssie, who roam around without practicing a definite profession. Particularly this last group is described in a negative fashion. In addition, the author distinguishes the Batrassi, slaves of the boyars, Romanian landed gentry. The Gypsies have supposedly become sedentary and are active in all kinds of professions. Many passages indicate with little subtlety that even these Gypsies cannot escape the blemish of their heritage. The Gypsy slave was a widespread phenomenon in Moldavia and Wallachia (currently Romania). De Chalmot (1789) already mentions this in his entry on Gypsies. According to him, there was not a boyar or nobleman in the eighteenth century who did not own at least three or four Gypsy slaves, while the most important people had many hundreds in their service.[14]

The element of fraud is brought in consistently in discussions of the horse trade. De Chalmot (1789XI:2911) even suggests that this was an important cause of the government's negative attitude toward Gypsies. The way people have perceived the role of Gypsies in horse trading provides a good illustration of the premise stated in the beginning of this section. The illegalities which pervaded this market must have been taken as a matter of course probably because inflating prices or "trickery" must have been part of horse trading, and every dealer, Gypsy and non-Gypsy, must have operated in that way. Otherwise one cannot explain why, through the centuries, people kept buying horses from Gypsies. However, no one bothers about this contradiction in scholarly literature until after the Second World War. Such inconsistencies easily found their way into the negative interpretation of the Gypsy lifestyle. The "explanation" of fraud in the horse trading business usually pointed toward the backwardness of the farmers who were tricked again and again. In addition, it was claimed that the psychological qualities of the Gypsy played a decisive role. The Gypsy supposedly sensed without fail how a potential buyer was to be approached (Block 1936:117).

Many other professions worthy of closer examination are mentioned in the encyclopedias, but for the sake of brevity, these must be passed over. What does need to be mentioned is that almost every encyclopedia reports that Gypsies visited markets and fairs yearly in order to perform as acrobats, magicians, dancers, and musicians (once again, occupations which require highly developed skills), while the older women foretold the future by reading cards and palms. Particularly this chiromancy, predicting the future by reading the lines of a human hand, has always appealed to the imagination. The encyclopedia of Witsen Geysbeek (1861) even goes so far as to claim that the old Gypsy women were not afraid to resort to murder in order to make their predictions come true.

Art

The only appreciation which the Gypsies have really gained has been in the area of art. However, this appraisal is often presented in the form of an indestructible stereotype: the Gypsies' fiery temperament combines with their musical virtuosity so that they can express their unbridled existence. Up to the twentieth century, the folkloric side of the Gypsies' means of expression has been highlighted. For instance, we read that Gypsy dancers were held in high regard in Russia; indeed, there are even examples of distinguished gentlemen who asked such gifted Gypsy girls to marry them. The improvisational talent of the Hungarian and Balkan Gypsies (mostly on the violin) in particular has generated many exhaustive descriptions.[15]

In the 1930s, when music encyclopedias begin to focus on the characteristics of Gypsy music, it starts to be emphasized that the Gypsy, rather than being creative, often copies and reproduces, which although particularly noticeable in music extends to other activities as well. The explanation for this is as follows: Gypsies in middle or Western Europe have been displaying their arts and crafts at fairs since the fifteenth century, capturing the citizenry's interest in music, dance, and magic. They partially take over the role of wandering acrobats and jugglers and give the ancient profession of musician a new "unprecedented exotic flavor" by singing in a strange language with "grace notes, trills, and timbres which are undeniably Asian." This view also argues that the musicians preferred to concentrate on and adapt to local melodies and rhythms for commercial reasons. That is why Gypsy music is seen more as a specific way of performing, a style of singing and playing that already exists among the local population, rather than an indigenous music which belongs to the tradition brought along by the traveling musicians themselves. Indeed, this is the way they entered European history, as itinerant musicians, socially abused, but much admired as musical craftsmen (Grote Winkler Prins 1979, XX:455). On the one hand then, there is a laudatory emphasis on the fact that all Gypsy music has an expressive vitality in common, and that Gypsies saw to it that the Spanish flamenco was handed down. On the other hand, it is claimed again and again, particularly during the last decades, that they do not possess an original musical culture.

A similar development can be observed with the ideas about the literary traditions of the Gypsies, as those ideas develop through time. In 1906, Vivat's illustrated encyclopedia manages only to report that there are poets among the Gypsies, and with that, we have the first encyclopedia to mention this aspect. One of the first Gypsiologists who examined Gypsy fairy tales and songs is the linguist Miklosich (1875:V). After this author, Schwicker (1883:159–187) praised the poetry and the narrative skills of Gypsies, deviating for the first time from his shining example, Liebich (1863:97), who found their poetry *"dürftig und armselig"* (meager and pitiful). Wlislocki must also be named as a great animator and popularizer in this branch of Gypsiology (1890:310ff.). This author, who was more blinded than enlightened by his "observations made through participation," left the beaten path at this point and collected many folktales, songs, poems, and fairy tales from Gypsies.[16]

In 1923, the *Oosthoek*, which apparently had learned little, and was badly informed on contemporary literature, writes that Gypsies do not have a literary tradition. In the second edition in 1932 an addition is made: ". . . except for fairy tales and stories which display little that is special." And suddenly, in the fourth edition in 1953, the Gypsies are seen as musical, cheerful, lively people, with a talent for reciting, arts, crafts, and languages. Moreover, they have a treasury of Eastern fairy tales and songs which is of utmost importance. The role of Gypsies as storytellers with a repertoire of hundreds of legends and other folktales also comes into focus in the seventies. The 1979 *Grote Winkler Prins* is even the first to devote a long section to the popular literature of Gypsies. However, the Gypsy's originality is denied again. There is talk of imitation and a mixture of motifs and subjects of foreign origins "without Indian traces," as it were, the sediment of the cultures which they have encountered during their travels. Essentially, this attempt at appreciation proves to be yet another negative interpretation, because little justice is done to the individuality of Gypsy culture.

Conclusions

The question as to the source of the representation of Gypsies in Dutch encyclopedias, which we raised in the introduction, can be answered very simply. The knowledge upon which this representation is based is taken straight from the scholarly works which existed at the time. Whatever is presented in these works is adopted without criticism from the original source. Grellmann's work in particular has had a pivotal function. This does not apply to the first two encyclopedias, one by Luïscius (1724–1734) and one by Hübner (1748), whose fairly short entries were based upon sixteenth- and seventeenth-century chronicles. After De Chalmot (1789), who based his entry of sixteen columns entirely on Grellmann, the tone is set for a long time. The importance of Grellmann's work can be seen in the fact that there are seven editions and three translations (English 1787, 1807; French 1788, 1810; Dutch 1791): a remarkable feat for that time. Although Grellmann was not the first to publish a book devoted entirely to Gypsies (see, for example, Fritschius 1660 and Thomasius 1671), he does retain the honor of having written the first standard work on the subject. He was the one who incorporated in his study all the knowledge which was available at the time. Thus he became an authority for practically all who published works on Gypsies after him. The degree to which he links up with the previous representation of Gypsies and to which he added new elements to this representation remains a question which cannot be answered fully at this point. Besides the originality of his work, its importance lies mainly in the compilation and popularization of different kinds of stereotypes. This is proved, among other things, by the fact that many of the opinions concerning Gypsies which are formulated later can already be found in their rudimentary or expanded form in Grellmann's work. Moreover, very few authors neglect to at least mention him; in fact, many of Grellmann's negative characterizations are copied down literally later on. For the French-German fields of language this produces an unmistakable genealogy, whose importance wanes only after the Second World War.[17] A tentative genealogy, according to which each "new" author relies to a great extent on the previously mentioned author(s) often plagiarizing unashamedly, looks like this: Grellmann (1783–1787) — Kogalnitchan (1837–1840) — Liebich (1863) — Schwicker (1883) — Wlislocki (1890) — Popp Serboianu (1930) — Block (1936) — Bloch (1953) — Clébert (1961–1964). Further research in this area should focus on completing this genealogy with, among others, English and American works.[18]

It is striking that the way the information is collected influences the representation of Gypsies only slightly. For example, the observations through participation of authors such as Wlislocki and Block, who insist upon completely different methods, produce practically the same images (aside from the Gypsy's literary tradition, which they both put down in writing) as their "unenlightened" colleagues propound. Aside from a few exceptions, the demonstrable negative and positive shifts in the representation of Gypsies are caused mainly by disciplines which did not concern themselves primarily with the "subject" Gypsies: incipient physical anthropology with its skull measurements and criminology, both disciplines which grew mainly in the first half of the nineteenth century. It has only been in the past thirty years that the more critical sociology, anthropology, and social psychology have transformed the representation of Gypsies from "the outside" and even partially demythologized it (see, among others, Acton 1974 and Okely 1983).

Encyclopedias are generally distinguished from scholarly/scientific works by the outdated concepts and representations which continue to appear in them. Editors are slow in accepting recent studies, particularly those which deviate from the norm, such as the social-scientific research from about 1960 onward, which concentrates on the marginal and minority position of Gypsies. An extreme example is found in the *Christian* (1929, 1961, 1977) and *Catholic* (1983, 1955) encyclopedias. These hold tenaciously to the work of the antirevolutionary Dutch political leader Abraham Kuyper (1907–1908), who was exceptionally negative not only about Gypsies but also about Jews and other groups. The encyclopedia *Thieme* from 1984 proves that outdated views are not limited to encyclopedias with a religious character. Thieme's encyclopedia presents a number of backward ideas about Gypsies which we do not find in the recent editions of encyclopedias such as *Oosthoek, Spectrum*, and the *Winkler Prins*. Those encyclopedias emphasize, at least from the 1960s onward, the Gypsies' position as a discriminated minority through the ages.

Now that the question about the origins of the ideas concerning Gypsies has been answered as fully as possible, we would like to dwell upon a general mechanism which is active in the development of a representation. Studies of minority groups show again and again that stereotypes do not appear out of the blue. In fact, they originate from prejudices which are already present albeit not yet crystallized. We speak of stereotypes only when these prejudices are standardized and accepted collectively. In relation to the representation of Gypsies, the following development seems plausible: ideas about this group already existed in the fifteenth century in Europe. These ideas became more and more negative, leading to generally accepted stereotypes in the eighteenth century. The largely negative content of these stereotypes (Gypsies are work-shy, they steal, lie, are not trustworthy, and so on) proved to be threatening enough to the accepted norms and values of the societies in which the Gypsies were trying to find a niche that they could easily be used to justify behavior which was aimed against this category of people and their cultures.

Both the attempts to exterminate Gypsies in the seventeenth and eighteenth centuries and the attempt to reeducate them in colonies at the end of the eighteenth and beginning of the nineteenth century could be defended in this way. This last idea fits in perfectly with the absolutist pursuit of a number of "enlightened" rulers to create a uniform state. Beginning in 1761, Austrian empress Maria Theresa and her son, who was also her successor, tried to forcibly "civilize" the Gypsies in order to make them accept a sedentary lifestyle (see, among others, Hohmann 1981:43). In their wake, the scientific interest in Gypsies increased, resulting in Grellmann's work. It is the latter who "demonstrates" that Gypsies are an untrustworthy, childish people, who can only reach a degree of higher civilization through careful guidance. The rationalizations which he presented in his work began to lead a life of their own as stereotypes, and they were soon used to justify the "civilization offensive" which was launched on several fronts. Later works, in which Grellmann's prejudices were continued, produced practically the same images. Even those who wished the Gypsies well, who thought they could rid themselves of their prejudices by traveling and living with them, like Wlislocki and Block, did not manage to escape the impressions which had been handed down. At times, people went even further and interpreted an initially positive impression in a negative way at the last moment. We can see this mechanism operate very clearly in the representation of the musical talents of Gypsies. Although they are praised for the virtuosity of their performances, particularly in the nineteenth century, once musicology, and subsequently the encyclopedias, takes a critical look at their repertoire, it is soon "demonstrated" that their music totally lacks originality, and that its nature is reproductive rather than creative. The same supposedly goes for their oral tradition, whose imitative character is continually emphasized.

Leaving aside the question of whether "imitation" and "originality" are valid concepts in this context, as they quickly lead to the chicken/egg argument, it must be noted that other performing arts and folktales never have to answer to such requirements.

During the nineteenth century it became clear that the forced, and thus one-sided, process of emancipation was doomed to failure. The outcome of these attempts to civilize the Gypsies were blamed on the group itself. Many came to the conclusion that they were a bad lot. It was thought that the only way to liberate the group was through intermixing and assimilation. Later, it was added that, as a people, they have an incorrigible character which is not worth a good effort. The early anthropologists who studied the Gypsies' national character, and after them, the ethnologists who were interested in "degeneration," both produced the rationalizations which were needed to show that Gypsies were a despicable people or race, inclined to criminality. It is not until the second half of the nineteenth century that the idea of intermixing is dropped. The concept of race begins to dominate at this time, and intermixing is now seen as the primary cause for "degeneration"; thus, socially speaking, the group is definitely relegated to the position of incorrigible pariah. Particularly the area of criminology, which also blossoms at this time, gratefully uses the new "scientific" insights to label the Gypsy as an innate criminal who has no right to a place in society. The Nazis continued this line of thought to its extreme. They denied those Gypsies who had "degenerated," because they had intermixed with "German vagabonds" among others, any right to a dignified existence. In this way, the prejudices concerning Gypsies which Grellmann gathered in a "scientific" manner were intermixed with theories developed by anthropologists, linguists, and others. In the new situation arguments which were developed during the emancipation to defend the idea that Gypsies should be raised, as it were, socially, have been turned into arguments to justify discrimination. With this the stereotyping of Gypsies acquired such an obdurate character that a comparison with anti-Semitism forces itself on our minds, but that is a subject for further research.

Afterword 1995:

The (more extensive) Dutch version of this essay was written in 1988. Since then, we have published several books and articles which elaborate on topics which are dealt with here. We mention especially the dissertation of Wim Willems: *Op zoek naar de ware zigeuner. Zigeuners als studie-object tijdens de Verlicting, de Romantiek en het Nazisme,* Utrecht 1995 (In Search of the True Gypsy. Gypsies as Objects of Research during the Enlightenment, Romanticism, and Nazism), to be published in English within two years, which offers a detailed analysis of the ideas of Grellmann, Borrow, and Ritter and their contribution to the stereotyping of Gypsies. To what extent these ideas were put into practice is elaborated in Leo Lucassen's dissertation on the Dutch situation: *En men noemde hen zigeuners'. De geschiedenis van Kaldarasch, Ursari, Lowara en Sinti in Nederland: 1750–1944* (Amsterdam/Den Haag 1990) (And They Were Called Gypsies) and his forthcoming book on Germany: *Zigeuner. Zur Genese eines polizeilichen Oberbegriffs in Deutschland (1700–1940)* (Böhlau-Verlag, Köln-Wien 1996). Together with Annemarie Cottaar we recently published a photo-textbook on the Dutch history of the Gypsies and caravan dwellers from 1868 onward: *Mensen van de reis. Woonwagenbewoners en zigeuners in Nederland 1868–1995* (Zwolle 1995) (Travelling People: Caravan Dwellers and Gypsies in the Netherlands, 1868–1995). Our main English and German publications since 1990 have been published in *Immigrants & Minorities* 11 (March 1992); the *International Review of Social History* 2 (August 1993); *Ethnologia Europaea. Journal of European Ethnology* 23 (1993); and *1999. Zeitschrift für Sozialgeschichte des 20. und 21. Jahrhunderts* 10 (1995), no. 1. See also our contributions in R. Muchembled, ed., *The Roots of Western Civilization: Popular Culture* (Danbury, CT, Grolier, 1994); Robin Cohen, ed., *The Cambridge Survey of World Migration,* vol. 5: *Migration in Europe, 1880–1950* (Cambridge, CUP 1995); and in Linda A. Bennet, ed., *Encyclopedia of World Cultures* IV (Europe) (Boston, G. K. Hall 1992).

NOTES

1. The forerunners of encyclopedias, the so-called dictionaries, are included as well. Obviously, the most specialized encyclopedias (technical, art, and so forth) are left out of consideration. The entries are: Bohemians, Egyptians, Gypsies, Heathens, Tsiganes, and Zigeuners. Our selection is based upon the dictionaries and encyclopedias which can be found at the Royal Library in The Hague. The central catalog of this library was consulted in order to complete the research. Although this catalog is by no means complete and although we were unable to study all the works listed in the Royal Library, we do consider them to be representative. For the complete list of about sixty encyclopedias, we refer to our Dutch article (Willems and Lucassen 1988).

2. Considering the extensive work which has been done on this subject, we have limited ourselves to those sources which are cited most often in the encyclopedias and which can be found in the Dutch libraries.

3. Of course, one cannot use this source as a basis for making general statements about representation in all strata of society. More specialized research is needed for this. For instance, Leo Lucassen's doctoral research focuses on the attitudes of several Dutch governments and the Dutch population.

4. Earlier works also describe the Gypsy's features; however, these descriptions do not amount to more than a crude sketch. It is only after the middle of the nineteenth century that the Gypsy is described in more detail. The descriptions are frequently based upon anthropometric research. See Liebich (1863:20), Schwicker (1883:104–105), whose work is largely based on the former, and also Wlislocki (1890:164).

5. Particularly the work of Friedrich Max Müller (1823–1900), who thought for a long time that he had arrived at the essence of humankind by means of language classifications, has encouraged the belief that something like an Aryan race supposedly exists, with Indian ancestors, interconnected by a common language. At the end of his life, he came to reconsider this idea. He began to realize that the existence of Aryan languages does not necessarily imply that people who speak this language have the same (Aryan) ancestors. In this way, he saw to it that the Aryan myth was reconsidered. At that time, however, his ideas had already become widespread (see Mosse 1980:42–44; Poliakov 1979:209).

6. This characteristic is first mentioned in the *Winkler Prins Encyclopedia* of 1954, which seems strange when we realize that already at the end of the eighteenth century, research had been done in Germany on the shape of German skulls (Blumenbach 1793:3–4), and that this research was continued intensively from the middle of the nineteenth century onwards. The results of this research

were, as far as we know, first mentioned by Diefenbach (1877:106). For an extensive survey, see *Kraniologische Studien*, Wlislocki 1890: 163, note 1.

7. Grellmann names, among others two seventeenth-century Dutch traveling accounts (1787:329–332): J. Nieuhoff, *Zee en lantreizen door verscheiden gewesten van Oostindien* (1653–1672) (Sea and Country Travels Through Several Regions of East India), Amsterdam 1682; and A. Rogerius, *Open-deure tot het verborgen heydendom op de Cust Chormandel* (The Open Door to the Hidden Heathendom on the Coromandel Coast), Leiden 1651. Grellmann did not copy the last title quite correctly. The actual title is: *De open-deure tot het verborgen heydendom ofte waerachtig vertoogh van het leven ende zeden mitsg. de religie ende godsdienst der Bramines op de cust Chormandel, ende de landen daar omtrent* (The Open Door to the Hidden Heathendom, or the True Account of the Life, Morals, and Religion of the Brahmins on the Coromandel Coast and the Surrounding Countries).

8. For instance, the 1870 *Winkler Prins Encyclopedia* writes: ". . . they grovel before the powerful of the earth." Liebich (1863:18), on the other hand, claims that Gypsies always hang on to their pride, something which supposedly distinguishes them from the Jews (who are considered obsequious). Wlislocki (1890:10) repeats this word for word, but later on in his book, when the character of the Gypsies is mentioned (*"keineswegs ein erfreulicher"* [by no means pleasing], p. 166), they suddenly appear to be marked by *"entwürdigende Kriecherei in Thun und Wesen"* (a demeanor of self-degrading servility).

9. *Katholieke Encyclopedie* 1938-25:591; 1955-25:320, but also the *Christelijke Encyclopedie* 1961-VI:679; 1977-VI:697. The nineteenth century witnesses the spreading of the idea that the criminality of the Gypsies has increased particularly because they have intermixed with indigenous criminals and antisocial characters. This "degeneration thesis" can already be found in Dirks (1850:152–153). Later, this thesis is worked out by such German (Nazi) scholars as Robert Ritter (1937; 1938). Even after the Second World War, there are some who continue to be influenced by this racist idea; see, among others, the opinions of Arnold (1958; 1965), Van Kappen (1965:7, 139), and finally, Küther (1976:25).

10. Avé-Lallemant 1858–1862-II:52, note 3. As far as we can tell at this moment, this author is one of the first to examine the Gypsies from a criminological point of view. They do not yet appear like this in Jageman's "criminallexicon" (1854).

11. De Goeje 1903. In this short article about Gypsy words in the Dutch language, De Goeje provides the first initiative toward an inventory of the influence of Romani (the language of the Gypsies) on Dutch. The only source which he uses is a *Bargoense* (language of thieves) word list made in 1860 by M. Verwoert, prison director of the city of Utrecht. De Goeje admits that his list

is not all-inclusive: "These are just a few notes, without the least claim of completeness" (p. 26).

12.   There is general agreement on this subject as well, starting at the beginning of the eighteenth century. Gypsies were heathens who lacked any kind of religious feeling (see, for example, Salmon 1733:503 and Grellmann 1787:141). The latter is well known for the following statement: *Es fällt ihm eben so leicht, mit jedem neuem Dorfe seine Religion zu verandern, als andern Menschen, ein anderes Kleid anzuziehen* (It is as easy for him to change religion with every village he passes as it is for other people to change clothes).

13.   The representation of this subject is based largely on Grellmann: *Man denke aber nicht, dass die Werkstätte des Schmiedes beständig vom pochenden Hammer wiederhaller, oder andere ihren andern Verrichtungen so fleissig obliegen* (Do not think that the smith's workshop echoes constantly with the sound of pounding hammers, or that [other Gypsies] are diligent in any other way) (1787:112). And yet Grellmann, an unimpeachable source in this respect, praises the Gypsies highly for their craftsmanship (1787:84). However, he undercuts these skills earlier in his work, claiming that the Gypsies only make small objects because heavy forging would take too much of an effort (1787:82). This opinion was adopted by, among others, Schwicker (1883:118), Wlislocki (1890:198), and Kuhinka (1957:80ff.).

14.   This serfdom lasted until the middle of the nineteenth century. Besides the landed gentry (boyars), both the king and the church made use of Gypsy slaves. In Transylvania, slavery was already abolished in the eighteenth century (Péysonnel 1765:11–12; Grellmann 1787:90; Kogalnitchan 1840:17–18; Vaux de Foletier 1970:86–89; Vossen 1983:55–57).

15.   For instance, the *Algemene Muziek Encyclopedie* of 1963 (and 1984) relates the beautiful anecdote of Bihari, a Gypsy violinist, who was praised highly by Liszt in 1821 for his virtuosity. This violinist had a servant carry his violin in front of him on a satin pillow; the most beautiful moment of his life occurred when he moved Queen Elisabeth of Hungary to tears with his playing.

16.   After Wlislocki, Aichele and Block (1926) in particular enriched the general knowledge about Gypsy fairy tales. This part of Gypsy culture was further explored by Kuhinka (1957:93–127) and recently by Uhlik and Radivic (1977).

17.   Martins-Heuss (1983) does a similar analysis, based on German scholarly works from the nineteenth century onward. She attempts to show that "the Gypsy" does not exist; instead, there is a representation of Gypsies which is constructed by a dominating society. Many of the dreams and nightmares of that society can be recognized in this representation. Although this study supports our conclusions in many ways, there are certain drawbacks to it. The most important one is that the author, in our view, uses debatable psycho-

analytic assumptions which make the greater part of her interpretations questionable (for other works in the area of German, see, among others, Hohmann 1980 and 1981).

18. Despite the fact that these have, in part, produced the same stereotypes, it is difficult to fit in most of the English works. They depart from the direction taken by continental works in that they barely pay attention to Gypsies in central Europe, concentrating instead on England and India (see, for example, Leland 1891 and 1893; Smart and Crofton 1875; Woolner 1914). The "godfather" of this English branch is Borrow. His most important work deals with Spain (1841), but he also wrote a number of books specifically on the English situation (1851 and 1857). From 1888 onward, the importance of this branch becomes known through the *Journal of the Gypsy Lore Society*.

REFERENCES

Acton, Thomas A.
  1974 *Gypsy Politics and Social Change*. London and Boston: Routledge and Kegan Paul.
Aichele, Walter, and Martin Block
  1926 *Zigeunermärchen*. Jena: Diederichs.
Arnold, Hermann
  1958 *Vaganten, Komödianten, Fieranten und Briganten*. Stuttgart: Verlag Georg Thieme.
  1965 *Die Zigeuner. Herkunft und Leben im deutschen Sprachgebiet*. Olten und Freiburg: Walter-Verlag.
Avé-Lallemant, Friedrich Christian Bernhard
  1858–
  1862 *Das deutsche Gaunerthum* (four volumes). Leipzig: Brockhaus.
Black, George Fraser
  1974 *A Gypsy Bibliography*. London: Folcroft. (first edition Edinburgh University Press, 1914)
Bloch, Jules
  1953 *Les tsiganes*. Paris: Presses Universitaires de France.
Block, Martin
  1936 *Zigeuner. Ihr Leben und ihre Seele, dargestellt auf Grund eigener Reisen und Forschungen*. Leipzig: Bibliographisches Institut. [English edition: *Gypsies: Their Life and Customs*. New York: D. Appleton-Century, 1939.]

Blumenbach, Johann Friedrich
1793 *Decas altera collectionis suae craniorum gentium illustrata.* Gottingae: publisher unknown.

Borrow, George
1841 *The Zincali; or, an Account of the Gypsies of Spain.* London: John Murray.
1851 *Lavengro; the Scholar—the Gypsy—the Priest.* London: John Murray.
1857 *The Romany Rye.* London: John Murray.

Clébert, Jean-Paul
1964 *De zigeuners.* Antwerpen-Zeist (first edition, Paris: Arthaud, 1961; English edition London: Vista Books, 1963).

De Goeje, M. J.
1903 "Zigeunerwoorden in het Nederlandsch," in *Album Kern.* Leiden: Brill.

Derlon, Pierre
1981 *Geheime geneeskunst van zigeuners.* Deventer: Ankh-Hermes (first edition: Paris 1978).

Diefenbach, Lorenz
1877 *Die Volksstämme der Europaischen Türkei.* Frankfurt am Main: Christian Winter.

Dirks, Jeroen
1850 *Geschiedkundige onderzoekingen aangaande het verblijf der heidens of Egyptiërs in de Noordelijke Nederlanden.* Utrecht: C. van der Post.

Fritschius, Ahasverus
1660 *Diatribe historico-politica de Zygenorum origine, vita ac moribus.* Jenae: Georg II Sengenwalds.

Grellmann, Heinrich Moritz Gottlieb
1787 *Die Zigeuner. Ein historischer Versuch über die Lebensart und Verfassung, Sitten und Schicksale dieses Volks in Europa, nebst ihrem Ursprung.* Göttingen: Johann Christian Dieterich (first edition: Dessau und Leipzig, 1783).

Gross, Hans
1904 *Handbuch für Untersuchungsrichter als System der Kriminalistik.* München: publisher unknown.

Hohmann, Joachim Stephan
1980 *Zigeuner und Zigeunerwissenschaft.* Marburg/Lahn: Reihe Metro.
1981 *Geschichte der Zigeunerverfolgung in Deutschland.* Frankfurt: Campus.

Kogalnitchan (Kogălniceanu), Michael
1840 *Skizze einer Geschichte der Zigeuner.* Stuttgart: J. F. Cast'sche (first [French] edition Berlin 1837).

Kuhinka, Ernest M. G.
1957 *Zigeuners, geschiedenis van een zwervend volk.* Rotterdam: Wyt.
Küther, Carsten
1976 *Räuber und Gauner in Deutschland.* Göttingen: Vanderhoeck & Ruprecht.
Kuyper, Abraham
1907– *Om de oude wereldzee* (2 volumes). Amsterdam: Van Holkema & 1908 Warendorf.
Leland, Charles Godfrey
1971 *Gypsy Sorcery and Fortunetelling.* New York: Dover (first edition: London 1891).
1893 *The English Gipsies and Their Language.* London: Kegan, Paul, Trench, Trübner & Co. (first edition: 1873).
Liebich, Richard
1863 *Die Zigeuner in ihrem Wesen und in ihrer Sprache.* Leipzig: F. A. Brockhaus.
Liégeois, Jean-Pierre
1983 *Tsiganes.* Paris: La Découverte/Maspéro.
Lombroso, Cesare
1887 *Der Verbrecher in Anthropologischer, ärtzlicher und juristischer Beziehung.* Hamburg: publisher unknown (first [Italian] edition: 1876).
1894 *Neue Fortschritte in den Verbrecherstudien.* Leipzig: publisher unknown.
1902 *Die Ursachen und Bekämpfung des Verbrechens.* Berlin: publisher unknown.
Martins-Heuss, Kirsten
1983 *Zur mythischen Figur des Zigeuners in der deutschen Zigeunerforschung.* Frankfurt am Main: Haag + Herchen.
Miklosich, Franz
1872– *Über die Mundarten und die Wanderungen der Zigeuner Europa's.* 1881 Wien: Kaiserliche Akademie der Wissenschaften.
Moormann, Julius Georg Maria
1932 *De Geheimtalen.* Zutphen: Thieme.
Mosse, George L.
1980 *A History of European Racism.* New York: Harper & Row (first edition 1978).
Münster, Sebastian
1550 *Cosmographia universalis* (lib VI). Basilaea: Henrichus Petri.
Okely, Judith
1983 *The Traveller-Gypsies.* Cambridge: Cambridge University Press.

Paspati, Alexandre G.
   1870 *Études sur les Tchinghianés ou Bohémiens de l'Empire Ottoman.*
         Constantinople: Antoine Koroméla.
Péysonnel, Charles Claude de
   1765 *Observations historiques et géographiques sur les peuples barbares
         qui ont habités les bords du Danube et du Pont-Euxine.* Paris: Tillard.
Pittard, Eugène
   1908 "L'Étude anthropologique des tsiganes," *Journal of the Gypsy Lore
         Society* 1:37–45.
Poliakov, Léon
   1979 *De arische mythe.* Amsterdam: Arbeiderspers. (First [French] edition:
         Paris: Calmann-Levy, 1971).
Popp Serboianu, C. J.
   1930 *Les tsiganes.* Paris: Payot.
Ritter, Robert
   1937 *Ein Menschenschlag.* Leipzig: Georg Thieme.
   1938 "Zur Frage der Rassenbiologie und Rassenpsychologie der Zigeuner
         in Deutschland," in *Reichsgesundheitsblatt*22:425–426.
Rüdiger, J. C. C.
   1782–
   1793 *Neuester Zuwachs der teutschen, fremden und allgemeinen Sprach-
         kunde in eigenen Aufsätzen, Bücheranzeigen und Nachrichten.*Leipzig
         und Halle: publisher unknown.
Salmon, Thomas
   1733 *Hedendaagsche historie of tegenwoordige staat van alle volkeren*(deel
         V, Turksche ryk in Asia en Afrika). Amsterdam: Isaak Tirion.
Schwicker, Johann Heinrich
   1883 *Die Zigeuner in Ungarn und Siebenbürgen.* Wien und Teschen: K.
         Prochaska.
Smart, Bath Charles, and Henry Thomas Crofton
   1875 *The Dialect of the English Gypsies.* London: Ascher & Co.
Swinburne, Henry
   1779 *Travels through Spain in the Years 1775 and 1776.* London: P.
         Elmsly.
Thomasius, Jacobus
   1748 *Gründliche historische Nachricht von denen Ziegeunern.* Franckfurt
         und Leipzig: publisher unknown. (First edition: Lipsiae 1671.)
Twiss, Richard
   1776 *Voyage en Portugal et en Espagne fait en 1772 & 1773.* Berne; (first
         [English] edition: London: G. Robinson, T. Becket and J. Robson,
         1775).

Uhlik, Rade, and B. Radivic
1977 *Zigeunerlieder.* Leipzig: publisher unknown.
Van Kappen, O.
1965 *Geschiedenis der zigeuners in Nederland.* Assen: Van Gorcum.
Vaux de Foletier, François de
1970 *Mille ans d'histoire des tsiganes.* Paris: Fayard.
Vossen, Rüdiger
1983 *Zigeuner: Roma, Sinti, Gitanos, Gypsies zwischen Verfolgung und Romantisierung.* Frankfurt am Main: Ullstein.
Willems, Wim, and Leo Lucassen
1988 "Beeldvorming over zigeuners in Nederlandse encyclopedieën (1724–1984) en hun wetenschappelijke bronnen," in Pieter Hovens and Rob Dahler, eds., *Zigeuners in Nederland. Cultuur, Geschiedenis en Beleid.* Nijmegen/Rijswijk: Ministerie van Welzijn, Volksgezondheid en cultuur, 5–52.
Wlislocki, Heinrich von
1890 *Vom wandernden Zigeunervolke. Bilder aus dem Leben der siebenbürger Zigeuner.* Hamburg: Act.-Gesellschaft.
1891 *Volksglaube und religiöser Brauch der Zigeuner.* Münster: Aschendorff.
Woolner, A. C.
1914 "The Indian Origin of the Gypsies in Europe," in *Journal of the Panjab Historical Society* 2:118–137.
Yoors, Jan
1967 *Wij zigeuners.* Brussel-Den Haag: Manteau, (First [English] edition, New York/London: Simon and Schuster, 1967).

Johnny Faa and Black Jack Davy:
Cultural Values and Change in Scots and American Balladry
(1980)

Christine A. Cartwright

The question of cultural function is one of the central concerns of oral-narrative research as well as one of the most complex and problematic. Faced with a narrative such as "The Gypsy Laddie" (Child #200), which has been among the most popular ballads in the English language for well over two hundred years, one of the most useful approaches a scholar can take is to examine the nature and sources of its hold upon the emotions and memory of English-speaking people. The ballad's plot and motifs have remained remarkably consistent, while the emotional tone and interpretation placed upon them have varied greatly. Why do we sing it? Why do we like it? Why have thousands of singers retained certain motifs and motif sequences, while feeling free to make quite individual changes in others? Have most singers liked and remembered the ballad for the same reasons, or does the variation in focus and interpretation indicate a corresponding variation in their understanding of and response to the ballad narrative? Does the same plot line serve different psychological or cultural functions for different singers?

I

"The Gypsy Laddie" was first collected in Scotland, and appeared in print for the first time in Ramsay's *Tea-Table Miscellany*, published in 1740.[1] It is the tale of a lady of high degree who abruptly abandons wealth, security, marriage, and motherhood when a band of Gypsies come singing to the door while her lord is away from home. Attracted, in most texts, by her beauty, the Gypsies cast a spell upon her; in a few versions she recovers when her lord, hearing the news from the servants, comes to bring her home, but in most she chooses to remain as she is. The ballad ends with the hanging or slaying of the entire Gypsy band (or all but one, who tells the story).

It is always difficult to reconstruct the cultural function of a narrative for people now dead, but through a combination of textual analysis and historical and sociological study, it is possible to make some educated guesses about the principal reasons for the ballad's popularity in eighteenth-century Scotland. We do not find traveling-salesman stories circulating in groups that take a relaxed view of casual adulteries, nor do we find priest, pastor, and rabbi jokes where no religious tension exists. In this case, we have a ballad in which several male members of an itinerant minority, racially and culturally distinct from the dominant population, abduct a rich, pretty wife and mother belonging to that dominant population, usually by means of a spell. The degree to which the lady is responsible for her own actions is left ambiguous in almost every published text, for, though bespelled at the opening of the ballad, her will and her wits seem very much her own when she refuses to return to her lord at its close. The ballad's narrative tension, then, seems to spring from a two-edged threat presented by the Gypsies: their [perceived] invasion of and imposition upon Scottish culture, with all of their disturbing, foreign values and ways, as well as their potentially threatening attractiveness.

We know that there was indeed a Gypsy population of considerable size in Scotland shortly before records of the ballad's existence began to appear. They were abruptly ordered out of the country by an act of the Scottish Parliament in 1609, and there are records thereafter of Gypsies (including three by the name of Johnne Faa, the name borne by the Gypsy chieftain and lover of the lady in many of the Scottish ballad texts) being hanged for having "remanet within this Kingdome."[2] While the parliamentary decree does not offer much detail or explanation of its grounds, the trials of Gypsies found within Scotland's borders after its enactment cast a good deal of light upon Scottish opinion of Gypsies in general. The court records of one Gypsy trial contain the court's observation that it should be leisum to all his Maiesteis guid subiectis, or ony of thame, to caus tak, apprehend, imprisone, and execute to death, all maner of Egyptianis, alsweill men as wemen, as cowmone, notorious, and condempnet Thevis, only to be tryit be an Assyse, that thai are callit, knawin, repute, and haldin Egyptianis . . .[3]

The equation here between "Gypsy" and "thief" is explicit, wholesale, and final: if one was known to be a Gypsy, the law presumed that he or she was also a thief.

The congruence between this blatant, official assumption and the assumptions expressed in later exoteric lore concerning Gypsies is too great and too widely supported to be ignored as a factor in the early cultural functions of "The Gypsy Laddie." Legend and legal action all over Great Britain in the nineteenth century show clearly that Gypsies were generally associated with child-stealing, curses, theft, fortune-telling, and the seduction of young women. They have long been considered dirty and their lifestyle squalid; they have been believed to possess arcane knowledge and powers, and their dark hair and eyes, ornaments, bright clothes, and distinctive music have connected them, in Scottish and English eyes, with the dangers and temptations of exotic cultures outside of northern Europe and away from Christianity. Given these associations and reactions as part of the climate in which the ballad was born, its tale of a white woman abducted by Gypsies (sometimes robbed, sometimes bedded, and invariably placed under a spell) must have evoked a powerful complex of cultural anxieties and concerns.

Certainly there must have been an element of outright ethnic fear and hatred, especially during the years (however many there were) of the ballad's life prior to its first appearance in print, when Gypsies were still numerous enough to warrant immediate, practical concern for the safety of one's valuables, horses, and womenfolk. Probably by Burns's day, when the nobility had so allied themselves with French and English manners and customs that it was no longer respectable for a Scot to speak or write Scots, a certain amount of nostalgia also entered into popular response to the ballad: nostalgia for the days when laird and tenant alike were proud to be Scottish and resisted the infiltration of foreign views and ways. But perhaps most deeply and consistently of all, the Scottish ballad texts seem to focus on the controlled, formulaic expression of the ambivalence long felt in Scotland toward the Eastern, Latin, and tropical cultures which they sailed to for trading purposes, [and encountered at home] when the Gypsies came and stayed.

For eighteenth-century Scotland, as for any seafaring nation, it was an economic necessity that the men be willing and able both to encounter and to resist the delights of foreign ports. The love of adventure was basic to Scotland's survival—provided the men (a) came home, and (b) had a home to come back to. The men could not be encouraged by their culture to hate or fear cheap rum and dark-eyed beauties or to shun the roving life, for someone had to sell the wool and the herring and bring home the silks and spices. Neither could the women be encouraged to enjoy them, for someone had to raise the children and maintain a stable home while the men were away. The Gypsies' presence in Scotland brought several of the most potent dangers and temptations of foreign ports into Scotland itself, and what a Scotsman could comfortably encounter overseas he could not comfortably leave his wife and children to cope with at home; what was good for the gander was not good for the goose. Faced with the foreign music, the spices, and the "black, but very bonny" beauty the Gypsies bring to "our lord's gate" in most of the extant Scottish texts, the lady reacts as many a Scottish sailor did and becomes a "rantin, rovin" lassie. Surely one of the great currents of narrative tension in the ballad is this inversion of right order: the lord coming home to find that the "out there" has come here; the husband trying desperately to restore the stability of his home and family, and the wife who should have kept it stable in his absence becoming the rover.

Robert Burns and the historian Robert Chambers, both of whom influenced Child's interpretations of the ballad's functions, assert that it was generally understood as a romantic tragedy, involving the unhappily married Lady Jean Cassilis and her lover Lord John Faa, who disguised himself as a Gypsy in order to elope with his old true love.[4] Chambers tells the story in great detail, claiming that it circulated as local legend in Ayrshire, and assumes that it is based upon an actual historical occurrence.[5] Child's own research, however, led him to conclude that Chambers's account had no basis whatsoever in fact; he quotes letters of Lord Cassilis's which indicate that he and his lady lived in harmony all their lives and that she was never abducted by any Gypsies, genuine or otherwise. Certainly the ballad texts themselves never suggest that the Gypsy was anything but a Gypsy; on the contrary, textual evidence indicates that both the Gypsies and the spell were considered genuine. It is possible that Chambers's version is a Victorian or even a literary creation: a kind of bowdlerization of what was otherwise a disturbing and distasteful picture of romantic and sexual union across ethnic, social, and cultural barriers of a very serious kind. It is also possible that, for inland Ayrshire [where there was no longer a strong Gypsy presence], the question of conflict between true love and arranged marriage was more and more pressing and more in need of expression than the fears and temptations connected with the foreign. Quite possibly, the picture of a Scottish noblewoman shedding her silks, donning a plaidie, and setting her bare feet in the Clyde for the sake of her old true love, whose name was evocative of an older and more Scottish Scotland, was tremendously moving and powerful in the days when Edinburgh spoke more French than Scots. Whatever the relationship between Chambers's version, actual Ayrshire legend, fact, and the ballad, it seems clear that the ballad functioned as a forum for the expression of a number of delicate, intertwined cultural anxieties, centering upon what can happen when the foreign invades the home.

II

The ballad is as popular in America as in Great Britain, but the central concerns of its singers underwent a sea change when it crossed the Atlantic. Textually, the ballad lost the glamourie or Gypsy spell, with its threat of the supernatural and the arcane; there were few or no Gypsies around for the immigrants to worry about, and wilderness life offered enough concrete dangers to take one's mind off spells. The Gypsy chieftain lost both his foreignness and his band, and most often appears as a lone traveler. (Apparently, as Barre Toelken remarked, a red-blooded American Gypsy doesn't need any help in capturing a lady's affections.[6]) The lord frequently becomes older, and the lady younger; more focus is placed upon the verbal exchange and conflicting claims in what is clearly seen as a romantic triangle, in which the singer is free to identify with any of the three participants.

The conserved core of the Scots/English narrative, as it consistently appears in the 193 American texts I have examined, is as follows: the Gypsy rides by (often "through the woods") singing so loudly, beautifully, or gaily that the lady's heart is immediately "charmed." He asks her to go with him, and she readily complies, frequently taking off or changing her shoes or "boots of Spanish leather." Her husband hears the news when he arrives home that night and immediately sets out in pursuit, catching up with the lovers at a river (occasionally a bog, a lake, or the "dark and dreary" sea). He begs his lady to come home, offering a threefold appeal: first to her desire for the security of his "house and lands" or "the gold I have," second to her love for her baby, and third to her sense of identity, propriety, or happiness as his wife. She refuses all three pleas and affirms the finality of her decision to remain with the Gypsy. The endings are diverse, but the common Scots/English stanza in which the lady compares the feather bed of the past with the ground she will now sleep on almost always appears in some form.

Several major changes in cultural function are clearly at work in this basic narrative. The meeting between the lady and the Gypsy received a very different context in America: he is no longer an outsider who intrudes into the lord's house while the lord is not there to guard it. In no text I have seen does he even ride *out of* the woods into a settled area, which might have indicated that he was considered an outsider. Instead, the Gypsy Davy or Black Jack Davy is simply passing by, riding *through* the woods, coming "whistling by," or crossing the field or the plain, and more or less inadvertently charms the lady with his singing. The home the lady leaves is apparently *in* the woods, field, or plain, or next to the road, if she is at home at all when she hears the Gypsy singing. She is never intruded upon, invaded, or abducted by any sleight or force; she is asked if she would like to come along and does so by her own free choice, quickly made and rarely reversed, though sometimes regretted.

Clearly, the complex of ideas and images associated with the Gypsy has changed from a frightening, dirty, destructive, and foreign one to something more delightful and worthwhile. Where, in the Scottish texts, the singers described the lady having to wade a river, sleep in "an auld reeky kilt," "the ash-corner" or "a tenant's barn," drink in taverns, sleep "wi' the black crew glowering owre me," and even being made to "carry the Gypsy laddie," stanzas begin to appear in American texts about sleeping under the stars or singing songs beside a campfire. The American lady may declare, "I wouldn't give a kiss from the Gypsy's lips for all of your lands and money," indicating that the singer is quite clear about her motive for leaving her husband. In Scottish texts, it is only the glamourie which makes the lady see "glamour," an illusory beauty, in Johnny Faa and his life; her proper place, the place of health and sanity and right order where she belongs, is clearly with her family. The American ballad has lost the certainty of that assumption.

The lady's choice, in every aspect but the adulterous, is in fact the choice that settled America. Where a land must be settled, the love of adventure and the willingness to roam become positive cultural values for women as well as for men, and the lady's decision to leave the established society for the wilderness could no longer be seen as a choice that only a bewitched woman would make. Some texts give enough descriptive emphasis to the intangibles the lady is choosing—love and freedom—to suggest that these had become the most moving and significant factors in her decision, for some American singers.

The effects of early American cultural context upon the ballad narrative are most clearly visible in characterization: the interactions between Gypsy, lady, and lord are often structured and phrased so that they resemble what must have been a common interaction between a suitor, a girl, and her father in the days when America was being settled. A young man wanting to move west, or to emigrate to America from Europe, had much the same life to offer his bride as does the ballad's Gypsy; inspired by the promise of furs, ore, and rich farmlands free for the taking, many must have used the same persuasive appeal in courtship:

> Oh come with me, my pretty little one,
> Oh come with me, my honey;
> Swear by the beard upon my chin
> That you'll never want for money,
> That you'll never want for money.[7]

Black Jack Davy's gay singing, and the sword, gold, or bugle "by his side" which he sometimes swears by in place of his beard, characterize him as an attractive adventurer: a free, independent man who bears upon or within his own body the wherewithal to make a woman happy.[8] One of the great attractions America's West held for men was that strength and enterprise were enough to make a good life—or at least were far more likely to be enough than they were in the mines and tenanted fields cf Europe. This image of Black Jack Davy opens the ballad so frequently that it is probably safe to consider it intrinsic to the ballad's meaning and functions in America.

Black Jack Davy charms; he does not spellbind. All direct mention of adultery disappears from American texts, and the romantic connection between the lovers is emphasized rather than the sexual. Several texts borrow a verse from the early Anglo-American courtship song "I'm Seventeen Come Sunday" to describe the meeting between the Gypsy and the lady:

> "How old are you, my pretty little miss?
> How old are you, my honey?"
> She answered him with a tee, hee, hee,
> "I'll be sixteen next Sunday."[9]

The lady's response to Black Jack Davy is usually in keeping with the general atmosphere of courtship rather than seduction. Her firm, composed assurance that she can indeed leave her home and family to go with the Gypsy, and her comparison of the feather bed she has had with the "cold, cold ground" on which she will now sleep must have allied her, by the bond of recognizable experience and emotion, with a large number of pioneer brides. She is frequently called "this fair young girl," "my pretty fine miss," or "my pretty little one." Babes or no babes, she is more of a lassie, by description, than a lady. The high number of texts in which she and her choice are cast in a positive light suggests that this resonance of ballad with experience was strong enough to overshadow the adulterous nature of her commitment to the Gypsy. Many of the texts we now have in print, collected from oral tradition, may have evolved at a time when Americans "needed" to sing about the risks and sacrifices of pioneer marriage more than they "needed" to sing about temptation, adultery, and the breakdown of the nuclear family.

The lord is often described in terms that suggest a formal, distanced relationship to the lady and perhaps a discrepancy in age between them. He is called "her old landlord," "her own grim (or Ingram) lord," and "her old man." This last term has had ambivalent connotations in

American slang throughout the ballad's lifetime, having been used of bosses and fathers, as well as of husbands.[10] In one text, in which the *abcb* rhyme scheme is otherwise consistent, this verse concludes "her old man's" search of the "pretty little one":

> So he rode all night 'til the broad daylight,
> Until he came to the water;
> He crossed and he looked on the other side,
> And there he spied his darling,
> There he spied his darling.[11]

The obvious rhyme here is "daughter."

In Scotland, the narrative tension is largely generated by the juxtaposition of the glamourie with the lady's apparently sound-minded refusal to return home; each hearer must decide whether her seduction was of the will or of the heart. The American ballad has settled that question: in every text, the lady goes freely and deliberately. Narrative tension in the American ballad turns upon the question, "when, if ever, is it all right for a woman to make this choice?"

The resolution of this question is therefore the crux of most of the individual textual variations made by American singers. The group of texts described above, in which the lady is young, the lord older, and the Gypsy an attractive bachelor, constitutes the clear majority among the texts I have examined, but singers have handled this question in a number of other ways. Some texts defend the marriage and deplore the lady's abandonment of her family and may focus either upon the lady or upon the lord as the central character in doing so. Others cast the ballad narrative as a woman-to-woman warning against wanton infidelity or simply against getting mixed up with footloose men. It may be sung as a men's song about the experience of abandonment, which follows the lord's actions and feelings with tremendous empathy. Other singers focus upon the comparison of the two men and the lady's relationship with each.

Those whose hearts lie with the lord may sing in the first person, making him the "I" of the ballad. Even where this is not done, the amount of direct address spoken by the lord is frequently very high in these texts:

I rid all day and I rid all night,
And overtook my daisy.
I found her laying on a cold river bank
In the arms of a Gypsen baby.[12]

* * *

Last night on a bed of down you lay
Your baby lay by you.
Tonight you will lie on the cold, cold clay,
With the Gypsy lad beside you.

Take off, take off your costly glove
That's made of Spanish leather,
Your hand I will grasp in a farewell clasp,
'Twill be farewell forever.[13]

* * *

And it's fare you well my dearest dear,
And it's fare you well forever,
And if you don't go with me now,
Don't let me see you never.[14]

Several texts collected from oral tradition in the early twentieth century
give only a verse or two to the lovers' meeting, another to the lady's
refusal to return and devote the rest of the song entirely to the lord.
Many include a verse in which he weeps at the sight of his wife in the
Gypsy's arms. These texts strongly characterize the lord as a loving
husband, good provider, and responsible father, while making it very
clear that the lady prefers the Gypsy's kisses to the solid qualities of her
husband.

He returned home that very same night
To take care of his baby.
He rode twelve miles in this lone state
And married another lady.[15]

> He mounted on his iron-gray horse
> That was so young and gaily,
> He rode back to rock his babes
> And dream of his lady,
> And dream of his lady.[16]

Those texts that give their allegiance to the marriage but their focus to the lady often share this opinion of the lord and of the "true love" that leads the lady to forsake lands, home, baby, and husband for the Gypsy's kisses. Many sing of her final regret for her foolish decision at the end of the song as she looks back upon the wealth and comfort she once enjoyed.

> O once I had a house and lands
> And jewels very costly O,
> Now I sit me down in rags
> Beside the Gypsy draily O.[17]

The texts that applaud the lady and the Gypsy as a satisfying, culturally acceptable pair of lovers make great effort, through symbolism and descriptive contexting, to explain, justify, and remove the stigma from her choice. In addition to their molding of the lord and lady into father and daughter and the Gypsy into a suitor, these texts may have the lady declare:

> I never loved you in my life,
> I never loved my baby;
> I never loved my own wedded lord
> As I love the Gypsy Davy.[18]

The majority of these texts end with the cold ground/feather bed comparison, thus closing the ballad on a note of commitment and willing sacrifice; of, as Bertrand Bronson said, "all for love, or the world well lost."[19]

The fullest feminine counterpart to the strong focus upon masculine concerns achieved in the texts sung "by" the lord is found, not in the pro-Gypsy texts but in those that tell the story as a warning from one woman to another. The pro-Gypsy texts generally give equal time to all

three characters, while the narrator remains in the background, but the
women's warning texts often include at least one verse in which the
narrator addresses the listener directly.

> Now all ye wives that hear this tale
> Be content to be a lady,
> And never let your hearts be set
> On a careless drunken Davy.[20]

* * *

> Oh soon this lady changed her mind,
> Her clothes grew old and faded,
> Her hose and shoes fell off her feet,
> And left them bare and naked.

> Just what befell this lady now
> I think it worth relating
> Her Gypsy found another lass,
> And left her heart a-breaking.[21]

* * *

> There are seven sweet Gypsies in the North
> They are calling to sweet Baltimore,
> They'll sing you a song that will charm your heart,
> And cause you to leave your husband.[22]

Each of these warnings, though given varying emphasis and
expression, concerns the temptation to abandon that which is lasting for
a temporary or even illusory attraction. In at least one family (the
Ingersolls of Pike County, Illinois, and Scarsdale, New York, one of
whose members sang for Dorothy Scarborough in the 1930s), the
"careless drunken Davy" text was traditionally sung by the women for
one another. The Ingersolls' version is humorous, rhythmic, and
memorable; as a shared event or traditional performance, it may have
taken the place of moralizing and serious discussions, effectively
communicating a message about temptation which was difficult for the

mature to explain and for the young to understand. It may also have functioned as a moral and cultural reference point for the married women of the family, for whom the pressure of stagnation in a stable relationship and lifestyle was more imminent, and the danger of succumbing to the longing for freedom, for rest and change, or for a way to reassert one's individuality may sometimes have posed a real and pressing threat. Coyote tales, in which the main character indulges all kinds of desires that one cannot afford to act out as a member of a close-knit family and community, may be used by the Navaho to teach children how to view and handle these desires, to reaffirm cultural principles and mores for the adults, and to allow all members of the audience (and the storyteller) to experience possibilities which they are discouraged from pursuing in their own lives.[23] Similarly, "Black Jack Davy" may provide a controlled context in which women—and men—may play with and discuss the cultural taboos on adultery and abandonment and the circumstances under which one might be tempted to break them. It would seem that singers may have made use of the ballad's basic structure as a vehicle for the expression of specific ways in which these taboos have touched, or threatened to touch, their own lives.

Probably the most widely shared characteristic of American texts is the use of parallel construction in the scenes of courtship and confrontation. The list of things the lady is leaving is often repeated twice or even four times: the Gypsy asks her if she will leave her house and lands, her baby, and her lord, and she agrees; her husband asks her how she can leave them, and she affirms that she has done so. This device appears more often than not in the texts I have examined and is apparently satisfying for singers of all the interpretive persuasions outlined above. Whether the lady's choice is seen as a right to be celebrated or as a temptation to be deplored and feared, the risk and sacrifice it involves remain a powerful center of attention.

This parallelism is often strengthened by a second repetition: the lady takes off or changes her shoes or gown to show that she is ready to go with the Gypsy and takes off her gloves in final farewell to her husband.

> "Well, you'd better leave your house and land,
> You'd better leave your baby;

You'd better leave your own landlord
And go with Black Jack Davy
And go with Black Jack Davy."

She put on her high-heel shoes
All made of Spanish leather
And then she kissed her sweet little babe
And then they parted forever,
And then they parted forever. (verses 4–5)

"Have you forsaked your house and land?
Have you forsaked your baby?
Have you forsaked your own true love
And gone with Black Jack Davy,
And gone with Black Jack Davy?"

"Yes, I forsaked my house and land,
Yes, I forsaked my baby;
Yes, I forsaked my own landlord
And gone with Black Jack Davy,
And gone with Black Jack Davy."

"You pull off those fine, finger gloves
That's made of Spanish leather
And give to me your lily-white hand
And we will part forever,
And we will part forever."

She pulled off her fine, finger gloves
All made of Spanish leather;
She gave to him her lily-white hand
And they were parted forever,
And they were parted forever. (verses 9–12)[24]

The textual linking between lord and Gypsy may be further strengthened
by similar promises made by both. The Gypsy frequently swears that
she "never will want for money," while the lord asks if she will not
return to "the gold I have," the usual house and lands, or to some rich

gift ("a silken bed and covers," "a room so neat") which he promises to give her.

The taking off or changing of clothing may also function as a symbol both of her rejection of the lord's provision and of her readiness to share the Gypsy's possessionless state. By this action, she expresses her trust in his ability to keep her from wanting for money—whether "want for" is understood as lack or desire. It also may symbolize her transference of sexual commitment and relationship and her gift to the Gypsy of "a' the coat gaes 'round." The lord's common farewell request for her ungloved hand in parting is in some sense his recognition that he will no longer be able to ask her to take off her glove or anything else and his acceptance of her right to transfer that privilege to the Gypsy, which she did at the beginning of the ballad by the shedding of her shoes. The clothing motif thus links material providence with sexual submission as important cultural signals of romantic commitment. Combined with the motif of the feather bed versus the cold ground, it expresses the transition which is taking place in terms of who will provide for her, whose bed or arms she will sleep in, and for whom she will take off her clothes.

These consistent, repetitive elements of the ballad narrative thus act as a cameo of some of the delicate, emotionally charged questions about love and marriage which seem central to its cultural functions in America. Is it ever acceptable for an unhappily married woman to be rescued by a lover, or is this release only for daughters and not for wives? Is it likely that a man willing to "rescue" another man's wife will be faithful to her himself, or is a relationship begun in adultery likely to end in it? Can a woman expect emotional stability from a footloose man, or will it be as hard for him to remain with one woman as it is to remain in one place?

These are some of the questions troubling to women which an individual singer, listener, family, or community might express and explore through singing "The Gypsy Laddie"; questions troubling to men are here as well. Can a man who gives a wife a nice home, money and pretty things, children, and security expect that, in return, she will remain happy, faithful, and loving? There is perhaps a note of bewilderment and despair in the lord's questioning of his wife, which many men find painfully familiar:

> O haven't ye got gold in store
> And haven't ye got treasures three
> Haven't ye got all that ye want
> And a bonnie bonnie boy till amase ye wi.[25]

A single man may identify positively with the Gypsy, but he may also recognize a common male fear in the lady's final bitter words which appear in many texts collected from male singers:

> Once I had a house and land
> A feather bed and money,
> But now I'm come to an old straw pad
> With nothing but Black Jack David.[26]

Will a woman who follows a man for true love's sake really remain with him if she does "want for money" after all? Can a man ever hope to be loved for who he is rather than for what he gives?

III

Before World War II, when the majority of the texts consulted for this study were collected, divorce was still scandalous, and runaway wives a rarity. Love that failed or ended was cause for sadness and in many situations also cause for shame, because adultery and abandonment simply were not supposed to happen. Since the advent of Rogerian and Gestalt therapy, however, these taboos have been breaking down. Many psychologists and marriage counselors have begun to view marriage as a growth stage: an arrangement made in order to enrich the lives of both parties, which can and should be dissolved if it ceases to do so. The picture of the ideal marriage put forward in the 1960s and 1970s, on television as well as in lay psychology and marriage books, is actually not far distant from the relationship enjoyed by the lady and the Gypsy in the ballad texts that favor it: it is based on love, rather than the need for security or propriety; it is "free and easy" rather than difficult; and it is begun by mutual agreement, with equal value placed upon the woman's right to decide for herself what is best for her own life. It has also become fairly common and culturally acceptable, as it was during the settling of America, to choose to live without houses and lands and financial stability. Many a young "gypsy" and his lady—in Europe as well as the United States—have backpacks, sleeping bags, an adventurous spirit, and not much else, seeking quite literally after the same kinds of happiness which the lady and the Gypsy in the ballad seek.

More than ever before in American culture, it is also becoming common and culturally acceptable for a woman to leave her husband and even her children for any or all of the reasons expressed in various texts of "The Gypsy Laddie." She may leave to get away from her traditional role and responsibilities; to get out from under her husband's protection and provision, if she finds them stifling; to seek whatever intangible qualities she longs for in her own life; or simply to take a lover. Material security is becoming increasingly available to women as salaries and job opportunities are equalized. The taboos probably do not need to be sung about as much because they exert far less pressure upon American lives than they once did. The drama of abandonment and adultery is readily available all around us, and the risk of scorn and poverty once involved in leaving one's husband has declined almost to the vanishing point.

Cartoonist Gary Trudeau, creator of the famous *Doonesbury*, a nationally syndicated strip which focuses on current political and cultural issues and tendencies, expressed some of the more literal connections between ballad and life today in a September 1979 episode. Joan Caucus, Jr., a college student, arrives unexpectedly at her mother's apartment, after not having seen or heard from her mother in several years. She is greeted at the door by her mother's lover, who calmly invites her in, and soon a stunned Joan Sr. is rushing home from her law office to face the child she abandoned. "After ten years of being a wife and mother," she explains, "I still didn't know who I was. And I wasn't getting help from your father. So one day I walked out the kitchen door and flagged down two passing college boys on a motorcycle."[27] *Doonesbury*, it should be remembered, is considered funny as well as true.

Though "Black Jack Davy," like other traditional ballads, is not sung as widely today as it was prior to World War II, it is still comparatively well known. A variety of traditional versions have been recorded by popular artists, including Jean Ritchie, Woody and Arlo Guthrie, and Bryan Bowers, and it is therefore not uncommon for people under the age of thirty to have heard two or three different kinds of texts. In order to gain some insight into the current functions of the ballad in American society, I conducted two small studies in Eugene, Oregon, a medium-sized city on the West Coast with an economically and educationally varied population. I first made a random check among approximately fifty people familiar with at least one version of the ballad, which most had learned at school or summer camp as children or heard from a recording or from friends or local singers. I asked each person to tell me what the ballad is about and found tremendous correlation between the answers I received and the lifestyle and values chosen by each of my informants. The young people I talked with, many of them poor and decidedly footloose, most frequently answered, "It's about a man and a woman who fall in love and go traveling together." Most of the married people, both young and older, answered, "It's about a woman who leaves her husband for another man, " often adding, "and then wishes she hadn't." One thoughtful young man, whose own wife had recently left him for her lover, taking their two-year-old son with her, answered, "It's about decision making, and the importance of choosing on the basis of inner needs and values, rather than on the basis of material needs."

In the second study, I sang my subjects five versions, ranging from Child's A text of the early eighteenth century through the spectrum of resolutions and narrative perspectives present in American tradition and including a new version written and recorded by a Scottish poet and musician (Mike Heron, co-founder of the Incredible String Band) which was fairly well known in the United States in the 1960s. I gave my subjects no prompting but allowed them to guide the conversation after each song. (This study, like the first, was carried out in the field, with no formal announcement that it was being done. The interactions took place in markets, parks, and living rooms, and sometimes formed a part of a longer ballad-singing session or conversation.) Heron's version, sung in a style and meter approaching the Irish jig, is a joyful, almost pastoral treatment of the ballad narrative, sung primarily by Black Jack Davy himself. It drew exclamations of enthusiasm and preference over other versions from very nearly all the subjects. It seems to complete and make explicit the process of resolution begun long before, through description and characterization, in the largest group of field-collected texts I had examined: the reshaping of husband into father, wife into

daughter, and adultery into wilderness romance. Heron's version opens
with Black Jack Davy singing alone:

> Black Jack Davy is the name that I bear;
> Been alone in the forest a long time,
> But the time is coming when my lady I'll find,
> And will love her, and hold her,
> Singing through the green, green trees.

> Well, the skin on my hands is like the leather I ride,
> And my face is hard from the cold wind,
> But my heart's a-warm with a softness that
> Will charm a fair lady,
> Singing through the green, green trees.

At this point the voice of Black Jack Davy is joined by a young
soprano, and the middle verses are sung as a duet.

> Well, fair Eloise rode out that day
> From her fine, fine home in the morning,
> With the flush of dawn all about her hair,
> Drifting, floating,
> Singing through the green, green trees.

> Well, sixteen summers was all that she'd seen,
> And her skin was soft as the velvet,
> But she's forsaken her fine, fine home,
> And Black Jack Davy's
> Singing through the green, green trees.

> Last night she slept on a fine feather bed
> Far, far from Black Jack Davy,
> But tonight she'll sleep on the cold, cold ground,
> And will love him, and hold him,
> Singing through the green, green trees.

The next two verses are sung by male voices.

"Saddle my mare, my fine grey mare!"
Cried the lord of the house next morning.
"For my servants tell me my daughter's gone
With Black Jack Davy
Singing through the green, green trees!"

Well, he rode all day and he rode all night,
But he never did find his daughter;
He heard from afar, come drifting on the wind,
Two voices, laughing,
Singing through the green, green trees.

Black Jack Davy sings the final verse solo:

Oh, Black Jack Davy is the name that I bear;
Been alone in the forest for a long time,
But now I've found my lady so fair,
And I love her, and hold her,
Singing through the green, green trees.[28]

Heron's version was known to several of my subjects and was the immediate favorite both among those who knew more than one version and those who heard this one first from me. Apparently its resolution of the ballad's broken taboos and cultural conflicts—between true love and marriage and how one can respond when their claims conflict—is highly satisfying, perhaps relieving, for the children and grandchildren of the singers whose texts were collected in the 1930s and 1950s. Most of my subjects delighted in the clear, unquestioned "rightness" Heron gives to "the virgin and the Gypsy" as a couple who almost recognize, rather than choose, one another as the partner each has been waiting for, and his removal of the troubling question of the lord's pain and the effect of the lady's choice upon him from the song. Many subjects' words and faces clearly indicated that this version of the narrative was both attractive and important for them, and many asked me to sing it twice and three times, to write it down, to come and sing it for friends, to give it to them so that they could remember and keep it.

This resonance of textual preference with lifestyle and personal values seems to have some bearing on the recorded versions of the ballad as well. Bryan Bowers, who recorded a more traditional version in 1977, gave—like Heron—more spoken lines and dramatic focus to the Gypsy than I found in any of the pre–World War II texts I examined. It is perhaps worth noting that, at the time of recording, both Bowers and Heron were single, traveled a good deal, and would have been considered members of the counterculture, both by appearance and lifestyle and by self-description. Jean Ritchie, on the other hand, recorded one of the most powerful of the women's warning version as a wife and mother.

The tastes, fears, and concerns of the audience and of individual singers are a formative and not yet well studied area for ballad scholars to consider. Further work with specific clusters of cultural concerns might bring us to a better understanding of the ballad as a genre and of the cultural values expressed, questioned, and defended in particular texts. Ballad scholarship will benefit from, and be made more useful by, increased and better attention to ethical, ethnic, and psychological contexts in its study of ballad evolution and cultural function.

NOTES

1. "Johnny Faa, the Gypsy Laddie," Ramsay's *Tea-Table Miscellany*, vol. iv, 1740. Rpt. (from the edition of 1763, p. 47) in Francis James Child, *The English and Scottish Popular Ballads* (Boston: 1882–1898), vol. 2, pp. 65–66.

2. The records of this and other Gypsy trials are to be found in Robert Pitcairn, *Criminal Trials in Scotland, From A.D. M.CCCC LXXXVII To A.D. M.DC.XXIV, Embracing the Entire Reigns of James IV. and V., Mary Queen of Scots, and James VI. Compiled from the Original Records and MSS., with Historical Notes and Illustrations.* 4 vols. (Edinburgh: William Tait, and London: Longman, Rees, Orme, Brown, Green, and Longman, 1833), vol. 3, p. 201.

3. Pitcairn, *Criminal Trials in Scotland*, p. 201.

4. Child is apparently following Robert Burns's assurance, given to the editor of *The Scots Musical Museum*, that "neighboring tradition strongly vouches for the truth of this story." Child quotes this passage, and notes that Lady Cassilis's name was inserted in the *Museum*'s text at Burns's direction.

5. Robert Chambers, *The Picture of Scotland* (Edinburgh: n. pub., 1827), 2 vols., n.p. Quoted in Alexander Whitelaw, *The Book of Scottish Ballads*,

Collected and Illustrated, with Historical and Critical Notices (Glasgow: Blackie & Son, 1857), p. 28.

6. Barre Toelken, "How Ballads Change: An Illustrated Lecture," in *The Oregon Curriculum: Literature I*, series ed. Albert R. Kitzhaber (New York: Holt, Rinehart & Winston, 1969), phonodisc @4809406, 12" LP.

7. [Footnote missing in original. But this is probably "Black Jack Davy," as sung by Bryan Bowers (W. Va.), *The View from Home* (Chicago: Flying Fish, 1977), phonodisc S037. Arranged by Bryan Bowers, as in note 16 of Cartwright's paper "Black Jack Davy: Cultural Values and Changes in Scots and American Balladry," *Lore & Language* 3:4/5 (1981), 153–188.]

8. [Footnote missing in original.]

9. "Black Jack Davy," Dorothy Scarborough, *A Song-Catcher in the Southern Mountains* (New York: Columbia University Press, 1937), p. 412 (b); text, p. 218. "Sung by Selma Clubb, South Turkey Creek, Leicester, N.D., c. 1932." Rpt. in Bertrand Harris Bronson, *The Traditional Tunes of the Child Ballads*, 4 vols. (Princeton, N.J.: Princeton University Press, 1952) vol. 4, text 126, p. 249.

10. See John S. Farmer and W. E. Henley, *A Dictionary of Slang and its Analogues Past and Present: a Dictionary Historical and Comparative of the Heterodox Speech of All Classes of Society for More than Three Hundred Years*, 5 vols. (London: Routledge & Kegan Paul, 1902; rpt. New York: Kraus Reprint Corp., 1965), vol. 4, p. 99.

11. George and Gerry Armstrong, "Black Jack Davy," on *Simple Gifts: Anglo-American Folksong*, Folkways Records FA2335, 12" LP.

12. "I'm Seventeen Come Sunday, or The Gypsy Laddie," Sharp MSS., 4615/3224, Clare College Library, Cambridge. "Sung by Mrs. Margaret Calloway, Burnsville, N.C., September 16, 1918," Rpt. in Bronson, vol. 4, text 7, p. 204.

13. "Gypsy Laddie," Robert Shifflett, LC Archive of American Folk Song 12,004 (A2). Rpt. in Bronson, vol. 4, text 83, p. 231.

14. "The Gypsy Laddie," Child's text 200-J. "a. Written down by Newton Pepoun, as learned from a boy with whom he went to school in Stockbridge, Massachusetts, about 1845. b. From the singing of Mrs. Farmer, born in Maine, as learned by her daughter, about 1840." Child, vol. 2, p. 72.

15. "Gypsy Davey," Helen Hartness Flanders, *Ancient Ballads Traditionally Sung in New England*, 5 vols. (Philadelphia: University of Pennsylvania Press, 1963), vol. 3, p. 207. "'Recited by Oliver Jenness, Chase's Pond Section, York Village, Maine, as learned from his grandfather, who was born in York, Maine. Mr. Jenness was 89 years old.' M. Olney, collector; September 25, 1947."

16.   Buck Buttery, "Black Jack Davy," on LC Archive of American Folk Song 11,909 (B24), collected by Marvin Wallace. Rpt. in Bronson, vol. 4, text 116, pp. 244–245.

17.   Mrs. Oleava Houser, "Gypsy Draily," on LC Archive of American Folk Song 11,908 (B34), collected by Mary Celestia Parker. Rpt. in Bronson, vol. 4, text 102, p. 238.

18.   "Gypsy Davey," John Harrington Cox, *Traditional Ballads Mainly from West Virginia* (Cambridge, MA: Harvard University Press, 1939), p. 31; and 1964 (ed. George Boswell), p. 40. Rpt. in Bronson, vol. 4, text 9, p. 205, with the following note appended: "Also in Dorothy Scarborough, *A Song-Catcher in the Southern Mountains*, pp. 414 (G) and 224. Contributed in 1925 by Mrs. Margaret Widdemer Schauffler of New York City; obtained from Miss Lucia Sanderson, Cleveland, Ohio, who learned it from an English-woman. Tune noted (From Mrs. Schauffler's singing?) by Frances Sanders, Morgantown, W. Va."

19.   Introduction to "The Gypsy Laddie," vol. 4, p. 198.

20.   "The Lady's Disgrace," Scarborough, p. 413 (F); text, p. 233. "Sung by Mrs. Genevieve Ingersoll, Scarsdale, N.Y., c. 1932. Learned from her grandmother's cousin, of Pike County, Ill.; traditional in her family." Rpt. in Bronson, vol. 4, text 32, pp. 214–215.

21.   Jean Ritchie, "Gypsy Laddie," on Folkways recording FA 2301 (A1), ed. Kenneth S. Goldstein, 12" LP. Also in Bronson, vol. 4, text 38, pp. 116–117.

22.   [The Gypsy Laddie], Arthur Kyle Davis, *Traditional Ballads of Virginia* (Cambridge, MA: Harvard University Press, 1929), pp. 591 (D) and 427. "Contributed by John Stone, November 3, 1920, from the singing of Misses Fannie and Hattie Via, State Junction, Va.; they learned it from Mrs. Orilla Keeton in Albemarle County." Rpt. in Bronson, vol. 4, text 91, p. 234.

23.   See Barre Toelken, "The 'Pretty Languages' of Yellowman: Genre, Mode, and Texture in Navaho Coyote Narratives," *Genre* 2:3 (September 1969), pp. 211–235.

24.   "Gypsy Davy," Mellinger Edward Henry, *Folk-Songs from the Southern Highlands* (New York: J. J. Augustin, 1938), p. 110. "Sung by Mrs. Samuel Harmon, Cade's Cove, Tenn., August 12, 1930." Rpt. in Bronson, vol. 4, text 125, pp. 248–249.

25.   [The Gypsy Laddie], Gavin Greig MSS., I, p. 154; text, book 14, vol. 4, p. 77. Also in Greig and Alexander Keith, *Last Leaves of Traditional Ballads and Ballad Airs* (Aberdeen: University of Aberdeen, 1925), p. 218 (Ib). "Sung by J. W. Spence, Fyvie, April 1906." Rpt. in Bronson, vol. 4, text 45, p. 219. (Note that this informant is male. This verse appears in question and answer form in another text collected in the north of Scotland, published in John Ord,

The Bothy Songs and Ballads [Aberdeen: Paisley & A. Gardner, Ltd., 1930], p. 411, but the name of the singer is not given.)

26. "Black Jack David," Brown MSS., 16 a 4 J (bis). Also in Jan Schinhan, ed., *The Frank C. Brown Collection of North Carolina Folklore*, vol. 4, *The Music of the Ballads* (Durham, N.C.: Duke University Press, 1957), p. 88. "Sung by Dr. I. G. Greer. Collected by C. Alphonso Smith and Thomas Smith, n.d. Another copy, unidentified in the Brown MSS., 16 a 4 J, nearly identical with this, probably also from Dr. Greer." Bronson, vol. 4, text 120, p. 246.

27. G. B. Trudeau, "Doonesbury," September 22, 1979. United Features Syndicate; *Eugene Register-Guard*, Eugene, Oregon, Section C, p. 8.

28. Mike Heron, "Black Jack Davy," sung by Robin Williamson and Likki Lambert. The Incredible String Band, *I Looked Up*, Elektra 74061 ET-84112, 12" LP.

THE CONTRIBUTORS

Thomas Acton is the author of several books and papers on Gypsies and is currently professor of Romani Studies, University of Greenwich, England.

Sarah Burns got her B.A. from the University of Chicago, M.A. from the University of California, Davis, and Ph.D. from the University of Illinois, Champaign-Urbana. She has published quite a few articles on nineteenth-century American art as well as the books *Pastoral Inventions: Rural Life in Nineteenth-Century American Art and Culture* (Temple University Press, 1989) and *Inventing the Modern Artist: Art and Culture in Gilded Age America* (Yale University Press, 1996).

Christine A. Cartwright was born in Chicago in 1955. She attended the University of Oregon where she worked under Barre Toelken and obtained a B.A. Honors in 1976 for her thesis, "The Role of Literature in Character Development and Value Clarification." By 1979 she had completed a master's degree in English at the University of Oregon. In 1980 she commenced her Ph.D. work in folklore at Memorial University of Newfoundland. Shortly before her death in an automobile accident in 1983, she completed her Ph.D. dissertation, "Charismatic Culture in St. John's, Newfoundland: A Cross-Denominational Study of Religious Folklife in Three Groups." Her early interest in literature brought her into the world of folklore via balladry, a topic that interested her even while she read, thought about, and wrote her dissertation on folk religion. Dr. Cartwright's work was not limited to ballads and folk religion. While at Memorial University of Newfoundland she was the editor in chief of *Culture and Tradition* from 1981 until 1983. In addition, she published articles and reviews on the subject of material culture.

Martti Grönfors, professor of sociology at the University of Kuopio, Finland, with a specialty in deviancy, was born in Finland and studied sociology, criminology, and social anthropology in Finland, New Zealand, and Britain. He has done research on Gypsies, gays, HIV, and community mediation; his prime research interests are minority issues and the sociology and anthropology of law and gender. His current research, "Men, Masculinity, and the Culture of Violence," is a cross-cultural examination of male identity and its relationship to violence. His partner, Sari Vesikansa, researches youth and education. They have a foster child, Naftali, from Sri Lanka. He can be reached at Jatasalmentie 11, 00830 Helsinki, Finland. Tel.: 358-0-788739; fax: 358-0-7592098; email: martti.gronfors@uku.fi.

Rena M. Cotten (Gropper) has been interested in the Roma since her under-graduate days. Her doctoral dissertation was one of the first by an anthropologist, and the ongoing continuities and changes she began to describe were the subject of her book *Gypsies in the City*, published in 1975. She has also written articles in the same field. She was selected as president of the Gypsy Lore Society for two five-year terms and helped to establish the North American chapter, which subsequently absorbed the parent organization.

Will Guy, born in 1940 in London, is currently lecturer in the Department of Sociology at the University of Bristol, England. He has been involved in research about Roma since 1969, when he began working on his doctoral dissertation on the Czechoslovak government's assimilation policy, concentrating on the period from 1958 to the present. From 1969 till the mid-1970s he worked closely with Eva Davidová, then of the Czechoslovak Academy of Sciences in Prague, and with the Svaz Cikánů-Romů (Gypsy-Rom Association), mainly in eastern Slovakia, northern Moravia, and Prague. He attended the first World Romani Congress in 1970 as interpreter to the Czech delegation. He also collaborated with the Czech photographer Josef Koudelka on Koudelka's book *Gypsies*. In the mid-1970s Guy did research on Travellers in Scotland, mainly around Glasgow, where the first local-authority caravan site for Travellers was being established. Since the revolutions of 1989 in Eastern and Central Europe he has been following the experience of the Roma in what is now the Czech Republic and Slovakia, returning there in 1989, 1991, and 1997.

Ian Hancock is Main Representative for the Romani people in the United Nations Economic and Social Council (Category II), and to

UNICEF and UN-DPI. He is president of the International Rroma Foundation, Inc., cofounder of the Romani Jewish Alliance, Inc., and a member of the Project on Ethnic Relations Romani Advisory Council (Princeton, New Jersey), the Anne Frank Institute, the National Conference of Christians and Jews, Inc., the Center for the Study of Ethnic and Racial Violence, the Global Organization of People of Indian Origin, Inc., and a number of other related organizations. Between 1985 and 1987 he was Special Advisor on Romani-related Affairs to Elie Wiesel, then chair of the U.S. Holocaust Memorial Council. He has served as a member of the U.S. Department of State's diplomatic team at the Warsaw meeting of the Organization for Security and Cooperation in Europe, and he lectures widely on racism and human rights. His publications on Romani issues number over one hundred. He is currently professor of English and linguistics at the University of Texas at Austin. Information on Rroma may be obtained from The Secretary, The International Romani Union, Manchaca, Texas 78652-0822, USA, or via e-mail from Romnet, <xulaj@mail.utexas.edu>.

Milena Hübschmannová was born in Prague and studied Hindi, Urdu, and Bengali at Charles University. The similarity of these languages to Romani inspired her to learn that language as well; since it was taught nowhere at the time, she learned it among the Roma. She graduated in 1956 and went to work as an editor at a radio station before attending the Oriental Institute and the Institute for Sociology. After the Russian invasion of Czechoslovakia in 1968 she was without work for several years, then in 1976 began teaching the Slovak variety of Romani at the School of Languages in Prague. Since 1991 she has been teaching a five-year course of Romani and Romani studies at Charles University. Over the years she and her daughter have spent a lot of time in Romani settlements as well as in Indian villages collecting tales, songs, proverbs, and narratives of traditional life. She has been widely published.

After taking an honors degree and qualifying as a teacher, **Cathy Kiddle** worked as a lecturer in Exeter College of Art before taking up a job as education director of "Welfare State" theater company. Based in the north of England, the company toured all over Britain and Europe. While traveling, Cathy Kiddle made contact with Gypsy families and support groups and was invited to become joint field officer for the Romany Guild and A.C.E.R.T. (Advisory Committee for the Education of Romanies and other Travellers) in London.

This initial contact has led to continuing educational work for the last twenty years with Gypsy and other Travellers, first in London and subsequently in Devon, where Kiddle has been responsible for the development of the county Traveller Education Service.

A writer as well as a teacher, Cathy Kiddle has published a book as well as several articles concerned with education, the family, and the Gypsy.

Alaina Lemon is an anthropologist who researched Romani history, language, and social life in Russia for two and a half years with Roma from several different dialect groups, after studying Romani with Roma in Chicago. The present essay draws from the first few months of interviews and from archival research before the 1991 coup attempt. Lemon has recently finished a dissertation at the University of Chicago titled "Indic Diaspora, Soviet History, Russian Home: Performances and Sincere Ironies in Romani Cultures." It traces, among other things, how Roma who are not professional singers or dancers identify with as well as contrast themselves to the performers described here. Her next project relates Romani experience to Russian social and cultural constructions of race and criminality. She is currently (1996–1999) with the Michigan Society of Fellows and the Department of Anthropology at the University of Michigan.

Born in 1959, **Leo Lucassen** got his Ph.D. from Leiden University in 1990 and is attached as fellow of the Royal Netherlands Academy of Arts and Sciences to the History Department in Leiden. Apart from his dissertation, he has published several articles on Gypsies and Travellers. For his main publications in this field, see the afterword of his article in this collection.

Peter Manuel is an ethnomusicologist teaching at John Jay College and the Graduate Center of the City University of New York. He has published extensively on popular and traditional musics of India, Latin America, and elsewhere. An accomplished sitarist, he also plays flamenco guitar and jazz piano.

Carol Miller reports: "In the early seventies, after teaching at various two-year colleges around the Seattle area, I followed the Machvaia I knew to California. Since then, when possible, I have been involved in their social life, parties, and ceremonials with the purpose of documenting Machvaia rituals and attendant beliefs. These efforts have been personally financed by sundry part-time jobs over a thirty-year period and they have been both my work and my pleasure."

Dan Pavel, who was born in 1958 in Cluj-Napoca, Romania, teaches at the Faculty of Political Studies and Public Administration at the University of Cluj and is the director of the Center for Political Analysis and Geopolitical Prognosis. He founded and was deputy chief editor of the weekly *22*, and of the first political science journal in Romania, the monthly *Sfera Politicii*, and the quarterly *Polis*, in Bucharest. He has published two books in Romania: *Bibliopolis: Essay on the Metamorphosis of Books* in 1990 and *Adam's Ethic: Or, Why Do We Rewrite History?* in 1995.

Bertha B. Quintana was born in New York City and received her graduate training in cultural anthropology at New York University. She was appointed to the faculty of Montclair State University in 1961, where she served as department chair and professor of anthropology for thirty years. A specialist in the culture of the Gypsies of southern Spain, Dr. Quintana has conducted extensive fieldwork among the Gypsies of Granada, a long-term research endeavor that included her pioneer anthropological study of the traditional themes and deep song of the Andalusian Gypsies as well as subsequent ongoing studies of *gitano* adaptations to cultural change. She was a founding member of the North American chapter of the Gypsy Lore Society, was elected its first president (1978, 1979), and served as a member of the board of directors until 1994. Dr. Quintana's other professional affiliations include the American Anthropological Association, the Society for Psychological Anthropology, and Society for Applied Anthropology. Upon her retirement in 1991, Dr. Quintana was designated professor emerita of anthropology by Montclair's board of trustees.

Diane Tong is the author of *Gypsy Folktales* and *Gypsies: A Multidisciplinary Annotated Bibliography* in addition to various articles.

She is currently concentrating on her photography and can be reached at 67 Park Avenue, New York, NY 10016, USA; email address <dianetong@delphi.com>.

Nidhi Trehan, born in India, received her master's degree in public affairs in August 1994 from the University of Texas at Austin. Her thesis adviser and mentor was Professor Ian Hancock of the Department of Linguistics. Currently, Trehan is a researcher at the European Roma Rights Center in Budapest, Hungary, where she is investigating the state of human rights for Roma in Central and Eastern Europe.

Gabrielle Tyrnauer holds a Ph.D. in anthropology and Asian studies from Cornell University. She is presently associate director of the Refugee Research Project at McGill University in Montreal, where she is also an Associate of Living Testimonies, a project that gathers videotaped testimony of Holocaust survivors.

She began her research with American Gypsies in the late 1970s with a study of Gypsies in the northwestern U.S. This led to a publication for the Washington State American Revolution Bicentennial Commission, *The Gypsy in Northwest America*, Tacoma, 1977. While a visiting scholar at Harvard University, she studied social change among the Boston Gypsies.

This was followed by a period of fieldwork with German Sinti under the auspices of the Deutscher Akademischer Austauschdienst, a German government exchange program. The article reprinted in this volume is the first publication based on this research. It was followed by a report written for the U.S. Holocaust Memorial Council, *The Fate of the Gypsies during the Holocaust* (1985). Various publications followed, including *Gypsies and the Holocaust*, the first bibliography of its kind (Montreal, 1989; 2nd ed. 1991). She is currently writing a book on Gypsies and the Holocaust.

Saga Weckman, a Romani speaker from a traditional Gypsy family, a former Gypsy activist, and a founding member of the Finnish Romani Association, retired after a lifelong career in broadcasting administration. She was an adult high school graduate and subsequently studied sociology at the University of Helsinki. She has written many articles on Gypsy issues with an emphasis on Gypsy education, has participated in numerous delegations on Romani affairs both in Finland and abroad, and has conducted research on Gypsy issues. Widowed, she devotes most of her time to her large kin group. She can be reached at Puuskaniementie 20, 00850 Helsinki, Finland. Tel.: 458-0-6985290.

Wim Willems, born in 1951, got his Ph.D. from Leiden University in 1995. He has written numerous books and articles on Dutch Eurasians, minorities, and (together with Leo Lucassen) Gypsies. For his principal publications on Gypsies, see the afterword of his article in this collection. He is currently coordinator of the Centre for the History of Migrants at the Institute for Migration and Ethnic Studies of the University of Amsterdam.

Permissions Acknowledgments

Every effort has been made to secure all necessary permissions for the selections included in this volume. The author would appreciate any additional information concerning sources.

Thomas Acton, "Using the Gypsies' Own Language: Two Contrasting Approaches in Hungarian Schools." Reprinted, with changes, from *Traveller Education* 22 (1987): 11–15, by permission of the author.

Sarah Burns, "Black•Quadroon•Gypsy: Women in the Art of George Fuller." Reprinted, with changes, from *The Massachusetts Review* 26:2–3 (Summer/Autumn 1985): 405–424, by permission of the author and the publisher. ©1986 The Massachusetts Review, Inc.

Christine A. Cartwright, "Johnny Faa and Black Jack Davy: Cultural Values and Change in Scots and American Balladry." Reproduced by permission of the American Folklore Society from JOURNAL OF AMERICAN FOLKLORE 93:370, October–December 1980. Not for further reproduction.

Martti Grönfors, "Police Perception of Gypsies in Finland." Reprinted, with changes, from *International Journal of the Sociology of Law* 9:4 (November 1981): 345–359, by permission of the author and the publisher.

Rena M. Cotten [Gropper], "Sex Dichotomy Among the American Kalderaš Gypsies." Reprinted, with changes, from *Journal of the Gypsy Lore Society* 30:1–2 (January–April 1951): 16–25, by permission of the author.

Will Guy, "Ways of Looking at Roma: The Case of Czechoslovakia." Reprinted, with changes, from *Gypsies, Tinkers and other Travellers*, ed. Farnham Rehfisch (London: Academic Press, 1975), 201–229, by permission of the author and the publisher.

Ian Hancock, "Duty and Beauty, Possession and Truth: 'Lexical Impoverishment' as Control," by permission of the author.

Milena Hübschmannová, "Economic Stratification and Interaction: Roma, an Ethnic Jati in East Slovakia." Reprinted, with changes, from *Giessener Hefte für Tsiganologie* 3–4 (1984): 3–28, by permission of the publisher.

Cathy Kiddle, "Pictures of Ourselves." Reprinted, with changes, from *Heresies* 6:2 [Issue 22] (1987): 58–60, by permission of the author.

Alaina Lemon, "Roma (Gypsies) in the Soviet Union and the Moscow Teatr 'Romen.'" Reprinted, with changes, from *Nationalities Papers* 19:3 (Fall 1991), 359–372, by permission of the author.

Peter Manuel, "Andalusian, Gypsy, and Class Identity in the Contemporary Flamenco Complex." Reprinted, with changes, from *Ethnomusicology* 33:1 (Winter 1989): 47–65, by permission of the author and the publisher.

Carol Miller, "American Roma and the Ideology of Defilement." Reprinted, with changes, from *Gypsies, Tinkers and other Travellers*, ed. Farnham Rehfisch (London: Academic Press, 1975), 41–54, by permission of the author and the publisher.

Dan Pavel, "Wanderers: Romania's Hidden Victims." Reprinted from *The New Republic* (March 4, 1991), 12–13, by permission of the publisher.

Bertha B. Quintana, "'The Duende Roams Freely This Night': An Analysis of an Interethnic Event in Granada, Spain." Reprinted, with changes, from *Papers from the Fourth and Fifth Annual Meetings, Gypsy Lore Society, North American Chapter*, ed. Joanne Grumet (New York: GLS, 1985), 122–128, by permission of the author.

Nidhi Trehan, "Roma in the Hungarian Educational System: Still the Invisible Minority" [Afterword to article by Thomas Acton], by permission of the author.

Gabrielle Tyrnauer, "'Mastering the Past': Germans and Gypsies." Reprinted, with changes, from *Genocide and Human Rights: A Global Anthology*, ed. Jack Nusan Porter (Lanham, MD: University Press of America, 1982), 178–192, by permission of the author.

Saga Weckman, "Researching Finnish Gypsies: Advice from a Gypsy." Reprinted, with changes, from a paper read at XI International Congress of Anthropological and Ethnological Sciences, Quebec, Canada, August 1983, by permission of the author.

Wim Willems, and Leo Lucassen, "The Church of Knowledge: Representation of Gypsies in Dutch Encyclopedias and Their Sources (1724–1984)." Reprinted, with changes, from *100 Years of Gypsy Studies*, ed. Matt T. Salo (Cheverly, MD: GLS, 1990), 31–50, by permission of the authors.